Praise for
Strategic Fund Development, Third Edition

"Few people understand the totality of fundraising strategy like Simone Joyaux. In the third edition of *Strategic Fund Development* Simone provides must-have insight into effective decision-making models that will lead you to well-managed and successful development efforts. Most important about this new edition is the insight you will gain to engage board members, staff, and volunteers in meeting organizational goals."

—Ted Hart, ACFRE

"Highly functioning nonprofit philanthropic organizations are the cornerstone of any democratic society. With her truly holistic approach toward fundraising and organizational development, Simone presents great insights in building those organizations. This makes her one of the most influential fundraising thinkers globally. This is not a book for North American fundraisers only. It is a must-read for anyone, active at any level, in any nonprofit organization anywhere in the world. By the way, for those who think fundraising is just learning some techniques to raise money, this book explains how wrong that is."

—Ilja De Coster, Senior Fundraising Consultant
and Managing Partner, EthiCom, Belgium

"An indispensable resource! This is the one reference book that I recommend to the students in my course on fundraising campaigns at the Université de Montréal. The book presents a great variety of key features while it interlaces methodology with practical approaches. As such, it is an outstanding resource for any philanthropic endeavor, and it will contribute to the successful planning of great fundraising campaigns."

—Dominique Richard, Executive Director,
Muscular Dystrophy Canada, Québec division

"Simone, thanks again for motivating me, reminding me of my responsibilities as a person and a professional. Thanks for the intellectual workout too often missing in the day-to-day grind."

—Wendy Zufelt-Baxter, MA, CFRE, Campaign Coaches, Canada

"When the Fundraising Management Certificate curriculum was recently revised, I immediately added your book as required reading for my course. The course focuses on the nuts and bolts of running a fund development office. Your book stresses the need for organizational infrastructure and strong fundamentals, just the message I wanted to deliver. And it reminds students that fundraising professionals must play a broad and strategic role in an organization. I wish it were required reading for CEOs!"

—Cathy Mann, CFRE, Academic Coordinator and
Instructor, Ryerson University, Chang School;
Fundraising Management Certificate Program
and Principal, Cathy Mann & Associates

Strategic Fund Development

Strategic Fund Development

Building Profitable Relationships That Last

Third Edition

SIMONE P. JOYAUX, ACFRE

WILEY
John Wiley & Sons, Inc.

Published by John Wiley & Sons, Inc., Hoboken, New Jersey.
Published simultaneously in Canada.

Wiley also publishes its books in a variety of electronic formats. Some content that appears in print may not be available in electronic books. For more information about Wiley products, visit our web site at www.wiley.com.

Library of Congress Cataloging-in-Publication Data:

Joyaux, Simone P.
    Strategic fund development : building profitable relationships that last / Simone P. Joyaux.—3rd ed.
        p. cm.
    Includes bibliographical references and index.
    ISBN 978-0-470-88851-3 (hardback); ISBN 978-1-118-06225-8 (ebk.);
    ISBN 978-1-118-06226-5 (ebk.); ISBN 978-1-118-06227-2 (ebk.)
    1. Fund raising. I. Title.
    HG177.J69 2011
    658.15'224—dc22

                                                                        2010053523

Printed in the United States of America

10 9 8 7 6 5

Pour Georges qui aurait été si fier de me voir auteur comme lui.
C'est la troisième édition, mon Père!

For the six Joyaux siblings, the Big Kids and the Little Kids.
We were never in one book together. Separated by years
and two editions of Dad's blockbuster.

Contents

Foreword

Dear Reader,

This Foreword was written by Tim Burchill—professional colleague and personal friend—and originally appeared in the second edition of *Strategic Fund Development* (2001).

Tim died suddenly on February 20, 2007. Beyond our reach now. Always remembered with admiration, gratitude, and great affection.

It seems fitting to keep Tim's foreword for this third edition. First, because of what he said: He so well understood the intent of the book. Second, because his name represents so much of what is good and important about this sector.

As always, thank you, Tim.

In this second edition of her cogent and popular *Strategic Fund Development*, Simone P. Joyaux, ACFRE, writes that "visioning is a lively process of sharing what people most care about in a way that creates enthusiasm and shared commitment, a collective sense of what matters to the organization and its participants. . . . Your organization's vision is a snapshot of your desired future."

Another contemporary observer of organizational planning and leadership, Joel Barker, author and futurist, offers a prescription for organizations of all kinds, from governments to multinationals, and from highly endowed universities to grassroots not-for-profit agencies:

- Organizations with vision are powerfully enabled.
- Organizations without vision are at risk.

Simone Joyaux provides those of us who labor in the vineyards of the philanthropic sector with invaluable tools and concepts for translating organizational vision into reality. As one who has enjoyed the privilege of being a colleague of Simone's in various venues, I view this volume as but one more component of the innumerable contributions she has made to not-for-profit organizations and their stakeholders over the past quarter century.

A foreword is probably not the place to summarize key points of a book. But three central messages in this volume are so critical to a proper perspective of the philanthropic sector that they warrant highlighting:

1. Success in securing philanthropic gifts is not the result of master techniques, deploying the latest technology, or enjoying the most hallowed tradition. Simply

stated, successful philanthropic fundraising is the product of the intentional, strategic, and consistent building and nurturing of relationships with an ever-expanding pool of stakeholders.

2. "No organization can survive on mission and vision alone."
3. Even as the practice of fundraising is emerging as a true and recognized profession, volunteers remain critical to the fundraising process and to the validation of the legitimacy of not-for-profit organizations.

Too much of the literature available in the field today gives scant attention to these three essential paradigms. Yet they constitute the very heart and soul of Simone Joyaux's writing.

It has been my privilege to work closely with Simone Joyaux in recent years: as fellow members of two boards of directors—the Association of Fundraising Professionals (AFP) and CFRE International—and as fellow faculty members in the Saint Mary's University of Minnesota MA in Philanthropy and Development program. In every venue—as well as in this book—she gives evidence of her limitless commitment to advancing the field of philanthropy. She is a true steward of philanthropy.

Tim J. Burchill, CFRE
President, The Metanoia Group
Executive Director, Hendrickson Institute for Ethical Leadership
Founder and Senior Faculty, Saint Mary's University of
Minnesota MA in Philanthropy and Development
Winona, Minnesota

Preface

Do You Need This Book?

This book is *not* just about fundraising.

Yes, fund development is the frame for this book; it's right there in the title. But the foundation of the book is building effective and sustainable organizations. In fact, parts of this book are pretty much stand-alone publications on specific topics. For example:

- Chapter 3 focuses on your *internal operations*. Use this chapter to learn about organizational culture and good decision-making. Learn what it means to define your organization's values and why those matter. Use conversation as a core business practice and use questions to stimulate conversation. Do all this well and you'll be stronger.
- Chapter 6 focuses on *institutional strategic planning*. This chapter tells you just about everything you need to know to do effective strategic planning in any organization. Forget fund development. Use this chapter—and its many examples—to carry out strategic planning at your organization. Strategic planning answers questions like: Why do you matter? Where are you going? How will you get to where you're going? And this chapter shows you how to decide all this and how to develop your plan.
- Chapter 8 explains *how to work with volunteers*. Apply these enabling functions well, and you and your volunteers will be far more successful. Use these strategies to get the best governance and fundraising performance from your board members.

Should you buy this third edition if you already own the second edition? You'll find lots of new stuff:

- More about leadership—in a separate chapter in this new edition.
- More about the fundraising professional—in a separate chapter in this new edition.
- More about fund development planning—including measures and tips to involve your board members in the process and implementation.
- Lots of new examples—keep the second edition for its examples, and check out the new examples in this third edition, posted on the book's companion website: strategic plans, fund development plans, surveys, and more.
- New introductory chapter—highlighting key elements of fund development.

- Lots more cage-rattling questions—to stimulate you, your colleagues and board members, and the profession and sector. (Let's agitate and make change!)
- And a website for the book with even more examples.

It's interesting, writing a third edition of this book. Certainly it's easier. I'm not starting from the beginning. I'm not creating something totally new. Instead, I'm editing and adjusting and adding. People call this book a "classic" and a "standard" in the profession. Professionals tell me they still use the book regularly, dog-eared copies resting near at hand. For sure, I don't want to change so much that readers lose what they value.

For me, much of the second edition includes some favorite, always-useful learnings and insights. You'll find resources, citations, and quotations that are a decade or more old. But old sure doesn't mean out-of-date. My sources—for inspiration and quotations and information and learning—span many years. I continue using them because they're good, regardless of the publication date. I continue quoting Shakespeare and Confucius, too, despite their age.

So I'm not starting from the beginning, writing this third edition. But I've changed in the intervening years. I've learned more and questioned more—and I keep learning and questioning.

I've connected with more professionals and volunteers around the world—speaking at conferences, developing curricula, serving clients. I read more research because there's more to read now. I still consume books and publications—and not just in philanthropy.

All this challenges and stimulates me. I know that philanthropy is my life's work. I know who I am and accept myself with better understanding and greater grace. I know why I do what I do and with whom I want to do it, whether colleagues, friends, or clients.

All this is reflected in this third edition of *Strategic Fund Development*. You'll find more examples and new tools. You'll find different ways to approach the same old things we always have to do. You'll find affirmation for some of what you do. But you'll find challenges—even harsh challenges—to other things you do (or don't do).

Strategic Fund Development: Building Profitable Relationships That Last is really a book of many parts, a resource beyond fund development, as well as a resource for fund development. *Strategic Fund Development* is the precursor to *Keep Your Donors*—it's the prequel, if you will. The two books belong together.

Back in 2000, when writing the second edition of this book, I said I was worried and frustrated. I still am. Even more so now. What frustrates and worries me?

- Treating philanthropy as a financial transaction and a means to achieve the organization's mission.
- Inadequate donor centrism and relationship building.
- Poor engagement of board members, too often stimulated by inadequate enabling by staff.
- Lousy governance, even from the supposedly sophisticated and experienced organizations and board members.
- Excessive focus on *how* rather than sufficient focus on *why*.
- Continuing sense of entitlement on the part of nonprofits/nongovernmental organizations (NGOs).

Actually, my frustrations and worries are a pretty long list! Just check out my pet peeves (and personal rants) on my home page at www.simonejoyaux.com. Check out my professional tips there, too.

Yes, I'm frustrated and worried. But I'm also optimistic. Keep your own faith; I do. Keep challenging yourself, others, and me, too! Keep learning. Use frustration and worry. Together, we can make changes. Together, we can strengthen fund development, organizations, and communities. Together, we do make a difference.

Why bother? Because the reward is organizational success, not just survival. And organizational success matters because strong philanthropic organizations make a bigger difference in their communities. That's what matters.

A Note on This Book's Companion Website

Throughout the book, I refer you to the companion website, which is new to this third edition (separate from my own website at www.simonejoyaux.com). The companion website includes all appendices for this book. For a list of appendices, by chapter, see the list at the end of this print edition.

Please visit www. wiley.com/go/strategic and enter "strategic123" to download an array of sample surveys, strategic plans and fund development plans, and other useful information.

Simone P. Joyaux, ACFRE
www.simonejoyaux.com

Acknowledgments

Just like we say when recognizing donors, "This book was made possible by the generous contributions of many."

First, I start with Tom Ahern. Not because he is my life partner but because of his profession: donor communications specialist. He's taught me to write better, much better. He challenges me professionally. He reads and edits my stuff—including three editions of this book. Thank you, colleague Tom.

Thanks to Sarah C. Coviello, CFRE, excellent collegial resource. Always there to brainstorm and strategize with me; to explore angles and directions. And thanks to dearest friend, Sarah, always there to support me.

Thanks to my clients and my volunteer gigs that graciously gave me permission to use work we produced together: Audubon Society of Rhode Island, Steel Yard, United Way of Dutchess County, Wethersfield (CT) Library, Women's Fund of Rhode Island, Women's Foundation of Southern Arizona, and the YMCA of Greater Providence. Thanks, too, to the Jewish Community Foundation of Southern Arizona.

Thank you to the cohorts at Saint Mary's University. You challenge and engage and inspire me. And you give me great ideas and quotes for my writings.

Thank you to the authors and scholars and practitioners in the philanthropic sector. Your research and experience informs my own work.

Most especially, thank you to all who give their time and money and passion in order to build strong, healthy, and vibrant communities.

And finally, thanks again to Tom, this time as my life partner. Best friend and playmate. Passionate philanthropist. Together, we yell our family battle cry and fight for change.

About the Author

Simone P. Joyaux, ACFRE, is recognized internationally as one of the most thought-ful, inspirational, and provocative leaders in the philanthropic sector. She's an expert in fund development, strategic planning, and board development. She teaches philanthropy at the university level, speaks at conferences worldwide, and regularly serves on boards.

Strategic Fund Development: Building Profitable Relationships That Last is considered a classic that deserves regular updating. Her book *Keep Your Donors: The Guide to Better Communications and Stronger Relationships*, received rave reviews. She has also written chapters in *Philanthropy in 7 Words* and *The Fundraising Feasibility Study* and is a Web columnist for *The Nonprofit Quarterly*.

As a volunteer, Joyaux founded the Women's Fund of Rhode Island, a social justice organization. She has been recognized as Rhode Island's Outstanding Philanthropic Citizen.

Simone's website is full of free downloadable resources. Her weekly blogs and free e-news provide professional tips, pet peeves, and personal rants.

CHAPTER 1

Let's Start Here

An Important Introduction

Philanthropy is the act of individual citizens and local institutions contributing money or goods, along with their time and skills, to promote the well-being of others and the betterment of the community in which they live and work. Philanthropy can be expressed in informal and spontaneous ways or it can also be expressed in formal, organized ways whereby citizens give contributions to local organizations, which in turn use the funds to support projects that improve the quality of life.

—European Foundation Centre, Brussels

Where to Start

Should all books begin at the beginning, especially professional books? My book *Keep Your Donors: The Guide to Better Communications and Stronger Relationships* (co-authored with Tom Ahern; John Wiley & Sons, 2008) began at the beginning, even using that title for the first chapter: beginning at the beginning.

So what's the beginning to this third edition of *Strategic Fund Development*? I'll start with a mini overview of definitions, resources, and happenings. Not all-inclusive nor even fairly comprehensive. Just some thoughts and perceptions that set the context for what comes next.

What's Happening Out in the World

Does that sound too big? Well, it isn't. This is the place to start: the environment in which you and your organization operate.

Think about world events like the great recession (its name in the United States) or the global economic crisis (with its own acronym, GEC). The economy affects your community and your organization.

Think about demographics and lifestyles. What do you know about Baby Boomers, Millennials, and gender differences? What are the implications for serving your clients and hiring employees? What trends affect your fund development program and marketing/communications? Think about politics and public policy.

How will legislation and regulation affect your clients and donors, your programs and advocacy?

How about technology? Think about the Internet, Google and googling, YouTube, and social media. What's the effect on your programming and administration, your relationship building, and your marketing/communications? And there's more, of course: Think about war, safety, security, science, and religion. Think about all the elements in your environment that you cannot control but do have to manage. See Exhibit 1.1, a tiny snapshot just for fun. How out of date is this snapshot as you read it right now or again in six months or later?

Exhibit 1.1   Tiny Snapshot of What's Happening in the World

Ten Trends You Have to Watch

1. Globalization under fire.
2. Resources feeling the strain.
3. Trust in business running out.
4. A bigger role for government.
5. Shifting consumption patterns.
6. Management as a science.
7. Asia rising.
8. Industries taking new shape.
9. Price stability in question.
10. Innovation marching on.

Curious about what this means? Read "The 10 Trends You Have to Watch," by Erick Beinhocker, Ian Davis, and Lenny Mendonca, *Harvard Business Review* (July–August 2009). "After a full year in heads-down crisis mode," many business executives think the result is a "restructuring of the economic order." What do you think? How do these affect your nongovernmental enterprise (NGO) and its environment? Read the article. Check with McKinsey & Company as it tracks these forces.

Five Trends That Will Reshape the Nonprofit/NGO Sector

1. Demographic shifts redefine participation.
2. Technological advances abound.
3. Networks enable work to be organized in new ways.
4. Interest in civic engagement and volunteerism is rising.
5. Sector boundaries are blurring.

Curious about these? Read "Convergence: How Five Trends Will Reshape the Social Sector," by Heather Gowdy, Alex Hildebrand, David La Piana, and Melissa Mendes Campos of LaPiana Consulting (November 2009). What do you think?

Where do you get your information about what's happening in the world? What research sources help you the most? How do you nurture strategic conversations to talk about issues, trends, and their implications for your community and your organization?

By the time you read this book, resources I suggest may no longer exist or may not be so great. But you'll find more. That's part of your job. For now, here are just two examples:

1. Pew Research Center (www.pewresearch.org): Nonpartisan fact tank that provides information through public opinion polling on the issues, attitudes, and trends shaping the United States and the world.
2. Center on Philanthropy, Indiana University (www.philanthropy@iupui.edu): Resource center for increasing the understanding of philanthropy and improving its practice through research and education.

Visit the various associations and resource centers around the world that focus on the nonprofit/NGO sector. Look at their research and publications. Then go beyond the nonprofit/NGO sector. Stay on top of business theory and happenings in the for-profit sector. Check out my home page blogs and "newsyletter" for recommended research, resources, and readings. See the booklists and links on my website at www.simonejoyaux.com.

Defining Philanthropy and Fund Development

Years ago when speaking in Mexico City, I heard philanthropist Don Manuel Arango Arias talk about philanthropy as "freeing the talent of the citizenry." That goes well with my favorite definition of philanthropy, coined by Robert L. Payton, that philanthropy is "voluntary action for the common good."[1] Consider, too, what other leading sector experts say: John Gardner talks about "private initiatives for the public good," Lester Salamon refers to "the private giving of time or valuables . . . for public purposes" and Robert Bremner notes that "the aim of philanthropy . . . is improvement in the quality of human life."[2]

Philanthropy is not defined by wealth. Everyone can give. Many choose to give. And it is hoped that organizations value all donors and respect all gifts. As Alfre Woodard says in the preface to *Robin Hood Was Right*, one of the best books you'll ever read: "Giving isn't a posture reserved for the rich or powerful. It is the responsibility and privilege of every man, woman, and child to participate in the task of building more just and humane societies."[3] The concept of justice—too often excluded from philanthropy—broadens our horizons.[4] The common good demands our attention. And Woodard continues, "Charity is good, but supporting and creating social change are about power. Power can infuse lives with purpose and dignity. That opens up the possibility of joy. The life of the giver, as well as that of the receiver, is transformed."[5]

While the word *philanthropy* comes from the Greek, the philanthropic tradition is neither a Western invention nor Western-dominated. Think about Islam's Zakat. Think about Confucianism and Buddhism. Imagine the earliest societies working together to help each other.

What Is Fund Development?

Hank Rosso described fundraising as the servant of philanthropy.[6] I don't much like the term *fundraising*. I prefer *fund development*, which seems more strategic and encompassing.

What's most important is that philanthropy and fund development belong together. Fund development helps engage people in philanthropy. Do your staff and board members understand this partnership? Do your staff colleagues and board members honor fund development as much as they honor philanthropy?

When I combine philanthropy and development, here's my definition. Philanthropy means voluntary action for the common good, freeing the talents of the citizenry. Fund development is the essential partner of philanthropy. Fund development makes philanthropy possible by bringing together a particular cause and donors and prospects who are willing to invest in the cause.

Perhaps it's called "development" because we never find the answer . . . only questions that lead to more questions.

—Cohort 20, Master of Arts in Philanthropy and Development, Saint Mary's University of Minnesota

---

The goal of fund development is to acquire donors of time and money who stay with the charity. This is done through the process of relationship building. With the donor at the center, fund development nurtures loyalty and lifetime value, thus facilitating philanthropy. You know if your relationship building works, because your retention rates and the lifetime value of your donors and volunteers increase.

Philanthropy and Mission

Philanthropy—and its essential partner, fund development—do *not* merely serve your organization's "greater purpose" or its "true mission." Your organization's mission is *not* just about saving the whales or feeding and sheltering the homeless or educating youth. Your organization has two missions: saving the whales + philanthropy and fund development. Or educating you + philanthropy and fund development. Never forget this!

Some Basic Definitions and Distinctions

Constituents are different from prospects, but there are similarities. Prospects may not be what you think (or hope) they are. Maybe you've confused prospects and the predisposed. Your organization needs a shared vocabulary to move conversation and decision-making forward. Try these:

Constituent: Someone who relates to or cares about your organization. Can be an individual, business, service organization, mosque, or other entity.

Constituency: Group of constituents.

Stakeholder: Not so different from a constituent. Someone who has a direct interest in your organization or your cause. *The AFP Fundraising Dictionary* has a nice angle: "a person who has a special interest in the activities and decisions of an organization."[7] Stakeholders are actually interested in the decisions that your organization makes. Do you think your organization understands that? What would happen if your organization actually reported on the decisions it makes? What would happen if your stakeholders actually watched your organization make decisions? Would your organization perform better if stakeholders were watching how the sausage really got made?

Predisposed: An individual, business, or some other entity whose interests and actions suggest a possible inclination or susceptibility toward your organization's cause or mission. "Suspect" is common fundraising terminology. But who wants to hear anyone referred to in such a pejorative manner? So I've invented this alternative term. In *The AFP Fundraising Dictionary*, a suspect is defined as "a possible source of support whose philanthropic interests appear to match those of a particular organization but whose linkages, giving ability, and interests have not yet been confirmed."

Prospect: An individual, business, or some other entity that has demonstrated an interest in your cause or organization. The individual has raised his or her hand by buying your services or asking to join the mailing list. In some manner, in some way, the individual, business, or entity has signaled an interest in your cause and your organization. Think of a prospect as a constituent who has moved along the constituency development continuum and is now considered qualified to receive a request of some sort. For example, a request to join your board or to give a financial contribution. The Visual Thesaurus (www.visualthesaurus.com) uses the phrase "the possibility of future success," also defined as somebody or something with potential.

Donor: Here comes our favorite definition, right? Donor: an individual, business, or some other entity that has given a gift of time or money or service to your organization. (So when this book refers to "people," I mean individuals, foundations, corporations, civic groups, whatever.) A donor of time is usually called a volunteer. But remember, a volunteer is a donor. Donors may be called contributors and investors, too.

And just a little P.S. What's a customer? Someone who uses or pays for goods or services. Watch the little diagram at www.visualthesaurus.com shift. Follow the other words for customer, for example: client, consumer, patron, user, subscriber, frequenter, business relation.

Naming the Sector and Its Organizations

Over the years, many have questioned the sector's name. It seems strange to define an entire sector by what it isn't and what it doesn't do (e.g., "not-for-profit" or "nonprofit" or "nongovernmental"). Others have proposed alternative terms like "independent sector" or "third sector." But these terms never seem to stick. I suspect "nonprofit" and "nongovernmental" are here to stay. And it isn't a battle I want to fight. In this book, I use nonprofit/NGO.

How about those terms "earned" and "unearned" income? "Unearned" references charitable gifts. Hey, nonprofits "earn" those gifts through very hard work! I say "income" with two subsets: revenue (referencing fees and tuition and box office, etc.) and public support/charitable contributions. Both equally earned, thank you!

By the way, it's okay that organizations generate excess income over expense. In fact, healthy organizations do just that. I wonder how well those outside the sector understand that. Actually, I wonder how many outside the sector understand how the nonprofit/NGO sector is financed. I wonder how well those outside (and inside) the sector understand the financing conflicts, the lack of capitalization, the inadequacy of resources, and the inappropriate expectations forced upon the sector.[8]

Why Does This Sector Matter?

The third sector has been called the "keystone of a caring society,"[9] as contrasted with the for-profit and government sectors, which might not be so caring. The nonprofit/NGO sector is essential for the "spirit and character of our society and for the freedom and fulfillment of each of us."[10] So says Waldemar A. Nielsen in his marvelous paean to the sector. The third sector is comprised of a myriad of organizations large and small, focused on education and human services, arts and culture, public society/benefit and health, and more. The third sector is essential to a healthy community.

Nielsen describes the sector as doing three key things:

1. Delivering a wide range of services to people—often bridging the gap between government investment and actual community needs.
2. Strengthening the other two sectors—the for-profit marketplace and government—often producing corrective and compensatory effects.
3. Serving as a humanizing force—offering people an opportunity to give. (Nielsen uses the phrase "an outlet for the nearly universal impulse to altruism."[11])

More than two decades ago, Nielsen ended his remarks with the following: "The Third Sector is now in serious difficulty—under simultaneous assault by inflation, government regulation and competition and the negative effects of some misbegotten tax policies. [The Third Sector's] own mismanagement of its affairs is another worrisome problem. To preserve its freedom and vitality will require a long determined and persevering struggle by all of us who are committed to the preservation of a humane, compassionate, and free society in this country. That cause is eminently worth fighting for."[12]

What might you say today? Something very similar. The third sector is in serious difficulty. As the saying goes, *plus ça change, plus c'est la même chose.*[13] The more things change, the more they stay the same.

Think about Nielsen's statement that the nonprofit/NGO sector provides corrective and compensatory benefits to the marketplace and government. During his 1979 remarks, Nielsen cited Kenneth Boulding, noting that without the nonprofit sector, the economy would quickly develop "conditions that would be widely regarded as pathological . . . [the economy] might easily produce distributions of income which would be regarded as unacceptable."[14]

Isn't that where we are in 2010, as I write this third edition? In the United States, this unjust economic situation has been developing for many years. And there's injustice everywhere in the world. As Nielsen said, the nonprofit sector is the counterbalance to government and the for-profit sector. A critical role of the nonprofit/NGO sector must be questioning the status quo. A major role for the sector must be advocating appropriate public policy.

Nonprofits and Democracy

Without a doubt, the nonprofit/NGO sector plays a critical role in creating and sustaining democracy.[15] Through voluntary association, citizens gather together and question, rally, and act.

In his nineteenth-century examination of life in the United States, Alexis de Tocqueville wrote extensively about voluntary associations. Beginning with the act of associating, de Tocqueville notes:

> *The most natural privilege of man, next to the right of acting for himself, is that of combining his exertions with those of his fellow creatures and of acting in common with them. The right of association therefore appears to me almost as inalienable in its nature as the right of personal liberty. No legislator can attack it without impairing the foundations of society.*[16]

De Tocqueville goes on to say:

> *In democratic countries the science of association is the mother science; the progress of all the others depends on the progress of that one. Among the laws that rule human societies there is one that seems more precise and clearer than all the others. In order that men remain civilized or become so, the art of associating must be developed and perfected among them in the same ratio as equality of conditions increases.*[17]

Through the right of associating, people push back against issues as diverse as laws and elected officials, corporations and their acts. By associating voluntarily, people exercise their right to question and critique, advocate and lobby. As associations—not just individuals—people can hold accountable their government as well as the marketplace.

Look at the movements that forced government to change and forced the for-profit sector to change somewhat. Think about the antismoking and environmental movements. Think about the Civil Rights movement. Look at the marriage equality movement and the antiwar movement. Remember the fall of the Berlin Wall. Look at the freedom movements around the world.

Citizens voluntarily engage in nonprofit organizations. NGOs fight and fight hard, including protests and litigation. And change happens. With change sometimes come—one hopes—stronger democracies and more justice. Thanks to the third sector. But still more must be done. The third sector must fight harder. More nonprofits must join in.

What stops NGOs from embracing their role in democracy? Why doesn't the sector step up and fight harder? Lots of reasons: Insufficient time. Not enough resources—after all, big funders (especially foundations) don't always support advocacy and public policy work. Why else? Fear of donor reaction. Lots of donors give to direct service and don't want to make systemic change. Systemic change means questioning the status quo, and lots of donors *are* the status quo. Why else? Regulatory threats. For example, the U.S. government invents laws and regulations to reduce the advocacy power of nonprofits. And nonprofits often don't find the wherewithal and motivation to fight this. On and on it goes.

The nonprofit/NGO sector does not live up to its potential to fight government. But let's not just blame the sector. The people—our donors and volunteers and voters—must stand up and speak out on behalf of the sector and on behalf of democracy, which is reinforced by this unique sector. The time is always now.

Why Does This Sector Matter? Redux

Read Michael Edwards's book *Small Change: Why Business Won't Save the World*.[18] It's his response (critical, fortunately) to the philanthrocapitalism movement. It's his challenge (come on, people, let's wake up) to society. It's an invitation (a much-needed battle cry) to you and me to fight.

> *For a society so enamored of capitalism, the United States is particularly vulnerable to the fascination of social entrepreneurship and philanthrocapitalism. I must ask my international colleagues if they are so easily seduced. I hope that they aren't. And I'm sad that the United States is.*

Like me, Edwards wants to provoke conversations so there's public discourse. And through public discourse, we can hear each other, learn from each, and ensure a stronger future for philanthropy and its results.

In sum, philanthrocapitalism claims that the "traditional ways of solving social problems do not work, so business thinking and market forces should be added to the mix."[19] Or, in other words, "business thinking and market methods will save the world."[20] (And make a lot of money for a limited number of people, too!)

Now, that's where I get stuck, and so does Edwards: the excessive admiration for business thinking and market methods. Let's see. ... Would that be General Motors' almost-bankruptcy and the 2010 BP Gulf oil spill?

I guess all those philanthropic responses to natural disasters, civil rights, poverty, education, the arts—from NGOs and millions of people—don't count for much? Weren't sufficiently efficient? Didn't produce meaningful and long-lasting results?

It's human to want quick solutions and facile answers. Nonetheless, it reflects a dangerous naïveté and a lack of understanding about what is required to make change. For example: This philanthrocapitalist approach hopes to fix the problems caused by capitalism. Honestly, I'm not trusting that. This approach fixes problems but doesn't change the underlying systems like racism or sexism. I want more than Band-Aids; I want real change. Moreover, philanthrocapitalists represent only a small portion of our society, but hold a disproportionate amount of control. That doesn't work for me. I believe everyone should and must have access. Philanthropy—and the value of the nonprofit/NGO sector—is about social transformation. Edwards justifiably asks, "Can these new approaches transform societies, or do they simply treat the symptoms of social problems in more efficient ways?"[21] I know my answer. What's yours?

Sure, philanthrocapitalism can make a difference. It can find cures for various diseases and produce jobs. But that doesn't fix the systemic issues that confront our society—things like greed and inequality, fear and prejudice, privilege and disadvantage.

Few areas of business expertise translate well into the very complex social and political problems, where solutions have to be fought for and negotiated—not produced, packaged, and sold. And, so far at least, there aren't many philanthrocapitalists who are prepared to invest in the challenges of long-term institution building, the deepening of democracy, or the development of a different form of economy in which inequality is systematically attacked.[22]

Economic growth doesn't fix racism, sexism, homophobia, and the fundamental inequities of our world. Economic growth doesn't fix poverty, either—just look at the growing disparity in income over the past few decades. As Edwards notes, "no great social cause was mobilized through the market in the twentieth century."[23] And I don't believe that the market will *ever* mobilize any great social transformation. But that's okay. That's okay as long as philanthrocapitalists quit promoting their excessive value and societies stop looking for quick fixes. Business thinking is different from nonprofit/NGO sector thinking. Capitalism—even philanthrocapitalism—focuses on the financial bottom line first. The bottom line in the nonprofit sector is different. The bottom line is mission, not money. The bottom line is the common good, not the marketplace's good. The result is social transformation, not reinforcement of the status quo. Certainly, nonprofits need to follow some good business practices, to stay healthy. But the bottom line is fundamentally different.

Edwards asks us to reflect on what is meant by the nonprofit sector, often called civil society. He defines civil society as "the things we do together, not because we want to make a profit or earn a material reward, but because we care enough about something to take collective action.... [Civil society] provides a space free of government control and the pressures of the market, a space in which private citizens can organization for public work.... It's that independence that enables civil society groups to hold government and business accountable for their actions and to act as crucibles for new or unpopular ideas, for democratic politics and the birth of social movements, and for speaking truth to power."[24]

Compare Edwards's remarks to Nielsen's. Look at de Tocqueville's commentaries. Read the recommended articles about the nonprofit sector's role in democracy. Review my monograph about "philanthropy's moral dilemma." What do you think? Are you ready for renewed battle? I hope so.

We must reject the idea—well intentioned, but dead wrong—that the primary path to greatness in the social sectors is to become "more like a business."

From *Good to Great and the Social Sectors: A Monograph to Accompany* Good to Great, by Jim Collins (New York: HarperCollins, 2005), 1

A Sad Truth

"Is there something in society's subconscious that expects nonprofits to operate in 'poverty-like ways'?" That question was a showstopper in the Cohort 20 classroom (Master of Arts in Philanthropy and Development, Saint Mary's University of Minnesota), summer 2010.

We were talking about the starvation mentality in so many nonprofits. You know, things like: really old, rather dysfunctional computers; such poor wages that employees cannot afford a reasonable mortgage and may have to visit the soup kitchen for a meal. We talked about the chronic underfunding of necessary infrastructure and overhead. We ranted against Guidestar, Charity Navigator, and their ilk that rate nonprofits based on spurious ratios. We recognized that inadequate infrastructure causes employees to work excessively long hours with poor tools and insufficient professional development. And we realized how hard it is to explain this to boards that make decisions.

There in the classroom, members of Cohort 20 explored why this happens. Who decided that 90 percent of the charitable gift must go to direct service, thus starving the organization and its employees of necessary resources? Who decided it was okay to pay less than a living wage to people who work in nonprofits?

One cohort member asked: "Does society think nonprofit employees should be paid low wages because then the employees will relate better to the clients?" Another cohort member observed: "Why does a willingness to accept lower wages (much lower wages than for-profits) seem to be an indicator or qualification for one's job in the nonprofit sector?" This is terrible. And unjust.

Is this a holdover from religion? (Although why should religious orders take a vow of poverty?) Is this some implied mandate from government that because the nonprofit sector gets certain benefits, the working conditions and wages can be lousy? What's going on?

I believe in a living wage for everyone, including employees in the non-profit/NGO sector. I believe that adequate infrastructure is necessary to support the programs and services provided to fulfill the mission. And by the way, I believe that competent people work in the nonprofit sector, just like competent people work in the for-profit sector. I also believe that there are incompetent performers in both sectors. I also expect that wages in the nonprofit/NGO sector will not be outrageous. I think it's a violation of the integrity and ethics of the nonprofit/NGO sector to pay the excessive salaries, benefits, and bonuses found in some for-profit jobs. That said, I have no problem with a decent wage, a *darn* decent wage for nonprofit staff.

It's time for the sector to fight this. It's time for nonprofits to invest in infrastructure and demand fair wages for their employees. It's time to stop honoring the unrealistic expectations of government contractors and scared boards. I believe we can explain this to our donors. Let's get it together and make change.

Basic Principles of Fund Development

What are the key messages that you want your staff and board members to understand? How do you define the basic principles of fund development? Here's my current list—current, I say, because as time passes, maybe I'll modify it. To check for any modifications, visit my website at www.simonejoyaux.com. For now, read on. Use Appendix 1-A, "Basic Principles of Fund Development," on this book's website to stimulate conversation with your staff and board. Make sure everyone is using common vocabulary for your conversations. Check the definitions earlier in this chapter.

Culture of Philanthropy

The right attitude matters as much as anything. Culture refers to the personality and attitude of your organization. A culture of philanthropy means that everyone accepts and celebrates the beauty of philanthropy and donors, no matter the type or size of the gift. It's your job as a leader to nurture a culture of philanthropy in your organization. See Chapter 3 for more.

Donor-Centered Organization

Successful fund development requires donor centrism.[25] Focus on the donor or prospective donor. "It's not what your organization is selling; it's what I'm buying that counts. I'm interested in my interests, my motivations, and my aspirations. Match those and then I'll give to you. Otherwise, leave me alone!"

Don't universalize your own passion. Not everyone is interested in your cause, no matter how convincing you are. Do not try to convince them! That's offensive. Instead, find those who share your passion.

Emotions as Key Decision-Makers

Giving is an emotional act not a financial transaction. Your organization is the means by which donors live out their own interests and aspirations. Your organization is the conduct to achieve the donor's desires.

Neuroscience and psychological research document that all human decisions are triggered by emotions.[26] Then rationale steps in.

Emotion is multi-dimensional: it focuses on a person's core goals, directs attention and interest, arouses the body for action, and integrates social group and cultural factors. It is thus a central component of meaning making.

From "Emotional Dimensions of Watching Zoo Animals: An Experience Sampling Study Building on Insights from Psychology," by Olin Eugene Myers Jr., Carol D. Saunders, and Andrej A. Birjulin, Curator: *The Museum Journal* 47, Issue 3 (July 2004): 299–321

Research from the direct mail industry says that people give in response to one or more of seven emotions: greed, guilt, anger, fear, flattery, exclusivity, and salvation. These really resonate with me. And for those who say, "Those emotions are so negative," get over it. They're emotions, feelings—neither positive nor negative. (By the way, I imagine that both Mahatma Gandhi and Martin Luther King Jr. were angry, very angry. And look what they accomplished.)

People move from one emotion (e.g., anger) to hope, by using your agency as the means to make change. Tom Ahern refers to this partnering of emotions as "twin sets."

Importance of Volunteers

Remember, philanthropy is defined as voluntary action for the common good. Volunteer participation is critical. Engage volunteers, including board members and others in the fund development process.

Make sure your staff effectively enables volunteers to participate in this meaningful work of identifying, cultivating, and soliciting. See Chapter 8 for a complete description of enabling volunteers.

Trespassing

Don't do it! Don't ask your board members and other volunteers to trespass on their personal and professional relationships. Don't you do it, either.

This favor exchange doesn't focus on donor interests, instead relying on personal relationships. What happens once the favor giver or receiver feels no further reciprocal obligation? Or when the solicitor asking for the favor is no longer affiliated with your organization? Instead, use connections to identify those who might be predisposed to your cause. If you cannot qualify them as prospects (and it's their choice!), then leave them alone. Nurture relationships between prospects and your organization, getting them ready to be asked and asked again.

Permission Marketing

Effective fund development is like permission marketing: People opt in or opt out. Seth Godin explored this term in his 1999 book of the same name. Godin contrasts permission marketing to interruption marketing, the traditional advertising/marketing approach. You know, the billboards and glitzy ads—and sending me a newsletter that I didn't ask for.

Godin observes: "Rather than simply interrupting a television show with a commercial or barging into the consumer's life with an unaccounted phone call or letter [or in fundraising, the uninvited newsletter or a solicitation], tomorrow's marketer [and top-notch fundraiser] will first try to gain the consumer's consent to participate in the selling process."[27]

So you identify the predisposed—those you suspect might have interests similar to your cause or organization—and introduce yourself.[28] Then, if the person (or corporation or foundation, etc.) expresses interest, that gives you permission.

Permission marketing is the privilege (not the right) of delivering anticipated, personal and relevant messages to people who actually want to get them ... treating people with respect is the best way to earn their attention. Permission doesn't have to be formal but it has to be obvious.

From a blog by Seth Godin called "Permission Marketing" on January 31, 2008, www.sethgodin.com

---

Visibility

Visibility does not produce more contributions. Everyone focuses on his or her own interests. Your agency can be more and more visible—but if I'm not interested, I'm not paying attention. And I sure won't send money. Just take a look at Exhibit 1.2, "Simone, Sports, and the Myth of Visibility."

Exhibit 1.2   Simone, Sports, and the Myth of Visibility

First, here's the backstory.

Every spring in the United States, March Madness, engulfs sports enthusiasts. This is the month for the annual collegiate basketball playoffs. The actual formal title is the National Collegiate Athletic Association (NCAA) basketball championship. Board members change board meeting dates to stay home and watch the games on television. Television networks battle with big bucks fighting for the rights to televise. Employees talk about the games at work. And apparently, all the media participate in March Madness at equally frenzied levels. Headlines, feature stories, newscasts. Evidently this is quite a show. I, however, don't pay attention. Why? Because I'm not interested.

I don't like sports. I don't watch them—nope, not even the Super Bowl thing. I don't engage in sports chatter. Often I don't know if a sports team is football, basketball, or baseball. Actually, I had to get my sister to verify that I correctly recited the backstory! So here's my story about the NCAA basketball championship.

In March a few years ago (see, I don't even remember which year!) my sister Nicole called me. I could tell she was very excited.

"Hey, Simone, I know you don't pay any attention to sports, but guess what?"

"What?" I responded with no enthusiasm whatsoever.

"MSU is one of the teams in the final game of the NCAA basketball championship!"

Unless you're familiar with the NCAA basketball championship, you probably wonder what MSU is. It's Michigan State University. I'm an alumna and so are most of my siblings. But it's bigger than that. My dad was a professor at MSU. I grew up in East Lansing, Michigan, home of MSU. The campus dominated the landscape because of its land mass and numbers of students. My family socialized with MSU professors. I visited my dad in his office at MSU, beginning, I assume, in my infancy.

I'm actually very interested in MSU! I even approach strangers wearing Spartan sweatshirts. You would think, given my deep attachment to MSU, that I would have noticed its name blaring at me in such a highly promoted activity as the NCAA basketball championship. But I didn't. Even though I'm very interested in Michigan State University, I didn't even notice its name when it was all over every single form of sports media for weeks. Because I—along with all other people—pay attention to what interests oneself, and little else.

(continued)

(Continued)

Here's another sports example: World Cup football, probably the major sporting event worldwide. In June 2006, Tom and I were visiting our home in Valros, France, a tiny village in the Languedoc region. There was a big outdoor movie screen in the center of the town square. Traffic no longer passed that way. This was really weird.

I asked a neighbor what was going on. He looked at me strangely, very strangely. *"Mais madame, c'est le Coupe du Monde ce soir. Et l'équipe de France joue."* Ah, the French team—les Bleus—was playing in the World Cup. The World Cup of soccer. Soccer, the biggest sport worldwide. The World Cup arguably the biggest global sporting event. The outdoor screen in Valros stayed up for two games, the semifinal and the final. In Paris, people crowded the Champs-Elysées to watch the final game on big screens. That's the year that Zinédine Zidane head-butted the Italian player in the chest. Les Bleus lost.

What's the moral of these stories? People pay attention to what interests them, and little else. If sports don't matter to you, the NCAA March Madness basketball playoffs or World Cup football, among the world's most heavily publicized events, simply disappear.

Source: Modified from *Keep Your Donors: The Guide to Better Communications and Stronger Relationships*, by Tom Ahern and Simone Joyaux (Hoboken, NJ: John Wiley & Sons, 2008).

It's okay if someone doesn't know who your agency is or what it does. Tell them, if they seem interested. That's identifying the predisposed. By the way, do *not* solicit someone unless you know for sure that the person knows about your agency.

Where do you need to be visible? Among your current donors, because you want to build their loyalty. Absence does *not* make the heart grow fonder—it's out of sight, out of mind! Nurture these donor relationships. Do you need more convincing? Are you hounded by board members who talk about community awareness? Is some marketing/public relations firm telling you it can help increase your marketplace position, thus making it easier to raise more money? Just read Tom Ahern's comments in Appendix 1-B on this book's website.

Give before Asking

You have to give first. *You* means each board member, the CEO and development officers, and fundraising volunteers. Why? Because you cannot represent an agency or cause without demonstrating your own financial and volunteer investment.

Every board member can afford to give a financial contribution every year—whether it's 5 euros, 500 Indian rupees, or 50,000 Kuwaiti dinars. I once listened to a single mother on welfare tell her fellow board members to quit patronizing her. "I can give, even if it's only two dollars. Just don't compare my gift size to someone else's gift size."

Yes, volunteering time is giving. But that gift of time does not substitute for a gift of money. Both are necessary. Both are expected of all board members.

Give to the best of your personal ability. And make this nonprofit/NGO one of your top commitments.

Ask to Receive

Why do most people give? Because they are asked. It's really that simple. But ask only those who are interested. Ask the right prospect for the right amount at the right time for the right project in the right way with the right solicitor.

An Individual Giving Program

Build an individual giving program. Each year, individuals, not foundations or corporations, give the largest portion of philanthropic gifts in North America. What about elsewhere? What's happening in your country? Can you afford to ignore—or postpone—the importance of individual participation? By the way, in my experience, individuals are more loyal donors than foundations or corporations or any other source of charitable gifts. Yes, individuals continuing giving, even in a bad economy.

Profession

Fund development is a profession. Like any profession, fund development relies on a well-researched body of knowledge,[29] has a code of ethical principles and standards,[30] and protects the public through voluntary certification[31] of professionals.

The documented body of knowledge and best practices guide the profession. Research tests new ideas, and validates and adds to the body of knowledge.

So what about personal opinions? You know, those comments about what your boss or your board member likes or doesn't like, but couched in terms of "what works" and "what is best." Qualified opinions from people who know the body of knowledge and possess the particular skills and expertise—those opinions matter. Strategic questions about the body of knowledge—exploring why and testing new ideas—they're okay, too. But personal opinions without knowledge and expertise are rarely germane, often distracting, and mostly inappropriate. Facts trump opinions. Expertise in the particular subject matters more than position and power. Personal opinion—without the body of knowledge—doesn't and shouldn't count for much.

Balanced Funding Mix

You know the maxim "Don't put all your eggs in one basket." Your organization needs a balanced mix of funding sources and solicitation strategies. That balanced mix fosters stability and credibility. However, a balanced mix does not mean equally apportioned between source and strategy. Different organizations have different funding models. For example, as a human services provider, your organization might rely more heavily on government contracts. Most educational institutions rely more heavily on tuition. Some performing arts institutions depend on box office receipts. Check out "Ten Nonprofit Funding Models"[32] in the spring 2009 *Stanford Social Innovation Review*.

Funding sources include individuals, foundations, corporations, governments, civic groups, and sometimes faith groups, too. Solicitation strategies include personal face-to-face solicitation[33] (the most effective and least expensive), direct mail, formal proposals, telephone, and fundraising events.

Just a reminder—to you and especially your board members: Whenever possible, the best way to solicit a gift is through face-to-face solicitation.

Fund Development Problems

Most fund development problems are actually *not* fund development problems. Most problems relate to other areas of operation. Good fundraisers and quality organizations identify and fix the real problems. See Chapter 4, which describes the best fundraisers as organizational development specialists.

Competition for Gifts and Donor Fatigue

Whenever fundraisers and organizations say they're "competing" for gifts, I twitch. And me twitching is not a good thing, not for me and not for others nearby. Twitching often leads to rants.

You're not competing for my money. I give to what interests me. And I'm not interested in most of your organizations. The same goes for most donors and prospects. People (and foundations and businesses and . . .) pay attention to what interests them. And that's usually where they give and volunteer, too.

On the other hand, there's a lot of congestion. Lots of worthy causes and lots of quality nonprofits/NGOs. Lots of messages bombarding you and me and all the others regularly. I pick what interests me. You and the others do, too.

Of course there are many dimensions to identifying interests and linking to those interests. Obviously, relationship building and fund development are not small activities. Yes, this is a lot of work. But the complaint of competition is an easy excuse and not particularly useful as a context for doing this work. Competition also seems to give organizations and fundraisers permission to avoid their own responsibility.

How about donor fatigue? I've never understood that one, either. Donors are tired of giving? Donors are tired of all the world's problems? How does that fit with loyal givers of time and money? I think donors are tired of getting solicitations from organizations and causes that aren't of interest to them. I think donors are frustrated that they don't know how organizations spend their gifts, what impact results from gifts. And why don't donors know this? Because organizations don't tell stories well, don't use donor-centered communications, and so forth.

Nothing Can or Should Substitute for Philanthropy

And I end this introductory chapter with a battle cry for nonprofit, nongovernmental charitable organizations: Nothing substitutes for donors.

I'm worried by what I see as an excessive focus on generating revenue by nonprofits. There's a new old chant in town: "Let's start a business where customers buy stuff and then we won't have to rely so heavily on donations!" Articles proclaim that nonprofits are "finally wising up."

It sounds like revenue is better than charitable contributions. Hey, we need both. Lots of both, revenue and charitable gifts. But increasingly, it seems that the reliance on donations is seen as somewhat demeaning. Even the term *nonprofit* suggests—in our capitalistic, profit-driven society—that to be nonprofit is less than. (As an aside: Notice the trend of hiring for-profit people to lead nonprofits. This worries me. See the section entitled "A Digression" in Chapter 4.) In summary, the revenue/charitable gifts equation seems to be: Revenue is better than charitable gifts. Customers produce revenue so customers are better, better than donors.

Generating Both Revenue and Charitable Gifts

Let's step back a moment. Since time began, many nonprofits have generated both revenue and charitable gifts. So the new news is pretty old—just more egregious with moneymaking entrepreneurs sneering about how to start business ventures. Theaters and symphonies produce revenue by selling tickets and refreshments. Museums generate revenue with admissions and gift shop sales. Colleges and universities charge tuition. Hospitals charge fees paid by insurance companies and government contracts.

In addition to revenue streams, these organizations run fundraising programs that garner charitable gifts. When I worked at Trinity Repertory Company, one of the top regional theaters in the United States, we generated 70 percent of our income from revenue and 30 percent from charitable gifts. Nonprofit hospitals, on the other hand, may get only 10 percent of their income from gifts. Revenue is great, as are the customers who produce the revenue. Nonprofits that can generate admissions, sales, and the like may well enjoy a more balanced financing stream.

Uniqueness of Nonprofits/NGOs

But nothing substitutes for donors and their charitable gifts. I repeat: Nothing substitutes for donors. And not because of the money. Donors are different from customers. The uniqueness of any and all nonprofits is philanthropy, voluntary action for the common good.

Voluntary action for the common good . . . the uniqueness and, yes, the strength of nonprofits. Individuals, families, businesses, service groups, and faith groups giving their time and their money to build strong communities. Moms and dads and little kids and teens volunteering in the soup kitchen and cleaning up rivers.

People with a little and lots of money giving gifts to help others. The woman who sent a few dollars to help a charity. The school kids who sent all the pennies they collected. The banker, the janitor, the nonprofit executive director, the pastor—all sending donations to causes they care about. And sure, Bill and Melinda Gates, too. Voluntary action for the common good. Nothing substitutes for these donors. I say "these donors," not their gifts. Again, it's not the money; it's the donors. It's the meaning of donors investing, committing, engaging in a cause.

Donors worry about the lives of others and the state of the world. Donors want to make a difference. And nonprofit charitable organizations are the means by which donors make that difference. Nonprofits/NGOs are the conduit for donors to live out their feelings and fulfill their aspirations. Nothing can substitute for these loyal donors. Nothing can substitute for voluntary action for the common good, not even buying things.

Customers and Donors

Are donors stickier than customers? Yes, says *Giving USA*.[34] Even in tough economic times, charitable giving still happens.[35]

Sure, revenue is good, but it doesn't substitute for charitable gifts. Sure, customer loyalty is great. I'm an ardent Apple fan. I'm a very loyal customer. But in a tough economy, I may not buy the newest iPod or the even newer laptop, which is so cool and better than the one I have.

I was a loyal customer of Michigan State University, my alma mater. But I'm not a customer any longer. I am, however, a donor. I'm a loyal donor. I've made a bequest in my will to MSU, too. Loyal customers are wonderful . . . those Apple buyers and Trinity Repertory Company subscribers. But the Trinity Rep subscribers who are also donors—now that's really something.

Customers and donors are not interchangeable, not even the really loyal ones. Yes, customers and donors have much in common. Just read Adrian Sargeant and Elaine Jay's book *Building Donor Loyalty* (Jossey-Bass, 2004). But customers and donors are not exactly the same.

Loyal customers can be affected by the economy. Customers can move on once their need is met, or in search of product enhancements. Ticket buyers may not buy tickets to the most challenging and controversial plays, even though that's the mission of the theater.

Donors, however, allow the theater to fulfill its mission rather than produce popular plays only. (Popular plays, subject to customer whim, are Broadway.) Donors give beyond a particular play because they're committed to the theater's mission. Donors give in tough economic times. Donors increase their gifts without the expectation of goods and services. Donors can be forever, even after death.

Fundraising Events Aren't as Good as Charitable Gifts, Either

Nothing substitutes for donors. And there's a parallel in fundraising itself: Nothing substitutes for charitable gifts, not even ticket purchases for fundraising events. Fundraising events cannot substitute for requesting a donation. The reality is that buying a ticket to an event is often about attending the event. If people are not interested in attending the event, they may not buy the ticket. And far too many fundraising events have no real connection to the cause, anyway; the event is just about making money. (Oh, don't even get me started on golf events!)

Also, in my experience, the economy affects fundraising events more than the economy affects charitable giving. Corporations back off of event sponsorship, but still may give a gift. Individuals don't buy tickets to events when times are tough, but these same individuals will still give a donation. The ticket is equated with the event. A donation—with no goods or services exchanged—is about the cause. So beware of too much focus on fundraising events.

In Conclusion

Spend more time on charitable gifts and donors. Beware of too much time focused on revenue generation—or overreliance on revenue, which is subject to the whim of customers. Nothing substitutes for donors. Nothing. Ever. Never.

Summary

This seems like a good way to end this introductory chapter. Thank you, Jeff Brooks, fundraising leader, from his July 29, 2010, blog at www.futurefundraisingnow.com.

If fundraising isn't important, you won't survive.

How important is fundraising within your organization?

Is it a necessary evil?

Is it the red-headed stepchild?

Is it an honored and celebrated part of what you do?

I've seen all of the above. And let me tell you: The more fundraising is respected and integrated with the organization as a whole, the better that organization does—financially and otherwise.

Fundraising is absolutely necessary to make all our good works possible, but it's more than that.

Fundraising is noble and good, but it's more than that.

Fundraising is just as important as program, but it's more than that.

Fundraising is itself a Good Deed of the highest order. Because it motivates people to become more conscious, evolved, effective, and integrated. No matter what else your organization does, if you are raising funds, you are making the world a better place by soliciting donors for funds.

The organizations that grasp this are the ones that will be raising the most money. Those that don't will fade away in the coming years. I know this will make me sound like a Republican, but market forces will take care of this for us. The clueless nonprofits will fail; the excellent ones will succeed. It's that simple.

CHAPTER 2

Positioning Your Organization to Survive and Thrive

The Four Relationships That Are Critical to Effective and Productive Fund Development (and Healthy Organizations)

Is everything okay? Unless you work in a nuclear power plant, the answer is certainly no (and if you work there, I hope the answer is yes). No, everything is not okay. Not in a growing organization. Not if your company is making change happen, or dealing with customers. How could it be?

And yet, that's what so many managers focus on. How to make everything okay.

We spend so much time smoothing things out, we lose the opportunity for change, or for texture or creativity.

Instead of working so hard to make everything okay, perhaps it is more helpful to work hard at living with a world that rarely is.

—Seth Godin's blog, January 4, 2009, at www.sethgodin.com

Most leaders and managers are task proficient to one degree or another. Organizational cultures emphasize task and results, and base most rewards and promotions on them. In the last 25 years, there has been an increasing interest in examining the processes by which results are obtained. . . . What has been largely missing is any focus on relationship and its importance in producing quality results. Even the current emphasis on process is not about human process, the dynamics of how we work and communicate with one another. . . . This presents a dilemma because, in actuality, nothing gets done except in relationship. Task, process, and results depend on it. Action does not occur in a vacuum. . . . Ignoring relationship and its dynamics is ostrich behavior of the most dangerous kind.

—Linda Ellinor and Glenna Gerard, *Dialogue: Rediscovering the Transforming Power of Conversation* (New York: HarperCollins, 1998), 176

Are You Slowly Going Out of Business?

How strong and effective is your organization? How well do you cope with demographic and economic changes? How effectively do you respond to societal and technological changes, and government challenges?

Here's the bottom-line question: How well does your organization adapt? What's your adaptive capacity? Or are you slowly going out of business?

What Questions Do Effective Nonprofit/NGOs Ask Themselves?

Here are just a few questions, only the tip of the proverbial iceberg. There are so many more, interspersed throughout this book, in *Keep Your Donors*, and at www.simonejoyaux.com. And of course, there are more questions beyond these references. Some of the questions here have yes/no answers. That's not so good. The best questions are more open-ended. You'll find those in future chapters. But for now, consider asking these questions in conversation with your colleagues in your organization:

- Does our organization have a vision and is it shared by staff, board members, and volunteers?
- Are we unique enough to make a difference and attract dollars?
- If contributions are slowing down, what is it about our organization that is failing to find an audience?
- What could we do to attract more volunteers?
- How do our stakeholders view us? Is this different from how we see ourselves?
- Does our agency focus only on the bottom-line financial goal or do we see the bigger picture?
- Is collaboration frustrating and merger or acquisition threatening?
- Does our board regularly discuss the implications of trends and the consequences of possible choices?
- Are we constantly ensuring that our organization is relevant?
- Does our fund development leadership (staff and/or consultant) insist that we address organizational development issues as part of improving fund development?

What Are the Questions That Effective Fundraisers Ask?

- Do I help my organization ask the right questions? Am I willing and able to take the risk? What stops me?
- Do I know enough about organizational development and the marketplace to help in areas that are not fundraising specific? For example: Do I know the newest strategies for recruiting, training, and enabling board members? Can I facilitate consensus decision-making and negotiate conflict? Can I develop community collaborations?

■ When I meet with my fundraising colleagues, do we discuss what can be learned from new business theory? Do we discuss community needs and collaborative ways to respond? Do we talk about managing change?

Answering questions like these honestly is only part of the challenge. Just as important is learning to ask the right questions, teasing out all the implications of each question, and nurturing a culture of learning throughout the organization. Keep reading and you'll find more and more questions, including questions about questions.

Changing the Way We Do Fund Development

Fund development is more than a set of strategies and techniques designed to get quick gifts. Yet most organizations value short-term, bottom-line contributions over the long-term returns made possible by building relationships. Boards focus on the cost to raise the charitable dollar. Development professionals spend lots of time pursuing the best direct-mail letter, the right special event, and the newest phonathon tactic.

Your organization will survive and thrive if it develops the four key relationships. This short-term approach is necessary but not sufficient to ensure your organization's continued health. An organization moving full speed ahead into the next millennium will need to develop four relationships:

1. Its relationship with itself. The task: creating the holistic infrastructure (culture and systems) that produces a healthy enterprise.
2. Its relationship with the community. The task: using strategic planning to ensure relevance and define marketplace position.
3. Its relationship with its constituents. The task: developing and strengthening relationships with individuals and groups so they are loyal supporters.
4. Its relationship with its volunteers. The task: carrying out the functions that enable volunteers to take meaningful action on behalf of the organization.

Finding Our Way in the Twenty-First Century

Too many nonprofits/nongovernmental organizations (NGOs) trade upon the presumed value of their missions and the bold implicit statement that "we do good." Yes, indeed, most nonprofit/NGO organizations do good work for their communities. But to continue and flourish, nonprofits/NGOs have much more to do: They must better understand their constituents and create lasting value for them. In a sense, your constituents—your community, your donors and volunteers, the people (or animals or places) you serve—are your shareholders.

Look at your own organization. Begin by asking the questions presented throughout this book. Identify other questions that will challenge your organization to think. Make sure you develop the four relationships essential to create a healthy institution (Exhibit 2.1): internal, community, constituents, and volunteers. Together, these relationships will produce more philanthropic dollars and long-term organizational health.

Exhibit 2.1   The Four Relationships That Ensure Organizational Survival and Health . . . and Fundraising Effectiveness

Your internal relationship creates the holistic infrastructure that produces a healthy enterprise. Your internal relations provide the foundation for all your work, allowing you to develop the other three relationships. Steps include: agreeing on shared values and creating a corporate culture and systems that reflect those values, ensuring individual and team learning, encouraging dialogue and shared decision-making, rewarding critical thinking, welcoming pluralism, building adaptive capacity, and accepting uncertainty and complexity.

Your relationship with the community ensures your organization's continued relevance and clarifies its position within the community. Nurture this relationship through ongoing strategic planning and implementation. Learn while doing. Steps include: identifying and responding to community need, effectively collaborating to meet community needs and eliminating redundant services and organizations, and regularly testing your mission.

Your relationship with constituents develops and strengthens connections with individuals and groups to produce loyalty. Effective relationship building is critical to any effective organization. Steps include: identifying and getting to know their interests and disinterests, motivations, and aspirations; finding the most appropriate and effective ways to communicate and cultivate; engaging diverse constituencies more fully with your cause and organization; creating extraordinary experiences for your constituents; evaluating their capacity to participate and readiness to be asked; designing the appropriate request; and asking.

Your relationship with volunteers enables them to take meaningful action on behalf of your organization. Volunteers expect to be adequately supported and involved. Steps include: understanding and using the concept of enabling; recognizing the functions necessary to support volunteers; recruiting staff who possess the skills, attitude, and knowledge to enable others to work effectively; and evaluating staff performance accordingly.

Philanthropy Builds Communities

Since the beginning of time, in every society and in all cultures, human beings have cared for each other. People, as individuals or gathered together in groups, voluntarily reach out to help others. This is philanthropy, described as voluntary action for the common good.

John W. Gardner[1] writes eloquently about the human need for community and the individual role in building community. One way the individual gains a sense of self is through continuous relationships with others. Community can confer a sense of belonging, and your organization can tap into this fundamental need. Belonging includes a recognition of mutual responsibility for the community and its members.

The individual supports the community through allegiance, commitment, and action. The healthy community (Exhibit 2.2) nurtures its members and provides a secure environment for growing. This community establishes expectations and standards wherein great things can happen.

Exhibit 2.2 Gardner's 10 Attributes That Define Community

1. *Wholeness Incorporating Diversity:* sharing a common purpose while welcoming different ideas and interests.
2. *A Reasonable Base of Shared Values:* sharing some core values and actively defending this common ground (possibly the most important attribute of community).
3. *Caring, Trust, and Teamwork:* creating a humane and respectful climate that accepts all individuals so together we can accomplish group purpose.
4. *Effective Internal Communication:* communicating freely and honestly with one another.
5. *Participation:* ensuring that there are leaders at every level and in every segment of the community; welcoming individuals and making sure they have a role to play.
6. *Affirmation:* building the community's morale through continuous reaffirmation.
7. *Links Beyond the Community:* reaching out to other communities; maintaining open, constructive, and extensive relations with the world beyond.
8. *Development of Young People:* enabling one's young people to develop fully, preparing them for future roles, instilling shared values, fostering commitment to shared purpose, and teaching them to preserve and renew the community's heritage.
9. *A Forward View:* identifying where uncertainty, complexity, and change will take the community.
10. *Institutional Arrangements for Community Maintenance:* developing the formal and informal infrastructures that maintain community.

Note: Use Gardner's attributes as a checklist to help support your strategic planning process (Chapter 6). Think about the implications of this checklist for your next case statement or fundraising letter.

Source: Reprinted with special permission of Independent Sector, a nonprofit, nonpartisan coalition of approximately 600 charities, foundations, and corporate philanthropy programs that advances the common good by leading, strengthening, and mobilizing the nonprofit community (www.independentsector.org).

Yet, this mutual responsibility often wavers. Many people feel alienated, disenfranchised, and contemptuous of society's failures. These individuals reject the community's attempts to strengthen itself, and they isolate themselves, accepting no responsibility for the community's health.

As Gardner observes, "no society can survive such abandonment by its members."[2] Instead, what is needed is an "active nurturing and rebuilding of community—in a spirit that honors both continuity and renewal."[3] Communities have both needs and wants. Needs may include the daily basics: food and shelter, education and employment, safety and health. Wants reflect the person's values and are often expressed through art, faith, and other means.

Taking Action—as Individuals and Organizations

Where people recognize and are moved by wants and needs, these same people may well organize a response. Think of this as community organizing, with its long and proud history.

For example, look at the history of religion, from charity work to social justice struggles. Think of the great movements throughout history. For example: the equity and nation-building movement led by Mahatma Gandhi and the U.S. Civil Rights movement led by Martin Luther King Jr.; the antismoking and environmental movements; the women's suffrage movement; the peace movements in countries around the world.

People get together, organize in their community, and start nonprofits/NGOs. Review "Why Does This Sector Matter?" in Chapter 1. Look at the history and proliferation of voluntary associations worldwide. Check out the Center for Civil Society Studies at Johns Hopkins University (www.jhu.edu/~cnp). Examine the work of the United Nations Statistics Division[4] (UNSD) regarding the sector.

What makes all this organizing, these movements, and these organizations different from for-profit and government agencies? Oftentimes, this organizing bridges the gaps left behind by government. Often this organizing is against government. Then, of course, there are the legal and regulatory benefits provided to this special sector by government. And the legal and regulatory restrictions mandated by government. Most importantly, there's the sense of mission in responding to the community, building community.

And finally—at least superficially—what makes nonprofits/NGOs themselves different is that they seek contributions. The process of seeking charitable contributions is called philanthropic fund development, only one component of which is fundraising, the art of asking. See Appendix 9-A, "Creating the Most Effective Fund Development Program for Your Organization," on this book's website.

An Expansion: Civic Engagement and Social Capital, Civic Capacity and Civil Society

What's the purpose of philanthropy? Building healthy communities. What's the purpose of nonprofit organizations, all those great NGOs? Building healthy communities. How does all this work? Try this scenario: Take some social capital and add a bunch of civic engagement. Those two together help produce civic capacity. Then civic capacity helps produce a civil society. And what about philanthropy, voluntary action for the common good? Acts like glue. Acts like a rallying cry.

CIVIC ENGAGEMENT   That's me and you, our neighbors and friends involved in our communities, whether it's our town or some other group we belong to. The word *civic* refers to the obligations each of us has by belonging to a community.

Civic engagement means people vote and volunteer. They participate in politics and advocate on behalf of others. They band together to build a stronger community. Of course, the degree of civic engagement goes up and down in any community or society at large. For years, the United States has had one of the lowest records of voter turnout in any voting nation. That's an example of bad civic engagement. Around the world, growing numbers of people volunteer; that's good civic engagement.

The nonprofit/NGO sector plays a critical role in civic engagement. People get together to form nonprofits to help others. NGOs bring people together for public discourse. And NGOs recruit people to volunteer their time and money to support important causes. All of this is civic engagement, a virtuous circle that happens when positive results continuously reinforce positive results.

SOCIAL CAPITAL Social capital is the theory that a person's networks[5] have value. Made au courant by Robert D. Putnam,[6] social capital refers to the people we know (networks), and what we do for each other (reciprocity). You use social capital every day. You meet with work colleagues to solve a problem. You borrow your neighbor's snow shovel because yours is broken. You belong to that professional association and network to make useful contacts and exchange important information. Social capital makes individuals and organizations more productive. Each of us has personal and public networks based on reciprocity, those mutually beneficial exchanges.

The theory of social capital identifies two kinds of reciprocity. One is the exchange of favors: "You do this for me and then I'll do this for you." The second kind of reciprocity is a general commitment to help others. "I'll do this without expecting anything specific in return—because someday when I need it, maybe someone will help me."

This second kind of reciprocity recognizes the mutual dependence and shared accountability that create healthy communities. And some of this is philanthropy. For example, you give a gift to your alma mater because education means so much to you and you want others to have that benefit. You volunteer at the local soup kitchen because you can imagine what it might mean to lose a job and not have enough money to buy food.

Here's how social capital works, inspired by Putnam's descriptions in *Bowling Alone*:[7]

- Social capital helps people work together to solve problems they all share. A lack of social capital would mean that most of us would just sit back and wait for others (perhaps too few) to try to solve the problem.

  I think of climate change and its effect on the planet. Regulations like car emissions standards can make things better; that's social capital. But we need a norm at the citizen level; that's even better social capital. Imagine a day when the peer pressure would be so great that no one would buy a gas-guzzling Hummer. And then our social capital would require that General Motors stop making them.

- The goodwill generated through social capital helps the community work smoothly. We buy things at stores assuming that the cashier isn't cheating us. You visit the library according to the posted hours assuming it will be open. To behave otherwise would produce dysfunction in daily lives.

- Social capital helps us lead happier and more productive lives. Trusting connections and deep bonds actually help us "develop or maintain character traits that are good for the rest of society."[8]

    Both experience and research show that social ties reduce isolation and stress, provide feedback to mitigate negative impulses, and help people develop empathy. Research even verifies the health effects of volunteering and giving money. Yes, really, honestly. Philanthropy is a feel-good business, emotionally and physically, according to medical science.

- Social capital also helps us learn and change. Through our networks, we meet diverse people and connect with different life experiences. We pass information around, often increasing its usefulness through our conversations. That same information exchange helps individuals, organizations, and communities achieve their goals. Effective nonprofits join this information exchange to support their own progress.[9]

Not only do you use social capital yourself, but you also watch its use daily. From religious congregations to school boards, sports leagues to civic groups, Internet networks to professional associations, and your own favorite nonprofits—all this is social capital in action, carried out through all those civil society organizations. Social capital produces civil society.

CIVIL SOCIETY "Civil society" refers to all the things people and organizations do together without being forced to do so. The term itself is very old, and commonly used everywhere in the world except the United States.

I think it's easiest to understand the term *civil society* as those organizations and individuals who come together voluntarily to build stronger communities. Or, as Alexis de Tocqueville said, "proposing a common object for the exertions of a great many men [and women] and inducing them voluntarily to pursue it."[10] Most importantly, these people come together outside the boundaries of government. The "outside of government" piece is critical. Government doesn't make us get together to build a hospital or found a museum. Government doesn't form trade unions or professional associations. In fact, many civil society organizations fight government—for example, the struggles for civil rights and the right to vote.

For some, civil society includes the broadest array of collective action—every kind of nonprofit/NGO, including charities, religious institutions, professional associations, trade unions, civic groups, academia, the arts, businesses, the media, and more. Others define a more limited view of civil society, focusing primarily on the nonprofit/NGO sector. But no matter what you include or exclude, civil society helps build stronger communities. And many of us believe that it's the spread of civil society worldwide that produces the most significant change.

Never forget the role of philanthropy and the nonprofit/NGO sector—in making change, in fostering democracy, in holding accountable the market and government sectors.

CIVIC CAPACITY Civic capacity is the ability of a community to identify its problems and fix them, and identify its opportunities and take advantage of them. The term most typically relates a town or city, and the duties and obligations belonging to that community.[11] Inherent in the concept of civic capacity is the coming together of diverse community voices, not just the select few who traditionally wield privilege and power. Sadly, all the right voices are too often absent from the table. And sometimes those at the table wonder why the community's civic capacity isn't so great.

Civic capacity depends on social capital and civic engagement. Civic capacity depends on a strong civil society, to partner with or fight against government. In sum, building community relies on the ability of individuals and groups to connect, to build bridges, to nurture relationships, and to work together for change. Healthy communities depend on civic capacity. Civic capacity is built through social capital (which helps increase civic engagement), civil society, and government. All this together produces a virtuous circle to build community.

And what happens when individuals and organizations ignore all these elements, civic engagement and social capital, civic capacity and civil society? Insular people and organizations focus only on their own interests and issues, disregarding anything beyond self-imposed boundaries. Those who are insular ignore new ideas or different experiences. Their inward, narrow-minded approach limits their own possibility for success, and distances them from connections that could generate meaningful relationships and build healthy communities.

That's a broken community. That's a broken world.

Challenging Philanthropy and the Nonprofit/NGO Sector

It's a simple formula that governs philanthropy: As community needs and wants increase and as the cost of providing services grows, more charitable giving is required. Some studies show that giving (money and time) may not be able to keep up with the demand. Much-needed organizations may fail, leaving unmet needs to threaten community health. Economies falter, creating more need for services and impacting the capacity to give. Yet, experience and other studies show increasing contributions of money and time.

Organizations and their fundraisers are right to wonder:

- Is there really an ever-increasing number of donors from whom we can expect ever-increasing dollars? Will there be in the future?
- How can we secure more volunteers to reach out to more prospects?
- How can we retain the loyalty of our donors?
- How do we make fund development decisions that best use the strengths and talents of our staff and volunteers?

To make [healthy communities] possible, we shall first have to rehabilitate the idea of commitments beyond the self. . . . Passive allegiance isn't enough today. The forces of disintegration have gained steadily and will prevail unless individuals see themselves as having a positive duty to nurture their community.

From *Building Community*, by John W. Gardner (Washington, DC: Independent Sector, 1991)

Organizations also worry about the political climate and the actions of governments on the local, national, and global levels. As governments disinvest in community services, nonprofits/NGOs step into the breach—and more charitable giving is required. And ultimately, charitable contributions can never compensate for the dramatic reduction in government financing of community services.

Research and experience clearly indicate that there are more prospective donors out there, in every community. Studies report that the reason many people do not give is because they've never been asked. More good news: Reports also say that some people would give more if they were asked to do so. Also, professionals know full well that donor loyalty is the key to success. Research and experience clearly explain how to build donor-centered organizations that use relationship building to nurture loyalty.

There is a lot to be done—supported by lots of tools to do the work, and do it well. But you need more than tools. You need an overarching understanding, a framework, a foundation. You and your organizations need the relationships described in this book.

Build an effective organization. Then an effective organization—led by its fundraiser—can build a donor-centered organization that nurtures donor loyalty. Start with these four relationships. Start now.

No More Entitlement

The halcyon days of unquestioning respect for nonprofit/NGO organizations are past. For decades, communities viewed nonprofit/NGO organizations with awe. Here were grouped all the kind and caring, the wise and farseeing. Philanthropic missions and values were held higher than other community activities. Operations and activities were above reproach. Much good was accomplished and most nonprofits/NGOs earned respect and deserved awe.

Both the first and second editions of the book included those words. I wouldn't change any of that. Then, in the first and second editions I went on to say: But we may be losing the edge we worked so hard to gain. We "may be losing"? Nope. We have lost.

Yes, indeed, nonprofits/NGOs, just like for-profits and government, can easily have feet of clay. A handful—albeit a growing handful—of organizations act improperly and illegally. Maybe once we would have said, "Oh, bless their hearts—they don't know what they're doing." But we cannot, should not, and would not say that anymore.

This sector is held to a higher standard. You can quibble about the unjustness of that. But the reasons the sector is held to a higher standard—I think I like those reasons.

I hate the scandals. I hate the illegal and unethical behavior. I want all those organizations and everyone in all sectors who behave this way—well, I want them caught and punished. And often (usually?) they are. But let's turn our attention to the other organizations in our sector. The less-than-effective ones. I'm most interested in those. Why? Because, too often, they don't get caught by others—unless volunteers and donors finally leave. Because too often, these organizations don't catch themselves—acknowledging their less-than-competent performance. Because these ineffective organizations harm other nonprofits and harm donors and volunteers and harm communities.

Some nonprofits manage inadequately and fight change. Others disregard general community needs and abuse power. Myopia stops many organizations from identifying ways to collaborate, merge, or close because of duplicated services or limited relevance. Too many organizations perpetuate weak boards and executive directors who don't have the right skills and knowledge—although some probably don't realize they are doing so.

Some nonprofits are really not organizations but rather programs. Someone has an idea and doesn't want to engage with an organization to develop that idea into a program within the organization. Or the organization doesn't welcome new, outside ideas for programs.

And dare I say it? Some nonprofits pursue unworthy missions, missions that don't add value to the community but are more like private interests and private clubs. Of course, these should fail immediately—as community-based, relevant nonprofits with too little support.

The volunteer and financial needs of all these organizations drain the community of energy, focus, time, and money. There isn't sufficient critical mass—of volunteers and money—to support all this. And that harms community rather than builds community.

So who has the courage to merge? Do you? Who has the courage to raise the toughest issues and reveal that the emperor may not have any clothes on? Do you? Which organizations are slowly going out of business—and either need to fix themselves or go out of business carefully and intentionally? Is that your organization?

Increased Scrutiny

The world has changed and will continue to change. Pretty obvious, right? People are increasingly skeptical as they see scandals and weak organizations. People are increasingly skeptical (and bored) because they're bombarded by message after message, each sincere, each importuning. People no longer assume that all nonprofits/ NGOs are necessary and do good. Governments question the sector more and more. And governments revise and add legislation and regulation in response.

To believe that whatever we do is a moral cause, and should be pursued whether there are results or not, is a perennial temptation for non-profit executives—and even more for their boards. But even if the cause itself is a moral cause, the specific way it is pursued better have results.

From *Managing the Nonprofit Organization: Principles and Practices*, by Peter F. Drucker (New York: HarperCollins, 1990), 85

Think about the following shifts.

YOUR DONORS   Your donors receive more requests for support than ever before. Now they are more discerning. They expect more from you, and you need to understand what their expectations are. Communications must be stronger (not necessarily louder) so that your request can be distinguished from others. Beware: Strong relationships with major donors alone are not enough. The level of intimacy between your organization and all your donors is the key to success.

Donors expect a certain level of sophistication and excellence in your fund development. Donors may not say it out loud—or even articulate it thus—but they expect a donor-centered organization with a comprehensive relationship-building program that nurtures loyalty. Your donors expect extraordinary experiences that link them to the meaning of your mission. Donors expect you to help them fulfill their aspirations. That's the summary. As for the detail[9]...

In some ways, it's harder and harder to secure a gift of time or money. Even donors of the smallest gifts can ask a lot of questions about your organization and their involvement. For example:

- Do I know this organization well enough to give, to give again, to give more?
- Does the organization know me well enough to have asked me for the right thing?
- How does this cause compare to my other interests?
- Does this organization meet my priorities?
- Is this request appropriate to my level of interest, readiness, and capacity to give?
- How well would giving to this organization meet my personal needs, fulfill my aspirations?
- Is this organization relevant and well-managed?

YOUR OPERATIONS   People—and that includes businesses, too—are increasingly intolerant of mediocrity in any area of operation, be it your service or the way you manage and govern. People expect quality service, and effective management and governance are expected.

Effective nonprofits/NGOs innovate. They seek out and apply appropriate new business theories to their operations. They design and maintain an infrastructure—corporate culture and systems—that provides for ongoing renewal.

While nonprofits sometimes lead in the development of products and services, nonprofits often lag behind in business management. Some NGOs reject management theory as suspicious or compromising, unfit for philanthropic organizations. Others embrace new theories wholeheartedly and then abandon them too quickly in favor of the next fad.

YOUR RELEVANCE   Organizations must have missions that respond to contemporary community needs and desires, and clearly communicate relevancy. Effective organizations test their missions regularly. Those institutions with only marginal value to the community will likely close because people will not volunteer or give enough. See Chapter 6, "The Second Relationship—With Your Community: Ensuring Your Organization's Relevance through Strategic Planning."

YOUR VOLUNTEERS   Good directions and personal follow-up with volunteers are not by themselves enough to produce the level of action required to move an organization forward. Volunteers—certainly those involved in your organization's governance and fund development—expect much more support from staff. And even if these volunteers don't expect this support, they need it, and often desperately.

Bottom line: Volunteers require good enabling to effectively do their work. So staff must be good enablers. See Chapter 8 for details about enabling.

YOUR GOVERNMENTS All levels of government worldwide scrutinize the non-profit/NGO sector. Legislative and regulatory bodies debate public policy and take more action than ever before. Some of this scrutiny is unjustified and the actions inappropriate. Regardless, nonprofits/NGOs need to cope with both the scrutiny and the results. With no more entitlement, life is much more difficult. Now more than ever, your organization will benefit if you develop the four relationships central to effective and productive fund development.

And a Little P.S.

Here's a challenge, perhaps, to your thinking. Where does the duty of loyalty lie? Do you expect your staff and board members to be loyal to your *organization*? I think not.

After a classroom conversation with Cohort 20 of the Master of Arts in Philanthropy and Development, Saint Mary's University of Minnesota, I think we all agreed that the duty of loyalty is to the values and mission, not to the organization. Maybe the organization needs to be fixed. Maybe the organization should close. But the values and mission might still be critical. Another organization might take on these values and mission. A new organization might start up.

Where does the duty of loyalty lie? To your donors or to your organization? I hope to your donors. That doesn't exclude your clients and that doesn't disregard your staff and volunteer colleagues. But your loyalty must be to your donors, their interests and aspirations.

Where else does the duty of loyalty lie? To your community. First, to your community.

Isolating Fundraisers and Fund Development

Most nonprofits/NGOs recognize how critical fund development is to the organization. Nonetheless, fund development is often isolated from other operations. Many staff and volunteers do not understand how intertwined fund development is with the overall organizational system.

Sometimes fundraising consultants and development staff choose to stay away from the rest of the institution. Other times, organizations deliberately keep fundraisers at arm's length from other areas of operation.

Location, Location, Location

I'll never forget the location of my first office as a development officer: at the end of a dead-end hallway. No one even passed by periodically. They had to want to come to my office. And that didn't happen with the program staff or even the marketing/communications staff.

Think about those development offices and buildings located on the hospital or university campus...far away from the heart of healthcare and education...far away from mission and impact. Sadly, that's emblematic of the whole situation, if you ask me.

What Are Fund Development Activities?

Early fundraising practice states that an organization needs three things to produce dollars: case, prospects, and volunteers. I wouldn't say only those three anymore. But I do know fundraisers that stop there. Or, rather, focus only on fundraising strategies and tactics, instead of the whole organization.

Too often fundraisers focus on strategies to meet the financial goals. Too often, bosses demand that fundraisers focus so narrowly. But that's not good enough. The fundraiser—the development operation—must help the organization develop the four relationships that strengthen fund development.

Specifically:

- Instead of helping the organization define its relationship to the community, development merely prepares the fundraising case by drawing from the organization's mission and program.
- Rather than ensuring good relations with all the organization's constituents, fundraisers focus on donor prospects.
- Development identifies, recruits, and provides logistical support to fundraising volunteers rather than enabling them.
- Rarely does the fundraiser help develop the organization's internal relations, because this seems to be the responsibility of the chief executive and board.

Fundraising Problems

When an organization asks, "Why isn't fundraising working?" it's generally something else in the institution that isn't working first. Fundraising problems generally stem from your organization's internal relations and your relationships with the community, your constituents, and volunteers. For example, you may lack fundraising volunteers because your board has not been properly recruited and trained. Or volunteers may not sell tickets to your special event because the event conflicts with organizational values.

More than 50 percent of the fundraising issues that stymie agencies are actually organizational development issues. This holds true even in major institutions with sophisticated development staff.

Unfortunately, many organizations and fundraisers do not realize what generally causes fundraising problems. Neither the organization nor the fundraiser understands that without the four critical relationships, fund development doesn't work well. Furthermore, neither the fundraiser nor the organization acknowledges the role of the fundraising executive in developing these four fundamental relationships.

Without a strong understanding of the four fundamental relationships and their relationship to one another, fundraisers sometimes recommend strategies that, at best, do not promote organizational health. At worst, these strategies harm the organization.

Sometimes these situations occur because fundraisers are not integrated into the whole organizational system. At other times, the fundraiser may not have sufficient knowledge and competency beyond fundraising tactics. Perhaps fundraisers (and particularly fundraising consultants) assume that the rest of the organization is doing fine. They restrict themselves—or are restricted by the organization—to that narrow view, the financial bottom line. Many fundraisers expect that chief executives will solve problems in the system, since they are responsible for institutional health. But that's an easy way out. This perspective relegates the fundraiser (and other organizational leaders as well) to the position of a specialist stuck in a private corner of a very complex, interrelated system.

Some Fundraisers Don't Lead

Even when organizations and fundraisers recognize the importance of the four relationships, the fundraiser may not be expected to help develop all these relationships. Many organizations separate the relationships and direct the work to independent specialists. For example, the marketing and public relations staffs deal with most constituents and communications. The chief executive addresses internal relations and strategic planning. The fundraiser focuses on donors and prospects only.

Even when organizations do expect the fundraiser to lead the institution in this work, the fundraiser may not be able to. The truth is, fundraising executives who are only technicians cannot solve organizational development problems. These professionals do not have the knowledge, skills, or experience to discern the issues.

Typically, these fundraisers identify the symptom as a fundraising problem and try to solve it as such. Frequently, the fundraising solution temporarily conflicts with the appropriate organizational development solution. Usually, the fundraising solution does not address the problem. Ultimately, inadequate or no progress happens.

We keep measuring and rewarding success based on the bottom line, the money line. We don't reward fundraisers as organizational development specialists, responsible for building the four relationships critical to philanthropy. With this faulty approach, we promote slowly (or quickly) going out of business.

Other fundraisers fully understand the problems. However, they are not allowed access to the organization to help resolve the problem. Again, inadequate or no progress is made.

What You Can Do Now

What is your best insurance against obsolescence? Change the way you do business. Forget the quick fix and pay attention to the fundamentals. Strengthen your relationships within your own organization and with your community, constituents, and volunteers.

Are you afraid your organization isn't ready for change? The need for charitable contributions can be a powerful motivator.

Clearly, the major motivation for institutional change should be meeting community needs. But if this is too threatening, use the need for increased contributions to get your organization to evaluate itself. Start by evaluating your fund development. If you do this evaluation well, you will examine the four relationships that are essential to effective fund development.

Since charitable gifts are a powerful motivator, the fundraising executive is in a powerful position. There is no better position from which to encourage self-examination and challenge complacency. There is no position with more need to address organizational health than that of the fundraiser. The fundraiser in your organization must be very knowledgeable about the institution's program and the community's need. No individual should be better able to develop and foster the four relationships essential to institutional health and fund development. (Indeed, the best fundraising executive is an individual well positioned to become a chief executive. Conversely, service first as an executive director can make a great fundraiser.)

Make Fund Development Part of the Larger System

Too often fund development and the fundraiser remain somewhat tangential to the rest of the system. Don't let this happen. Fully integrate fund development and the fundraiser into the organizational system. Then you have a better chance of raising more money.

The more parts your system has, the greater the complexity and uncertainty. What affects one function will affect another. A problem in one part of the system is usually stimulated or reinforced by a situation elsewhere. Certainly an action in one area will affect other areas. Partial solutions are rarely more than temporary.

> *In a complex world, there are no simple, bounded problems. Problems continually expand and spill over to involve every aspect of business. . . . The most basic assumption is that all organizations are complex systems that interact constantly and significantly with a host of other equally complex systems. The most important property of these systems is that they cannot be broken down into parts that have separate lives of their own. Thus, in an organization, no basic functions, departments, or objectives exist independently of one another . . . one obtains a highly distorted and seriously misleading picture of any part of a system if one attempts to study and manage it apart from the larger system in which it exists.*[12]

What can you do? Look at your own institution. In summary, the chief executive ensures a culture of philanthropy and donor-centered organization. More specifically, the chief executive must:

- Help board and staff to see the links between fund development and other institutional functions, to identify and resolve systemic issues at various points.
- Make sure members of the fundraising staff understand the program and relate well with the program staff.
- Involve your fundraiser in board selection, recruitment, and development.
- Insist that fundraising staff work with all other staffs, including program and marketing, to identify the agency's constituents, find out their interests and

needs, and brainstorm how the agency can respond. (And insist that those other staffs pay attention to philanthropy and development and the fundraiser.)

- Show your staff—the janitor, the receptionist, direct service personnel, trustees, chief executive, bookkeeper—the role they play in fund development.
- Listen to your fundraiser's thoughts about program quality and community perception.
- Expect your fundraiser to be actively involved in the community, serving on boards and exploring community issues, trends, and solutions.

Strengthen the Professional

During the past decades, fund development has become professional. There's a documented body of knowledge, best practices, and next practices. Education and training proliferate, teaching the history and philosophy of philanthropy as well as fundraising practice. Academics and practitioners conduct research. Our ethical codes, standards of practice, and certification programs enhance credibility.

As a result, the profession produces effective fundraising executives who are consummate managers and proficient technicians. They believe in their causes and the philosophy of philanthropy. They know how to create infrastructure, document activities, and delineate roles. These professionals mathematically project goals and analyze response rates. Using sophisticated solicitation strategies, fundraisers negotiate major gifts and write effective direct mail. Generally, these competent professionals support volunteers well with strategies that work today.

But what about tomorrow? Entitlement is over and there is increasing congestion when seeking gifts. Donors demand more, and communities examine nonprofits/NGOs more closely. Organizations that focus only on the fundraising bottom line will not increase charitable contributions. Fundraisers who seek a quick fix and pursue short-term techniques will not produce more money for the long term.

No matter who leads your fund development effort (development staff, executive director, consultant, or volunteer), this person must be more than a manager and fundraising strategist. Lots more. See Chapter 4, devoted entirely to the fund development professional.

In the quantum world, relationships are everything. . . . Power in organizations is the capacity generated by relationships.

From *Leadership and the New Science: Learning about Organizations from an Orderly Universe*, by Margaret J. Wheatley (San Francisco: Berrett-Koehler, 1992)

A Fundamental Truth

Pay attention to others first. Read lots more about this in Chapter 7, on constituency development. But I wanted to introduce the thought here, at the start.

In the first edition of this book, I started reciting this mantra: *It's not what you're selling that matters; it's what I'm buying that counts*. That's a fundamental marketing maxim. And it's well worth keeping in mind as you work to build the four critical relationships. This mantra maxim holds true no matter what you're doing: whether you are building a relationship with your community through strategic planning, strengthening your relationship with a candidate for trusteeship, enabling a volunteer to carry out fundraising activities, or strengthening the group dynamics among your staff colleagues.

What does this actually mean? Just look back at Chapter 1, basic principles. Read all about interest and donor centrism. If your organization wants my help as a volunteer or donor, you must interest me. Simply put, it doesn't matter that you do good work. It doesn't matter that you respond to a community need. If you do not meet *my* need—whatever it is—I won't participate in any significant way. I may give you a token gift for some reason, but don't count on more.

Marketing is a highly ethical concept that fosters relationships that share meaningful benefits between parties. There is a mutually beneficial exchange that—to be successful—requires understanding of and respect for personal interests and needs and wants.

On the surface, this is not a hard principle to grasp. But the problem is, organizations and boards and staff start assuming. You assume you know what interests me. I assume I know what you want. That's bad. Too many organizations and professionals just don't understand the principle well. And many organizations don't perform accordingly, even if they understand the principle.

Many charities refuse to acknowledge the basic marketing exchange in philanthropy. They assume their good cause justifies the request and motivates the gift. As a result, these organizations are not tapping the full philanthropic potential in their communities. These charities are losing donors.

The statement "It's not what you're selling that matters; it's what I'm buying that counts" seems to offend some organizations, their volunteers, and their staff. To some, this principle seems to suggest that prosperous donors and supporters are selfish. This principle may call to mind an individualistic culture, excessive competitiveness, and alienation from community. But self-interest need not be interpreted negatively. Psychiatrist Robert Coles explains: "There is an element of self-interest in serving others." Coles observes that this is both morally and psychologically acceptable; "unless individuals can really believe in something and immerse themselves in an activity, they won't have much to offer."[13]

See an example of this in Exhibit 2.3, the story of my dad's death and the fund I started.

Exhibit 2.3   A Personal Story That Illustrates the Key Principle: It's Not What You're Selling; It's What I'm Buying

---

In 1990, my father died suddenly of cancer. We discovered he was sick, and then he was dead six weeks later. He died in Michigan, before I could get there.

I arrived in East Lansing a few hours after his death. That afternoon, I phoned Michigan State University (MSU) and set up a scholarship fund for travel in a French-speaking country. The fund was named for my father, Georges Jules Joyaux. He had not yet been dead 10 hours.

Within a few weeks of Dad's death, I received solicitation letters from the national and local cancer societies. Timely and appropriate letters. Good fundraising efforts triggered by my father's death.

And I threw each of those letters away. Why?

Too soon? No. Too impersonal? No. (Although a personal call probably would have generated a nominal, one-time gift from me.) On paper, I looked like a prospect. But as it happened, I wasn't. The cancer societies sold certain, worthwhile things. But my interests were elsewhere.

They were selling freedom from pain, health, a cure for cancer so others would not suffer, as had my father and family. Protection so I might not die from this dreaded disease. Protection for my husband, my mother, my brothers and sisters, and my friends.

But what was I buying? Not health. I rarely give to health organizations. Certainly, I want everyone to be healthy, myself and loved ones included. But I'm not buying health. Not freedom from cancer. I am sorry my father died from cancer. It was ugly, as much of death is. But I'm not buying an end to cancer.

What did I buy that afternoon when I called MSU from the living room of my parents' home? My French heritage. Love and respect for different cultures, taught by my father. Joy of travel to other countries. Commitment to education as I look at all the teachers in our family.

A warmth toward MSU. My father came to the university as a young man from war-torn France. There, he met my mother and taught for 41 years. All six of us kids went to school there.

Love and admiration for my father, his vision of a world where pluralism is honored, his wit and sarcasm, his intelligence and eloquence, his strengths and weaknesses, his love for teaching and his students.

Cancer took him. But it did not define him.

So, my mother and the six Joyaux kids set up a scholarship fund in Georges's name. Each year, an MSU student receives funds to study in a French-speaking country. The country doesn't have to be France, only French-speaking. An academic curriculum isn't necessary. Traveling and experiencing are what count. My father always reminded everyone: "The most important thing is to step out of your linguistic ghetto and become aware that there are people who live, eat, learn, and make love in a medium which is not English."

It amuses me to think of Georges's reaction to his fund. He would laugh and make a smart remark. But he would remember the students. I think he would be pleased. With the scholarship, the students receive a description of my father and what he accomplished in his lifetime. I trust they read it.

I tell this story around the country when I teach and consult. I ask people what they think the cancer society is selling. People are so gracious. They use polite words and euphemisms. It takes a while before anyone gets to the nitty-gritty—protection from death. Better yet, protecting me personally from dying and protecting others I care about.

People are just as gracious when they talk about what I'm buying. They always emphasize the honoring of my heritage, my father, and his beliefs. Sure, that's a part of it. But then I laugh. Irreverently, I proclaim: "Just honoring my

(continued)

(Continued)

father and my heritage? No way. I bought a house in France and my dad can't visit. . . . This gift is about me and my interests. I love France, and I'm committed to pluralism."

You have to look deep. Get down to the essentials, not just the surface.

Enough said for now. Read on.

Summary

Your organization's survival and its success depend on four critical relationships: your internal relations, your relationship with the community, your relationship with your constituents, and your relationship with volunteers. Build these well, and you'll flourish. Ignore these relationships—even a little bit—and you'll struggle.

That's the bottom line: Develop the four relationships!

With these four in hand, you've pretty much got all you need. Then "just do it," as Nike says. But without these four relationships, fund development is neither effective nor productive over the long term. Then your organization will go slowly out of business.

More importantly, without these four relationships, your organization itself is neither effective nor productive over the long term. Then your organization should go out of business—and quickly! This is really hard work. Sometimes not as hard as you think. And sometimes harder than you think.

Actually raising money is the smallest part. First—and always—everything else has to work well. Start now.

CHAPTER 3

The First Relationship—Within Your Organization

Creating the Infrastructure That Produces a Healthy Organization

The greatest menace to progress is not ignorance, it is the illusion of knowledge.
—Daniel J. Boorstin[1]

The non-profits are human-change agents. And their results are therefore always a change in people—in their behavior, in their circumstances, in their vision, in their health, in their hopes, above all, in their competence and capacity. In the last analysis, the non-profit institution . . . has to judge itself by its performance in creating vision, creating standards, creating values and commitment, and in creating human competence. The non-profit institution therefore needs to set specific goals in terms of its service to people. And it needs constantly to raise these goals—or its performance will go down.
—Peter Drucker, *Managing the Non-Profit Organization: Principles and Practices* (New York: HarperCollins, 1990), 85

Making Your Organization Effective

Without good internal relationships—between the board of directors and staff, among staff, between departments and functions—your organization will most likely falter. And when these basics falter, your fund development program will surely falter as well. I call this the first relationship—referring to the internal operations of your organization, your organization's relationship with itself. The task is to create the holistic infrastructure that produces a healthy enterprise.

No organization can survive on mission and vision alone. Infrastructure provides the supporting systems and framework that allow your organization to pursue its vision and achieve its mission. Infrastructure defines how your organization conducts its work. Infrastructure is formal and informal, documented and casual. Infrastructure includes such activities as financial and personnel management, marketing and planning, and the behaviors and attitudes of staff and volunteers. Infrastructure, in short, amounts to your corporate culture plus your organization's systems.

Fund development is part of the infrastructure and, at the same time, depends on infrastructure for support. If the rest of your organization has problems, fund development will, too. For example:

- Poor quality in your services affects your ability to raise charitable gifts.
- Without good decision-making, your organization establishes an unrealistic fund development goal.
- Board members are reluctant to identify prospects or solicit gifts, because the board recruitment process doesn't talk about the board member's fund development role.

Development professionals cannot succeed by simply changing tactics; they must help cure the institution's ailments. As James Carville might say, "It's the organization, stupid."

From James H. Lewis, CFRE's review of the second edition of *Strategic Fund Development* as it appeared in *Advancing Philanthropy*, Fall 1997, Association of Fundraising Professionals, Alexandria, VA

The Fundraiser as an Organizational Development Specialist

Most fundraisers know that effective infrastructure is essential to effective fund development. How does this play out? First, donors prefer to give to well-managed and well-governed institutions. Donors expect organizations to manage money properly, comply with legal and regulatory requirements, make decisions effectively, and continuously improve services. All this is accomplished through infrastructure. Second, fundraisers use components of infrastructure to carry out development activities. For example, fund development uses planning to design activities. Fund development employs marketing and communications strategy to develop relationships with prospects and donors. Personnel practices help manage fund development volunteers.

The best fundraisers know more than just the basics of infrastructure. The best fundraisers are organizational development specialists. These fundraisers understand how and why an organization's infrastructure affects all of its activities, fund development included. The most effective fundraisers pay attention to corporate culture, respect systems, and learn about group behavior. These fundraisers identify and fix infrastructure problems and stay current with evolving management theory.

These highly competent fundraisers are change agents. They facilitate individual and organization-wide learning. These individuals build capacity for change. As organizational development specialists, they serve as scouts, identifying challenges and opportunities, and getting them on the table within the organization.

Operating as an organizational development specialist, the best fundraisers go back and forth between fund development, the institution, and its other parts.

These fundraisers assess fund development by looking at everything else in the organization, too—maybe even first. For example, see the fund development audit included in the second edition of this book, and posted at www.simonejoyaux.com. Note that the first questions focus on overall institutional health. Only at the end of the audit do questions focus on fund development specifics. Better yet, get yourself a copy of *The Fundraising Audit Handbook* by Guy Mallabone, MA, CFRE, and Ken Balmer, PhD.[2]

For another example of "everything else in the organization," review the governance assessment included in Appendix 6-B on this book's website. This survey approaches institutional health from the board's perspective. Questions are far-ranging but always focused through the prism of governance.

Fund development is, first, organizational development.

Big job, isn't it, serving as a development officer? And the job is bigger than many development officers think or do. That's why there's a separate chapter in this third edition devoted entirely to the development officer. (See Chapter 4.) Make sure you operate as an organizational development specialist, not just a great fundraising technician. Choose the right road—for you professionally and for your organization.

Role of Corporate Culture and Systems

Cultures form in any group, whether your book club, your board, or your organization. In fact, groups within a larger organization may have different cultures. Some of these cultures are explicit, but "most are implicit, understood but not spoken, residing in the language and habits of interaction between the people.[3]

Corporate culture refers to the personality of an organization and the way your members interact and behave. Although culture is too rarely discussed, it pervades an organization and is transmitted from one individual to another. Corporate culture is "the set of rarely articulated, largely unconscious, taken-for-granted beliefs, values, norms, and fundamental assumptions the organization makes about itself, the nature of people in general, and its environment . . . organizational culture consists of the set of unwritten rules that govern acceptable behavior within and even outside of the organization."[4]

Research shows that an organization's culture dramatically affects its effectiveness. Culture is pervasive, affecting all areas of the organization, including fund development.

Corporate culture refers to the behaviors that underlie group behavior. On the other hand, the term *systems* refers to the permanent structures in your organization. Systems direct the flow of what happens. Systems include core processes, management and governance hierarchy, and informal networks. Many systems are formal and documented. Others are informal but just as strong.

- Core processes are those that you cannot do without. They include such things as continuous quality improvement, performance measurement and control, financial and personnel management, and board recruitment and development.

- Hierarchy defines the relationships of individuals and groups, one to the other. Hierarchy assigns authority and accountability.
- Informal networks refer to an organization's practices. These networks are not codified or written down, but they do reflect your corporate culture. They describe what "everyone knows is the way we really do business."

Together, corporate culture and systems can produce either dysfunctional or healthy organizations. When both corporate culture and systems are effective, the organization flourishes. If corporate culture is dysfunctional, even well-designed systems won't operate well. However, a healthy corporate culture can compensate, to a large degree, for inadequate systems.

What's the culture in your organization? What's the culture you'd like to have? Introduce this topic in your organization. Begin the conversation by challenging assumptions and asking cage-rattling questions.

A DEEPLY MOVING STORY

Let your imagination put you in a grandstand at the Seattle version of the Special Olympics. There are nine contestants, all physically or mentally disabled, assembled at the starting line for the 100-yard dash. At the gun, they all start out, not exactly in a dash, but with a relish to run the race to the finish and win. All, that is, except one boy who stumbles on the asphalt, tumbles over a couple of times, and begins to cry. The other eight hear the boy cry. They slow down and look back. They all turn around and go back . . . every one of them. As you watch, one girl with Down's syndrome bends down and kisses him. You hear her say, "This will make it better." All nine link arms and walk across the finish line together. Everyone in the stadium, including you, stands up, and the cheering goes on for several minutes.

People who were actually there are still telling the story, four years later. Why? Because deep down we know this one thing: what matters in this life is more than winning for ourselves. What truly matters in this life is helping others win, even if it means changing our own course.[5]

When I read this story, I didn't think about philanthropy and the valuable work that the Special Olympics and the millions of nonprofits/nongovernmental organizations (NGOs) do every day. I didn't think about the wonder of a great development officer finding the right donor for a cause. Yes, all that is true. But what I thought about was the group culture among those contestants. I thought about the values that they share. I thought: "I want to work in a place where people treat each other like that, where people go back for each other and cross the line together." (By the way, *Clicks and Mortar* is one of my favorite books about organizational development, values, and culture. Read it!)

Concept of a Group

Visit www.virtualthesaurus.com. Watch how the word *group* morphs in the diagram. Consider synonyms like unit, whole, building block, part, constituent, and component part. Think about the groups you know, for example: book clubs and sports teams, professional associations and classrooms. These groups are brought together for some unifying purpose.

Organizations consist of many groups. There are teams of employees addressing selected topics and departments carrying out specific functions. Boards and committees focus on particular issues. Now look deeper. How about the female employees—do they sometimes behave as a group? How about the men? Your organization probably has generational groups, for example Millennials and Boomers. At their most basic, groups within an organization exist to talk and, typically, to do or decide something. So participation—through attendance and talking—is critical.

In some way, group participants opt in. Some group members may be more active, others less so. But the group members recognize some commonality and that creates a bond, albeit limited in some cases. On some level, the group exists only when it comes together. The group may come together virtually or face-to-face. But the group comes together in some manner.

Think about the nature of participation in a group and the subsequent obligation. Groups depend on participation. To be part of a group means you participate according to the expectations established by the group. All group members share accountability for group health. This accountability does not reside solely with the group's leader.

But too often, group members think it's okay not to attend and not to talk within the group. Is this acceptable? Can members of the group avoid interaction within the group? For example, is it okay to avoid conversation within the group but talk outside the group about group issues?

The answer is a resounding "no." To be part of a group requires interaction—and that interaction belongs within the group. And never more so than within an organization.

Consider this: What is the obligation of group members to encourage and enable interaction? An enormous obligation! Maintenance of group integrity is the responsibility of all group members. Facilitating participation belongs to all. However, there are introverts and extroverts. There are cultural differences. Some people may be uncomfortable speaking within the group and choose not to participate in conversation. Instead, they may share their thoughts with colleagues after the group meetings. In this scenario, great insights and useful information are shared one-on-one, without the advantage of comment and reaction within the full group. The value of the group, the synergy of more than one, is lost. Again, this is not acceptable.

Here's more: People from different cultures or positions may approach groups in different ways. Some people may feel uncomfortable and unsure about how to participate, so they remain silent. Sadly, the value of their perspective and experience is not added to the mix to enhance group learning. And again, this is not okay. And it gets worse: Think about differences in privilege and how they affect groups. Some members of a group have positions of authority that may inhibit or intimidate others in the group. Other members of the group may have personal privilege—like race/ethnicity, gender, generation, socioeconomics, sexual orientation—hat produces power and threatens others in the group.

Never underestimate the power of privilege—too often invisible to the privileged—and how it compromises good group dynamics. For more about invisible privilege, read articles by Dr. Peggy McIntosh, PhD. See also "Philanthropy's

Moral Dilemma," the final chapter in *Keep Your Donors: The Guide to Better Communications and Stronger Relationships*, also posted in a modified version at www.simonejoyaux.com.

Then there's the distraction factor. People join a group without making sufficient time to participate. These individuals are too busy or focused on other things. Yet attendance is critical within a group because a group is defined by its moments of coming together and interacting.

All these scenarios are troublesome. All these scenarios threaten group effectiveness. Effective groups depend on the participation of their members. That's not negotiable. Silence is not acceptable, nor is absence. Certainly absence occurs periodically. Naturally some members will speak more than others. But all members must attend regularly and must speak often. The challenge then is to create an effective group. It is helpful to understand group dynamics and the role of group behavior. It is useful to clarify roles, expectations, and relationships. It is essential to understand diversity—whether cultural or personality or anything else.

Take a look at Seth Godin's book *Tribes*. Read Seth's blog about tribes and what they mean. Apply Seth's concept of tribes to your work and volunteer experiences. Think about customers as a tribe (think Apple Computer!). Think about donors as a tribe. (The Steel Yard, [www.thesteelyard.org], calls its tribe members Yardies.) Now look closely at the various groups in your organization. What makes these groups work well or not so well? Think about corporate culture. Examine the systems. Pay attention to the behaviors of individuals within the group. Analyze group dynamics. And work hard to fix the problems, capitalize on effectiveness, and celebrate success.

Group behavior can be altered only by changing corporate culture.

Role of Group Behavior

Group behavior affects the way your organization makes decisions, how well you identify and resolve issues, and how you negotiate conflict. Group behavior affects the willingness of employees and volunteers to stay with your organization and your ability to recruit new employees and volunteers.

Effective fundraisers use group behavior to get the job done well. They understand enough theory to encourage positive behaviors and control negative ones. Consider these potentially harmful group behaviors:

- Your development committee is too fragmented to discuss really challenging issues.
- Your board is so cohesive that members rarely question or disagree on anything, thus compromising the quality of your decisions.
- Program staff don't honestly express their concerns about how money is raised, so your organization cannot create a united philanthropic case for the community.
- Group interactions are full of conflict and game playing, so fund development volunteers leave.

- Almost everyone is concerned about a new program, but no one says so aloud in the group, so you launch a program that no one thinks should be done.
- Your board members don't speak candidly with each other. In fact, dysfunctional politeness reigns! This avoidance stops conversation about giving and fund development expectations of board members.

Keep in mind that group behavior reflects corporate culture just like individual behavior does. Although theory can explain group behavior, only corporate culture can change group behavior.

Much is published about group behavior. Three theories—group dynamics, groupthink, and managing agreement—are particularly important for your organization to understand.

GROUP DYNAMICS   In groups that function effectively, members feel some linkage, one to the other, and to the group as a whole. This linkage produces the cohesion that is necessary for the group to operate successfully. In fact, the degree to which group members are linked defines the level of group health.

The theory of group dynamics[6] describes linking forces as:

- Member satisfaction from participating in the group.
- Degree of closeness and warmth felt between members of the group.
- Pride of membership in the group.
- Ability of members to address the crises that face the group.
- Degree to which members of the group express their ideas and feelings honestly.

Take a look at the groups in your organization. How do these dynamics operate within your board, among your staff, within the development committee, between the development committee and the board? To what degree are your group members linked?

GROUPTHINK   Some cohesion is necessary for a group to operate effectively. Start with shared values, for example. Add in a level playing field for sharing information and expertise. But consider what happens when a group is too cohesive. Members abdicate their independence and objectivity and support group norms without question. Other group members may mask their real feelings in deference to the consensus.[7]

This is groupthink, "a mode of thinking that people engage in when they are deeply involved in a cohesive ingroup, when the members' strivings for unanimity override their motivation to realistically appraise alternative courses of action. . . . Groupthink refers to a deterioration of mental efficiency, reality, testing, and moral judgment that results from ingroup pressures."[8]

Groupthink produces a number of unfavorable results.

- Group members are pressured to avoid expressing arguments against group positions for fear of being considered disloyal.
- Members censor themselves, suppressing their own doubts about the wisdom of group consensus.

- Certain members make sure the group doesn't get information that could interfere with the group's cohesion.
- Group members see only unanimity and assume that silence signifies agreement.
- Members rationalize the group's judgments and ignore warnings and disregard assumptions.
- Members believe in the group's own morality and disregard the ethical consequences of decisions.
- The group endorses stereotypes, seeing outsiders as adversaries or competitors who are weak and stupid.
- The group sees itself as invulnerable, encouraging excessive optimism and risk taking.[9]

Now look at the groups in your organizations. Do you ever see examples of excessive cohesion?

[Organizations] frequently take actions in contradiction to what they really want to do and therefore defeat the very purposes they are trying to achieve . . . a major corollary of the paradox . . . is that the inability to manage agreement is a major source of organization dysfunction. . . . Organization change and effectiveness may be facilitated as much by confronting the organization with what it knows and agrees upon as by confronting it with what it doesn't know or disagrees about.

From "The Abilene Paradox: The Management of Agreement," by Jerry B. Harvey, *Organizational Dynamics* 3, Issue 1 (1974): 63–80

MANAGING AGREEMENT   A particularly interesting theory of group behavior is called "managing agreement." Most people know something about its opposite, managing conflict. Fewer understand managing agreement—and it is just as difficult.

Jerry Harvey calls this the Abilene Paradox, based on an unwanted family trip to Abilene. Harvey summarizes the trip this way:

Here we were, four reasonably sensible people who, of our own volition, had just taken a 106-mile trip across a godforsaken desert in a furnace-like temperature through a cloud-like dust storm to eat unpalatable food at a hole-in-the-wall cafeteria in Abilene, when none of us had really wanted to go. In fact, to be more accurate, we'd done just the opposite of what we wanted to do.[10]

What a horrible story. But groups and organizations do end up in Abilene regularly. Maybe it's the fund development event no one wanted but thought everyone else did. Or the fund development brochure, donated by a great copywriter and designer, which everyone knows (but doesn't say) is too slick and polished for the organization's values and desired image (Exhibit 3.1).

Exhibit 3.1 Six Elements That Express the Inability to Manage Agreement

1. Individual members of the organization agree, privately, about the situation or problem.
2. Individuals agree, privately, about the steps necessary to cope with the situation or problem.
3. Organization members don't clearly communicate their desires and/or beliefs to each other. They communicate the opposite, causing the group to misperceive what everyone actually believes.
4. Based on the inaccurate and invalid information they have transmitted to each other, these individuals make group decisions that are contrary to what they really want to do. Consequently, the group produces results that conflict with the organization's purposes and desires.
5. By taking these counterproductive actions, organization members are frustrated, angry, irritated, and dissatisfied with their group or organization. These individuals then form subgroups with those they trust and blame others for the organization's dysfunction.
6. The cycle repeats itself with greater intensity if people don't deal with their inability to manage agreement.

Source: Adapted from Jerry B. Harvey, "The Abilene Paradox: The Management of Agreement," *Organizational Dynamics* 3/Issue 1, 63–80, © 1974, with permission from Elsevier.

As Harvey notes, organizations "frequently take actions in contradiction to what they really want to do and therefore defeat the very purposes they are trying to achieve.... [A] major corollary of the paradox ... is that the inability to manage agreement is a major source of organization dysfunction.... Organizations change and effectiveness may be facilitated as much by confronting the organization with what it knows and agrees upon as by confronting it with what it doesn't know or disagrees about."[11]

Has your organization ever visited Abilene? How did this happen? More importantly, *why* did this happen? How will you avoid trips to Abilene in the future? Who in your organization will take the risk to challenge the trip to Abilene? What's your role?

Components of an Effective Infrastructure

Effective organizations regularly evaluate their infrastructure to determine if a particular component operates well and contributes to institutional health. Organizations examine infrastructure by conducting self-assessments or by commissioning independent audits. You can incorporate ongoing assessment as part of annual operations. Also, a long-range strategic planning process evaluates infrastructure as well as program. (See Chapter 6.)

Generally, effective infrastructure includes the following components:

- Planning and assessment (strategic planning is the method to create the first relationship, relationship with community; see Chapter 6).
- Marketing and communications.
- Human resource development (staff and volunteer).
- General business management.
- Corporate governance.
- Financing (revenue and charitable contributions—and charitable contributions demand donor centrism).
- Quality assurance and continuous quality improvement (which includes customer centrism).

What's missing? What would you add to an effective infrastructure? How do you design your infrastructure—including corporate culture and core systems—to meet the complex, changing environment and escalating community needs? I choose to talk about these eight components:

1. Shared values.
2. Art of leadership.
3. Commitment to process.
4. Learning organization (personal mastery, mental models, shared vision, team learning, and systems thinking).
5. Ongoing conversation.
6. Participatory decision-making.
7. Well-managed change (including adaptive capacity).
8. Culture of philanthropy.

All organizations—no matter the type or size, whether for-profit or NGO—need these eight attributes. And an NGO needs one more: a strong culture of philanthropy. Together, these eight components described here will help you develop your organization's relationship within itself. This internal relationship is the first of four defined in this book, all of which are essential to effective organizations and productive fund development.

Shared Values

The first component of an effective infrastructure is shared values. Shared values are the foundation for your organization's internal and external relationships. Shared values are the most critical element for building any type of community, and your organization is a community.

Your organization's life begins with shared values. In fact, values precede the birth of an organization and certainly precede mission.

A value is an enduring belief that a specific mode of conduct is personally or socially preferable to another. A value possesses intrinsic worth, desirability, and utility to the individual or group.

In her article, "Decision-Making in Ethics," Barbara H. Marion, CFRE, presents the theory of tiered values. Each of the tiers is built upon the preceding one.[12] Moral values, says Marion, are the first tier. These values are the "primary, unvarying bedrock rules of individual conduct that result from culture, experience, and training." These individual values are "unconditional, forming the life philosophy of the individual." Second-tier values are "consciously and deliberately [taken] to form our personal code of honor based on principles such as truth-telling, love of country, respect for others, protection of the weak, and tolerance." The third tier of values reflects the professional's standards of practice.

Psychologist Louis Edward Raths formulated a seven-step process to determine values.[13] A true value subscribes to each of these seven elements.

1. *Prized and cherished.* A value is something that the individual or group prizes and cherishes.
2. *Publicly affirmed.* The individual or group must be willing to publicly affirm the value.
3. *Available alternatives.* A value is not mandated. One must be free to choose other alternatives.
4. *Chosen intelligently.* A true value is chosen after intelligently considering the consequences.
5. *Chosen freely.* Individuals and groups choose values freely after considering consequences.
6. *Action.* A true value means acting on one's belief. The final test of a value is action.
7. *Repeated action.* A true value demands repeated action in a consistent pattern.

Individuals have values. These values guide our actions and judgments. Our values are the standards that influence us as we make choices among alternative courses of action. Our values are relatively permanent frameworks that shape and influence our behavior.

Groups, too, have values. Groups form when individuals congregate through common interests or a shared purpose. But first and foremost, individuals congregate because of shared values, those fundamental beliefs that are not negotiable.

Groups operate best through consensus and unity of purpose and action. But even with unity of purpose and action, groups can still flounder if the individuals do not share values. Shared values are the essential glue, and this means that the individual's values must match those of the collective entity.

A group's values have two parts. First, some of the values reflect the group's purpose or mission. Second, other values describe how group members relate to each other, how members behave and act, and how the organization conducts its business.

Because groups are comprised of individuals, the group must articulate its values to ensure some commonality. Don't assume that everyone shares the same values. Group articulation of organizational values assures the individual that her or his values fit well enough with those of the collective entity. These values then provide a framework that guides the actions and judgments of the group.

The values of an organization are, generally, articulated as second- and third-tier beliefs. The group deliberately defines its shared code for behaving and operating. These articulated shared values help the group decide its actions, interact among its members and constituents, and choose its consequences.

Operating with Values

Effective organizations possess clearly articulated values and behave in accordance with these values. Values form the foundation for all organizational activities, choices and decisions, and actions. Values are management and governance tools that:

- Help test mission and determine vision and program.
- Serve as a screen to determine the worthiness, appropriateness, and robustness of all operations.
- Provide the framework for policies and procedures, program delivery system, communications, and fund development strategies.
- Evaluate whether new people align with organizational values and are invited to join.

In their study of visionary companies,[14] James C. Collins and Jerry I. Porras observe that companies last specifically because they have clearly articulated values. These values remain fixed even while business goals and products, strategies, and practices change in response to the changing world.

The authors quote Ralph Larsen, then CEO of Johnson & Johnson, who states: "The core values embodied in [Johnson & Johnson's] Credo might be a competitive advantage, but that is not *why* we have them. We have them because they define for us what we stand for, and we would hold them even if they became a competitive *dis*advantage in certain situations."[15] These most effective organizations continually distinguish between that which is core—unchanging and constant—and that which can and often should change.

Effective organizations discuss how a value affects a particular decision. These organizations identify value conflicts and have a process to make ethical decisions. These organizations regularly assess whether behavior is aligned with values. And these organizations ask individuals to leave who do not publicly affirm and act upon the group's values.

As groups grow and change—when some people leave and new people join—the values still form the foundation for existence. But be wary. Sometimes the values lose their position in the forefront of the group. Perhaps the new people and incumbents did not discuss the values, so the values did not provide that critical screening for invitation or not or opting in or out. Groups must keep their values alive, practiced and promoted.

Values, the nonnegotiable tenets against which we measure the worthiness of our choices.

From *Clicks and Mortar: Passion Driven Growth in an Internet World*, by David S. Pottruck and Terry Pearce (San Francisco: Jossey-Bass, 2000), 1

Articulating Organizational Values

Many groups (or organizations) do not identify their values. When an organization doesn't articulate its values, individuals may behave at cross-purposes. Individuals may join the group without sharing the group's values. Conflict arises and decision-making falters. Rather than too much cohesion, as in groupthink, there isn't enough to move the group forward.

Other organizations do articulate their values. These organizations distribute their value statements to all employees and display their values everywhere: printed in brochures and annual reports, posted on walls, and given to customers and vendors.

The problem is, organizations (and their people) often forget the values. The values statement is just a piece of paper rather than an active part of organizational infrastructure. In this situation, the organization may follow some (or even all) of its articulated values, but not consciously. This, too, is problematic.

Usually there are two reasons why organizations don't use their values.

First, the process of articulating values involves only a small group of people. Perhaps senior management, a special task force, or the board of directors alone determines values. There is little or no ownership, because those affected by the results do not participate.

Keep in mind: A group's values belong to the group. That means that all members of the group participate in the deliberation. Only then can the group choose intelligently and freely. Then choosing happens over and over throughout the organization's decision-making and actions.

Second, there is no mechanism to use the values as part of operations. Values don't work unless consciously institutionalized. For example, the values statement shapes dialogue at meetings. The values statement helps you evaluate how you deliberate, make choices, and take action. Then, Raths's "action" and "repeated action" are not lost.

To articulate your shared values, bring group members together and talk. Through conversation, the group identifies its shared values. Together, the group examines how the values might affect all activities. Sometimes an objective facilitator encourages the group to question itself more readily. Summarize the results and draft the statement. The entire group reviews the draft before adopting the values as institutional policy.

Sometimes, because of geography or organization size, all group members cannot get together. In this case, use alternative methods to engage all group members in the process. For example, the YMCA of Greater Providence connected with all 400 employees and volunteers. First, a team of volunteers and staff developed multiple statements to test values. Then a survey asked which statements represented values of the YMCA.

Survey results produced 21 values statements that the majority of employees and volunteers shared. The CEO and planning consultant used these independent statements to write a narrative that described the YMCA's values. The result was five values:

1. *Respect:* All people have worth and value.
2. *Caring:* We are sensitive and nurturing.
3. *Honesty:* We trust and earn the trust of others.
4. *Responsibility:* We use our resources to serve the diverse community.
5. *Change:* We are future oriented and inspired by change.

But the Y didn't stop with these statements. Each statement included an explanation. For example:

> *Respect: All people have worth and value. As individuals and as an organization, we:*
>
> > *believe that people are basically good, want to do their best, and can learn, change and grow*
> >
> > *reach out and embrace the full diversity of individuals and families, regardless of ability, age, income, faith, lifestyle, physical challenge, race, or ethnicity*
> >
> > *create opportunities for people to be meaningfully involved through challenging responsibilities and individual and team participation*

See the Y's complete values statement in its strategic plan (Appendix 6-O), posted on this book's website.

The Women's Foundation of Southern Arizona (WFSA) brought together its full board and staff to articulate shared values. Individuals took the risk to speak honestly and share opinions. The resulting values statement helped board and staff members decide if subsequent conversation focused on the degree to which the organization behaved in accordance with these values, and what strategies would help enhance alignment with values.

Within a month of its founding, the original steering committee of the Women's Fund of Rhode Island (WFRI) met to define values for the new organization. After intense group dialogue, the facilitator gathered up the various notes and drafted a values statement. The founding steering committee reviewed, edited, and formally adopted the values statement. Based on the group's shared values, the founding steering committee then articulated the mission statement.

Certainly, the Women's Fund founding steering committee had in mind the general purpose or intent of this organization. But defining mission was not the first step. First, we had to identify our shared values and clearly articulate the fundamental beliefs of why we gathered together. With that foundation in place, we were better able to define mission.

The Women's Fund of Rhode Island continually tests its programs and grant-making against its values. At its 10-year anniversary, WFRI reviewed its values. The end result: some consolidation, some adjustment—but still the same founding intent.

See Exhibit 3.2 for the values statement of the Audubon Society of Rhode Island. See the original values statements for Equity Action and the Women's Fund of Rhode

Island in *Keep Your Donors* and also located at www.simonejoyaux.com. Visit their respective websites for updates and more information (www.rifoundation.org and www.wfri.org, respectively).

Exhibit 3.2 Values Statement of the Audubon Society of Rhode Island, Over 100 Years of Education, Conservation, and Advocacy

---

The following values guide ASRI decisions and actions. These values belong to everyone in the organization.

Natural World

Nature is a web of symbiotic relationships. We value the deep connectedness of all things. We appreciate the natural world and its biodiversity. We recognize that preservation of the natural world is essential for human life.

Good Science and Sound Knowledge

Objective empirical science sets the standard for the preservation of natural systems. We promote good science and sound knowledge. We believe that people deserve to be fully informed.

Civic Engagement, Community, and Action

Civic engagement—acting individually and collectively—is essential to sustainable development and global stewardship of the earth's resources and the environment. We recognize human responsibility to the global environment. We believe in grassroots collaborative action in order to live in harmony with nature.

Excellence and Permanence

Integrity, trustworthiness, and quality are essential to permanence. We pursue excellence in every area of our work. We successfully adapt due to our external focus, network connectedness, inquisitiveness, and innovation. We are committed to future generations, passing on a strong organization and a sustainable environment.

Respect, Diversity, and Access

The earth and all living organisms deserve respect. Our world and its people are rich in diversity. We embrace inclusion and access regardless of race, ethnicity, culture, language, gender, age, socioeconomics, physical challenges, sexual orientation, or any other difference. We embrace inclusion and access regardless

(continued)

(Continued)

of differences in background or life experience. We welcome ideas and provide opportunities to our guests, donors, volunteers, and employees.

Tradition and Accomplishments

The past provides important perspective and insight for today and tomorrow. We respect our history, honor our accomplishments, and embrace change for the future.

Source: Courtesy of the Audubon Society of Rhode Island (www.asri.org).

For more examples, see the values statements included in the sample strategic plans posted on this book's website. Of course, a strategic plan begins with a clear statement of the organization's values. The values guide everything that the organization does. The values bring together staff, board members, and other volunteers. And naturally, the values set the stage for the strategic plan. P.S. Organizations do not (and should not) redo their values too often. (The same holds true with mission, by the way.) Values are long-term foundational attributes, not ever-changing items that vary based on who is in the room at the moment.

Managing Value Conflicts

Value conflicts are inevitable in the life of an organization. Sometimes participants in the organization find that their values conflict with those of the group. Sometimes a particular situation puts organizational values in conflict, one with another.

Participation in an organization may constrain an individual's values. To avoid possible conflicts between the individual's values and those of the organization, communicate your organization's values before confirming an individual's participation. By joining, the individual agrees to subscribe to and support the organization's values.

Even longtime participants may suddenly find themselves in conflict with the organization's values. If the individual is unable to change the group—in a reasonable period of time and in a reasonable manner—the individual must leave the group. The individual cannot stay and agitate and disrupt the group. If necessary, the group must ask the individual to leave.

Sometimes, there may be a conflict between the values of an organization. Now the decision is really tough. A particular choice or situation forces a conflict between the organization's articulated values. For example, a bank offers your organization a contribution that will fund much-needed services for youth. You won't have to charge the youth at all, thus supporting your value of being financially accessible. However, the bank's hiring and lending practices penalize the poor and people of color. This conflicts with your values of diversity and respect for others. What will you do?

As Marion observes, "Questions of right and wrong are easy: do not kill; do not steal; do not cheat. So are ethical questions until the choice is between competing values and one must choose which course of action is more righteous."[16] The group decides which is the best choice, given competing values. To choose, the group talks together. Decision-making guidelines are also helpful. Marion proposes an ethical decision-making process that incorporates the following steps.

1. Clarify the problem.
2. Identify the key competing values at stake.
3. Identify the players and stakeholders.
4. Identify the most plausible alternatives.
5. Imagine the potential outcomes.
6. Evaluate the potential outcomes.
7. Decide on a course of action.
8. Test the decision.
9. Implement the decision.
10. Evaluate the results or consequences.
11. Modify policies and procedures.

Marion has an additional step, located between steps 8 and 9: Share the decision with someone else. This step is automatic in a group decision-making situation.

Aligning Behavior with Values

Articulating shared values is relatively easy. Finding consensus, particularly around this core, shouldn't be too difficult. Otherwise, why (and how) would you all have gotten together in the first place? The real challenge is aligning behavior with values. To use the oft-repeated cliché, we have to "walk the talk." Once the organization articulates its values, make the values part of the corporate culture. Keep the values alive through behavior, through formal and informal assessment and feedback, and through organizational policy, procedure, and systems.

Your organization can use several strategies to help people understand and behave according to group values.

- When you interview candidates for board and staff positions, share the values statement and describe how these values are displayed in the actions of the organization and its individuals. Emphasize that all staff and board members must adhere to these values when working with your organization.
- Include the criterion "adheres to our stated values" as part of the performance appraisal for staff and board members.
- Help each person within the organization hold himself or herself accountable and extend that accountability to his and her colleagues. Provide feedback to each other when behavior does not appear to support the organization's values.
- Begin meetings by asking attendees to pull out the values statement and read it silently.
- When a difficult situation arises, review the values statement to set the stage for deliberation.
- Annually assess the degree to which behavior is aligned with values. Use a survey to compare individual and group behavior to each value. The survey

asks respondents to rate their own individual performance and the performance of various teams or groups within the organization.

- Every three to five years, use the strategic planning process to reevaluate values and assess how well the organization is behaving. Convene group discussions and circulate surveys.
- Examine organizational policies and procedures to ensure that they reflect values. As necessary, develop new policies and procedures to support values.
- Compare performance to values when you appraise the performance of staff and volunteers.
- Periodically, start a board meeting with a quick review of values. At the end of the meeting, discuss how the group's behavior and actions reflected the organization's values.
- When you face a particularly difficult decision, talk about your values first. This discussion will offer you insights into decision-making.

Some Core Values

There are values that make groups and organizations function better. These values include such things as respect, honesty, and responsibility. Values that are essential to groups but may appear to conflict one with the other include a commitment to the group agenda rather than a personal agenda while at the same time respecting different opinions and agreeing to disagree.

Finally, there are the values that reflect your organization and its founders. Some differ from organization to organization; others may be similar but expressed differently.

Challenging Values

Group effectiveness depends on some form of common bond and an alignment of some shared views and values. Yet, this may suggest groupthink, exclusion, or totalitarianism to some.

If a group articulates its shared values and uses these as a foundation for the organization, does this produce homogeneity? Will the group only seek out clones of its existing members? Clearly this would not be advantageous. To survive in the next millennium, organizations must respond to a complex, changing, and uncertain world. Exclusionary practices and homogeneity threaten survival.

A group can share values and still avoid conformity.

Avoid homogeneity and conformity by taking the following steps:

- First, involve everyone in the process to produce shared values. The collective, collaborative process co-creates values.
- Second, encourage group members to speak honestly.
- Third, include pluralism, diversity, and individual creativity as organizational values. Make sure your values speak to developing the individual's full potential.

It is helpful for the group to establish values that support inclusiveness in ethnicity, gender, age, and experience.

Using Values in Fund Development

Naturally, your fund development program must operate in accordance with your organization's values. The need for a dollar cannot compromise your organization's values. For example:

- You are a theater company with a resident corps of actors. You believe that these actors are the best in the business. You do not endorse the concept of stars. For a fund development event, your theater company would *not* host a national touring production with famous actors.
- You are a youth organization that develops self-esteem and life skills for teens. You offer teens alternatives to street activities and substance abuse. You probably would *not* solicit gifts from alcohol manufacturers or distributors.
- Your organization values diversity. You believe in gender, generation, and ethnic diversity. You would be uncomfortable if men chaired most of your fund development activities.
- You are a homeless shelter. Hundreds of your donors give gifts of $50 or less. You also have affluent donors who represent the corporate and social sector of your community. If you plan a fund development event with a ticket price of $250, you might also plan a fund development event with a more accessible ticket price.
- You are a community development corporation, building affordable housing. A marketing firm donates the design and production for your case statement. The result: just plain stunning to look at, but far too glossy and high-end. The piece doesn't reflect your organization's values. Big mistake: You forgot to share your values with the firm prior to the work.

These are fairly straightforward decisions regarding values. But consider the following. Initiate a conversation with your own board and colleagues—and get ready for some emotional discussion. You may find that, sometimes, your values conflict one with the other. Now it's really hard.

- As a social justice organization, you hold your endowment in socially responsible investments that reflect your values. But this investment approach reduces your endowment, thus risking financial health and organizational sustainability. What is your values-based decision?
- Would your organization—no matter your cause—accept a gift from a tobacco company? The U.S. courts have found the tobacco industry guilty of conspiracy to harm people and guilty of falsifying information distributed to the public. But the gift would allow you to do good work. What is your values-based decision?
- If you were an environmental organization, did you accept a gift from Exxon after the *Valdez* oil spill? Would you accept a gift from BP or Transocean or Halliburton after the spring 2010 Gulf of Mexico oil debacle? Sure, these spills were not intentional—although major questions about negligence abound. Still,

the money would allow you to do good work, including lobbying for stronger regulation to fight future spills of this nature. What is your values-based decision?

- As a fund development executive, would you accept a bequest made to you and your family from a donor to your agency? Over the years, the agency donor had become a dear friend to you personally. What is your values-based decision?

In addition to complying with the organization's values, you should articulate specific values for fund development. Why? Because fund development is susceptible to the appearance (and sometimes the reality) of inappropriate behavior. Increasingly, people are suspicious of fund development practice. Respond by articulating values for your fund development program.

The fund development profession has already defined some values by establishing codes of ethics, standards of professional practice, and donors' rights. Your organization can use these. For example, hire only a fundraiser who belongs to a professional association and subscribes to an ethical code. Communicate the code, standards, and donors' rights to your various constituents, not just your donors.

Talk with your volunteers and staff about their values for fund development. Involve the development committee, board, and staff. Discuss how your fund development values could affect fund development activities and decisions. Then adopt the values as organizational policy.

Use the Association of Fundraising Professionals (www.afpnet.org) Code of Ethical Principles and Standards of Professional Practice and the Donor Bill of Rights as a starting point for your organization's conversation. See www.afpnet.org. And check out the other professional associations around the world, many highlighted at www.simonejoyaux.com.

The Art of Leadership

Leadership is the second component of effective infrastructure. Effective fundraisers are good leaders. They lead the fund development function, and they lead organizational development.

Leadership guarantees that your institution develops the four relationships central to an effective organization and critical to productive fund development. Leaders facilitate the ongoing process to develop, sustain, and renew these relationships. In this third edition of *Strategic Fund Development*, I explore the topic of leadership in Chapter 5.

Commitment to Process

Have you ever asked a group of people, "Who likes process?" Some wave their hands enthusiastically. Some don't. Actually, lots of people frown. But building strong organizations and nurturing relationships are all about process. Effective management and governance require process.

Process takes time. Process can be messy. Process involves more than one person, sometimes lots more than one person. And that means diverse opinions and conflicts and conflict management and ... And all that is pretty stressful and tiresome.

C'est la vie. That's life. Embrace process. Just take a look at Exhibit 3.3, a blog from Seth Godin.

Exhibit 3.3 The Reason Social Media Is So Difficult for Most Organizations

It's a process, not an event.

Dating is a process. So is losing weight, being a public company, and building a brand.

On the other hand, putting up a trade show booth is an event. So are going public and having surgery.

Events are easier to manage, pay for, and get excited about. Processes build results for the long haul.

Source: Seth Godin's blog on December 10, 2009. Read all of Seth's blogs at www.sethgodin.com.

When you visit www.visualthesaurus.com and click on "process," watch the web it weaves, connections like: outgrowth, work, work on, procedure, cognitive process, mental process, operation, unconscious process, cipher, manage, handle, deal, care.

I clicked on one of the connections and then these words came up: juggle, coordinate, come to grips, handle (and mishandle), conduct (and misconduct). Yet another click gave me: harness, rein in, maneuver. And my writing partner would gasp at these: channelize and becharm.

No wonder some people don't like process. But commit to it you must. Then do it well.

The Learning Organization

This great business theory changed my professional life. For that reason, I include the learning organization as a central component of an organization's internal relations.

Effective organizations are always learning, and the best fundraisers lead the crusade for learning. They know that organizational health and fund development depend on how well (and how quickly) the organization learns.

A learning organization is a way of operating. Learning means enhancing one's capability—as an individual and as an organization—to achieve desired results. Peter Senge[17] (1990) notes that for organizations to excel in the future, they must tap people's willingness and ability to learn. Through learning, we continually re-create ourselves.

There are two types of learning, adaptive and generative. Effective organizations use both.

1. Adaptive learning means you modify existing operations, thereby producing an altered concept.
2. Generative learning means you create something previously unknown from current experience and information. Generative learning is the most stressful for an organization because it is unfamiliar.

Becoming a learning organization is no easy task. To do so, Senge says, you must build an infrastructure that includes five specific disciplines: personal mastery, mental models, shared vision, team learning, and systems thinking (Exhibit 3.4). Woven together, these disciplines create the learning organization.

Exhibit 3.4   Five Disciplines of a Learning Organization

1. *Personal mastery:* Personal development of the individuals in the organization.

    An organization will learn only if the individuals within it learn, too. Each individual must commit to lifelong learning. Personal mastery means we each commit to self-examination, patience, and an objective view of reality. Every individual can achieve a special level of proficiency in her or his personal and professional life.

2. *Mental models:* Deeply held paradigms that affect choices and action.

    Individuals and groups hold assumptions and generalizations that influence their view of the world, shape their decisions and actions, and affect their interpretation of what is possible. Often, we fail to use new insights because they conflict with our fundamental images of the world. Effective individuals and groups learn to see their own mental models, examine them, and encourage others to examine and influence these models.

3. *Shared vision:* Common aspiration held by the group.

    Together, an organization's stakeholders create their shared vision, thereby building a sense of commitment. Shared values, common vision, and a sense of identity bind these stakeholders together.

4. *Team learning:* Working together for action.

    Teams develop intelligence and ability that is greater than the sum of the team members' individual abilities. Team learning starts with dialogue where members suspend their assumptions so that the group discovers insights not available individually. Dialogue also helps the team identify its own behaviors that may undermine learning.

5. *Systems thinking:* Process for seeing the whole.

    Systems thinking focuses on the whole and how its parts relate one to the other. Systems thinking helps us reflect upon, talk about, and understand the forces and interrelationships that affect the behavior of various systems. This discipline helps organizations see how to change systems more effectively.

Source: From Peter M. Senge's work.

Senge observes that the individuals who contribute most to your organization are those who practice these disciplines. Through practice, individuals enhance their own ability "to hold and seek a vision, to reflect and inquire, to build collective capabilities, and to understand systems."[18] As the practitioner becomes more proficient with the discipline, she or he finds new ways of seeing and doing.

The challenge then is not only to learn what you need to know but also to unlearn what you no longer need. That means eliminating the habits, practices, and assumptions that once worked—even those that may have accounted for past successes—to make room for new methods that better fit your new circumstances.

From "The Art of Smart" by Anna Muoio, *Fast Company*, July–August 1999

Systems Thinking Is the Cornerstone

Systems thinking means seeing interrelationships rather than linear chains. You see a whole whose parts relate and operate for a common purpose. You see processes of change rather than snapshots of activity.

Systems thinkers don't tolerate functional silos. You know what silos look like: development and program staff only rarely talk to each other; bookkeeping tracks the numbers but doesn't see its role in donor communications; employees focus on their own responsibilities and don't talk about other areas of operation. Systems thinkers understand there's a real hazard operating within a vacuum.[19]

Silos = systems failure.

—A bumper sticker from Cohort 20, Master of Arts in Philanthropy and Development, Saint Mary's University of Minnesota

---

Systems thinking helps your organization understand how its actions create current reality. Then, as a learning organization, you define your future vision and design the infrastructure that will move you from your current reality to your future vision.

Systems include both detail complexity and dynamic complexity. *Detail complexity* refers to many individual variables that seem not to be related. *Dynamic complexity* focuses on the whole system and its interrelated parts. Dynamic complexity exists when the same action has dramatically different effects in the short run and the long run, when an action has different consequences in different parts of the system, or when obvious interventions have consequences that aren't so obvious.

Effective organization leaders recognize the importance of dynamic complexity. They see the whole system—fund development and organizational development—and its interrelated parts. They act as systems thinkers, seeing when and how a change in action or structure can generate significant and enduring improvement.

Systems thinkers know that each action produces a reaction. Action in one area will likely affect another area, producing both intended and unintended consequences. For this reason, systems thinkers learn to anticipate the reactions and trade-offs of a chosen action. These leaders identify high and low leverage points within a system and evaluate the potential impact before deciding how to act.

Systems thinking benefits organizations by helping them figure out the best leverage in complex situations. By approaching situations in a systemic way, people see what causes the problem and how it can be fixed. Senge views systems thinking as the cornerstone of the learning organization. Systems thinking relates and integrates the other four disciplines—personal mastery, mental models, shared vision, and team learning—into the whole organization.

Organizations are complex systems that interact constantly and significantly with a host of other equally complex systems. The most important property of these systems is that they cannot be broken down into parts that have separate lives of their own. Thus, in an organization, no basic functions, departments, or objectives exist independently of one another.

From *Framebreak: The Radical Redesign of American Business*, by Ian I. Mitroff, Richard O. Mason, and Christine M. Pearson (San Francisco: Jossey-Bass, 1994)

The bottom line of systems thinking is leverage, says Senge. He goes on to observe that while people often think they need more information to address issues today, the opposite may be true. People may actually have so much information they have trouble deciding what is most important. And systems thinking helps distinguish what is most important. Now look at your organization. Consider how an action in one part of the system will affect another area, whether sooner or later.

- How might the diverse, sometimes conflicting or competing relationships among clients, donors, trustees, staff, and other volunteers affect budgeting?
- What might be the effect of a new service on current services and their delivery?
- What would be the short- and long-term effects on your fund development of discontinuing a service?
- How might changing community demographics affect your board composition?
- How could your marketing strategy for a particular service affect donor perception and public image?
- How will the actions of your maintenance staff affect your ability to solicit funds from donors?

Create Your Learning Organization

Practitioners say there are five major benefits when you function as a learning organization.

1. Your organization adapts more readily and rapidly to the changing environment.
2. People are considered the organization's top assets, creating intellectual resources and producing innovation.

3. Your organization becomes its own "community brain," which generates, integrates, and organizes information, knowledge, and wisdom.
4. Your organization creates its own conversations that, by linking the organization's knowledge, produce learning.
5. The parts of your organization cooperate to help the larger whole survive and grow. Together, the organization enhances its capacity to achieve desired results.

To create your own learning organization, use the five disciplines of personal mastery, mental models, shared vision, team learning, and systems thinking (see Exhibit 3.4). Review the earlier information in this section. Then, design an infrastructure that incorporates the attributes of a learning organization, described in Exhibit 3.5.

Exhibit 3.5   Attributes of a Learning Organization's Infrastructure

- The organization involves all stakeholders. People are free to choose within recognized boundaries. (Peter Block notes in his book *Stewardship* that even in the most empowered organizations there are still bosses who set the boundaries.)
- The organization uses learning (and its five disciplines) as a major strategy for organizational success, and devises ways for the organization to practice and learn from its mistakes. This process of practice and learning happens while you carry out daily operations, but it is separate from operations.
- Stakeholders share an overall view of the system and see their own places in it.
- The organization clearly articulates values, mission, and vision, and develops these through an ongoing and honest participatory process.
- Corporate culture and core systems are based on stewardship. Responsibility and authority are shared throughout the organization.
- A critical mass of organization members commits to redesign the infrastructure into a healthy system. Enough individuals share new insights and skills, thus passing on learning through the whole organization. This new learning belongs to the system and everyone in it, not to any single individual or small group of individuals.
- New concepts of leadership engage people throughout the organization. Leaders work toward personal mastery and participate in and facilitate learning.
- Personal mastery and team learning are key accountabilities for employee and volunteer selection and orientation. The reward and recognition system reinforces both accountabilities.
- People work together in learning situations, developing new strategies and techniques to address issues.

(continued)

(Continued)

- The communications system, ongoing conversation, and participatory decision making provide all constituents with a systemic view of the organization, helping everyone to understand individual and group contributions.
- People create ways to identify, share, and celebrate learning and results.

Source: Data from Phillip J. Carroll, "Infrastructure for Organizational Transformation at Shell Oil," *Collective Intelligence* 1, no. 1 (MIT Center for Organizational Learning), and from Carolyn J.C. Thompson, presentation at Systems Thinking in Action Conference, Boston, 1995.

Conversation Is a Core Business Practice

Pay attention to conversation because it can change your organization! Conversation helps you develop and renew the four relationships fundamental to effective organizations and effective fund development.

Conversation means an interchange of ideas in which two or more participate. But conversation is more. Consider this thought: "... it is in how we speak with one another that we experience respect from others and whether we are being heard."[20] Conversation is more than talking. Conversation:

- Is carried out face-to-face, in writing, and through technology.
- Includes casual, informal chatter and more formal discussion and formal dialogue.
- Uses discussion and dialogue as specific techniques to accomplish particular goals.

Humans are social beings. We connect through conversation. That's how we learn. Through conversations we build shared knowledge and generate new insights. We make commitments and organize for action.

Conversation happens between individuals and among groups within your organization and between your organization and its community. Your conversation can be formal and structured or casual and unstructured. Either way, conversation—even chance encounters—requires both intent and an initiator. Sometimes there is a purpose and desired result for the conversation. Other times, there may be no purpose but casual contact.

Conversation produces community, and a sense of community generates commitment.

Systems thinker Alan Webber[21] says that the most important work in the new economy is creating conversations. Systems thinking theory states that conversation is the chief management tool that makes learning happen. Through conversation, organizations learn and can then stimulate change. Just read Exhibit 3.6, an amazing story of conversation among the titmice and robins.

Exhibit 3.6   Conversation among the Titmice and Robins

Years ago bottles of milk were delivered to porch steps in rural England. The glass bottles had no caps and so the robins and titmice perched on the bottle lips and drank the cream. Generation after generation of robins and titmice enjoyed the cream.

One day, the bottles began arriving with cardboard caps. The robins and titmice perched again on the bottle lips, only to encounter a barrier to their enjoyment.

The robins finally flew away, never to return to the bottles. But the titmice learned to break through the cardboard caps with their beaks and continued to enjoy the cream.

The robins didn't learn to break through the milk caps but the titmice did. Why?

Robins are territorial birds. It's safe to assume that one robin figured out how to break through the cap on the bottle. But she stayed in her own territory and didn't share the information with her fellow robins.

Titmice are flocking birds. They hang out together. Somehow they communicate and share information. The first titmouse that learned to break through the cap shared it with the other titmice. And generation after generation of titmice continued to enjoy the cream.

Effective organizations are comprised of titmice, nonterritorial flockers, who regularly communicate and learn together. All those wonderful conversations help them organize for action.

Source: From a story told by Arie de Geus at the 1994 Systems Thinking in Action TM Conference and retold in his article "The Living Company," *Harvard Business Review* (March–April 1997).

Conversation is critical to organizational health and learning because it:

- Gathers information.
- Shares knowledge.
- Questions assumptions.
- Identifies implications and consequences.
- Generates answers.
- Builds understanding and linkages.
- Creates camaraderie.

Talking in Your Organization

Look at your own organization. Do you have lots of conversations? Is conversation encouraged, whether formal or informal? Is participation inclusive, extended to bring in more people and perspectives? Does conversation encourage questioning and innovation? Do individuals and groups learn through conversation?

Consider the following:

- How often have you watched one individual or a small group dominate discussion and control the decision?
- Have you seen groups make poor choices because participants did not talk enough about consequences?
- Have you ever gone along with a decision without asking enough questions because you assumed some other group had discussed the issue adequately?
- Do your board and staff talk about the tough issues such as eliminating programs or overcoming gender and ethnic bias?
- Are your trustees and staff uncomfortable with disagreement?
- Do any of your staff or volunteers withhold information from others, seeking to control decision-making?
- Do some individuals push their own personal agendas, ignoring the will of the group?
- Does your organization isolate discussion to a handful of people, thinking this is efficient and protects confidentiality?

Look at the design of your board meetings. Do you focus primarily on reports? Do you structure meetings for brevity, avoiding extensive conversation? In the haste to run good meetings, do your committees do most of the talking and then recommend action to the board, which reacts without much talking? The result may be efficient meetings. However, this also produces uninformed, disengaged, and bored boards.

The theory of "committees do the work and the board acts on committee recommendations" is fine for routine or straightforward decision-making. But when your organization must make judgments about uncertain and complex issues, you are best served if the board and its members engage fully. And full engagement at board meetings means conversation.

As the legal and moral corporate entity, the board must fully understand its choices. Committees may research and talk, but then they come to the board for extensive conversation, which helps produce good decision-making. The best boards talk lots about meaningful issues. The best boards do not tolerate the "reports only" format. But, as Rhode Island colleague Michael Fantom notes, "It's safe to listen to reports only; it's less risky. With reports only, there's no confrontation and no accountability."

Michael's comment is so true and very scary. The board is legally and morally liable for the health and effectiveness of the organization. Yet, boards avoid conversation because it's too risky and might ruffle someone's feathers—maybe the CEO's or the board chair's or that really powerful board member's feathers. The board avoids deep strategic conversation, thus avoiding confrontation and avoiding any accountability. Do you think your board knows it's doing that?

I use "conversation" and "dialogue" interchangeably in my writings and work. However, in theory, there is a difference: conversation is more informal; dialogue is a more formal and intentional process.

Pay attention to how people gather together in your organization. Do they get together only at formal, scheduled meetings? Or do they encounter each other casually and talk informally about issues that matter? Do people hang out with their department colleagues only or do they mingle across the boundaries of the organization?

Examine the physical layout of your organization. How does this layout affect conversation? Are people isolated in cubicles and are departments separated one from the other, or even in different buildings?

Think about the grapevine and gossip in your organization. Oh, how fast information travels through the grapevine. Use it. Use the grapevine, and the power of positive gossip, to share information and encourage conversation.

Sure, formal communication is important, but don't discount the parking lot conversations and the lunchroom chatter. Reinforce these conversations for the good of the organization. Pass on the news and share the questions. Encourage the exploration and value the insights.

In their article "Conversation as a Core Business Process,"[22] Juanita Brown and David Isaacs note that "thoughtful conversations around questions that matter might be *the* core process in any company—the source of organizational intelligence that enables the other business processes to create positive results." Brown and Isaacs quote Fernando Flores, who states that "an organization's results are determined through webs of human commitments, born in webs of human conversations."

The irony is that if conversation is a core business practice, why do so many organizations focus on "Stop talking and get back to work!"? Effective organizations work hard to encourage conversation. These organizations know that people (and the organization itself) learn and make better decisions because of conversation. Indeed, these organizations continually explore how to develop the attitude, systems, and processes to foster meaningful conversations. Fund development leaders also understand the value of conversation. They create opportunities for people to talk about strategic issues and bring up controversial topics.

Discussion and Dialogue Are Different

Formal conversation uses two techniques, discussion and dialogue, to help accomplish activities. While both are important to organizational health and learning, dialogue is the more critical and the less familiar.

There's a fair amount of discussion in most organizations. People pass information and opinions back and forth hoping to convince each other of a particular perspective. By trying to convince each other to accept an opinion, discussion does not seek "coherence and truth," said physicist David Bohm.[23]

Dialogue, on the other hand, sees the larger picture and seeks Bohm's "pool of common meaning." The purpose of dialogue is to move beyond the understanding of any individual and to explore the complex issues. To this end, dialogue is collaborative conversation (see Exhibit 3.7). People pool their information and experience, suspend personal assumptions, and avoid the need to persuade others.

Exhibit 3.7   What Does Dialogue Mean?

In learning organization theory, dialogue is a group process that helps produce organizational change. What do people do when they dialogue?

- Treat everyone as equals.
- Share information and experience without advocating one position or another.
- Suspend personal assumptions and really listen to what others say.
- Identify hidden questions and issues.
- Determine what lies behind opinions so that deeper understanding is possible.
- Integrate diverse perspectives into a new collective view.
- Learn together.

During dialogue, people observe their own thinking processes and mental models. As each person reflects upon and shares his or her views, group understanding deepens. People notice inconsistencies, fragmentation, incoherence, and polarities. People seek the patterns and missing pieces.

Then shift happens. Participants integrate their diverse perspectives into a new collective view. Together, people are transformed so they can make decisions that transform the organization. Peter Senge calls this shift "metanoia."

Effective dialogue, contrasted to discussion, requires the intent and support of the group. Your organization engages the right people, erring on the side of inclusiveness rather than exclusiveness. Dialogue accepts everyone as equal, without any power structure. Dialogue uses face-to-face interaction to enhance perception and build teams.

In their book *Dialogue: Rediscovering the Transforming Power of Conversation*, Ellinor and Gerard[24] present a continuum for dialogue versus conversation.

Dialogue	Discussion/Debate
Seeing the *whole* among the parts	Breaking issues/problems into *parts*
Seeing the *connections* between the parts	Seeing *distinctions* between the parts
Inquiring into assumptions	*Justifying/defending* assumptions
Learning through inquiry and disclosure	*Persuading, selling, telling*
Creating *shared* meaning among many	Gaining agreement on *one* meaning

Ellinor and Gerard observe that interconnectedness and diversity are the bases for dialogue. "Dialogue rests on the idea that we live in a world that is collective in nature with interconnected parts."[25] First, dialogue helps people see the interconnections. Then dialogue helps people build the capacity to "leverage the team's inherent diversity."[26]

Good dialogue leads with uncertainty. You ask critical strategic questions and identify the unspoken questions and issues. Dialogue embraces pluralism and accepts diversity and its resulting paradoxes.

Dialogue is progressive. It moves throughout the organization, stimulating learning and producing change. Dialogue flows from a person's internal conversation to small groups. From small groups, dialogue moves to multiple groups. Finally, multiple group dialogues produce large-scale impact. You make dialogue practical by discussing the implications for your organization. This is learning.

Whether you use discussion or dialogue may seem a fine distinction, but effective organizations use dialogue to focus and deepen the ongoing conversations that Alan Webber describes as critical for organizational success in the growing knowledge economy.

Conversation Supports Strategic Thinking

As an aside, organizations that survive think strategically. Conversation, especially the dialogue form, stimulates strategic thinking.

Strategic thinking is a group process, dependent upon the highest-quality collective thought. That's why leaders bring people together and encourage them to ask questions. Strategic thinking depends on this ongoing conversation to support organizational continuity, promote creativity, facilitate transition, produce learning, and generate change.

Thinking strategically means understanding why, not just what and how. When you think strategically, you consider the whole system, its various parts, and their interconnectedness. You see dynamic complexity rather than focus on details. You consider the implications of information and the consequences of choices. You transform information into knowledge and then knowledge into learning.

Thinking strategically allows individuals and organizations to identify and resolve dilemmas by shifting the context in which they are understood. Organizational members explore long-term complex issues that are important to the organization's survival. This exploration helps people examine their assumptions (Senge's mental models) about what drives the organization and its various stakeholders and how the dynamics of the larger community affect the institution.

Strategic thinking means asking the right questions. Clear, challenging, and penetrating questions elicit creative thinking. By questioning current assumptions, an organization can change the assumptions. Shifts in assumptions then produce innovation. Use conversation and dialogue to stimulate strategic thinking in your organization. Conversation and dialogue help improve the quality of thinking together because individuals shift awareness and notice more.

Through dialogue—not discussion—organizational members identify patterns, recognize barriers, distinguish issues, and find new opportunities. Dialogue helps people explore the connections between ideas, not just the ideas themselves. Participants observe differences rather than conflicting views, thereby bringing new insight to the whole.

Questions are catalysts for change. Questions bring people together. Questions attract people and resources to your organization.

A reminder: Decide if dialogue is or is not necessary. Many times a decision belongs to a single individual or small group; no dialogue is needed. Be vigilant, though, because there are many more situations when good dialogue is beneficial.

Create Conversation in Your Organization

Effective organizations develop and sustain an infrastructure that allows conversation to happen. Here are some ideas to help your organization create conversations.

1. Identify the essential qualities that make conversation good, and promote these qualities in your organization.
2. Identify the one question that, if you all answered it together, would help your organization create conversations.
3. Create a spirit of inquiry before you begin conversations.
4. Make sure the environment is safe so it's risk-free to ask questions and question assumptions.
5. Differentiate between dialogue and discussion and make sure both happen.
6. Know when conversation is unnecessary because decisions are routine.
7. Involve as many persons as possible, making sure that conversation happens between various individuals and groups within your organization.

Start by asking the individuals in your organization to identify the qualities necessary for conversation. Compare your organization's list to Exhibit 3.8, qualities commonly identified by people in different settings.

Exhibit 3.8   Qualities Essential to Good Conversation

- Safe to speak honestly.
- Mutual risk taking.
- Respect for everyone in the room.
- Participants' perceptions change.
- Empathy with one another.
- Sense of exploration.
- Climate of discovery.
- Common language.
- Pluralism and diversity among participants and opinions.
- Challenges the way participants think.
- Energy and synergy within the group.
- Feeling of intimacy and shared values.
- Topic really matters to the participants individually.
- No one judges.
- Build on each other's remarks.
- When conversation ends, participants want to talk more.

Once your organization has identified the essential qualities, ask people: "Do we create conversations that reflect the qualities we desire?" Together, figure out why and why not. Talk about how you can promote the essential qualities within your organization. For example:

Ask yourselves if it is lack of faith and trust that stops your organization from creating conversations that reflect these qualities. Perhaps individuals worry that while they seek good conversation, others in the group do not.

Ironically, experience shows that most people seek the same qualities in conversation, and certainly the majority in any group does. It appears, then, that people must make a leap of faith and behave in keeping with these qualities. Since most people want these same qualities, someone must take the risk and act accordingly.

Together, examine your organization. What core question, if answered, would allow real learning conversations to become the norm rather than the exception? Remember, the question might not have anything to do with conversation itself. The question simply stimulates your organization to identify and eliminate the barrier to good conversation.

Consider these five questions:

1. How do we create a safe space for conversation that produces individual and organizational learning and results in good decision-making?
2. What can I do to ensure that I recognize (and question) my own mental models?
3. What do I have to lose by creating good conversation myself?
4. How can I better convey who I am without fear?
5. How do the parts of our organization relate to the whole?

Create a spirit of inquiry among the members in your organization. Begin by talking with the group. Ask yourselves: "How can we create a spirit of inquiry here and now?" Together, define the traits that characterize this spirit. Establish general guidelines to use as you create conversations. Here are a few examples:

1. Meet in a place with no distractions.
2. Make sure people feel relaxed and comfortable.
3. Give everyone a chance to talk. Help people find out what they share in common.
4. Respect people's experience and expertise.
5. Ask questions that stimulate thinking and help people look deeply into the situation.
6. Make sure everyone recognizes that the dialogue might produce some discomfort. And that's okay.
7. Use diagrams, tape recordings, and other tools to help people understand the connections between the various thoughts presented.[27]

Asking the Right Questions

What is a right question? Are there actually wrong ones? Yes, when using conversation as a core business practice, there are right and wrong questions. Here's the point: Good conversation and dialogue depend on good questions. The questions we ask are as important as (sometimes more important than) finding the right answers. The best questions open minds and stimulate change. The right questions bring people together in hopes of decision-making and action.

And the wrong questions? They stymie conversation, distract attention from what's important, frustrate people, and stop dialogue.

By the way, what irony: people who have all the answers when they don't even know the questions.

What are the right questions? The right questions are those that engage people in exploration, learning, innovation, and change. The right questions are open-ended and avoid bias. These questions likely do not have an immediate or easy answer. That's the point. These questions probe the most difficult challenges and the most intriguing opportunities for your organization. These questions can refresh and reform your organization.

Asking questions means we must suspend our own assumptions about "what is right" and "what is best." We need to listen to others and question our own assumptions rather than advocate for our own opinions. Consider what our colleague Karla A. Williams, ACFRE, says: "Pursuit of knowledge is based on asking questions and questioning the answers." And I would add, "asking the questions that matter in the first place."

Strategic questions create dissonance between current experiences and beliefs while evoking new possibilities for collective discovery. But they also serve as the glue that holds together overlapping webs of conversations in which diverse resources combine and recombine to create innovative solutions and business value.

From "Conversation as a Core Business Process," by Juanita Brown and David Isaacs, *Systems Thinker* 7, no. 10 (December 1996–January 1997): 4

Too often, we only probe the surface when asking questions. We don't question our own assumptions. We ask the obvious questions. The challenge is to ask the deeper questions and question those questions to learn more.

Brown and Isaacs note that "the quality of our learning process depends on the quality of questions we ask."[28] Asking the questions that matter requires some skill. It takes skill to explore the questions, question the inherent assumptions, and discover new questions of meaning. People develop these skills by talking together and practicing more.

In learning organization theory, learning is both an individual and a group process. Group learning is where the added value is most critical because the organization learns and can then change. Brown and Isaacs go on to say, "Clear, bold, and penetrating questions that elicit a full range of responses tend to open the social context for learning. People engaged in the conversation develop a common concern for deeper levels of shared meaning."[29]

Peter Drucker identified five key questions. Then he brought together several thought leaders[30] to explore his questions in a little book called *The Five Most*

Important Questions You Will Ever Ask about Your Organization. And what are those questions?

1. What is our mission?
2. Who is our customer?
3. What does the customer value?
4. What are our results?
5. What is our plan?

It's just as simple as that—or just as complicated. Drucker, with his colleagues, explores the meaning of each question and the parts of each question. What a great tool for annual self-assessment, and planning priorities for the year. What a great tool to wake up the somnolent.

And when you get really good at exploring the right and meaningful questions, move on to the cage-rattling ones. The cage-rattling questions may be scary and risky. Need ideas? Take a look at this great little book by Whitney and Giovagnoli: *75 Cage-Rattling Questions to Change the Way You Work* (New York: McGraw-Hill, 1997). The authors offer "shake-'em-up questions to open meetings, ignite discussion, and spark creativity." Questions like:

- What drives your best customers [and best donors] crazy and what makes them exceedingly happy? Why?
- What false or outdated assumptions do people operate under at work?
- If you came up with a brilliant idea, who or what might prevent you from implementing it?
- Which of these concepts—teamwork, learning organization, continuous improvement, leadership and quality—is the biggest joke at your company?

Ask tough and cage-rattling questions ... questions that are a product of a fair dose of curiosity, a sense of humility, the strength to challenge the status quo, and the willingness to share ... including the willingness to relinquish privilege, resources, and power.

—Kelly Hurd, Cohort 19, Master of Arts in Philanthropy and Development, Saint Mary's University of Minnesota

---

Worried that your organization won't appreciate questions, especially cage-rattling ones? Consider these 13 questions—about asking questions—raised by cohort colleagues at Saint Mary's University (www.smumn.edu/philanthropy.aspx). Which ones might work in your organization?

1. Why are people afraid of the cage-rattling questions?
2. To what degree do people fear cage-rattling questions? Or do they resist cage-rattling questions out of fear of the answers?

3. Why are cage-rattling questions so scary? How can we strengthen the way we ask these questions? (Perhaps the questions are so big that people get lost in them. Maybe breaking these questions down into smaller parts might help.)

4. Why is there so little movement on asking, exploring, answering? Where (and why) is there resistance? Is it fear of questions, fear of change, or fear that there will be no answers?

5. Why do we resist? Why are we afraid? What do we fear? Of all our fears, what is the largest and why?

6. Why do I care so much? Why don't they care enough (and who said they didn't)?

7. What circumstances tend to instigate cage rattling? (Forced out of one's own comfort zone? Exploring unique or different experiences and cultures? Presence of other cage-rattlers? Willingness to be self-aware and open?) How can we appropriately use these circumstances?

8. To what degree is the element of surprise—or permission—important in the success of asking cage-rattling questions?

9. How comfortable are you "being lost"? Are we willing to be uncomfortable—to talk and question and be questioned?

10. What is the difference between truth and fact?

11. What does trust mean and why does it matter?

12. What does it mean to be part of a community? What are we entitled to and obligated for if we are part of a community?

13. What is exploitation? Why do we have it? Why do we tolerate it?

Now for some examples of meaningful (and sometimes cage-rattling) questions that apply to just about any nonprofit/NGO:

1. If your organization went out of business tomorrow, what would be the cause? What will it take to prevent this?

2. What change—if made in your organization—would most enhance your organization?

3. What does the community expect from your organization and are you willing to adapt to these needs?

4. What difference would it make to the community if your organization closed?

There are so many more questions. What would you add? Explore these questions from my classrooms in the Master of Arts in Philanthropy and Development, Saint Mary's University of Minnesota.

1. How and why does an organization/group/board fall apart when once it is effective?

2. What is the nature of communication that builds understanding? How can we do this in our organization?

3. How do we frame strategic questions for each generation?

4. How do we meet the multiple interests, emotions, and motivations of our volunteers and donors over time and as they change?

5. How do we incorporate noble failure to build an adaptive, effective organization?

6. How do process and results relate? What is their relative importance?

7. How do we enable a risk-friendly culture within the board and management?
8. How does what we do today affect future generations?
9. How do we avoid excessive fascination with cage-rattling questions, thus not holding ourselves accountable for ideas and action?
10. What is development's role in change and leadership?
11. How do we change potential energy into action?
12. How do we create cultures of accountability?
13. How do we change dysfunctional politeness and cultures of congeniality?
14. How do we get and give permission for candor?
15. How do we build reflection into our work?
16. What is our role—as leaders—in the organization's ecosystem? How can we make the greatest possible impact?
17. How do we develop relationships within the ecosystem?
18. How and what can we learn from others (e.g., within our organization, outside our organization, and with other organizations)?
19. How can we partner with others?
20. How can we balance independence with interdependence?
21. Where are our organizations on the spectrum between minimum requirements and good practice? How might we improve the position and standing of our organization?
22. To what degree does the organization's credibility affect our faith in and willingness to invest in the cause?
23. To what degree and in what ways do we allow philanthropic opportunities to impact other decision-making in the organization?
24. To what degree and in what ways does the nature of our fundraising metrics depersonalize the very nature of true relationships?
25. How vulnerable is an organization if it depends increasingly on great fundraising technicians and less on leaders who can look beyond fund development?

How do we help ourselves and others feel comfortable being uncomfortable?

—Cohort 20, Master of Arts in Philanthropy and Development, Saint Mary's University of Minnesota

---

Interested in good questions for governance? See Appendix 3-A on this book's website for questions about building an effective board. For questions about philanthropy, privilege, and power, visit Resources | Free Download Library at www.simonejoyaux.com. And for still more questions, see *Keep Your Donors: The Guide to Better Communications and Stronger Relationships.*

One final item: Are you ready to use conversation as a core business practice? Are you ready to use questions to stimulate conversation, learning, and change? To a large degree, the process of asking questions is about sharing power and tolerating complexity. Can you do it?

Evaluate your readiness using these several yes/no questions generated through conversation with colleagues in the Master of Arts in Philanthropy and Development at Saint Mary's University of Minnesota.

1. Can you judge the optimum time to ask which questions within which group?
2. Do you possess sufficient experience and knowledge to help answer the questions?
3. Can you help personalize possible answers to the particular situation or organization?
4. Are you comfortable pushing around multiple questions and diverse answers?
5. Are you comfortable creating new answers?
6. Do you value the fact that the questions and answers keep changing?
7. Do you question your own assumptions and do you welcome that questioning by others?

Participatory Decision-Making

This is the sixth component of the organization's internal relationship. Decision-making means choosing. And choosing really means picking between the anticipated consequences of each choice. An individual or a group selects one among several possibilities.

Effective organizations choose well. Their decision-making combines the five components of the organization's internal relationships: shared values, leadership, commitment to process, learning organization, and ongoing conversation.

When appropriate (and this should be more frequently), effective organizations involve multiple people in the decision-making process. These organizations know that certain decisions require group decision-making. For example, corporate governance is a collective act, done by the group called the board. In fact, no single individual within the board—including the board chair—has any more authority than any other. So any governance decision is a group decision. For more information about corporate governance and the concept of the collective, visit www.simonejoyaux.com. Click on Resources and visit the Free Download Library.

Effective organizations also recognize the distinct advantages of participatory decision-making, even when not required. These organizations know that group decision-making brings together diverse opinions, experiences, and expertise. Together, the result can be greater than the sum of the individual parts. These organizations recognize that participatory decision-making builds group understanding and develops support for and ownership of the choice. Also, the process of group decision-making contributes to individual, group, and organizational learning.

Check out Sheena Iyengar's book The Art of Choosing *for the science behind choosing (New York: Hachette Book Group, 2010).*

Systems thinkers and learning organization theory focus on listening to learn rather than to answer. The process of asking and listening helps us know each other better and allows us to work together to create better solutions. The process of engagement and participatory decision-making most often produces better solutions than lone ranger behavior.

In *Clicks and Mortar*, Pottruck and Pearce observe:

I want the engagement of everyone in the company . . . but the business requires that I also have the ability to move fast, to make decisions quickly when I need to . . . leadership is not only about facilitation or consensus, it is about ultimate responsibility. Even as I encourage dialogue and listen carefully to everyone who contributes, my responsibility is to make decisions that are the best for the whole of the business, and to continue to have the participation of those who disagree with me.

It requires that I understand other people's points of view—and that I can acknowledge our differences. . . . Acknowledging resistance does not mean giving up your own point of view. It doesn't mean that other people have to have their way. It merely means that they know they have been genuinely heard and considered, even if the hearing and considering do not change your decision.[31]

Some Distinctions in Decision-Making

Not all decisions require participation. Some decisions belong to just one person. Sometimes one person is assigned to make the decision all alone. Don't waste time when participation doesn't add value. But remember, deciding that a decision requires participation is a strategic decision itself.

Here are some scenarios for a sole decision maker:

- The head of maintenance selects a Dyson vacuum cleaner. She didn't get permission to buy a new one. She managed her own budget and determined agency needs.
- The events planner decided the menu for the donor thank-you party without talking with anyone else.
- The chief financial officer selected the auditor. Oops! Is that really her decision? In good governance, that's a board decision, usually recommended by a specific board committee.

Moreover, there are some distinctions in the nature of participation in decision-making. For example:

- *Information to inform the decision-making process.* The decision maker listens to the perspective of others—but then makes the decision on her own. For example:
  - The chief executive officer invites her senior management team and members of the development office to help interview candidates for the new chief development officer. The staff provides their feedback to the CEO and the CEO makes the decision. The decision belongs solely to the CEO.
  - The newsletter editor queries staff for story suggestions—but chooses the topics himself.
- *Input into the decision-making process.* The decision maker invites input from others—and uses that input to make the best decision. For example:
  - During the strategic planning process, all agency staff complete an assessment of internal systems. Retreat attendees review the assessment results and use this input to make decisions about the future.

- The property manager must schedule resurfacing the employee parking lot. He asks staff for suggestions about the most convenient (or least inconvenient) times. Then he makes the decision.
- *Helping make the decision.* A group of people makes the decision together. They talk together. They may examine information and input from others. The decision maker(s) explore(s) trends and implications. Then the decision-making group decides, often by voting. For example:
  - At the strategic planning retreat, attendees (including board members, some staff, and even some community people) review assessments, input, and information. Retreat conversation focuses on all this data. Together the group decides key directions and priorities for the future.
  - The CEO establishes a task force and gives it authority to figure out how to strengthen communications between departments. The task force, comprised of volunteers at all staff levels, develops a plan within those boundaries. The smart CEO accepts that plan.

Strategic Decision-Making

For the purposes of this text, strategic decision-making refers to those choices that are not routine and repetitive. Instead, these decisions are characterized by uncertainty and risk. These decisions are very important to your organization. And, according to decision-making theory, they possess certain attributes.

- Strategic decisions are critically important to your organization's success and failure.
- These decisions commit major resources, thus directing and limiting activities throughout the organization.
- Strategic decisions have a dual orientation, involving the worlds both inside and outside of your organization, and may take you into a new area of work.
- Strategic decisions affect the entire organizational system, not just one part.
- The results of a strategic decision—whether good or bad, intended or not—will likely not be known for some time.

The decisions that affect the future of our civilization and of the human race are, increasingly, made in a group context ... when people convene in groups, a new entity is created, with its own dynamics and complexity, and "its" decisions cannot be predicted even from a thorough knowledge of its constituent members.

From *Group Decision-Making*, by Walter C. Swap and Associates (Beverly Hills, CA: Sage, 1994)

Exhibit 3.9 compares routine (category I) and strategic (category II) decisions. This descriptive list can help you decide which decisions would benefit from whose participation.

Exhibit 3.9   A Categorization of Decision Characteristics

	Category I Decisions	*Category II Decisions*
Classifications	Programmable, routine, generic, computational, negotiated, compromise	Nonprogrammable, unique, judgmental, creative, adaptive, innovative, inspirational
Structure	Procedural, predictable, certainty regarding cause/effect relationships, recurring, within existing technologies, well-defined information channels, definite decision criteria, outcome preferences may be certain or uncertain	Novel, unstructured, consequential, elusive, and complex; uncertain cause/effect relationships; nonrecurring; information channels undefined; incomplete information; decision criteria may be unknown; outcome preferences may be certain or uncertain
Strategy	Reliance upon rules and principles, habitual reactions, prefabricated response, uniform processing, computational techniques, accepted methods for handling	Reliance on judgment, intuition, and creativity; individual processing, heuristic problem-solving techniques; rules of thumb, general problem-solving processes

Source: From Harrison. *SPB-HARRISON MANAGER DECISMAKE PRS 3ED*, 3E. © 1987 South-Western, a part of Cengage Learning, Inc. Reproduced by permission (www.cengage.com/permissions).

The Process of Decision-Making

There is much more to decision-making than the outcome. Generally, the decision-making process includes the following components:

- Identifying who needs to participate in the decision-making process and why.
- Designing the decision-making process.
- Determining who will facilitate the decision-making process.
- Articulating the issue, its scope, and the context for decision-making.
- Talking about trends and implications.
- Identifying alternatives and their implications and consequences.
- Talking about implementation strategies, time frames, and accountability.
- Deciding.
- Informing people of the decision and its impact on them.
- Monitoring progress of action.

- If necessary, modifying action.
- Evaluating action and talking about key learnings for the next decision.

The process produces a choice. Because each choice has its own consequences, decisions involve risk. The more important the decision or the larger its scope, the greater the risk. When you decide, you choose your preferred consequences.

As Peter Drucker observes, "Every decision is a commitment of present resources to the uncertainties of the future. . . . [The laws of probability mean] that decisions will turn out to be wrong more often than right. At the least, they will have to be adjusted."[32]

Of course, decision-making doesn't end with the choice. Then it's time for action. Someone is designated to implement the decision, to take action. Without action, there is no decision-making.

Effective decision-making relies on effective group behavior, described earlier in this section. Effective decision-making also depends on trust. Groups, whether small teams or large organizations, function because there is trust. When you trust, you are confident in the reliability of persons or things without making careful investigation. You believe the person or thing will not fail in its duty. In *Managing the Non-Profit Organization: Principles and Practices*, Drucker describes trust as predictability, knowing what to expect of someone. For Drucker, this is mutual understanding but does not require either mutual love or respect.

Dissent and Decision-Making

Conflict is inevitable. It's part of all human interaction and certainly part of group decision-making. Individual experiences, perceptions, and expertise make people see things differently.

Conflict is also healthy. It helps keep a group lively and alive.

Yet, organizations struggle to avoid conflict. Many staff see dissent as a challenge to management's authority. Too many volunteers avoid disagreement as though it were an affront to politeness.

Fight dysfunctional politeness!

This is the wrong way to do business. Good decision-making rarely happens without conversation, and good conversation often produces differing opinions and disagreement.

If it seems really easy to decide something important, it would probably be best to hold off. The more important the decision, the greater the risk. And risky decisions should cause lots of questions and disagreement. Then people better understand the choices and consequences. Keep in mind: Dissent helps your organization explore issues, create understanding, develop mutual respect, and learn.

Mary Parker Follett[33] observed that dissent within an organization does not beg the question who is right or what is right. Rather, each participant is giving his or her best answer to the question she or he perceives. What the group needs to ask is: Which question are we trying to answer? Drucker reinforces this when he observes that the most important part of effective decision-making is asking what the decision is really about.[34]

That's why organizational members are responsible for asking the questions worth asking. By asking the right questions and exploring the possible answers, each individual gains understanding. Through understanding, the group learns. By pulling together different pieces of various responses, the group produces the best decision.

Conflict isn't resolved by keeping it quiet. In fact, silence really means consent—so beware! Conversation (both discussion and dialogue) tackles conflict and helps groups make good decisions. If the decision that needs to be made is important enough, the decision-making process will benefit from multiple people talking. Through conversation, people and groups share diverse information, opinions, and experience.

Resolving conflict by creating shared understanding (not necessarily agreement) generates unity and commitment. Organizational health also depends on the group's ability to work through the mess of disagreement and conflict. The challenge, then, is to use the benefits of conflict and to minimize the negative effects.

Effective groups differentiate between acceptable and dysfunctional conflict. They use acceptable conflict to help make the best decisions and minimize dysfunctional conflict. Dysfunctional group conflict usually arises from one or a combination of the following factors:

- Attempt of one individual or subgroup to hold power over another.
- Lack of consensus about organizational values, vision, and direction.
- Low tolerance for diversity.
- Feelings of competition for resources and rewards.
- Different goals.

Dialogue should involve considerable conflict and disagreement. It is precisely such conflict that pushes [people] to question existing premises and make sense of their experience in a new way.

From "The Knowledge Creating Company," by Ikujiro Nonaka, *Harvard Business Review* (November–December 1991)

Securing Consensus

After all the conversations, make a decision. The best group decisions result from consensus. But contrary to popular perception, consensus does not mean unanimity, nor should consensus produce the lowest common denominator. Instead, consensus decision-making is a highly effective, win-win process. Although consensus decision-making is more time consuming, it generally produces a longer-lasting result. Groups make decisions through high-quality conversation, communication, and equal access to influence, exploration of alternatives and implications thereof, and supported by a series of agreements.

First, the group clearly identifies what is being decided. Second, the group agrees to the process for decision-making. Then, the group proceeds with the content of actual decisions. Often, the group makes the decision by voting. But the voting happens only after sufficient dialogue. In dialogue/conversation everyone is heard, information is transformed into knowledge, and individuals and the organization have learned. Naturally, the resulting decision may not be the first choice for every group member. However, each participant has been heard and has had the chance to influence others and learn together. Participants recognize that the process has been fair and open, and that the resulting decision reflects the best thinking by those involved.

Ultimately, the quality of decision-making is judged on the success of implementation. And successful implementation depends on the group's shared sense of ownership for both the decision-making process and the resulting decision. (See Appendix 3-B on this book's website, a great outline about consensus decision-making from the Association of Junior Leagues International, www.ajli.org.)

Well-Managed Change

Managing change is the seventh component of your organization's internal relationship for the new millennium. To survive well, effective organizations manage continuity, change, and the transition between the two. The intersection of these three management functions is the point of highest organizational vitality.

In this book, change refers to the external trappings as well as the internal transition that people go through to live with the change. As William Bridges observes, "unless transition occurs, change will not happen."[35] For change to work, people have to let go of the current reality and accept a new vision. They have to envision the way things are supposed to be in the changed organization.

Yet, change is really hard. In fact, the more successful you are, the harder it is to change. After all, if things are going well—for you personally or for your organization—why would you want to change? But ongoing learning—producing Senge's moments of metanoia—require constant questioning and challenging. So the only way to do this is to unlearn. Or to hide away those old learnings so you're open to new ones.

Usually, change is either adaptive or innovative, just like learning is either adaptive or generative. (See "The Learning Organization" earlier in this chapter.) Adaptive change may be the most conservative, reflecting only a modest alteration in the status quo. Also, this type of change may be relatively easy to accomplish.

But suppose you build a true learning organization—thus developing an ongoing capacity to adapt. Your ability to continually adapt would create an organization that continually changes. Imagine that: a series of small incremental changes and periodic larger changes, all accumulating to produce overall dramatic change.

Then there's innovation, considered a higher degree of change. Typically, this is the most challenging to execute and the most worthwhile and useful to organizational health and survival.

If you're willing to get lost, you may find a way out.

—JoAnne Akalaitas, American theater director and writer

But again, picture a true learning organization, an organization built to adapt. A truly adaptive organization would be less discomfited by change, more accustomed to adjustments, and better prepared for dramatic change. Surely this could be an organization "built to last," as described by Collins and Porras later in this chapter.

By the way, effective strategic planning (presented in Chapter 6), produces change. So part of good strategic planning is well-managed change. And, without the elements in this chapter—creating an effective internal relationship—effective planning doesn't happen and neither do learning and change.

Building Adaptive Capacity

Effective organizations make change by building their adaptive capacity. Adaptive capacity is a skill, and happily, a skill that individuals and organizations can develop. Adaptive capacity means "taking the initiative to make adjustments for improved performance, relevance, and impact. Fundamentally, [adaptive capacity] is the ability to respond to and instigate change."[36]

It's a complex world both outside and inside your organization. Just think about demographics, socioeconomics, technology, social mores, safety and security, nation building, fundamentalism, the environment, globalization. Think about group dynamics and dissent, conversation and decision-making, and leadership or the lack thereof.

Think about how fast things change and what doesn't change. Examine the impacts on your personal and professional life, the lives of your clients and donors and volunteers, the impact on communities near and far. How do organizations ensure relevancy? How do relevant organizations survive? How does it all work and how do you cope when it's not working so well? The short answer is: by adapting as appropriate. Or going out of business very carefully.

Carl Sussman describes four qualities that define what it means to be an adaptive organization: external focus, network connectedness, inquisitiveness, and innovation.

1. *External focus.* Pay attention to what's happening outside your organization. Reflect back on systems thinking: everything is connected; what happens in one part of the system will affect another part of the system. Remember dynamic complexity, too.

Your organization has to build connections, stay connected, observe and listen and share and engage. Isolated, insular organizations will die—and should die. Sussman says, "Adaptive capacity includes the ability to generate or initiate change—challenging the organization's external circumstances. This level of change, particularly, may require the organization to forge relationships that extend beyond its borders."[37]

2. *Network connectedness.* Your organization is part of a community, a network of connections necessary to create healthy community. See, again, how this relates to systems thinking and learning organization theories . . . that web of connectedness that produces meaning and results. You'll succeed in partnership with others—from communications to cooperation to collaboration (and even merger).

Says Sussman, "Perhaps the fullest realization of organizational potential occurs when nonprofits occupying their special niches, either by conscious design such as strategic alliances or simply through the aggregation of independent efforts, create the potential for system-level effects that advance their missions more effectively than would be possible in isolation."[38]

The term adaptive capacity *refers to an organization's ability to change: in response to changed circumstances—survival—and in pursuit of enhanced results—creation.*

From "Making Change: How to Build Adaptive Capacity," by Carl Sussman, *Nonprofit Quarterly*, Winter 2003

---

3. *Inquisitiveness.* What more needs to be said? This book is made up of questions and asking questions, and pursuing "why" more than "how." Questions generate conversation that generates learning and produces change. Review the distinction between dialogue and discussion. Embrace learning organization theory. Develop your own—and organization-wide—*folie du pourquoi.*[39]

4. *Innovation.* Innovation is about creating something new. You're no longer reacting, but rather initiating. The most adaptive nonprofits/NGOs change in order to remain relevant and effective.

The Change Process

Organizational change may change core systems. But sometimes important change demands adjustments to corporate culture.

Changing corporate culture is harder because it requires adjusting individual and group attitudes and then modifying individual and organizational behavior. Changing core systems (i.e., policies, procedures, and structure) is easy by comparison. And sometimes, change is even bigger—transformational. Like changing your mission. Now that can be really hard.

Top-down change probably doesn't really happen. Sure, the leader can order change, but that doesn't mean others support it or do it. No matter the official policy or the leadership mandate, change requires grassroots activist support. Change depends on engaging your organization's diverse constituents. Change results from the melding of constituent understanding and commitment, influence and action.

Effective organizations accept change as a vital and essential part of individual and organizational life. These organizations accept change and develop their infrastructures to support change. The most effective organizations seek leaders who are comfortable with change and can manage it well. Actually, these leaders welcome change as long as it is stimulated by organizational learning.

In the same way, effective fundraisers know that change is part of fund development. These fundraisers are comfortable and prepared—whether or not donors change interests or community needs shift, whether or not volunteers alter their priorities or need different kinds of support, and so forth.

Managing change means managing courage.

Reacting to Change

Certainly hesitancy and anxiety are part of every change process. Suspicion may also be a part. And in some situations or in certain organizations, mistrust may rear its ugly head. Recognize this. Identify which is happening, even if it's all four. Respect the reality and then you can manage it.

Generally, individuals and groups react to change in three ways. Some passively resist. Others aggressively undermine. Still others sincerely embrace the change. Just remember, change happens more easily when people are predisposed to it. So your organization may need to change its corporate culture about how people react to change.

For example: In learning organizations, people recognize the world's ambiguity and uncertainty and expect the same in the organization. They know that the organization's ongoing learning will likely generate change. If you are not yet a learning organization, you might find support for change because people are dissatisfied with the status quo or because they recognize potential alternatives.

But what about those who resist? John Kotter and Leonard Schlesinger have identified four primary reasons. First, the resister fears losing something of value. Second, she or he misunderstands the change and its implications. Third, the resister does not believe that the change makes sense for the organization. Fourth, the resister has a low tolerance for change.[40] You'll have to face the resisters if you want change to happen. You can't ignore them.

Building Support for Change

Effective organizational leaders build commitment to the change process. Once the attitude for change is in place, behavior can change.

The first behavioral adjustment comes from the top. This means your management and your organization's trustees. According to Jeanie Daniel Duck, these leaders must ask themselves, "If we were managing the way we say we want to manage, how would we act? How would we attack our problems? What kind of meetings and conversations would we have? Who would be involved? How would we define, recognize, compensate, and reward appropriate behavior?"[41]

Successful change involves stakeholders throughout the process. Use the strategies of learning organizations, ongoing conversation, and participatory decision-making. Include stakeholders in deliberations. Seek their opinions. Listen to their perspectives. Use their input. Make sure they understand the resistance to change. Encourage them to identify strategies to overcome the resistance. Ensure that stakeholders help implement and evaluate the change strategies.

Communicate change with stakeholders directly and frequently. Provide updates on progress and challenges. As often as possible, communicate face-to-face. Talk about the need for change. Explain the process for change. Describe the plan for change. Remind people that change is normal and part of business as usual. Create the opportunity for questions and encourage feedback. Talk about how the current processes affect mission, vision, and program. Describe how the proposed changes will improve program and achieve vision.

As human beings we accept change that enhances our sense of well-being—our identity. Any change that threatens our basic identity is resisted. That is the law of human nature.

From *Leading Consciously: A Pilgrimage toward Self-Mastery*, by Debashis Chatterjee (Newton, MA: Butterworth-Heinemann, 1998), 145

Effective leaders remember that change is intensely personal. Change relates to each individual as well as the group together. Change is successful when each individual understands and accepts his or her role in change and acts accordingly. Individuals and groups within the organization must understand their connection to the overall system. People need to know about any new roles, relationships, processes, expectations, and required skills.

While change is a standard part of organizational life, change does require patience. Leaders provide both support and consistent pressure. Duck allows that "once a week, people could visit Pity City. But they weren't allowed to move there." With this same balance of support and pressure, another change agent notes, "We carry the wounded and we shoot the resisters."

Managing the Change Process

Duck outlines eight steps for managing change:

1. Establish context for change and provide guidance.
2. Stimulate conversation.
3. Provide appropriate resources.
4. Coordinate and align projects.
5. Ensure congruence of messages, activities, policies, and behaviors.
6. Provide opportunities for joint creation.
7. Anticipate, identify, and address people problems.
8. Prepare the critical mass.

Consider how this plays out. Well-managed change requires that everyone understands the meaning and reason for change. Leaders explain why, from their viewpoint. Through conversation, everyone in the organization talks about why the change is necessary. People get together and ask questions, talking about what will happen if the organization does and doesn't change.

Well-managed change demands appropriate resources. If your organization needs more staff, different systems, or new rules to support change, provide them. Make sure activities are coordinated and carefully integrated to complement each other and the change process. Along with this, make your messages, policies, and behaviors congruent with the change. Get ahead by anticipating people's needs, concerns, and problems. Figure out ways to address these issues immediately.

Throughout the change process, gain people's commitment to change by involving them in the diagnosis of situations and identification of solutions. Give people the chance to work together and create new ways of doing things. Make sure you build a sufficient number of people who are committed to the change process.

See Exhibit 3.10 to try an even more no-nonsense approach, proposed by Price Pritchett and Ron Pound.[42] This may provide the extra push that your organization and your development function need.

Exhibit 3.10   No-Nonsense Approach to Change

1. Promote the vision and focus on the future. Don't waste precious time and resources looking backward.
2. Demonstrate unwavering commitment, and practice what you preach. You don't road test culture change; you just do it. The world is uncertain and complex. If your culture doesn't adapt rapidly, everyone loses.
3. Shake the group up. Show everyone that the old culture is incompatible with what is to come.
4. Involve everyone but expect casualties. Engage stakeholders in identifying, designing, implementing, and evaluating change. Make them responsible for changing group culture. Show that you care. But remember you can't make everyone happy. Old behaviors that conflict with the new culture have to go. Let go of the people whose attitude and behavior could sabotage the change your organization needs. Better to lose them than risk your organization's health.
5. Don't let the existing culture control your new approach. Honor history when it helps. Otherwise, get rid of any traditions that stop change.
6. Change infrastructure. Eliminate out-of-date or unnecessary policies and procedures. Create new practices.
7. Bring in new people. Don't hesitate to remove those who fight change. It's harder to convert resisters than it is to bring in new people who will embrace the changing culture.
8. Encourage eccentricity. Reward questions and unconventional acts. Reward those who welcome pluralism.
9. Create a critical mass of like-minded people so you can carry out big changes. Give your best people the big jobs.
10. Honor loyalty to the organization when the loyalty is demonstrated appropriately. Stop loyalty to the past culture. People who feel threatened don't mind fighting dirty to keep things the way they are.
11. Communicate more and more. People need to hear the logic and rationale behind the decision to change. Tell them what is coming and how they will be affected. Cheerlead!
12. Make things happen fast. You cannot afford months or years for staff and volunteers to catch the spirit and change their behavior.

Source: Adapted from *High-Velocity Culture Change: A Handbook for Managers*, by Price Pritchett and Ron Pound (PRITCHETT, LP, 2000). Adaptation used with full permission of PRITCHETT, LP. All rights are reserved.

In summary, don't lose your nerve! That's a fitting phrase, used by Robert H. Miles in his article "Accelerating Corporate Transformations (Don't Lose Your Nerve!)." Through his research, Miles found that "the biggest barrier to corporate transformation was getting organizations to execute their bold new ideas quickly."[43]

To paraphrase Miles, organizations must launch a transformation both boldly and rapidly. Unfortunately, "speed brakes" slow things down during a transformation process. While these speed brakes don't matter much during regular business, Miles's speed brakes can derail transformation. Miles notes that "to accelerate transformations, managers need to release each of these brakes, in a particular order."[44]

- Speed Brake #1: Cautious Management Culture: Compel all executives to confront reality and agree on ground rules for working together.
- Speed Brake #2: Business-as-Usual Management Process: Run a no-slack launch on a parallel track with regular systems; make sure there are early, visible victories.
- Speed Brake #3: Initiative Gridlock: Limit the company to three or four initiatives.
- Speed Brake #4: Recalcitrant Executives: Compress launch to quickly engage key executives and to identify and confront those not on board.
- Speed Brake #5: Disengaged Employees: Rapidly cascade the changes to all employees to boost engagement.
- Speed Brake #6: Loss of Focus during Execution: Anticipate and defuse post-launch blues, midcourse overconfidence, and the presumption of perpetual motion.[45]

Understanding Transition

Sometimes it actually seems easy to move forward with change. The vision is in hand. The organization has outlined strategies to move from current reality to the new vision for the future. Everyone is committed. "It's a go. Let's push the button!" But don't forget transition. As noted earlier, transition is essential for change to result. In their article "Leading Transition: A New Model for Change,"[46] William Bridges and Susan Mitchell define transition as internal, "a psychological reorientation that people have to go through before the change can work."

Transition isn't automatic. People have to get through the transition before the change is actually accomplished. Bridges and Mitchell note that transition includes three distinct processes or phases—and each is distressing to people. First, people need to say good-bye to the old ways. Sometimes letting go may be relatively easy because the old ways as less than satisfactory. Other times, letting go is troublesome because people see those old ways are familiar. Leaders help people through this phase by "marking the ending" with a symbolic event or activities.

After letting go, people "shift into neutral." They've let go of the old but have not yet started anew. This "neutral zone" is confusing and worrisome. During this time, leaders must be particularly visible, accessible, and communicative. Don't rush through the neutral zone. It's a time for thinking, learning, and clarifying the reasons for change.

Finally, it's time to move forward and start anew. People have let go and come to closure about the old ways. These individuals have survived the neutral zone, developing energy and finding the creativity to move forward. They hit the third phase in strong stride.

Starting anew is risky. People must behave differently, risking false starts and even mistakes. The organization must facilitate and support all three phases of transition. The organization must operate in accordance with its values and provide guidance and a risk-free environment. Always remember, some people will not make it through the transition. They're unable to let go of the past. Still others will be so anxious that they'll never get out of the neutral zone and move forward. Those individuals who do not make it through the transition should not stay in the organization.

Changing through Dynamic Stability

In his article "Change without Pain,"[47] Eric Abrahamson urges organizations to avoid the disruptive change that can tear them apart. Instead, Abrahamson recommends interspersing dramatic change with smaller initiatives, what he calls "dynamic stability." This approach to change reduces organizational overload and chaos, thus reducing resistance.

Try Abrahamson's tinkering and kludging to make changes in your organization.

Dynamic stability is defined as "a process of continual but relatively small change efforts that involve the reconfiguration of existing practices and business models rather than the creation of new ones."[48]

First, try tinkering. Take a look at what you are already doing. Examine your existing programs, services, structures, and processes. Then modify here and there. Adapt. Abrahamson observes that this tinkering doesn't guarantee successful change. However, tinkering is less costly and stressful, capitalizes on existing resources, and typically produces results more quickly. Then try kludging. Kludging is like tinkering but on a larger scale with more parts. Organizations capitalize on their internal resources but also go outside their own boundaries, adapting from other organizations and external observation.

Pacing is another critical factor in dynamic stability. Instead of changing as much as you can as quickly as possible, slow down. Personalize the pace of change to your organization, some quicker and some slower. Learn when to rest and when to push forward quickly.

Abrahamson offers four guidelines for dynamic stability:

1. "Reward shameless borrowing." First play around with what already exists within your organization. As a final resort invent from scratch.
2. "Appoint a Chief Memory Officer." Change is great but only if you learn from the past. Your chief memory officer remembers the past so you can avoid repeating mistakes while tinkering and kludging.
3. "Tinker and kludge internally first." It's easier and more stable if you tinker and kludge inside first. Then with experience, venture outside your own boundaries.

4. "Hire generalists." Generalists possess a wide range of skills, and this diversity promotes open-mindedness, innovation, collaboration, and a combining of experience and information that is critical. Abrahamson calls generalists "boundary spanners."

Appreciative Inquiry

Dr. David L. Cooperrider[49] proposes "appreciative inquiry" as an organization-wide context for innovation and change. Much of organizational theory—including change—examines the challenges and threats and outlines how to respond. Contrarily, appreciative inquiry focuses on positive affect, cognition, and interaction. In other words, typical management inquiry organizes around the problem to be solved, whereas appreciative inquiry organizes around the "solution to be embraced."[50] Appreciative inquiry seeks to generate new knowledge, thus allowing the organization to learn, to envision a new future, and to change into that future. Through this process, organizations discover and understand what works well, and then foster innovation.

Cooperrider articulates four principles for appreciative inquiry.

1. "Inquiry into 'the art of the possible' in organizational life should begin with appreciation." Begin first with what works. Discover, describe, and explain the "exceptional moments" in your organization. These moments give life to the functioning system and activate the competencies and energies of workers.
2. "Inquiry into what's possible should be applicable." Use the results of your appreciative inquiry to generate knowledge within the organization and to build shared learning.
3. "Inquiry into what's possible should be provocative." An organization can be anything its members want it to be. Also, an organization can learn to guide its own evolution.

    Cooperrider notes that appreciative inquiry becomes provocative "to the extent that the learning takes on a normative value for members. In this way appreciative inquiry allows us to use systematic management analysis to help the organization's members shape an effective future according to their own imaginative and moral purposes."
4. "Inquiry into the human potential of organizational life should be collaborative."[51]

Appreciative inquiry seeks out the very best of "what is" to help ignite the collective imagination of "what might be."

From *Appreciative Inquiry: A Constructive Approach to Organization Development*, by David L. Cooperrider (Cleveland, OH: Department of Organizational Behavior, Weatherhead School of Management, Case Western Reserve University, 1993), 5

Appreciative inquiry focuses on two basic questions:

1. "What in this particular setting and context makes organizing possible?"
2. "What are the possibilities, expressed and latent, that provide opportunities for more effective (value-congruent) forms of organizing?"[52]

There are four steps in appreciative inquiry:

1. Discover and value what makes your organization work. Think about when commitment was at its highest, examine those factors, and determine why.
2. Envision your future. Once you have discovered what was best, your mind begins to look at future possibilities. Think about what might be. Create a positive image of your desired future.
3. Engage in dialogue. Only through this conversation can you ask the right questions, question assumptions, discover shared meanings, and learn together. Through dialogue you create consensus.
4. Construct the future through innovation and action. Cooperrider notes that appreciative inquiry "creates a momentum of its own." The desired future is grounded in the realities of what worked. This grounding produces the confidence to "try to make things happen."

Cooperrider's comments about appreciative inquiry sound a whole lot like learning organization theory: Inquiry is questioning, learning is change, and working together is how to build strong and effective organizations. And all of this is about the way you relate within your organization—across departments, without silos, between individuals and groups, supported by adequate infrastructure.

Think about Amazon.com

"It's important to be stubborn on the vision and flexible on the details."[53] So says Jeff Bezos in a *Harvard Business Review* interview. Bezos talks about life at Amazon, commenting on organizational culture, errors of omission, and other mistakes.

For Amazon, "information perfection and customer obsession" are central to organizational culture. "First, we are willing to plant seeds and wait a long time for them to turn into trees. . . . We're not always asking ourselves what's going to happen in the next quarter."[54] Instead, Amazon focuses a lot on the things that won't change. "For our business, most of [the things that don't change] turn out to be customer insights . . . what's important to the customers. . . . Another thing that we believe is pretty fundamental is that the world is getting increasingly transparent—that information perfection is on the rise. If you believe that, it becomes strategically smart to align yourself with the customer."[55]

Bezos says that the biggest strategic mistakes a company can make are errors of omission: "The times when companies were in a position to notice something and act on it, had the skills and competencies or could have acquired them, and yet failed to do so." So Amazon "maximize[s] the number of experiments . . . per given unit of time," thus "reducing the cost of experiments."[56] And all those experiments generate learning and change.

And here's something Bezos commented on, which really resonated with a client of mine: Don't confuse good process management with bureaucracy. Amazon focuses on "defect reduction and execution," and Bezos says that's one reason the company is so successful for its customers. He goes on to explain: "When you are inexperienced with disciplined process management, you initially think that it's equivalent to bureaucracy. But effective process is not bureaucracy. Bureaucracy is senseless process."[57]

A Culture of Philanthropy

The eighth and final component of your organization's internal relationship is a culture of philanthropy. A culture of philanthropy refers to your organization's attitude toward philanthropy and fund development.

Look back to the earlier section of this chapter describing corporate culture. What does "culture" mean? The attitudes, beliefs, customs, practices, and behaviors that characterize your organization. Culture is pervasive, affecting all areas of an organization. An organization's culture may be great or toxic. Through your work and volunteer life, you've undoubtedly seen both.

Remember, your organization's culture dramatically impacts its effectiveness. Keep in mind what Pottruck and Pearce say:

> *Everything else can fall away; the industry and products and circumstances may change; but an abiding culture can serve as the custodian of dreams for your company team, and for the customers on whose faith you build your house of business. It is an unchanging constant in the midst of a tornado of change, and it is something people want badly. It allows us to offer choice to those who work here and for those we want to work here ... to live and work by their values, and who will toil together toward something larger than themselves. . . . The company, at its best, can be a vehicle for everyone to make a difference.*[58]

As a charitable organization, an essential part of your corporate culture must include philanthropy. Not the strategy but the culture. Why is a culture of philanthropy so important? Because philanthropy is not just about raising money. Philanthropy is not just another management function. Philanthropy is part of the mission of the nonprofit/NGO organization. You're not just a zoo; you're a zoo and a philanthropic organization. Indeed, it might be said that successful nonprofits/NGOs pursue two missions: program and philanthropy.

Organizations that operate with a culture of philanthropy understand three things: the value of organizational culture, the importance of philanthropy, and the inextricable link between philanthropy and fund development.

Keep in mind: Without philanthropy, nonprofits/NGOs cannot survive. Whether it is the volunteer board of directors, other volunteers, or charitable gifts, nonprofits/NGOs depend on some form of philanthropy. But philanthropy does not last long without fund development, because fund development is the process to encourage philanthropy. Together, philanthropy and fund development form a virtuous and perpetual circle.

Effective organizations incorporate a culture of philanthropy as part of organizational culture. Each volunteer and every employee feels it. Clients and donors recognize it whenever they connect with the organization.

But Too Often, There Is No Culture of Philanthropy

The program staff is too busy to share client stories with the development officer. Worse, the program staff looks askance at the development staff. The program staff—maybe the marketing staff, too—think that development is like selling used cars, pushy and somewhat sleazy. Come on. Be honest. How do other staffs look at you? What do they think about fund development?

Board members are happy to delegate fund development to someone else, whether a committee or staff. Too many board members view development with distaste. Still others think that philanthropists are only the wealthy. These organizations have not yet developed a culture of philanthropy. As a result, organizational success is compromised.

Within a culture of philanthropy everyone in the organization—from the janitor to the board chair—understands that philanthropy and fund development are critical. Furthermore, each individual understands that she or he has a role in the process.

First and foremost, everyone is an ambassador. As an ambassador for the organization, everyone does his own job well. Everyone understands how all the various jobs in the organization create one integrated system. Everyone talks positively about the organization within the community. Most especially, everyone treats all of the organization's customers (clients, donors, volunteers, community people, etc.) with care and respect.

In a culture of philanthropy, everyone understands that if the organization's programs are weak, it doesn't matter what the fundraiser does. Everyone knows that if board members don't talk about the organization with their friends and colleagues, it doesn't matter how hard the executive director tries to raise funds. Each person knows that if the receptionist isn't sufficiently helpful, the best direct-mail solicitation will not be as effective as it can be.

When your employees and volunteers live a culture of philanthropy, they respect the development staff and respect the fundraising function. Everyone sees philanthropy as beautiful, and embraces fund development as the essential partner of philanthropy.

(P.S. A culture of philanthropy does *not* mean that every single staff person and board member has to ask for money. A culture of philanthropy does *not* mean that other staffs have to add fundraising functions to their workloads. Nor does a culture of philanthropy mean that all board members must be wealthy or even affluent. A culture of philanthropy is about attitude and behaviors, not more job tasks.)

Building the Culture of Philanthropy in Your Organization

Consider, first, the questions that you might ask yourself about building a culture of philanthropy. Here are some examples:

1. How do the people in my organization define philanthropy? How do they define fund development? What are the differences in thought and attitude when describing these two functions?
2. What is organizational culture and how would the people in my organization define our culture?
3. What effect does organizational culture have on our organization's operations and effectiveness?
4. What effect does our organizational culture have on philanthropy and fund development?
5. What are our values regarding philanthropy and fund development and how do we develop systems and processes to reinforce these values?

6. How can we enhance our organizational culture to best reflect our values?
7. How can we engage staff and volunteers in meaningful conversations to foster a culture of philanthropy?
8. How can we modify these questions and add more questions?

Review this chapter and make sure you have the skills and knowledge to build the necessary infrastructure. Take a look at your colleagues within the organization. Which of them has the skills and knowledge to do this work? How can you enhance your skills and knowledge together?

Think long and hard about how you will initiate conversations about organizational culture and the culture of philanthropy. Consider formal and informal conversations. Think about extending the conversations and engaging more people.

When the time is right, bring together some of your organization's leadership to initiate the conversation. Evaluate the effectiveness of the conversation and outline your next steps.

Think about formal training opportunities and informal chats about the meaning of philanthropy and fund development. Engage staff in storytelling about clients and organization accomplishments.

Encourage the honest sharing of concerns and discomfort about fund development. Host a "complain and whine" session about fund development with staff and volunteers. You'll find that much of what they say is justified—and you'll want to make sure that your fund development program avoids those inappropriate behaviors. Some of what they say reflects a lack of understanding about best practices—so you can inform them. A small part of what they express describes their own fears—and you can help overcome these.

Think about Forgiveness

And maybe first, think about forgiveness. Actually, think about forgiveness a lot—whether you're trying to convince others of the culture of philanthropy or something else altogether.

In April 2010, I was speaking at the Association of Fundraising Professionals (AFP) Québec Chapter. I spoke in English. Sadly, despite a French father, I am not bilingual. Nonetheless, we seemed to have a good time together, the workshop guests and me.

Building a culture of philanthropy was one topic we discussed. First, we all expressed concern about the disconnect and sometimes conflict between program and development staff, a fairly common occurrence in my experience and theirs, too. I kept saying it is our job to fix this, our job to enable change, our responsibility as development officers to lead the creation of a culture of philanthropy. I asked, "How will we help build this culture of philanthropy?"

The first response came from a man sitting midway back in the auditorium. "Forgive them," he said.

I was stunned. Gasping. And I said so.

"Forgive them," I repeated.

And then I knew. I faced myself. And I confessed to my colleagues there in Montréal: "I'm angry at them for not understanding. I'm angry that they don't recognize the beauty of philanthropy and the integrity of ethical fund development."

I walked up the auditorium aisle and asked the speaker to write down his name. I told him—and everyone there—that I was going to quote him. That his remark meant so much to me.

"Forgive them."

First, forgive them. Otherwise we cannot advance the conversation. First, forgive them. Otherwise my anger will leak through, and that's distracting and rude and unfair.

How do we build a culture of philanthropy? "Forgive them," said Nick Mantello in Montréal.

"Forgive them" is a pretty good starting point in many situations. Start there, and learning and change are more possible. "Forgive them" won't work always and it won't work forever. At some future point, something else might well be necessary.

But for now, "Forgive them," said Nick Mantello.

A Last Word on How to Build an Organization That Will Last

In a 1990 interview, the cofounder of the Hewlett-Packard Company, William R. Hewlett, talked about his life's work. "I'm probably most proud of having helped to create a company that by virtue of its values, practices, and success has had a tremendous impact on the way companies are managed around the world. And I'm particularly proud that I'm leaving behind an ongoing organization that can live on as a role model long after I'm gone."[59]

Hewlett was talking about organizational development—and so did the other 18 companies in a six-year study of timeless management principles, conducted by Jim Collins and Jerry Porras. The authors of *Built to Last* identified the differences between extraordinary companies and highly successful ones. And what did they discover? Timeless principles that distinguish the extraordinary company from the merely highly successful company. These principles shatter myths and reinforce the critical importance of organizational development.

Here are several of the 12 shattered myths:

1. "It takes a great idea to start a great company." Wrong. Some of the visionary companies began without any idea and others failed with their original ideas. And, as Collins and Porras note, "all great ideas eventually become obsolete."
2. "Visionary companies require great and charismatic visionary leaders." Wrong again. Indeed, high-profile charismatic leaders often hindered the company's development. CEOs of the visionary companies focused on building a strong company. The study showed that "the continuity of superb individuals atop visionary companies stems from the companies being outstanding organizations, not the other way around."
3. "The only constant is change." On the contrary. Visionary companies protect their core values pretty much forever, creating a stable foundation. But they change and adapt their products and services, assuring their relevancy. Collins and Porras call this preserving the core and stimulating progress.
4. "Visionary companies are great places to work, for everyone." Not at all. These companies are great only for those who fit well with the company's core ideology and its demanding standards. "Visionary companies are so clear about what

they stand for and what they're trying to achieve that they simply don't have room for those unwilling or unable to fit their exacting standards."

5. "[Visionary] companies make their best moves by brilliant and complex strategic planning." Sometimes. But then these companies also experiment, take advantage of opportunities, and work by trial and error. The authors comment that visionary companies "mimic the biological evolution of species," trying lots of stuff and keeping what works.

6. "The most successful companies focus primarily on beating the competition." Nope. Instead, visionary companies continually pursue the question: "How can we improve ourselves to do better tomorrow than we did today?"

7. "You can't have your cake and eat it, too." Oh, yes, you can. Visionary companies avoid the "the tyranny of the 'or'" and choose the "and." Visionary companies refuse to choose between A or B but try for A *and* B.

Built to Last notes that the company itself is the ultimate creation. It isn't the product or service. These are merely the vehicles for the company. This is about designing an organization—and visionary companies spend more time designing the organization than they do designing the product and services. And what about the stream of quality products and services? They come to fruition because of the outstanding organization.

[A] group of people get together and exist as an institution that we call a company so they are able to accomplish something collectively that they could not accomplish separately—they make a contribution to society.

From a speech by David Packard, given to Hewlett-Packard's training group on March 8, 1960, as quoted in *Built to Last* (New York: HarperBusiness, 2004), 56

To summarize:

The essence of a visionary company comes in the translation of its core ideology [core values and purpose] and its own unique drive for progress into the very fabric of the organization—into goals, strategies, tactics, policies, processes, cultural practices, management behaviors, building layouts, pay systems, accounting systems, job design—into everything *that the company does. A visionary company creates a total environment that envelops employees, bombarding them with a set of signals so consistent and mutually reinforcing that it's virtually impossible to misunderstand the company's ideology and ambitions.*[60]

Surely that's organizational development.

Fighting the Good Fight and the Right Fight

Yes, mission comes first, founded firmly on shared values. But creating a meaningful, effective, and sustainable organization makes the difference. Without the organization, mission doesn't survive. So leadership enables everyone to work together, creating the infrastructure that produces a healthy organization. Together you build and nurture this internal relationship.

I say again: Learning produces change. Change results from the linkages between and integration of questioning and conversation, conflict and dissent, fighting the good and right fights. And leadership enables all this to happen.

Alignment is important, but too much is not so good. Agreement is overrated—just think about that trip to Abilene. Conflict stimulates thinking and creativity. In fact, scientific research shows that "dissent will fire up more of an individual's brain, stimulating more pathways and engaging more creative centers. In short, more of what makes people unique, innovative, and passionate is available for use."

Moreover, the purpose of alignment isn't to create agreement and harmony. Instead, the purpose of alignment is to "sustain an organization's ability to fight for what really matters, and to pull everyone together again once the fight is resolved."[61] That sure sounds like well-managed change.

A peaceful, harmonious workplace can be the worst thing possible for a business. Research shows that the biggest predictor of poor company performance is complacency.

From "How to Pick a Good Fight," by Saj-nicole A. Joni and Damon Beyer, *Harvard Business Review* (December 2009)

Joni and Beyer observe in "How to Pick a Good Fight": "Conflict is healthful only when people's energies are pointed in the right direction and when carried out in a productive way." Just like there are good and bad questions, there's good and bad conflict. So fighting the right fights well helps produce learning and change—which in turn produce an organization that is relevant to the community.

Of course, the challenge is how to pick the right fight and fight it well. Joni and Beyer propose three principles to help pick the right fight.

- Make it material. Be sure this is a high-stakes issue that will motivate everyone.
- Focus on the future. Forget the past and who may have been to blame. Look to the future.
- Pursue a noble purpose. "The right fight connects people with a sense of purpose that goes beyond their own self-interest, unleashing profound collective imagination and abilities."[62]

Joni and Beyer go on to say, "A good future-facing fight has three qualities. It speaks to what is possible, shifting the debate away from what happened to what could happen. It is compelling, focusing people so intently on real, achievable benefit that they are willing to work through any associated costs and controversies. And it involves uncertainty, because if things are certain, there's no need to fight."[63]

See Exhibit 3.11 for an assessment tool to help you pick the right fight. Most of the concepts and language apply to nonprofits/NGOs. In some cases, you'll have to modify a bit.

Exhibit 3.11   Assessment Tool: When to Pick a Fight

How do you know when an issue is worthy of a fight? With your team, state the issue as specifically as you can and then ask a series of questions, structured around our "right fight" principles. If an issue passes each stage of the test, it merits a right fight.

1. Make It Material

Value: Does the fight involve something that has the potential to . . .
- save 15% or more of your resources or time for a year?
- allow you to charge at least 10% more than you now do?
- grow your sales or share of customers faster than the market?

If you answered yes at least once, the fight passes the value test. But if not, you should either restate the battle in bolder terms or address the issue with traditional alignment tools like quarterly plans.

Complexity: Can you resolve the issue by . . .
- relying on routine processes and common skills?
- calling in an expert to solve it for you?
- holding different people or parts of your organization accountable for separate pieces of the problem?

If you responded yes at least once, the issue probably isn't that complex and doesn't justify the stress of a right fight. However, the fight will pass the complexity test if you answer one of the following questions affirmatively.

Does resolving the issue require . . .
- careful balancing of multiple perspectives?
- different people to lead the process at different times?
- mutual accountability for the answer?

If the issue passes the value test but not the complexity test, try to settle it in a routine fashion.

Change: Will the solution require . . .
- the organization to work in a fundamentally different way?
- a new way to integrate big-picture perspectives with specialized local knowledge?
- new real-time information flow between different parts of the organization?

If you answered yes at least once, the change warrants a right fight. If your answers were all negative, it's probably time for a task force, not a fight.

2. Focus on the Future

Possibility: Is the issue about . . .
- sorting out the details of what happened in the past?
- determining blame or accountability for the organization's current circumstances?

A yes answer to either question is a red flag. Right fights should speak to what is possible, not what is past. To see if an issue passes the possibility test, ask the following.

Do we have an opportunity to . . .
- avoid the mistakes of the past and improve current circumstances?
- choose a course that increases the possibility of success?
- find the best way to turn a vision into a reality?

Charisma: Does the opportunity . . .
- require that significant innovation take place?
- create a vision that is exciting enough to get people to take risks and embrace change?

One yes answer here means that the possible benefits are real and achievable enough to compel people to work through the costs and controversies associated with a right fight.

Uncertainty: Does the issue in question . . .
- require you to respond to wild cards like new regulations or dramatic economic shifts?
- demand a response to unexpected changes in customer preferences, disruptive technologies, or channels?
- present choices where the best way forward is not clear?

If you answered affirmatively at least once here, a right fight is appropriate. But if the way forward is obvious, debate will just slow you down.

3. Pursue a Noble Purpose

Corporate values: Does the challenge . . .
- speak to more than making money?
- reflect a larger cause that is central to your organization's mission?
- flow directly from the values of the organization?

If you can't answer any of these questions affirmatively, see if you can translate an uninspiring objective into something more noble.

(continued)

(Continued)

Urgency: Will the process of solving the challenge . . .
- motivate employees to go above and beyond their ordinary responsibilities?
- generate plans that people throughout the organization can embrace?
- seem important enough that people are willing to dissent?

The more affirmative answers you get here, the more likely it is that people up and down the organization will work to find the best solution.

Respect: Will a solution to the issue . . .
- win respect and admiration from stakeholders outside the organization (including opponents)?
- produce an outcome that the average worker will be willing to bring up with friends?
- generate positive external press or recognition for the group?

At least one yes here indicates that you have a noble purpose. If you've gotten this far, your challenge has all the makings of a right fight.

Source: Reprinted by permission of *Harvard Business Review* from "How to Pick a Good Fight," by Saj-nicole A. Joni and Damon Beyer (December 2009). Copyright © 2009 by the Harvard Business School Publishing Corporation; all rights reserved.

Picking the right fight is only part of your work. You have to fight well, and leadership makes that happen. Think about the components of an effective infrastructure described in this chapter—for example, values and corporate culture, conversation as a core business practice and systems thinking, group dynamics and group process.

Examine Exhibit 3.12 for the principles of engagement proposed by Joni and Beyer.

Exhibit 3.12   Principles of Engagement

To determine how well a battle is being fought, ask yourself the following questions.

Rulebook

- Are there clear boundaries for conduct and behavior?
- Are people with dissenting points of view encouraged to speak up?
- Are mechanisms in place to keep the debate on a professional level?

Referees

- Is the leader neutral or genuinely open to differing points of view?
- Does the leader keep the debate on track and enforce the rules?
- Does the leader create the sense that competition is fact based and fair?

Playing Field

- Does each side of the debate have a realistic chance to win?
- Is it clear how a resolution will be reached—by a decision from the top, a majority vote, or consensus?

Gaps to Exploit

- Do different groups have different agendas based on their roles?
- Does each group have a specific objective champion?

Relationships

- Is there trust that individuals will deliver on their commitments and behave with integrity?
- Will leaders throughout the organization test perspectives up and down the hierarchy?

Energy

- Are tension levels high enough to promote optimal performance?
- Do leaders have a good sense of what people care about, and are those passions used to motivate performance?
- Do leaders routinely take the temperature and, if necessary, adjust goals and assignments to rebalance tensions?

Outcomes

- Can the leader give people bad news without damaging personal relationships?
- Is there dignity in losing, and is risk taking rewarded?

Source: Reprinted by permission of *Harvard Business Review* from "How to Pick a Good Fight," by Saj-nicole A. Joni and Damon Beyer (December 2009). Copyright © 2009 by the Harvard Business School Publishing Corporation; all rights reserved.

Derailment and Mistakes

Denis E. Waitley notes, "Mistakes are painful when they happen, but years later, a collection of mistakes is what is called experiences."[64] Make mistakes. Try new things—innovate—and make more mistakes.

When people deliver results and fight the right fights to the best of their abilities, they should gain something real and valuable, even when they end up on the losing side. To get people to step up and take risk, you have to reward risk taking itself, not just successful outcomes.

From "How to Pick a Good Fight," by Saj-nicole A. Joni and Damon Beyer, *Harvard Business Review* (December 2009): 57

And how about this: "Do we always have to avoid derailment? How about noble failure as a learning strategy? Indeed, how do we incorporate noble failure to build an adaptive, effective organization?" Thanks to Cohort 15, Master of Arts in Philanthropy and Development, Saint Mary's University of Minnesota.

Defining Success

What's success? How do you define it? What is success for your organization?

How about this definition? "Success is peace of mind, which is a direct result of self-satisfaction in knowing you made the effort to do the best of which you are capable."

That's from John Wooden,[65] a member of the Basketball Hall of Fame as both a player and a coach. What a great definition for success, applicable to an individual, to a team, and to an organization. Peace of mind because you made the effort to do your best.

In addition to the definition, Wooden created his "pyramid of success." He said that the heart of the pyramid is condition, skills, and team spirit. Get your own copy of Wooden's pyramid on the Internet.

Summary

If you want to raise more money for your organization, first strengthen your organization's internal relationship. This relationship relies on an effective infrastructure that produces a healthy corporate culture and sound systems.

Traditionally, organizations develop an infrastructure with such components as planning and assessment, marketing and communications, human resources, business management and governance, financing, and quality assurance/continuous quality improvement.

Effective organizations add eight more components to develop their internal relationship and move strongly into the future: shared values, art of leadership, commitment to process, learning organization, ongoing conversation, participatory decision-making, well-managed change, and culture of philanthropy.

First, these organizations articulate shared values and operate accordingly. Second, these effective organizations recruit and develop leaders who possess specific attitudes and skills and perform certain functions. Third, committed to process, the most effective organizations turn themselves into learning organizations, the fourth component. These organizations know that operating as a learning organization may well be the most critical attribute for survival.

Fifth and sixth, these organizations stimulate ongoing conversation and participatory decision-making, both essential to learning organizations. Well-managed change is the seventh component that effective organizations use to strengthen their internal relationships. And the culture of philanthropy weaves through it all.

CHAPTER 4

The Fund Development Professional

Choosing Your Road—Organizational Development Specialist or Just Another Fundraising Technician

Don't measure yourself by what you have accomplished, but by what you should have accomplished with your ability.
> —John Wooden, American basketball coach and member of the Basketball Hall of Fame as both a player and coach

Truth walks toward us on the paths of our questions. As soon as you think you have the answer, you have closed the path and may miss vital new information. Wait awhile in the stillness, and do not rush to conclusion no matter how uncomfortable the unknowing.
> —From the book *Maisie Dobbs* by Jacqueline Winspear
> (New York: Penguin, 2003), 32

Strengthen the Professional Fundraiser

I first expressed concern about the work of the professional fundraiser in 1997, in the first edition of *Strategic Fund Development*. Specifically, I was bothered by a tactical approach that developed technicians rather than a strategic approach that developed strategists. A decade later, Tom Ahern and I complained about the situation again in *Keep Your Donors: The Guide to Better Communications and Stronger Relationships*.[1]

The bad news: I haven't seen much improvement since that early complaint. The good news: I have seen more acknowledgment that there's a problem. Nonetheless, the focus still seems to be on fundraising techniques. So I'll express my concerns again, here in this third edition. And I'll expand more.

First, let's start slowly with a gentle introduction, some overarching competencies, and a job description. Next? Well, next is a bit more candid, rather like tough love day on my blog at www.simonejoyaux.com.

By the way, this challenge to the fundraising professional has resonated with colleagues from Australia to Kansas City, Missouri, USA. What do you think? Read on.

That Gentle Introduction

Entitlement is over—and has been for a long time. Nonprofits/NGOs proliferate. There's more congestion when seeking gifts. Donors demand more and communities examine nonprofits/NGOs more closely. In fact, the sector's credibility wavers more than in times past.

Ironically, organizations that focus mostly on fundraising as a financial transaction will likely not increase charitable contributions. Fundraisers who seek a quick fix and pursue short-term techniques will not retain donors and will not produce more money for the long term. And organizations that are satisfied with short-term results likely won't be around for the long term.

Leadership is the response to all these weaknesses and the answer to produce strong organizations. Leaders build effective organizations and strong communities.

And what about the professional who leads an organization's development function? She, too, must be a leader. Philanthropy and fund development require a leader, not merely a manager or technician. Leaders are more than managers and more than content experts. See Chapter 5 ("The Art of Leadership") and Chapter 8 (on enabling). In summary, your fund development leader helps the organization develop the four critical relationships described in this book. She understands how these relationships affect fund development.

Your chief development officer[2] is responsible for fostering a culture of philanthropy within the organization. With the CEO, your chief development officer assures that the organization's corporate culture and operations support fund development, and vice versa. Your chief development officer ensures that philanthropy and fund development are institutionalized throughout the organization. (See Appendix 4-A in this book's website for a sample job description. It is an electronic version that you can personalize to your organization.)

What do I want my professional footprint in this world to look like?

—Karen Denny, Cohort 19, Master of Arts in Philanthropy and Development, Saint Mary's University of Minnesota

---

Your development officer must possess the right knowledge, attitude, and competencies to develop the four relationships critical to institutional health—and therefore essential to fund development effectiveness and productivity. And this knowledge and these competencies—and the right attitude—are much broader than many people think.

As a profession, we have more work to do. As an individual, are you ready for this? As the boss hiring the development officer, do you know what to hire for? As a board, will you allocate the money? And as an organization, will you welcome this help to guide your organization?

Executive Competencies

What knowledge and competencies do effective fundraisers need? They demonstrate critical competencies identical to any other executive within an institution. These competencies can be summarized into broad categories adapted from William R. Bryan, PhD.[3] These are: commitment to results, business savvy, leading change, and motivating.

1. *Commitment to Results.* The competent executive builds the four relationships critical to organizational health. She or he is a systems thinker who is customer focused (and that includes donor centered) and goal driven. This individual identifies relevant information and helps transform this information into individual and organizational knowledge and learning. The executive is action oriented and innovative. She or he anticipates and solves problems and takes advantage of opportunities.

2. *Business Savvy.* The executive possesses comprehensive management knowledge as well as knowledge about the particular business and operations of his or her agency. Comprehensive management knowledge includes: nonprofit/NGO governance; values clarification and assessment; fiscal planning and management; strategic and program planning and evaluation; volunteer and staff development, role delineation, performance expectations and assessment, recruitment and training, and enabling; marketing and communications; and general management theory.

This competent executive is both a critical and strategic thinker and a competent decision maker. She or he manages and facilitates group behavior and decision-making and helps delineate responsibilities. The capable executive values pluralism and seeks diversity in all its forms, including diversity of culture, gender, and opinion.

And in fundraising, like any other profession, there is a specific body of knowledge required. See, for example, CFRE International (www.cfre.org), the baseline credential for fundraisers worldwide. Read the Test Content Outline, which describes the knowledge and skills expected of fundraisers. Evaluate yourself right now. Use this Test Content Outline as a screening and hiring tool. See more later in this chapter.

3. *Leading Change.* The executive is a flexible leader, possessing the skills and implementing the leadership functions presented in Chapter 5. She or he shares the values and vision of the organization and consistently displays integrity. She or he models behavior, develops people, and builds teams.

4. *Motivating.* The competent executive manages continuity, change, and transition. This individual knows how to influence and enable others. She or he is concerned about the impact of attitude and action on the organization and its participants.

Tough Love Day Is Here, Now

It's time to get ourselves together. There are fundraisers and there are organizational development (OD) specialists—the latter classified as change agents serving the entire organization and looking beyond the need for money. As my colleague Sharilyn Hale says, these change agents focus on "the broader goal of long-term health and deepened capacity."

Guaranteed: Every organization needs its own in-house organizational development specialists to survive and flourish. And the development officer should be one of these specialists.

Think about the fundraising challenges you face daily. Probably more than 50 percent of these issues are not fundraising problems at all.

What is organizational development? Organizational development is the process of making organizations work. Organizational development includes: preparing for and managing change in organizational settings, and managing individuals, groups, systems, and culture as the resources of an organization. What is a great development officer? Certainly not just a fundraising technician. It's about the organization, too. So great fundraisers combine fund development techniques and organizational development expertise.

Think about the fundraising challenges facing you daily. Probably more than 50 percent of these issues are not fundraising problems at all. These are organizational development issues that affect fundraising. Just being a good (or even great) fundraising technician cannot solve these other issues.

My advice to you?

- Transform yourself into an organizational development specialist. Move beyond operating as a fundraising technician.
- Own your own power and accountability. Enable (empower) others to do the same.
- Develop your own intellectual curiosity. Explore, practice, experience, and question. Then create your own vision, your own philosophical underpinnings for the work that you do.
- Work and volunteer in keeping with your own personal values and integrity.
- Question your own assumptions and those of others with whom you engage.
- Don't get seduced by political realities. Don't use them as an excuse.
- Be thoughtful and intentional. Consider models but don't be inflexible. Personalize.
- Lead. And lead change. And that means speaking up and speaking out.

The development office and staff have enormous power just because philanthropy is a revenue stream. Take on this inherent power and use it well—and that means embrace leadership. You. Go on. Lead.

Look at Your Organization

Fund development is about much more than asking for money. Consider these issues—all of which affect fund development, but none of which stem from fundraising.

- Is your organization sufficiently relevant to the community to secure support (e.g., respect, clients, board members, volunteers, goodwill, and also donors and gifts)?

- Does your organization effectively foster relationships with diverse constituents, including clients, donors, community decision-makers, media, regulators, and so forth?
- Are your staff effective enablers, empowering volunteers to do the best they can—volunteers of all kinds, including direct service, fundraising, board members, and so forth?
- How effective is your organization at planning and decision-making, and securing quality information to plan and make quality decisions?
- Does your organization regularly examine itself and the external environment, discussing the findings and learning and changing when necessary?
- How effective is your organization at clarifying roles and identifying necessary skills and distinguishing between governance and management?
- What do your leaders do and what do you do to develop leaders?
- What are the values and corporate culture of your organization?

These are all organizational development issues. Yet, each of these—and more—affects your organization's ability to raise charitable contributions. And each of these issues is connected, one to the other, in some manner.

How Technical Fundraisers Affect the Bottom Line

I'll say it again: Being a technician is not enough. It never has been. And if we ever needed a wake-up call, the global economic crisis that emerged in 2008–2009 sure should be that call, loud and clear. Whereas fundraising technicians can and often do succeed, staying at this technician level leaves you and your organization vulnerable. For instance:

- Your organization can be blindsided by events happening externally and even internally. Sooner or later these events will affect your fundraising activities and your donors.
- Your organization's mission may be out-of-date and your programs may no longer be important to the community. Eventually your constituents will notice and leave. Your donors will stop giving.
- Your donors may not feel close enough to your organization. Small gifts will not become larger ones and donors may not renew their gifts.

None of these situations is new. They were true yesterday and will be true tomorrow. The only difference may be in the quickness and frequency with which they occur, the time and effort it takes to recover, and the increasing frustration experienced by clients, donors, volunteers, and staff.

In all of these instances, an organizational development specialist would be a pivotal player. This accomplished fundraiser monitors activities and projects trends inside and outside the organization. She stays in touch with community needs and priorities to keep the organization relevant. She builds constituent loyalty through constant communications and cultivation.

One thing is certain. Thinking like a technician and focusing only on short-term actions won't increase revenue. Why?

- Most fundraising challenges stem from the organization and its operations, not from fund development. You must be able to discern the true nature of the situation in order to solve it.
- There's major fundraising congestion in communities. Your organization cannot distinguish itself with a better letter or a "more special" special event. Instead, you may need to overhaul fund development. You may need to change the way you do the business of your organization, and even what that business is.
- Finally, fundraising has never been solely about money. It has always been about relationships: understanding someone's interests and finding a match with your organization, or accepting their disinterest and moving on. Simply focusing on dollar goals, response rates, and prospect research won't work, without forging a deep relationship between the organization and the prospect.

The best fundraiser is fully aware of these realities. She uses her knowledge and skills as an organizational development specialist and enabler to help the organization learn and change.

Remember this: A fundraiser who is good at tactics will raise good money. A fundraiser who is good at tactics and strategy will raise great money. And the fundraiser who is an organizational development specialist, too? That fundraiser will raise really great money.

The Accomplished Fundraiser

Yes, the accomplished fundraiser is different from the fundraising technician. Whether by choice, limited skills, or organizational constraints, fundraising technicians spend their time targeting prospects and managing volunteers. These professionals develop the organization's stories into a case for fundraising support.

The best technicians believe deeply in their causes, understand philanthropy, and know how to create infrastructure, document activities, and delineate roles. These excellent technicians use sophisticated solicitation strategies, negotiate major gifts, engage donors, and provide competent support to volunteers.

On the other hand, the truly accomplished fundraiser is an organizational development specialist. She expects access to all parts of the organization and convinces the chief executive officer of this need.

The organizational development specialist is familiar with contemporary management theory and uses it to expand the organization's view of fund development and organizational development. She probes deeply into areas of the organization that fundraising technicians would consider out of bounds: areas such as board recruitment and designing programs that are relevant to the community. She actively participates in governance, organization-wide strategic planning and evaluation, community needs assessment, and marketing and communications.

What is a great development officer? Certainly not just a fundraising technician. Great fundraisers combine fund development techniques and organizational development expertise.

The accomplished fundraiser is a systems thinker, seeing both the forest and the trees. He knows what makes systems work and what makes them flounder. He's a consummate enabler, empowering volunteers and staff to participate meaningfully on behalf of the organization. He's a critical thinker, asking the tough questions about fund development, organizational operations, and relevance to the community. He's a strategist, who helps the organization determine where it wants to go and how to get there.

The accomplished fundraiser identifies relevant information and helps others understand the implications of the information. He anticipates and solves problems and takes advantage of opportunities across the organization.

The most accomplished fundraising professionals perform well in all four relationships proposed in this book. And these professionals involve staff and board in the process of developing relationships that support the organization.

The Road to Transformation

As for the process of transforming yourself, unfortunately there is no 10-step program to move from technician to accomplished fundraiser. This transformation is not as much about skill development as it is about attitude, expanded knowledge, and taking action. The transformation is neither orderly nor linear. Instead, you expand attitude, knowledge, and skill and take action simultaneously.

First is your own personal commitment. Your transformation depends on self-development. Honestly evaluate yourself. Commit the necessary time and effort to learn and grow.

Second is a willingness to expand your knowledge, in effect making your organization more dependent on you. Do this through self-study, continuing education, and conversation with colleagues.

For example, make sure you know enough about your organization's program and services so the program staff recognizes your value in this arena. Also, move beyond fund development and the nonprofit sector. Look elsewhere for your learning—and demand that your professional associations expand their continuing education beyond fund development and nonprofits. Learn lots about the theory and practice of management and organizational development.

Third is assertiveness[4] —convincing your organization to let you into the whole system. Be persistent, because convincing takes lots of personal conversations and repeated small and large acts on your part. Be patient. Change takes time and there may be some confusion and struggle along the way.

Fourth is a willingness to practice the knowledge, skills, and attitude of an accomplished fundraiser. One of the best ways to practice is serving as a board or committee member for another organization.

Why should you bother to be an organizational development specialist? Because that is what will make a difference in your organization and its health, vitality, and survival. And that is what will make a difference in your career as a professional also.

When you know what to do when there is something to be done—that is tactics. When you know what to do when there is nothing to be done—that is strategy.

From *The Ruins of Ambrai*, by Melanie Rawn (New York: Daw Books/Penguin, 1994)

What Do You Need to Know?

What must the fundraiser know? Not only what to do tomorrow, but how to think about tomorrow. What makes systems and people work, how, and why. You need some specific kinds of knowledge. You must possess certain competencies. And you have to embrace the appropriate attitude and behaviors.

Review the lists presented here. Reflect on this book and the four relationships proposed here. Think about how all this is interrelated and interconnected. Familiarize yourself with best practices in these areas—and look to the next practices. Talk with colleagues. Add more to these lists as you transform yourself. And practice, practice, practice.

Necessary Knowledge Areas

- General business management and nonprofit management and governance.
- Group and organizational behavior.
- Systems thinking and values clarification.
- Strategic planning and evaluation.
- Fiscal planning and management.
- Volunteer and staff development, role delineation, performance expectations and assessment, recruitment and training, and release.
- Marketing and communications.
- Leadership.

Necessary Skills of Organizational Development Specialists

- Facilitation skills.
- Conflict resolution skills.
- Proficiency as teacher and learner.
- Effective communicator (listening, informing, and helping to transform information into knowledge and learning).
- Critical thinker (anticipating problems, identifying solutions, and redirecting resources).
- Strategist (analyzing situations, identifying barriers and opportunities, capitalizing on strengths, and ensuring action and results).
- Effective motivator; ability to manage people well.
- Effective enabler. (See Chapter 8.)

Attitude and Behavior of Organizational Development Specialists

- Willing to share decision-making.
- Respectful and trusting of others.
- Trustworthy yourself.
- Welcome divergent opinions.
- Question your own assumptions.
- Flexible and comfortable with conflict and change.
- Commitment to process.
- Appreciate conversation and disagreement.
- Patient and persevering.

Learning Outside the Nonprofit/NGO Sector and the Fund Development Field

Throughout this book you'll find theories, authors, and reading recommendations outside the field of philanthropy and outside the nonprofit/NGO sector. Sometimes I incorporate the readings into the text. Other times, I just recommend titles and authors to you—and maybe include some brief annotation, hoping to intrigue you to go to the source yourself.

My advice to you and all professionals: Expand your horizons if you don't already. Then expand your horizons even more.

My biggest professional growth often happens outside the fundraising profession. Then I apply it to the fundraising profession. And, since I believe I'm supposed to be an organizational development specialist—not just a fundraising technician—then reading outside fundraising isn't negotiable. Moreover, reading outside the nonprofit/NGO sector is equally important.[5]

Maybe my interest beyond fundraising is because I moved from an executive director position to a development professional position. I was leery of the development position. I wasn't sure I'd like that limited focus. I certainly didn't want to give up leadership roles in strategic planning and board and management development. As time passed, I realized that I was a better fundraiser because of my experience as an executive director.

Here are three business/life books that I read while writing this third edition. These three books really hit me hard. I think every fundraiser, chief executive, and leader of any kind should read them:

1. *The Art of Choosing* by Sheena Iyengar (New York: Hachette Book Group, 2010)
2. *Distracted: The Erosion of Attention and the Coming Dark Age*, by Maggie Jackson (Amherst, NY: Prometheus Books, 2009)
3. *The Hidden Brain: How Our Unconscious Minds Elect Presidents, Control Markets, Wage Wars, and Save Our Lives* by Shankar Vedantam (New York: Spiegel & Grau, 2010)

Why are these books so important? All three are based on research. No weak personal opinions here. Instead, research and more research. Research about how the brain works—and that certainly affects the behaviors of clients, staff, board members, and donors. Research about multitasking and technology and our attention-deficient world—and that certainly affects how we nurture any of the relationships described in this book. Research about our unconscious biases—and that affects everything, including community building and philanthropy and fund development.

Each of the books provides easy-to-understand examples and stories that illustrate the research. Each of the books explains what the research means, why it matters, and what the implications are. Please read these three books. What you'll learn affects all of us and the future of our communities and world. And that's no exaggeration.

Fundraisers as Leaders

Should fundraisers be leaders? Is that part of the obligation? It's easy to say that everyone should be a leader. (Oh, that problematic word *should*.) I suspect that most people lead in some aspect of their lives at some point—and often regularly. But right now, let's focus on the kind of collaborative and empowering leadership presented in this book, and within the context of nonprofit institutions and the philanthropic sector. Yes, I think that—by virtue of position and role—fundraisers need to be leaders. And leaders must be organizational development specialists.

Moreover, I want fundraisers to be leadership leaders. Read Chapter 5, "The Art of Leadership," as a companion piece to this chapter about fundraising professionals. Read other books and articles about leadership. There's so much out there. Now decide how you define leadership and what kind of leader you plan to be.

Fundraisers and Power

One of the greatest challenges to effective (and good as opposed to bad) leadership is the nature and use of power. Fundraisers—development professionals—have enormous power within an organization. You control a revenue stream.

Some people suspect (and surely hope) that you have ready access to money. Maybe you print it in the basement during the darkest hours of the night. Maybe you have a secret stash of rich donors who give whenever you beckon. Maybe you know the mythical recipe and the special ingredients to get however much money whenever for whatever.

Of course, that's not true. You don't print the money in the basement. There's no secret stash of rich donors. And the mythical recipes are just that, myths. The truth is much easier and more difficult, both at the same time.

Nonetheless, fundraising professionals have enormous power. Why? Because you should know the body of knowledge. You should be an organizational development specialist. You really, really should be a change agent. And hopefully you are willing and able to take the risks[6] required of a change agent. (I know, lots of *shoulds* in the previous sentences. And I do try to avoid that word. But right now, I'm talking to you and me and there are some *shoulds* for us.)

Your power resides within the body of knowledge, experience, and expertise. Your power resides in your courage and commitment, and all that means leadership.

So the question is: How do you relate to this power? Think of all the other questions embedded within that question. For example: Do you recognize and accept your power? Do you understand the limits of your power? Are you willing and able to exercise your power? Are you comfortable questioning your power and the power of others? Are you committed to combining and expanding power? Do you willingly and eagerly empower others?

Those are just a few questions about your personal and professional power. Now think about the broader questions of power dynamics within your organization. Do staff and board recognize these dynamics and talk about them?

Too often those with power dismiss those without power. For example, donors who give the most might expect special privileges and a larger voice.

But, as colleague Sharilyn Hale, CFRE, notes, the opposite can also be true: Those with less power may reject those who give larger gifts or are more able to volunteer. This discomfort is just as harmful to the organization, negatively affecting donor relations and volunteer recruitment.

Sharilyn also makes another interesting observation: The proximity to traditional power that fundraisers often have can set them apart within their organization. Others in the organization may look askance at the fundraiser as she connects with prospects and donors with varying levels of privilege and hence power.

And still there's more about power, power within society. What is power and where does it come from? Why and how does privilege produce power? How does philanthropy empower and disempower? Read more about this in Chapter 5, "The Art of Leadership." See also "Philanthropy's Moral Dilemma," the final chapter in *Keep Your Donors*, and posted on my home page at www.simonejoyaux.com.

Defining a Profession

In the early 1980s, I joined the National Society of Fundraising Executives (NSFRE), now called the Association of Fundraising Professionals (AFP). I was the new chief development officer at Trinity Repertory Company in Rhode Island, one of the nation's top 10 regional theaters.

From the beginning, NSFRE told me that fundraising was a profession—and that a profession included these four elements: documented body of knowledge, continuing education, code of ethics, and some form of certification. I embraced that wholeheartedly.

Turn to Wikipedia[7] and you'll see this definition: A profession arises when any trade or occupation transforms itself through "the development of formal qualifications based upon education, apprenticeship, and examinations, the emergence of regulatory bodies with powers to admit and discipline members, and some degree of monopoly rights."[8]

Oops. That monopoly thing isn't so great. You know how governments feel about price controls and monopolies. I don't like them, either, actually. Bet you don't, either.

Wikipedia had an interesting list of "main milestones" to mark the evolution from occupation to profession. These milestones include: becoming a full-time job, establishing a training school, establishing academic education at universities, establishing local and national associations, introducing codes of professional ethics, and establishing licensing laws.

Another oops. Many of us professionals do not think that government should license fundraisers. Instead we believe in strong voluntary certification programs, for example the CFRE, FAHP, and ACFRE. And CFRE is the only baseline credential for fundraisers, and the prerequisite for the best advanced credentials, I think.

The Wikipedia entry also lists more than one dozen characteristics of a profession. For example, *skill based on theoretical knowledge*. Yes, there is a body of knowledge and we can learn it through reading and academic and continuing education.

Now consider this opposite, *indeterminacy of knowledge*: Some of the professional knowledge cannot be learned through rules and must be acquired through experience. Yes, experience is actually important. Other characteristics of a profession include some form of competence testing and codes of conduct and ethics.

And here's a curiosity in the Wikipedia list: One of the characteristics of a profession—domination by males. That's already out-of-date for the fundraising profession. Women dominate but are still paid less than men for the same work and same competencies. Male domination is declining in many other professions as well.

Take a look at this interesting *Harvard Business Review* article by Richard Barker,[9] "No, Management Is *Not* a Profession." Barker affirms that professions are comprised of "particular categories of people from whom we seek advice and services because they have knowledge and skills that we do not."

Barker explains that professions depend on an "asymmetry of knowledge" that is, overall, "relatively permanent." Professional bodies define what this knowledge is. And professional bodies certify that specific individuals are fit to practice that profession.

So that's the body of knowledge. But what interested me most about Barker's comment was the meaning of asymmetry: unreciprocal relationship, irregularity, imbalance. I visited www.visualthesaurus.com and found out that mathematics, for example, is asymmetric, lacking in symmetry.

Here's how I understand Barker's meaning: Consumers of a profession—me hiring a doctor, you hiring me as a fundraiser—cannot necessarily "judge the quality of advice" received. The knowledge is specialized enough. The knowledge is diverse, sometimes but not always obviously linked and easily put together.

Contrast that to buying a computer or a car—neither of which depends on professional advice in Barker's sense. The purchaser knows what she wants as a result of the purchase. But in the case of a profession, Barker notes that "we have no option but to trust the professionals with whom we transact."

[Society] relies on professional bodies to define what their members should know and to certify them as fit for practice.

From "No, Management Is *Not* a Profession," by Richard Barker, *Harvard Business Review* (July–August 2010), 55

This reminds me of the situation we fundraisers so often encounter: trying to convince our boss or board about the appropriateness of a particular fundraising strategy, the way to write donor communications, and so forth.

Fundraisers possess asymmetry of knowledge, not easily accessible to others. And unfortunately, too many bosses and boards don't recognize that. Instead of following the advice—because these bosses and boards actually have no capacity to judge the quality—they deny the validity.

And the real aggravation: Bosses and boards hold fundraisers accountable for results, but don't let the fundraisers make decisions based on the body of knowledge and their professional expertise.

Body of Knowledge

I believe strongly that there is a body of knowledge common to all fundraising—no matter the country, culture, type or size of organization. If this weren't true, there couldn't be international conferences with speakers from one country sharing knowledge and advice with fundraisers from other countries.

If we deny a common body of knowledge, then fundraisers couldn't work with diverse organizations in different cultures and countries. If we think fundraising is different in China and South Africa and Rhode Island, USA, then we are not a profession. That said, cultural distinctions, language differences, and life experiences require interpretation and sometimes personalization of the body of knowledge.

We've enjoyed the advantage of experiential knowledge for a long while now: practitioners doing the work, and leading practitioners documenting best practices. Now there's more research, scholarly research codifying the empirical base. Research stands behind the body of knowledge. That's good and necessary. Continuing education—coupled with academic education—assures the continual evolution of the sector and the fundraising profession.

If you expect to be a star in this profession, read the research. Regularly. Apply the learnings from research, explaining the value and implications to your organization's leadership. Talk about the trends and implications for your organization.

As the body of academic research grows, this knowledge must be fed into professional practice, where it can have an impact on performance.

From *Fundraising Principles and Practice*, by Adrian Sargeant, Jen Shang, and Associates (San Francisco: Jossey-Bass, 2010), xxiv

---

As a profession, we fundraisers (and the organizations and communities that we serve), need research, books, and articles by professional practitioners. We need textbooks and academic research. Any profession—including ours—needs continuing education and academic education. All of this helps develop our profession and us professionals.

Code of Ethics

Codes of ethics are all the rage—as if that will somehow stop Wall Street, BP, and their compatriots. Oh, if only it were so easy.

Fundraising professionals have long embraced codes of ethics, both the existence and the enforcement. Barker observes, "A professional body determines and enforces a code of ethics. This process is fundamental to the very existence of any profession, because it enables society to trust that members of the body are serving the public interest."[10]

There it is, the trust thing. I like the way Barker reminds us of the trusted position that any professional body holds. He likens this to a contract with society. "[Professional bodies] ... control membership in the professions through examination and certification, maintain the quality of certified ongoing training and the enforcement of ethical standards." And society benefits. Society is "rewarded," says Barker, "for its trust with a professional quality that it would otherwise be unable to ensure."[11]

By the way, I do not interpret Barker's article to mean that the same professional body must define ethics, provide training, and certify professionals. As a former chair of CFRE International, I appreciate the value of a separate certification body.

Voluntary Certification for Fundraisers

I believe strongly in certification. The CFRE (Certified Fundraising Executive) is the baseline certification for fundraisers worldwide. As stewards of the public trust, CFRE International (www.cfre.org) certifies those fundraising professionals who demonstrate the required knowledge and skills, and a commitment to the highest standards of ethical and professional practice.

The CFRE is a practice-based credential,[12] established through a job analysis done every five to seven years. The job analysis researches what fundraisers do by surveying a sample of these professionals working in countries around the world. In the official language of certification (a body of knowledge and profession in its own right), researching what fundraisers do means: the major domains of fundraising practice, the tasks performed within the domains, and the knowledge needed to perform the tasks. The CFRE exam tests the fundraiser's mastery of the knowledge areas that are directly linked to the tasks performed.[13]

See Exhibit 4.1 for the newly revised domains, tasks, and knowledge areas released in 2010, based on the most recent job analysis. Visit www.cfre.org and click on Exam Information to get the complete document, called Test Content Outline.

Exhibit 4.1   Major Domains of Fundraising Practice

Test Content Outline for the Credential of Certified Fundraising Executive (CFRE):

1. Current and prospective donor research
2. Securing the gift
3. Relationship building
4. Volunteer involvement
5. Leadership and management
6. Ethics and accountability

Source: Visit CFRE International at www.cfre.org.

I recommend that organizations use the CFRE Test Content Outline as a tool for identifying and screening competent development officers. For example, during a job interview, ask a candidate to explain how she carries out the listed activities. For example, use the CFRE Test Content Outline in the professional development plans and performance appraisals of your development staff.

In addition to CFRE, the baseline credential for fundraisers, some professional associations offer advanced certification. For example, the Association for Healthcare Philanthropy offers the FAHP. The Association of Fundraising Professionals offers the ACFRE. I believe the CFRE should precede these advanced credentials as an eligibility requirement to qualify for the advanced credential.

Is this your profession, your career—perhaps even your vocation? Are you a certified fundraiser? If not, why not? If I were hiring, I'd ask why someone has chosen not to be certified. That would be an interesting conversation. Other questions I'd ask applicants for a fundraising position in my organization:

1. Which professional association do you belong to? Why that one? (And if an applicant for a fundraising position wasn't a member of a fundraising professional association, I'd be really, really curious why.)
2. Which professional publications do you read regularly? Why those? (And if an applicant for a fundraising position didn't read something like the *Chronicle of Philanthropy* regularly, I'd be really, really curious why.)
3. Which are your favorite fundraising books and why? Which are your favorite nonprofit/NGO sector books and why? (And if an applicant doesn't name some of the major authors in our field, I'd be really, really curious why. Or what if the applicant hadn't heard of some of the major authors in our field?)
4. Which books outside the nonprofit/NGO sector have meant the most to you and why?

Excellence in Fund Development

I think there are many paths to excellence in fundraising—and the paths can criss-cross and intersect.

A true profession wants academic degrees, both undergraduate and graduate. A true profession requires ongoing research and professionals who read and use that research. A true profession demands continuing education—and professionals who participate in continuing education as audience, developers, and teachers. A true profession expects its professionals to read and explore, research and test, practice and define next practices, respecting experiential learning.

Not everyone will come to this profession with an undergraduate degree in fund development. Not everyone will pursue a graduate degree in philanthropy and development. That's okay. A liberal arts degree provides a great platform to build upon. A business degree can serve as a platform, too, as long as the business people understand that there are differences between the nonprofit and for-profit sectors. Experiential learning, continuing education, and certification are all paths to excellence.

A Digression

And on the topic of for-profit business people joining the nonprofit/NGO sector, allow me to rant. There seems to be a veritable movement for nonprofits to hire for-profit business people to lead organizations—often as CEO or as chief development officer. Have you noticed this? Some of our major foundations turn to individuals who've worked only in the for-profit sector. Some of our universities hire business people to lead their development operations. It seems like the new way to fix nonprofits.

And that's my concern ... a new way to fix nonprofits. It appears that too many nonprofits/NGOs think for-profit leaders possess special expertise and talent to make nonprofits stronger. It seems that some nonprofit boards think there's nothing unique about nonprofit organizations, no special experience or expertise required of nonprofit leaders.

A new way to fix nonprofits … as if nonprofits are more flawed than the government or the for-profit sectors. Nonprofits need fixing … as if the best way to fix them is to bring in the guy who ran the oil company or the gal who managed the bank.

As usual—certainly in the United States—the for-profit sector acts like it has the right answers and the best solutions. How did we get to this place? Why does our society embrace this approach? Why does society overvalue the for-profit sector and undervalue the NGO sector?

Fundraising as a Vocation

"Viewing fundraising through the filter of vocation can provide fundraising professionals with an added layer of context and meaning to their work and bring resulting benefits to the organizations they work for and the communities they serve."[14] So begins "The Song of the River: A Study of Vocation in the Lives of Fundraisers," by Sharilyn Hale, CFRE. This master of arts thesis "explores what fundraising professionals think about the concept of vocation and their experience of it within their work." And despite the diversity across gender, generation, nationality, and tenure, Hale's research shows that there is a "high level of consensus that the link between vocation and philanthropy is significant and requires professionals to consider their work within a larger philosophical framework."[15]

This seems a fitting way to end a chapter on fundraising professionals—and an interesting link to leadership, the next chapter. Why and how does vocation relate to philanthropy, to fund development, and to those who work in this field? Why and how does vocation relate to leadership, no matter the profession?

Defining the purpose of her thesis research, Hale says:

> *Numerous leaders in the philanthropic sector have challenged fundraising professionals to be more than mere fundraising technicians. These leaders suggest there should be a corresponding alignment of personal values, commitment, passions, and vision for the change we would like to see in the world. This challenge raises many questions and vocation may provide some of the answers.*
>
> *Paul Pribbenow suggests that vocational exploration and education is a major responsibility for the fundraising profession. He says, "[I]f we believe that we are called to serve the public practice of philanthropy, then educating each other about the meaning of that call seems like an essential aspect of our professional work" (1998). This study therefore is essential to continuing the dialogue about the nature of fundraising and the role of fundraising professionals, within a greater philosophical context.*[16]

Hale's research includes an analysis of the literature regarding vocation, organizational development, personal development, theology, psychology, professions, career planning, and human resources. She also conducted key informant interviews and an anonymous, self-administered survey with fundraising professionals.

The study does not intend to suggest that fundraising must be viewed in the light of vocation nor that professional fundraisers who claim vocation as part of their experience are morally or professionally superior. . . . [T]his project explores a concept that may provide an added layer of context and meaning to the work of fundraisers, at a point in history when many are seeking such layers in their work.

From "The Song of the River: A Study of Vocation in the Lives of Fundraisers," by Sharilyn Hale (master's diss., Saint Mary's University of Minnesota, 2004), 13

Consider these thoughts from "The Song of the River":

Spend some quality time around fundraising professionals and it won't take long for one or two to express the meaning and satisfaction they gain from their work. For some, this comes from generally knowing that, through their efforts, they are helping organizations achieve their missions, which in turn benefit society in a myriad of ways. For others, there is an added sense of personal calling they bring to their work. They claim fundraising is in fact an expression of vocation, motivating them, inspiring passion, and nurturing in them a sense of purpose and personal mission. . . .

Numerous leaders in the philanthropic sector have challenged fundraising professionals to be more than mere fundraising technicians. These leaders suggest there should be a corresponding alignment of personal values, commitment, passion, and vision for the change we would like to see in the world.[17]

Sharilyn concludes:

Philanthropic organizations, by their very nature, can be viewed as centres of vocation embraced and expressed. And those working in these organizations may be participating in vocation.

First, fundraising engages people in the purpose and practice of philanthropy, affirming a link between fundraising and vocation—where fundraising professionals may rightly view their work as a call to serve others. This vocational view can engage people in a process of personal and collective reflection.

Vocation can help fundraising professionals understand the value of their work to the world as well as the value of their work to themselves. . . . These professionals make connections between their values [and] passions and identify and understand how their call impacts those around them. They claim to be part of something bigger than themselves . . . yet embrace their call with humility and grace. . . .

Second, fundraising workplaces within philanthropic organizations would benefit from being supportive of vocation. A strong culture of philanthropy in an organization can prepare the way for a culture of vocation. Such a culture would provide a forum for colleagues to reflect and question each other on the role of fundraising in the community, both within and outside of the organization, and the meaning of the work.[18]

What do Sharilyn's comments mean to you? What questions does the concept of vocation raise for you and your organization? For example:

1. Does the concept of vocation enhance any and all professions? Are there particular professions that seem most appropriately linked to vocation? Why or why not? How and how not?
2. Does philanthropy itself (love of humankind and voluntary action for the common good) benefit from the concept of vocation? Why and how—or not?
3. What role might vocation play in your work and in the work of your organization?
4. How would you put this issue on the table and stimulate dialogue within your organization? In your professional association?
5. How might vocation relate to leadership? Why and how—or not?

P.S. from Sharilyn

What does Sharilyn think today, after investigating fundraisers and vocation in her thesis? Here's what she told me:

"In my mind, vocation is not about religion or theology but rather a framework for quality personal action. It is an intensely human need to find meaning, to experience meaning and connection with others. And work is and can be a wonderful avenue for this self and communal realization.

"I often reflect on a quote from Martin Seligman,[19] 'any job can become a calling, and any calling can become a job.' We choose each day. Sometimes we forget or get overwhelmed or bogged down or off track. And we make a different choice.

"Then when I stop for a moment and reflect and regroup, I sense the difference between working from one perspective or the other. I sense a difference in my attitude, my energy, the quality of my leadership, and the scale of my vision. Then I can make a better choice and start again. That is the value of vocation to ourselves, to our profession, and to our organizations."

Defining Your Philosophy

You decide. But decide you must, I think.

Beyond the body of knowledge and all that learning, there's your own philosophy. Your philosophy about philanthropy, your philosophy of work, and your behavior as a professional. I suspect that most truly committed professionals—in any field—ask themselves: Why do I choose to do this work rather than some other work? How does my approach to this work reflect my life's values and beliefs?

Given my philosophy, what kind of workplace do I seek? What do I expect from myself and my colleagues in that work environment? Where are my lines in the sand, those boundaries I cannot cross because of my philosophy? And with all this, what levels of risk am I willing and able to take: to live my philosophy, engage others in this journey of questioning and self-definition, and make changes if I must?

Is this still too vague, this philosophy thing? I'll use myself as an example. Here's just a portion of my professional philosophy that I try (and sometimes fail) to live out, whether speaking, consulting, writing, or volunteering.

Be more concerned with your character than your reputation, because your character is what you really are, while your reputation is merely what others think you are.

—John Wooden, American basketball coach and member of the Basketball Hall of Fame (www.coachwooden.com)

- Encourage conversation even when it makes people uncomfortable.
- Ask cage-rattling questions even though I know it makes people uncomfortable.
- Speak out even if it puts me at risk. (Ask my life partner Tom about the time I was alone in the airport with the soldiers and their machine guns, and the ethnic profiling at the screening point. Or how angry some people get when I talk about privilege, including my own invisible and unearned privilege as a white, heterosexual, well-educated, affluent person—my only disadvantage being my gender.)
- Encourage the release of nonperforming board members even though they're big donors. Because good corporate governance is good corporate governance, and bad performance is bad performance, regardless of money.
- Push fundraisers and CEOs to recognize the dynamics of privilege and power that we use every day in fund development (the words "major gifts," for example) and in governance (for example, executive committees)—and figure out how to modify that inequity.

So it begins with you. Examine yourself. Define your philosophy. Get ready to fight for it.

Mind you, this isn't about demanding that others agree with you. This isn't about convincing others or refusing to play. But this is about defining what you believe in and choosing to behave that way. Your philosophy is about the kind of workplace and community and world you want to help build and support. Your philosophy is about your role and accountability as a person and a professional, regardless of the particular position you hold.

What's your philosophy? It's yours. Not mine. Not hers. Not his. Yours. If you figure this out, work and life will be clearer. Not necessarily easier. But clearer.

Summary

I think of all this as organizational development work. Organizational life is all about organizational development work. Until we recognize this, how can we run effective organizations? Until we accept all this, how can we operate good development programs? We need to change the way we do fund development. We need to change the way we build organizations.

Why bother? Because the reward is a healthy, viable, and effective organization. Because the reward is organizational survival. And finally, because the reward is strong philanthropic organizations that make a difference in their communities.

Maybe you're an organizational development specialist already. And you've defined your philosophy and you're a leader, too. If so, keep it up and help develop others.

Maybe you want to transform yourself. If yes, go forth and do so. Examine yourself and outline a plan for change. Read this book. Read other books. Find yourself a coach and mentor. Do what it takes.

The best fundraisers are organizational development specialists, not just great fundraising technicians. The best fundraisers must embrace the obligations, the attitude and behaviors, and the knowledge and skills of leaders, too.

If not you, who?

CHAPTER 5

The Art of Leadership

A Critical Element of the First Relationship—Within Your Organization

Understand the importance of nonconformity. Leadership is about change, hope, and the future. Leaders have to venture into uncharted territory, so they must be able to handle intellectual solitude and ambiguity.

—C. K. Prahalad, Paul and Ruth McCracken Distinguished University Professor of Strategy at the University of Michigan's Ross School of Business. From "The Responsible Manager," *Harvard Business Review* (January–February 2010)

Leadership should be born out of the understanding of the needs of those who would be affected by it.

—Marian Anderson (1897–1993), celebrated singer of the twentieth century

What Is Leadership?

Chapter 3 described the first relationship that contributes to effective fund development: the relationship within your organization—creating the infrastructure that produces a healthy organization. I proposed eight key components of this relationship within your organization: shared values, commitment to process, learning organization, ongoing conversation, participatory decision-making, well-managed change, and culture of philanthropy and the art of leadership.

In this third edition of *Strategic Fund Development*, I devote an entire chapter to the exploration of leadership. Nonetheless, this is by no means a definitive description. Learning more about leadership is, I think, a joy and requirement of any professional, whether for-profit or nonprofit/nongovernmental organization (NGO).

Leadership is a critical component of effective infrastructure and your organization's internal relations. Effective and efficient fundraisers are good leaders. They lead the fund development function, and they lead organizational development. In fact, as I noted in Chapter 4, "The Fund Development Professional," I expect fundraisers to be leadership leaders.

Leadership guarantees that your institution develops the four relationships central to an effective organization and critical to productive fund development. Leaders facilitate the ongoing process to develop, sustain, and renew these relationships.

What is the leadership issue of our time? How can we create sustained solutions for complex systemic issues whose solutions cannot be mandated from the top? Asked another way: How can human communities productively confront complex issues where hierarchical authority is inadequate to bring about change?

From *The Fifth Discipline: The Art and Practice of the Learning Organization*, by Peter M. Senge (New York: Doubleday, 1990)

Defining Leadership

Leadership means the willingness and ability to lead and influence others. Leadership is about learning and change—so leaders are change agents. The best organizations are rich in leaders. This network of individuals creates a web to support your organization. Leadership acts as the glue that helps hold your organization together.

Because leadership exists to help accomplish group purpose, leaders are accountable to the group. Leadership depends on the shared values and vision of the group rather than an independent belief system and personal agenda of the leader. Robert K. Greenleaf describes this as the servant leader concept.[1]

Contrast this to an abusive concept of leadership where an individual ensures the outcomes he wants and prevents those he doesn't want. This person diminishes other people, enforcing power in order to bring about intended consequences in the behavior of others. This is done without concern for the rights and initiative of the others.

Another negative view of leadership is the vision of a parental figure who puts everything right. As John W. Gardner observes, "To some extent the conventional views of leadership are shallow, and set us up for endless disappointment. There is an element of wanting to be rescued, of wanting a parental figure who will set all things right."[2]

Peter Block, author of *Stewardship: Choosing Service over Self-Interest*,[3] uses the concept of stewardship to alter the conventional theory of leadership. Block's stewardship incorporates accountability, partnership, empowerment, and service. He notes that leadership means initiative and responsibility, without taking control and disempowering others. Leaders are partners. They retain initiative and accountability but avoid dominance and patriarchal oversight.

True leadership has people who follow when they have the freedom not to.

From *Good to Great and the Social Sectors*, by Jim Collins (New York: HarperCollins, 2005)

In systems thinking theory, the leader helps create a learning organization and leads the organization's learning. Traditionally, observes Daniel H. Kim, leaders are perceived to be out in front of everyone else, knowing all the answers. However, this conflicts with the concept of a learning organization. Experience shows that people learn by doing and learn by taking risks. When taking risks, people often make mistakes and that is part of learning.[4]

In the new world, Kim remarks, leaders are still out in front. However, these leaders are taking risks, making mistakes, and learning faster than others are.[5] The leader helps others learn. The leader of today and tomorrow develops a community of learners by reaching the learner inside each individual. This leader helps others question and overcome their limitations.

Kim goes on to say that in addition to leading the learning process and being open to making mistakes, the leader seeks the truth.[6] The leader lets everyone know that the truth is what she or he wants and expects to hear. The leader also ensures safety. An organization committed to learning must be a safe place. These organizations recognize that without a sense of safety, people will not take risks and will not tell the truth. In a safe environment where trust, commitment, and responsibility are shared, people will raise the tough issues and help the organization change.

Leaders Are Made, Not Born

Sure, circumstances and situations often produce leaders. But more importantly, leaders can be developed. Individuals can develop leadership skills and learn leadership tasks.

Just as leaders are obliged to develop new leaders, so are organizations. Effective organizations create a culture and an infrastructure that produce new leaders regularly. Effective organizations devote resources to leadership development.

Nonprofits/NGOs engage volunteers as well as paid staff. Ideally, an organization includes competent leaders in both staff and volunteers. Unfortunately, despite the best recruitment process, securing volunteers who are actually effective leaders cannot be guaranteed.

However, organizations can ensure that they hire leaders on staff. The board of directors hires a chief executive who possesses leadership attributes and skills and demonstrates the ability to carry out leadership functions and tasks. The board then expects that the chief executive will hire other leaders at all levels within the organization. And the CEO hires a leader to serve as chief development officer. This individual leads the development operation and serves as a key leader within the institution itself.

What Do Leaders Do?

Leaders carry out key functions and specific tasks. Effective leaders know leadership is an art as well as a developed skill. Committed leaders actually study leadership in order to improve their own performance. Happily, there's a wealth of writing on leadership, and more written regularly. There's more and more research about leadership, too.

Leadership should be more participative than directive, more enabling than performing.

—Marian Anderson (1897–1993), celebrated singer of the twentieth century

Each of the functions and tasks described here—compiled through various readings and my own perspective—is essential to help build the four relationships critical to effective fund development. More importantly, these functions and tasks are essential to develop a healthy organization.

The tasks are grouped into four function areas: people, organization, personal, and community.

1. The "people" function presents tasks that relate to the individuals within the organization.
2. The "organization" function focuses on tasks that bring people together as one entity, moving them forward to achieve the organization's mission and vision.
3. The "personal" function focuses on the leader herself or himself.
4. The "community" function highlights tasks that connect the organization to the external community.

As you review this list of leadership functions, ask yourself:

- How do I carry out these leadership functions as part of my life's work, no matter in which organization or sphere of life I operate?
- Have I developed the skills necessary to carry out these functions?
- How do I evaluate my own performance regularly, improving as necessary?
- How do I encourage leadership in others?
- How do I respect (and welcome) leadership by others?
- Does my organization know that these tasks are the responsibility of our leaders, and do we regularly evaluate the performance of our leaders?
- Does my organization talk about leadership regularly at the governance and management levels? Have we articulated together what we mean by leadership, how we will develop leaders, and how we will evaluate them?
- What is my organization's plan to foster continuity within its leadership and to assure succession?

What is my organization's plan to identify, cultivate, and develop leaders, and do we implement it effectively? As you review these functions, ask yourself another question—proposed in the Philanthropy and Development classroom at Saint Mary's University: What is the responsibility that comes with a certain level of seniority, expertise, experience, privilege, insight, and courage?

People Functions

1. *Value each individual.*
   Recognize the importance of each individual compared to her or his tasks or functions. Encourage personal mastery and self-fulfillment. Encourage diversity and pluralism. Welcome the unusual person and different idea. Consistently advocate for equity. Encourage each person's voice.
2. *Gather and develop others to be leaders.*
   Recruit leaders to join the organization. Help others within the organization exercise leadership. Choose the best and brightest to replace existing leaders.

Seek competence in others and in yourself. Recognize and celebrate leaders and leadership.

3. *Motivate others.*

   Encourage commitment, not just compliance, by engaging the collective beliefs of people in your organization and its mission. Align group and individual beliefs and actions.

4. *Exercise political judgment.*

   Manage the conflicting needs and desires of diverse constituencies, both internal and external.

5. *Remove obstacles—and empower others to do the same.*

   Eliminate barriers that prevent others from doing their jobs. Enable others to realize their full potential and aspirations. Anticipate problems, identify solutions, and redirect energies of self and others.

6. *Engage constituents.*

   Foster access and engagement through diverse strategies. Enlist constituents in conversation and questioning and decision-making. Build shared understanding and ownership.

7. *Promote the knowledge and skills, behavior, and art of the specific job as well as the organization's work.*

   Leaders ensure that people have the skills and information, support and resources to do the work. Leaders link each specific job to the organization's mission and direction.

8. *Enable others.*

   Chapter 8 describes 19 specific enabling functions. Leaders apply these to staff (and volunteers in nonprofit organizations). Learn all about these enabling functions. Then use them well.

Organization Functions

1. *Affirm values and set the highest ethical standards.*

   Ensure that the organization articulates its shared values. Communicate and model these values. Help the organization act in accordance with its values.

2. *See the entire system, the big picture, as well as its interrelated parts.*

   Think long-term as well as short-term. It's all about systems thinking, never about functional silos.

3. *Ensure pluralism and cultural competence.*

   Make sure the organization values and welcomes diversity. Build a healthy corporate culture. Ensure that the organization and its members can interface well with other cultures—whether those are corporate cultures or social cultures.[7] (See the discussion of multiple intelligences [MI] later in this chapter.)

4. *Build adaptive capacity.*

   Ensure that the organization—its individuals and teams—uses external focus, network connectedness, inquisitiveness, and innovation to both adapt and generate anew. Use adaptive capacity as a component of learning and change. Help everyone respect change, and change as needed. (See more about adaptive capacity in Chapter 3.)

5. *Assure the existence of vision, direction, and goals.*
Some say that the leader envisions direction and goals. Some say that the leader creates and nurtures vision through a process that engages people throughout the organization. Others say the leader has a vision and uses group process to test, refine, and build ownership for that vision.

But mostly, I hope that the organization itself—facilitated by the leader—regularly envisions. I expect the leader to engage the organization in a process to generate vision together.

When you become a leader, you lose the right to think about yourself.

—The Reverend Gerald Brooks, Grace Outreach Center, Plano, TX

---

6. *Institutionalize leadership.*
Create an infrastructure (corporate culture and systems) that supports leadership development. Assure that the organization designs and implements specific programs and activities so that others can develop and practice leadership.
7. *Ensure that the questions worth asking are asked—and engage people in conversation.*
Encourage intellectual curiosity. Encourage others to ask strategic and cage-rattling questions. Identify issues and focus the organization's attention. Engage people in conversation to support learning and change.
8. Have ideas and point the organization toward opportunities and solutions.
Articulate reality and anticipate multiple futures.
9. *Manage.*
Do leaders really manage? Should they?

At some time, someone started the myth that those who are good leaders typically are not good managers. In this myth, leaders see the forest but cannot see the trees. Leaders lead but they are not good at implementation and follow-through.

Nonsense. The most effective leaders see the forest and the trees. Maintaining perspective on the big picture as well as the small details is essential to get where you are going.

Leaders help themselves and others translate vision into the small steps to get there. Leaders acknowledge the challenges inherent within the detail and help manage process to accomplishment. Leaders set priorities, but mostly facilitate the process of setting priorities. Leaders devise plans, but mostly facilitate that process, too.

Leaders allocate resources, and ensure that resource allocation aligns with priorities and plans. Leaders organize and build the institution, keep the system functioning, make decisions, and facilitate the decision-making process.

Check out "The Responsible Manager" by C. K. Prahalad[8] in the January–February 2010 issue of *Harvard Business Review*. Dr. Prahalad's words read like a leadership manifesto:
- Humility in success and courage in failure are hallmarks of a good leader.
- Be unstinting in helping your colleagues realize their full potential.

- Assume responsibility for outcomes as well as for the processes and people you work with. How you achieve results will shape the kind of person you become.
- Expect to be judged by what you do and how well you do it—not by what you say you want to do. However, the bias toward action must be balanced by empathy and caring for other people.

10. *Build community.*
Unify the group and preserve trust within the organization. Use dissonance but diminish dysfunctional conflict.

11. *Listen and communicate.*
Find out what others think. Bring everyone to the table and make sure they have a voice. Inform, explain, and teach. Communicate why, not just what or how.

12. *Serve as a symbol within and outside the organization.*
Serve as the organization's chief spokesperson and diplomat. Promote the organization's unique character. Tell the organization's stories.

13. *Represent the group.*
Cross boundaries and build relationships between groups, organizations, and communities.

14. *Renew, change, and build a learning organization.*
Foster the process of individual and team learning, renewal, and change. Create a safe, risk-free environment.

15. *Keep it all going—and that includes implementation!*
Provide momentum and facilitate transformation. Balance continuity, transition, and change. Make sure that things are implemented.

16. *Create a legacy for the future.*
This isn't a personal legacy. This isn't about the leader; this is the organization's legacy. Create a sustainable organization. Leave a legacy of such things as a positive culture, useful infrastructure, strong relationships, effective leadership, and a solid reputation for the organization.

The best leader is a person who realizes—with all his/her frailties and failures—that there is a need to continually learn, show compassion, exhibit integrity, and enable others . . . all for the common good.

—Cohort 13, Master of Arts in Philanthropy and Development, Saint Mary's University of Minnesota

---

Personal Functions

1. Delegate but do not abdicate.
2. Be prepared to do anything you would ask of others.
3. Take risks and make mistakes.
4. Recognize and, as appropriate, change your own assumptions or paradigms (called mental models in learning organizations) and help others identify and change theirs.

5. Set high standards for yourself and others. Evaluate your own performance and change.
6. Welcome criticism. Learn from it.

As Dee Hock, founder and CEO emeritus of Visa USA and Visa International, observes, "Active critics are a great asset. Without the slightest expenditure of time or effort, we have our weakness and error made apparent and alternatives proposed. We need only listen carefully, dismiss that which arises from ignorance, ignore that which arises from envy or malice, and embrace that which has merit."[9]

Community Functions

1. *Assure that the organization is relevant to the external community.*
   Use ongoing strategic planning to assure relevance (or to help the organization close well if need be). See Chapter 6 on strategic planning.
2. *Perpetually connect the organization to the external community.*
   This external focus helps build adaptive capacity, listed as in Organization Functions, and reviewed at length in Chapter 3.
   Build knowledge alliances with organizations and community leaders to assure ongoing two-way conversation, information sharing, and learning. Collaborate with other organizations to meet community needs.
   Leaders also participate as volunteers in the community, encouraging the organization's employees to do the same.
3. *Build civic capacity in order to create a civil society.*
   Civic capacity refers to the ability of a community to identify the challenges and opportunities it faces, and to bring together the diversity of the community to address these issues effectively. Civic capacity is about empowering individuals and organizations across the three sectors (for-profit, government, and non-profit/NGO) to work together for the good of the whole. When a community is strong in civic capacity, the community welcomes traditional and nontraditional organizations and individuals to the table to share power.
   Effective leaders work to build civic capacity, for the good of the community, regardless of their own organization's role or position. Why? Because we all want to live in a civil society—and anyone who is a leader anywhere is committed to and invested in that.
4. *Assure environmental accountability.*
   Leaders build green organizations and help build a green world. As leaders connect their organizations to the external community, these leaders promote accountability to the environment.

The kind of leadership most effective today is similar to the kind of service that the best consultant gives a client: collaborative assistance that is both problem-solving and developmental. Its target is both the situation and the professional capability of the person.

From "Leading Transition: A New Model for Change," by William Bridges and Susan Mitchell, *Leader to Leader*, Spring 2000, 36

Leadership and Diversity

Call it diversity or pluralism—leadership sure is about multiplicity and inclusiveness. People experience life differently, and that experience produces different perspectives, conflicting opinions, and opposing beliefs.

Diversity is more than race/ethnicity, generation, gender, sexual orientation, socioeconomic status, and faith. But each of these certainly affects how people experience life. Diversity makes for a rich and complex world. Pluralism builds stronger communities and organizations.

As Pottruck and Pearce note, diversity is more than affirmative action, and its rationale is more than moral fairness. Diversity is "the practical ground of good business."[10] Significant diversity in the people of your organization brings significant diversity in the perspectives offered within your organization.

"Significant" is what is important. Effective organizations bring together people who may disagree on matters of substance. That's what adds value to the organization: enough diversity to ask questions, question assumptions, and question answers; sufficient diversity to stimulate breakthroughs and encourage change, to facilitate learning and reaffirm values.

Leaders know that their organizations must be innovative and cutting-edge to respond to this rich and complex world. For this reason, leaders encourage diversity. Leaders figure out "what it will take to make *sustainable, long-term* progress in gaining and keeping a diverse group of people."[11]

When Dee Hock talks about hiring, he is certainly mindful of diversity: "Never hire or promote in your own image. It is foolish to replicate your strength. It is stupid to replicate your weakness. Employ, trust, and reward those whose perspective, ability, and judgment are radically different from your own and recognize that it requires uncommon humility, tolerance, and wisdom."[12]

Leaders know, too, that diversity increases complexity and complexity produces ambiguity. Leaders know that people are often frustrated by complexity and threatened by ambiguity. So leaders help their organizations develop tolerance for both.

Leaders acknowledge and respect diversity, welcome and seek it out, and revel in pluralism.

But it's more than tolerance. Tolerance seems so limiting. Tolerance seems like "Okay, we'll accept diversity because it's the thing to do, but we don't much want to do it." Leaders actually welcome diversity. Leaders encourage diversity. Leaders expect and revel in diversity.

Encouraging diversity and tolerating complexity stand in direct opposition to complacency. Leaders fight complacency. They work against the status quo, or what Pottruck calls "incumbency."

In this vein, Porras and Collins[13] urge leaders to consider the following questions:

- What "mechanisms of discontent" can you create that would obliterate complacency and bring about change and improvement from within, yet are consistent with your core ideology? How can you give these mechanisms sharp teeth?

- What are you doing to invest for the future *while* doing well today?
- Do people in your company understand that *comfort is not the objective*—that life in a visionary company is not supposed to be easy? Does your company reject doing well as an end goal, replacing it with the never-ending discipline of working to do better tomorrow than it did today?

A Special Obligation of Leadership

True leadership means acknowledging privilege and its politics, and struggling for fairness. The best leaders know that invisible privilege (like socioeconomics, ethnicity, gender, sexual orientation) coupled with visible privilege (like their own hierarchical position) dramatically affect what happens everywhere.

Privilege and its politics affect the willingness to ask the essential and cage-rattling questions. Privilege and its politics affect group dynamics. Privilege and its politics affect the ability to take risk. Really, privilege and its politics affect everything.

First and forever, leaders challenge the status quo.

So privilege and its politics affect your staff and volunteers and the health and effectiveness of your organization. Privilege and its politics affect your community and its ability to build civic capacity and civil society.

In 1988, Peggy McIntosh, PhD, published her groundbreaking article "White Privilege: Unpacking the Invisible Knapsack."[14] McIntosh challenges us to recognize our own unearned and invisible privilege. She dares us to acknowledge that privilege is not a result of something a person has done. On the contrary, privilege is the result of "invisible systems conferring dominance on a particular group."

Think about it. Don't get angry. Just think about it. Some of us were born white. And in many, many countries, it's an advantage to be white. And those who are born white and male have even more advantage. For example, white men run most Fortune 500 companies. Yet women and people of color are just as smart, intelligent, competent, experienced, capable, able, willing, driven, educated. . . .

As McIntosh notes in her 2010 article "White Privilege: An Account to Spend," success has less to do with how hard one works than with the "systemic class and race privilege to which [one is] born." And let's add a couple of other privileges of birth, for example, gender and sexual orientation. In fact, invisible privilege is like being born into automatic affirmative action. So if you're born white, or heterosexual, or male, you have automatic privilege in many, many societies. If you're born all three, you win the lottery.

Of course, you didn't choose how to be born.[15] No one does. So this privilege doesn't make any individual guilty, merely privileged. And being privileged is important to recognize, acknowledge, and then use as McIntosh's account to spend . . . an account to spend to make change.

Perhaps what's hardest to understand is why the privilege system is so hard to see. Why, in fact, are we[16] the privileged taught not to see our own privilege? McIntosh says that the myth of meritocracy, a "two-part belief that underlies the ideology of the United States,"[17] stops us from seeing our own privilege. (You decide to what degree some or all of this ideology applies to your country.)

The Myth of Meritocracy

The myth of meritocracy works like this: "The first part: The individual is the only unit of society. The second part: Whatever an individual ends up with in life must be what he or she wanted, worked for, earned, and deserved. This is the U.S. myth of equal opportunity for all: Everybody succeeds on his or her own merits."[18]

This sure is the way that the United States works. Individual rights almost always trump community rights.[19] And how many times do you hear the phrase "pull yourselves up by your bootstraps," as if everyone even has boots to pull up by!

Brainwashed by the meritocracy myth makes it "easy to believe that if people do not succeed, it is because they are not worthy, either individually or as a group—for example, because they aren't smart or don't work hard enough. The myth of meritocracy says that if people work hard, they get ahead."[20]

But that simply isn't true. People are denied work because of their race and gender and sexual orientation—despite laws to the contrary. People are paid different wages because of their gender—despite laws to the contrary. Our society discriminates against people because of their faith, their physical or mental health . . . sometimes the list of discrimination seems endless.

Everyone probably knows the Chinese proverb: Give a man a fish and you feed him for a day. Teach a man to fish and you feed him for a lifetime. But in the social justice movement, there's an additional phrase: You have to give the person a place on the river to fish from. Teaching a person to fish isn't enough—unless you give the person a place on the river. And that, too, is privilege.

Too often, people are blind to the lives of others. Too often, we forget that each individual experiences life differently. Too often, we refuse to empathize with others.

With my privilege, I'm faced with deep obligation to act.

—Karen Denny, Cohort 19, Master of Arts in Philanthropy and Development, Saint Mary's University of Minnesota

---

The Greatest Leaders

The very best leaders know all this. True leaders recognize and acknowledge privilege. True leaders use their own privilege as an account to spend. Real leaders raise these issues and encourage safe conversation. The very best leaders work hard to manage and co-opt this reality. The very best leaders achieve fairness within their organizations. The great leaders fight the war for fairness in the world, too.

And the greatest leaders? Perhaps they fight the longest. As McIntosh notes, "We who are the most powerful [due to our privilege] can use our privilege to weaken systems of power and privilege."[21] Nothing else is acceptable. Nothing else is leadership.

In the courses that I teach at Saint Mary's University of Minnesota,[22] we talk lots about privilege and power. Together, the students and I ask the essential and cage-rattling questions, and go back home and do so again and again. Questions like:

- To what degree and in what way are/should/can nonprofits/NGOs be stabilizing forces of culture—while also questioning the status quo?
- What is the connection between power and impact?
- How do we help individuals, communities, government, and organizations feel deeply compelled to understand and confront the injustices that exist on a local and global scale?

Imagination is not only the uniquely human capacity to envision that which is not, and therefore the fount of all invention and innovation. In its arguably most transformative and revelatory capacity, it is the power that enables us to empathise with humans whose experiences we have never shared.

—J. K. Rowling, June 2008 Commencement Address at Harvard University

---

Leadership in Philanthropic Organizations

All the functions for people, organization, and community belong to all leaders, anywhere—and that includes leaders in philanthropic organizations.

But there's more, too. Nonprofit leaders demonstrate philanthropy through their own acts of giving time and money. NGO leaders recognize that philanthropy is not merely a means to achieve mission, but rather a meaningful activity itself. These leaders make sure that their organizations accept philanthropy as a core component of mission.

These leaders know that philanthropy and the philanthropic sector play a critical role in building civic capacity and creating civil society. Leaders in nonprofits/NGOs fight long and hard to strengthen the sector, nurture its credibility, and build a more just world.

And leaders in the philanthropic sector know that there are two kinds of philanthropy: mainstream philanthropy, the dominant version, and social change/progressive philanthropy, the oft-forgotten one. Neither is more important; both are needed. But mainstream philanthropy is more visible, more talked about, more documented ... it's mainstream.

Too many fundraisers aren't aware of social change/progressive philanthropy. Too many publications ignore social change/progressive philanthropy and focus exclusively on mainstream philanthropy. Too many nonprofit staff and board members cannot distinguish between the two.

What's the difference? "Traditional philanthropy is based on responding to, treating, and managing the consequences of life in a society with a capital-based economy. Progressive philanthropy ... analyzes and responds more to cause than effect. Progressive philanthropy supports ... social change ... [and] actions that seek to right the imbalances of an unjust society or unequal distribution of resources... often making people, institutions, and government uncomfortable. Progressive philanthropy ... challenges the assumptions that economic and social inequities are somehow unavoidable as the price of progress or prosperity."[23]

Philanthropic leaders choose where to be involved—mainstream or progressive philanthropy. That's a personal choice. Our communities need both philanthropies. But philanthropic leaders know about both types of philanthropy. And philanthropic leaders see how privilege and power relate to social change/progressive philanthropy.[24]

Culture is always about politics in the end.

Mohammed Moulessehoul, Algerian novelist.

Attributes and Skills of Leaders

Effective leaders possess certain attributes or attitudes. Leaders master learnable skills and behave in certain ways.

The art of leadership is liberating people to do what is required of them in the most effective and humane way possible.

From *Leadership Is an Art*, by Max DePree (New York: Dell Publishing, 1989), 1

---

1. Leaders willingly and eagerly accept and share responsibility. Believing in Block's stewardship and Greenleaf's servant leadership, leaders empower others by distributing responsibility and authority, even while retaining responsibility for the whole.
2. Leaders possess emotional, intellectual, and physical vitality and stamina. They are dependable, confident, assertive, adaptable, highly tolerant, and flexible. They are courageous, resolute, patient, and steadfast. And leaders are passionate—passionate about their organizations and missions, their constituents, and their communities.
3. Both visionary and practical, leaders lead through serving. They neither coerce others nor depend on official status or authority.
4. Leaders balance being out in front with following and supporting. They balance their own ego with the egos of others. Leaders acknowledge responsibility for failure and share responsibility for success.
5. Competent and knowledgeable in key fields, leaders know the organization and its work. Max DePree[25] refers to this as task competence. For him, this includes personal performance and achievement plus the potential for continuing growth and accountability. Self-aware leaders evaluate their own strengths and weaknesses and work toward personal mastery. Leaders continually strive for self-development.

6. Leaders seek diversity and nurture pluralism. They are comfortable with complexity, ambiguity, and uncertainty. They welcome and learn from the skills and experience of others.

7. Leaders are curious. They embrace the *folie du pouquoi*, asking why. In describing himself, Einstein said, "I have no special talents. I am only passionately curious."

8. Leaders encourage contrary opinion, are comfortable with disagreement, and accept conflict. Leaders recognize that creativity and innovation result from new opinions, conflicting ideas, and essential and cage-rattling questions. Leaders help identify the right fights and enable the organization to fight well. (See Chapter 3, Exhibits 3.11 and 3.12, for more about fighting.)

Strong leaders create the kind of conflict that can spark creativity and innovation.

From "How to Pick a Good Fight," by Saj-nicole A. Joni and Damon Beyer, *Harvard Business Review* (December 2009)

---

9. Even while they are achievement oriented, leaders commit to process and demand outcomes from process. Whether choosing "ready, aim, fire" or "ready, fire, aim," leaders make sure that their colleagues understand and own decisions. (By the way, I'm less and less interested in ready and then fire. Aiming is just too important.)

10. Leaders are intelligent and able to judge and act. They exercise good management and decision-making skills.

11. Leaders know that their individual behavior models the behavior of others. Leaders are trustworthy and trusting.

12. Leaders deal well with people and motivate themselves as well as others. Leaders are sensitive to others and respect and understand the wants and needs of their diverse constituents. Leaders understand group behavior as well.

13. Leaders communicate easily at all levels and with diverse constituents. They listen and hear. They tell stories and use symbols well. More importantly perhaps, as Seth Godin says in his book *Tribes*, leaders give people "stories they can tell themselves. Stories about the future and change."[26]

14. Leaders are ethical and honest. They are clear about their own beliefs and values regarding human nature, the role of the organization, measurement of performance, and so forth. Leaders are consistent in belief and practice, at work and in their personal lives. Leaders are disciplined and persevering.

Leaders surround themselves with other leaders to balance out their natural human frailty. Leaders are humble. They're proud of those with whom they share leadership.

—Wendy Zufelt-Baxter, Cohort 15, Master of Arts in Philanthropy and Development, Saint Mary's University of Minnesota

---

15. Leaders are excellent organizational development specialists and good managers.
16. Leaders possess multiple intelligences. For example, leaders possess both emotional intelligence and social intelligence, translated into high levels of competency. Do you think leaders should also possess creative intelligence? Are the best leaders more like innovative entrepreneurs than more traditional executives are? How about cultural intelligence? Keep reading!

Are leaders all this all the time? Of course not. Leaders try and fail in small and large ways. Leaders know this. But they continue to strive.

Leadership and Intelligences

The word *intelligence* comes from the Latin verb *intelligere*, "to understand" and "to choose between." That old standard, the intelligence quotient (IQ), measured how smart you were, with a focus on mental capabilities such as reasoning, planning, problem solving, understanding complex ideas, and learning from experience.

In the olden days, people pretty much focused on one intelligence only. But back in 1983, Howard Gardner[27] proposed multiple intelligences. Thus started the field of multiple intelligences (MI).

As I use it, the term intelligence refers to a set of human computational capacities. As humans, we have the ability to "compute" language, number, social relations, special relations, etc. We cannot directly see the intelligences. We observe them at work by observing individuals carrying out various kinds of behaviors and tasks.

From Howard Gardner, FAQ at www.howardgardner.com

Here's Gardner's explanation of intelligence:

Fundamentally, an intelligence refers to a biopsychological potential of our species to process certain kinds of information in certain kinds of ways. As such, it clearly involves processes that are carried out by dedicated neural networks. No doubt each of the intelligences has its characteristic neural processes, with most of them quite similar across human beings. Some of the processes might prove to be more customized to an individual....

From an evolutionary point of view, it seems probable that each intelligence evolved to deal with certain kinds of contents in a predictable world. However, once such a capacity has emerged, there is nothing that mandates that it must remain tied to the original inspiring content.[28]

Yes, we can learn and change. We can develop our intelligences. But, Gardner cautions, don't conflate the terms *intelligence* and *style*. They are different. "Styles refer to the customary way in which an individual approaches a range of materials—for example, a playful or a planful style. Intelligence refers to the computational power of a mental system—for example, a person whose linguistic intelligence is strong is able readily to compute information that involves language."[29]

Back to those multiple intelligences. Neuroscience and psychological research help us understand that intelligence extends far beyond the traditional IQ measure. Studies take us into new realms that seem unreal.

Here's a small note from a thoughtful book, *The Elegance of the Hedgehog* by Muriel Barbery. Madame Michel, a nondescript concierge in Paris, hides her thoughts, her feelings—her real self—from others. But truly, she's an observer of humanity, an explorer and a philosopher. She's continually angered by the people around her. For example, people's lack of self-awareness and blindness toward others angers Madame Michel.

At one point, she muses: "What is the purpose of intelligence if it is not to serve others? And I'm not referring to the false servitude that high-ranking state-employed flunkeys exhibit so proudly, as if it were nothing more than vanity and disdain. . . . [P]rivilege brings with it *true* obligations. If you belong to the closed inner sanctum of the elite, you must serve in equal proportion to the glory and ease of material existence you derive from belonging to that inner sanctum. . . . The only thing that matters is your intention: are you elevating thought and contributing to the common good. . . ."[30]

True leaders observe, inquire, respect, accept, appreciate, and model. True leaders bring these experiential learnings with them as they lead.

—Wendy Zufelt-Baxter, Cohort 15, Master's Program in Philanthropy and Development, Saint Mary's University of Minnesota

---

Emotional Intelligence

Let's start with emotional intelligence. Leaders possess a high degree of emotional competency. See Exhibit 5.1, which reads like a litany of leadership qualities.

Exhibit 5.1   Emotional Intelligence: A Primer

Emotional intelligence—the ability to manage our relationships and ourselves effectively—consists of four fundamental capabilities: self-awareness, self-management, social awareness, and social skill. Each capability, in turn, is composed of specific sets of competencies. Below is a list of the capabilities and their corresponding traits.

Self-Awareness

- Emotional self-awareness: the ability to read and understand your emotions as well as recognize their impact on work performance, relationships, and the like.

- Accurate self-assessment: a realistic evaluation of your strengths and limitations.
- Self-confidence: a strong and positive sense of self-worth.

Self-Management

- Self-control: the ability to keep disruptive emotions and impulses under control.
- Trustworthiness: a consistent display of honesty and integrity.
- Conscientiousness: the ability to manage yourself and your responsibilities.
- Adaptability: skill at adjusting to changing situations and overcoming obstacles.
- Achievement orientation: the drive to meet an internal standard of excellence.
- Initiative: a readiness to seize opportunities.

Social Awareness

- Empathy: skill at sensing other people's emotions, understanding their perspective, and taking an active interest in their concerns.
- Organizational awareness: the ability to read the currents of organizational life, build decision networks, and navigate politics.
- Service orientation: the ability to recognize and meet customers' needs.

Social Skill

- Visionary leadership: the ability to take charge and inspire with a compelling vision.
- Influence: the ability to wield a range of persuasive tactics.
- Developing others: the propensity to bolster the abilities of others through feedback and guidance.
- Communication: skill at listening and at sending clear, convincing, and well-tuned messages.
- Change catalyst: proficiency in initiating new ideas and leading people in a new direction.
- Conflict management: the ability to de-escalate disagreements and orchestrate resolutions.
- Building bonds: proficiency at cultivating and maintaining a web of relationships.
- Teamwork and collaboration: competence at promoting cooperation and building teams.

Source: Reprinted by permission of *Harvard Business Review* from "Leadership That Gets Results," by Daniel Goleman (March–April 2000). Copyright © 2000 by the Harvard Business School Publishing Corporation; all rights reserved.

In fact, according to research by McClelland and Goleman, excellent performers at work possess three domains of competency. These are intelligence quotient (IQ), expertise, and emotional intelligence. But emotional intelligence is the most critical performance factor.[31]

According to the research on high performance, the intelligence quotient is of limited importance. Expertise is important. And emotional intelligence is most important.

Emotional intelligence is what affects an individual's ability to learn emotional competence. This competence is a learned capability and results in outstanding work performance. An individual's emotional competence shows the degree to which that emotional intelligence has been translated into on-the-job capabilities.

Emotional competence depends on four elements of emotional intelligence: self-awareness, self-management, social awareness, and social skill. As Goleman notes,[32] good customer service is an emotional competence based on empathy, while the competence of trustworthiness depends on self-regulation.

Just because someone is high in emotional intelligence does not mean that she or he will learn the emotional competencies required for high performance at work. However, possessing high emotional intelligence does indicate the potential to learn the emotional competencies.

Just because you are high in emotional intelligence does not mean that you have translated that into emotional competence on the job. But leaders certainly have. Leaders display emotional competency and continually enhance it within themselves.

With information in hand about emotional intelligence and competency, leaders develop this understanding within colleagues in the organization. The best leaders develop ways to enhance emotional competency within workers.

SIX STYLES OF LEADERSHIP   Through further research, Goleman and his colleagues describe six styles of leadership resulting from the different components of emotional intelligence. Different styles of leadership clearly affect performance and results, and the research provides guidance about which style is most effective when. However, says Goleman, all six leadership styles have a measurable effect on organization climate or performance. (See Exhibit 5.2.)

To paraphrase Goleman,[33] the six styles of leadership are:

1. *Coercive leaders.* These individuals demand immediate compliance.
2. *Authoritative leaders.* These leaders mobilize people toward a vision.
3. *Affiliative leaders.* These individuals create emotional bonds and harmony within the organization.
4. *Democratic leaders.* These leaders build consensus through conversation and participation.
5. *Pacesetting leaders.* These individuals expect excellence and self-direction from those they lead.
6. *Coaching leaders.* These leaders develop their people for the future.

The research strongly suggests that leaders should be flexible, changing styles as the situation demands. Moreover, the research clarifies links among leadership, emotional intelligence, organizational climate, and performance.

EXHIBIT 5.2   Six Leadership Styles, Their Origin within Emotional Intelligence, When They Work Best, and Their Impact on Climate and Performance

	Coercive	Authoritative	Affiliative	Democratic	Pacesetting	Coaching
The leader's modus operandi	Demands immediate compliance	Mobilizes people toward a vision	Creates harmony and builds emotional bonds	Forges consensus through participation	Sets high standards for performance	Develops people for the future
The style in phrase	"Do what I tell you."	"Come with me."	"People come first."	"What do you think?"	"Do as I do, now."	"Try this."
Underlying emotional intelligence competencies	Drive to achieve, initiative, self-control	Self-confidence, empathy, change catalyst	Empathy, building relationships, communication	Collaboration, team leadership, communication	Conscientiousness, drive to achieve, initiative	Developing others, empathy, self-awareness
When the style works best	In a crisis, to kick-start a turnaround, or with problem employees	When changes require a new vision, or when a clear direction is needed	To heal rifts in a team or to motivate people during stressful circumstances	To build buy-in or consensus, or to get input from valuable employees	To get quick results from a highly motivated and competent team	To help an employee improve performance or develop long-term strengths
Overall impact on climate	Negative	Most strongly positive	Positive	Positive	Negative	Positive

According to the research data, the authoritative leadership style affects climate most positively. However, affiliative, democratic, and coaching styles follow closely. Nonetheless, Goleman stresses that no leadership style should be used exclusively and, "all have at least short-term uses."

Organizational climate—or working environment—has long been known to affect performance, and six factors influence climate. To paraphrase Goleman,[34] these factors are:

1. Flexibility: how free employees feel to innovate without red tape.
2. Responsibility: employee sense of responsibility to the organization.
3. Standards: the level of standards that people set within the organization.
4. Rewards: the sense of accuracy about performance feedback and the appropriateness of rewards for performance.
5. Clarity: how clear mission and values are to the people within the organization.
6. Commitment: the level of commitment to a common purpose shared by those within the organization.

All emotions are social. You can't separate the case of an emotion from the world of relationships—our social interactions are what drive our emotions.

—Richard Davidson, director, Laboratory for Affective Neuroscience, University of Wisconsin, as quoted by Daniel Goleman in *Social Intelligence: The New Science of Human Relationships* (New York: Macmillan, 2008), 83

Social Intelligence

All emotions are social. So in addition to emotional intelligence, there's social intelligence, the science of human relationships. Goleman[35] proposes two categories within social intelligence: social awareness (what we sense about others) and social facility (what we do with that awareness). (See Exhibit 5.3.)

With any intelligence, there's a range or continuum of expertise or accomplishment. Goleman notes that synchrony and primal empathy are basic, "purely low-road capacities" and empathic accuracy and influence combine both high- and low-road capacities. Importantly, Goleman notes that even though we may consider these soft skills, effective tests and scales exist to assess these intelligences.

The best leaders function at the highest levels of social intelligence. These leaders recognize themselves as part of the community. They're aware of others and are engaged. They embrace the servant leader concept.

As Goleman observes, "socially intelligent leadership starts with being fully present and getting in synch. Once a leader is engaged, then the full panoply of social intelligence can come into play, from sensing how people feel and why, to interacting smoothly enough to move people into a positive state."[36]

And to return to *The Elegance of the Hedgehog*, this time hearing the thoughts of the young girl Paloma, whose name we learn only at the book's end. She has equal voice to Madame Michel, the concierge. Indeed, she and Madame Michel are but the same voice at different ages.

Exhibit 5.3   Social Awareness

Social awareness refers to a spectrum that runs from instantaneously sensing another's inner state, to understanding her feelings and thoughts, to "getting" complicated social situations. It includes:

- Primal empathy: Feeling with others; sensing nonverbal emotional signals.
- Attunement: Listening with full receptivity; attuning to a person.
- Empathic accuracy: understanding another person's thoughts, feelings, and intentions.
- Social cognition: Knowing how the social world works.

Social Facility

Simply sensing how another feels, or knowing what they think or intend, does not guarantee fruitful interactions. Social facility builds on social awareness to allow smooth, effective interactions. The spectrum of social facility includes:

- Synchrony: Interacting smoothly at the nonverbal level.
- Self-presentation: Presenting ourselves effectively.
- Influence: Shaping the outcome of social interactions.
- Concern: Caring about others' needs and acting accordingly.

Source: From *SOCIAL INTELLIGENCE: THE NEW SCIENCE OF HUMAN RELATIONSHIPS* by Daniel Goleman, copyright © 2006 by Daniel Goleman. Used by permission of Bantam Books, a division of Random House, Inc.

Paloma is as lonely and angry as Madame Michel. And both save themselves through each other and through Monsieur Kakuro.

Bemused, Paloma says of Monsieur Kakuro: "It's really pleasant to listen to him talking, even if you don't care about what he's saying, because he is truly talking to you, he is addressing himself to you. This is the first time I have met someone who cares about me when he is talking: he's not looking for approval or disagreement, he looks at me as if to say 'Who are you? Do you want to talk to me? How nice it is to be here with you!' That is what I meant by saying he is polite—this attitude that gives the other person the impression of really being there."[37]

And Madame Michel reprises this same thought later: "When did I first experience the exquisite sense of surrender that is possible only with another person? The peace of mind one experiences on one's own, one's certainty of self in the serenity of solitude, are nothing in comparison to the release and openness and fluency one shared with another, in close companionship. . . ."[38]

Then the art of leadership must incorporate emotional and social intelligences, and people and community functions. And perhaps the art of leadership is the art of humanity and humanness.

Creative Intelligence

And here's another intelligence, possessed by innovative entrepreneurs: creative intelligence. According to researchers Jeffrey H. Dyer, Hal B. Gregersen, and Clayton M. Christensen, innovators are different from typical executives.

The researchers found two themes common to innovators: (1) They actively desire to change the status quo, and (2) they regularly take risks to make that change happen. In fact, innovators "steer entirely clear of a common cognitive bias called the status quo bias—the tendency to prefer an existing state of affairs to alternative ones."[39] In defiance of the status quo, innovators question, observe, experiment, and network more.

Researchers Dyer, Gregersen, and Christensen describe five discovery skills that innovators leverage to create new ideas.[40]

- *Discovery skill #1: Associating.* Associating—the ability to "successfully connect seemingly unrelated questions, problems, or ideas from different fields—is central to the innovator's DNA."[41]

Associating is related to how the brain manages information. The authors explain that the brain is *not* like a dictionary with a high-speed alphabetizing function.

Instead, the brain links or connects words and experiences. So, "the more diverse our experience and knowledge, the more connections the brain can make."[42] And, the more frequently we're exposed to different information and experiences, the more associations our brains make. As Steve Jobs says, "Creativity is connecting things."[43]

- *Discovery skill #2: Questioning.* Questioning—asking the essential and right questions—is part of the innovator's DNA.

How much more needs to be said about asking questions—and figuring out the right questions to ask? Provocative questions. Questions that challenge the status quo. Questions that generate more questions. Revisit Chapter 3, "The First Relationship—Within Your Organization." Check out all the questions throughout this third edition.[44]

- *Discovery skill #3: Observing.* Observing—carefully observing everyone and everything—is another skill of innovators. Innovators watch closely. They pay attention to the most common occurrences, especially when associated with their customers.

- *Discovery skill #4: Experimenting.* Experimenting—"construct[ing] interactive experiences and try[ing] to provoke unorthodox responses to see what insights emerge"[45]—is the fourth discovery skill. Innovators create an innovative corporate culture, encouraging others to participate in the process. Experimentation is risk taking—and risk taking recognizes the inevitability and importance of failure.

Innovators rely on their "courage to innovate"—an active bias against the status quo and an unflinching willingness to take risks—to transform ideas into powerful impact.

From "The Innovator's DNA," by Jeffrey H. Dyer, Hal B. Gregersen, and Clayton M. Christensen, *Harvard Business Review* (December 2009), 66

■ *Discovery skill #5: Networking.* And finally, networking—connecting with different individuals and groups—is the fifth discovery skill of innovators. Networking is such old news. But examine your own networks right now. How diverse are the individuals and groups you connect with, and how often do you do so? How often do you expose yourself to different ideas, beyond your own field and profession?

Of course innovators have lots of ideas, both good and bad. Focus on "lots"; that's what's important. Consider this blog from Seth Godin, marketing guru and all-around great thinker:

> *A few people are afraid of good ideas, ideas that make a difference or contribute in some way. Good ideas bring change; that's frightening.*
>
> *But many people are petrified of bad ideas. Ideas that make us look stupid or waste time or money or create some sort of backlash.*
>
> *The problem is that you can't have good ideas unless you're willing to generate a lot of bad ones.*
>
> *Painters, musicians, entrepreneurs, writers, chiropractors, accountants—we all fail far more than we succeed. We fail at closing a sale or playing a note. We fail at an idea for a series of paintings or the theme for a trade show booth.*
>
> *But we succeed far more often than people who have no ideas at all.*
>
> *Someone asked me where I get all my good ideas, explaining that it takes him a month or two to come up with one and I seem to have more than that. I asked him how many bad ideas he has every month. He paused and said, "None."*
>
> *And there, you see, is the problem.*[46]

Now think about your own organization and yourself, too.

Does your organization value innovation and innovators? What's the level of innovation in your organization?

What's the innovation quotient within your staff and board members? How do you rate yourself as an innovator? How would others rate you? How do you hire for creative intelligence (and emotional and social intelligences, too)? How do you evaluate your colleagues and those you hire and supervise?

What's your organization's plan to identify and hire those with creative intelligence? What's the plan to strengthen the discovery skills in you and your colleagues? For example, build your own associating skill by actively seeking out new experiences—from reading to travel to different music to . . . Well, you get it. Through their research, Dyer et al. found that the more often people tried to "understand, categorize, and store new knowledge, the more easily their brains could naturally and consistently make, store, and recombine associations."[47]

Strengthen your own experimenting skill by examining your own life first. What risks do you take? How do you gain new experiences? Here's a powerful finding from the research by Dyer et al.: Living outside your native country dramatically improves your discovery skills. In fact, "the more countries a person has lived in, the more likely he or she is to leverage that experience to deliver innovative products, processes, or business."[48]

By the way, creativity isn't just about the new and innovative. Creativity also means avoiding your habitual responses and the conventional solutions.[49] Sounds a lot like learning organization theory—learning and change—in Chapter 3.

And how do you manage all this? "Managing creativity involves a series of difficult balancing acts: giving people the freedom to come up with new ideas but making sure that they operate within an overall structure, creating a powerful corporate culture but making sure that it is not too stifling.[50]

How do innovators describe their motives? Jeff Bezos wants to "make history." Steve Jobs wants to "put a ding in the universe." Skype cofounder Kiklas Zennström wants to "be disruptive, but in the cause of making the world a better place."

From "The Innovator's DNA," by Jeffrey H. Dyer, Hal B. Gregersen, and Clayton M. Christensen, *Harvard Business Review* (December 2009), 66

Cultural Intelligence

And there's more: cultural intelligence (CQ).

Cultural intelligence allows individuals (and groups and organizations) to navigate different systems of culture. Culture refers to the beliefs, values, customs, traditions, norms—the way of life—of a group of people. A group's culture describes how its people see things, interact, behave, and make judgments about their world.

We all know that people in other communities[51] may do things differently than we do here, wherever our here is. And if we're visiting or working there, all will go more smoothly if we, the visitor, can observe and interpret the culture, and modify our behavior accordingly. This process is about suspending judgment, welcoming diversity, and being sensitive enough to anticipate the reactions of others.

"A person with high emotional intelligence grasps what makes us human and at the same time what makes each of us different from one another. A person with high cultural intelligence can somehow tease out of a person's or group's behavior those features that would be true of all people and all groups, those peculiar to this person or this group. . . ."[52]

P. Christopher Earley and Elaine Mosakowski present three sources of cultural intelligence:

1. *Cognitive (the head).* You *learn* about the beliefs, customs, and traditions (and taboos) about the other culture.
2. *Physical (the body).* Through your *demeanor and actions*, you show that you have "entered their world." You both "receive and reciprocate gestures that are culturally characteristic."[53]

3. *Emotional/motivational (the heart).* You actually want to do this—and you believe that you can. Interestingly, the authors note that "people who are somewhat detached from their own culture can more easily adopt the mores and even the body language of an unfamiliar host."[54]

I suspect that true leaders possess cultural intelligence, too. I imagine them able to observe and analyze their own lives and cultures, as well as those of others. I believe that true leaders find ways to welcome and feel some comfort in other cultures, amid different experiences. And I expect that true leaders empower their colleagues to develop a level of cultural competence that welcomes pluralism.

By the way, Earley and Mosakowski describe different cultural intelligence profiles (e.g., the provincial, the analyst, and the natural). And they offer a handy little tool to diagnose one's own cultural intelligence.

Leaders as Critical Thinkers

I think. You think. They think. We all think. But how often do we think about thinking and what thinking actually means? Check out the map at www.visualthesaurus.com. Thinking means forming thoughts and making judgments. Thinking links to reasoning and thought process.

Thinking is a mind process where we consider something carefully. And that's the problem, for your mind process or mine. Because a person's mind process is affected by his or her life experience—and that can lead to bias, a very human quandary but a quandary nonetheless.

Egocentric thinking results from the unfortunate fact that humans do not naturally consider the rights and needs of others. We do not naturally appreciate the point of view of others nor the limitations of our own point of view.

From *The Miniature Guide to Critical Thinking, Fifth Edition: Concepts and Tools,* by Dr. Richard Paul and Dr. Linda Elder (Dillon Beach, CA: Foundation for Critical Thinking Press, 2008), 21

Click again on the diagram at www.visualthesaurus.com. "Thought" links to view, sentiment, persuasion, idea, opinion, and belief. All that, too, links to one's own life experience and the focus on the self—one's own ego—and again the possibility of bias.

The risk actually gets worse. Just consider these two definitions from the visual thesaurus: a personal belief or judgment that is not founded on proof or certainty; and any cognitive content held as true.

Call these assumptions or mental models.[55] No matter. Here's the problem we face as human beings: Without conscious intent, much of our thinking is "biased, distorted, partial, uninformed, or down-right prejudiced. Yet the quality of our life and that of what we produce, make, or build depends precisely on the quality of our thought. Shoddy thinking is costly, both in money and quality of life."[56] The good news is that we can improve our thinking; we can think critically. Get help by reading *The Miniature Guide to Critical Thinking: Concepts and Tools* (www.criticalthinking.org).

To paraphrase the authors, critical thinking is both a skill and an art that you and I use to analyze and evaluate our thought process in order to improve it. Critical thinking is "self-directed, self-disciplined, self-monitored, and self-corrective thinking . . . requir[ing] rigorous standards of excellence and mindful command of use."[57] The process of critical thinking demands "effective communication and problem solving abilities and a commitment to overcoming our native egocentrism and sociocentrism."[58]

This highly useful mini guide challenges each of us to think most carefully, to examine our own biases, and to use specific steps to produce critical thinking. Paul and Elder explain the following important information.

- Elements of thought: purpose, question at issue, information, interpretation and inference, concepts, assumptions, implications and consequences, and point of view.
- Description of the essential intellectual traits: intellectual humility versus intellectual arrogance; intellectual courage versus intellectual cowardice, intellectual empathy versus intellectual narrow-mindedness, intellectual autonomy versus intellectual conformity, intellectual integrity versus intellectual hypocrisy, intellectual perseverance versus intellectual laziness, confidence in reason versus distrust of reason and evidence, and fairmindedness versus intellectual unfairness.
- Checklist for reasoning, accompanied by questions to examine our own thinking and criteria that you and I can use to evaluate our reasoning.
- A description of the three levels of thought, which should scare each of us into embracing critical thinking.
- A list of the universal intellectual standards, and questions to help you and me use these standards.
- A template for problem solving: a useful tool in so many situations.
- Tools to analyze and assess research—and more.

Leadership means critical thinking, not just plain thinking with its risk of ego. Leaders are critical thinkers. No critical thinking, no leadership. Leaders learn critical thinking and teach it. Leaders facilitate critical thinking. Leaders overcome bias and help others do the same. Leaders enable others to use critical thinking.

Leaders as Reflective Practitioners

Leaders are reflective practitioners. Leaders create an organizational climate that encourages individual and group reflection. Also, leaders help others develop their capacity for reflection.

"Reflection is the art of listening to our inner voice for insights about a question and accessing intelligence that may go beyond our personal knowledge or experience." So says Robert Gunn.[59]

Gunn reminds us that our thinking creates our reality. He also notes that as humans, we have a unique gift: the power to change our thoughts. As we change our thoughts, so our reality will change. To reflect upon one's history, experience, actions, and their implications helps us understand, and then allows us to create a new future. Reflection can help us create our reality.

As reflective practitioners, leaders have a deep understanding of themselves and strive to understand those around them. These leaders strive to create communities of reflection, thus expanding understanding and learning. As Gunn notes, these leaders serve others as well as themselves.

Gunn proposes a set of questions to help the reflective practitioner become aware of his or her thinking habits:[60]

- Am I responding to my own ego?
- Do I allow myself some quiet time to reflect (or am I booking my schedule fully, going from one project or meeting to the next without a break)?
- Am I asking questions of others to elicit a full understanding of their thoughts or statements?
- Am I thinking in terms of puzzles rather than crises?
- Do I look for blame or innocence in what others tell me?
- Do I spend time thinking about issues or jump to conclusions as rapidly as possible?
- Am I comfortable admitting that I do not know the answer?

Paul Pribbenow,[61] CFRE, speaks and writes about professionals as reflective practitioners. Paul encourages each of us to reflect on the work that we do, to better understand the why, not just the how. Paul challenges us to find ways in which we can become reflective practitioners, committing the time and focus to this important endeavor. And finally, Paul invites us to speak reflectively with each other, with colleagues across the diverse sectors, sharing with and learning from each other.

Leaders as Communicators

Read any business book. The job of leaders is to make information "useful and meaningful to others, as a way of moving them toward committed engagement in [the organization]."[62] That's not much different than the theory that communication is a two-way endeavor and begins with listening.

In *Clicks and Mortar*, Pottruck and Pearce state: "As a leader, every day I try to remember that others will tolerate my point of view, but they will act only on their own. Accordingly, part of my job is to reconcile those points of view, to try to help everyone, including myself, gain a more insightful view of reality. In this work, listening is every bit as critical as speaking. Two-way communication is vital."[63]

But too often people confuse listening as the precursor to answering, rather than listening as a way of learning. How many times have you watched someone prepare his answer while listening to another, rather than truly listening to hear and learn? How often have you done that yourself?

Pottruck and Pearce talk about listening as an "attitude with a single focus: the more I *am known* by those I want to follow me, and the more I *can know* them, the greater will be our ability to do great things together."[64] Approaching listening with this attitude allows the leader to reaffirm that others are "real partners in the enterprise," being heard *and* sharing accountability.

Conscious leaders have the ability to listen simultaneously to three dimensions of language—the factual, the intentional, and the transformational. They pick up factual details with the precision of the scientist, gain insight into the intention of the speaker with the imagination of a poet, and are willing to be transformed by what they hear with the zeal of a pilgrim.

From *Leading Consciously: A Pilgrimage toward Self-Mastery*, by Debashis Chatterjee (Newton, MA: Butterworth-Heinneman, 1998), 113

Pottruck and Pearce note that effective leadership communication incorporates three separate elements: speaking, listening, and engagement. Speaking and listening are learnable skills. But engagement requires a genuine interest in others, a respect for their diversity, and a desire to hear what they feel and believe.

Engaging others does not take away the authority of the leader, nor does engagement compromise the leader's ability to make quick decisions. Leadership is about ongoing conversation and participatory decision-making. Leadership is about making decisions that are best for the whole organization, regardless of any single individual's opinion.

As Pottruck says, "Even as I encourage dialogue and listen carefully to everyone who contributes, my responsibility is to make decisions that are best for the whole . . . and to continue to have the participation of those who disagree with me. It requires that I understand other people's points of view—and that I can acknowledge our differences."[65]

People make a commitment to their leader. Indeed, there are no leaders without followers; and to be a follower, one commits to a leader.

Pottruck and Pearce wrestle with the relationship between the leader and follower. They turn to business coach and author Noel Tichy.[66] Tichy explains that people seeking to commit need basic information to make their decision. And people constantly seek reinforcement of that basic information throughout their lives in the organization.

And what is this basic information? People want to know *who* the leader is and *where* the organization is going. They expect the leader to answer these questions well, and to answer them again and again. Pottruck and Pearce add another element of basic information: *why* the organization is going there. So leaders communicate who they are personally, where the organization is going, and why it is going there. Leaders do this over and over, in ways that can be heard and understood by their colleagues.

By the way, one final thought about leaders and communication—from colleague Gary Kelsey:[67] "Don't mistake leadership for strong talking."

The day [people] stop bringing you their problems is the day you have stopped leading them. They have either lost confidence that you can help them or concluded that you do not care.

From *My American Journey*, by General Colin Powell, U.S. Army (Ret.) (New York: Random House, 1995), 52

Chaordic Leadership: Understanding Complexity

Some say that understanding complexity is the principal science of the future. And just what is complexity? It's "autocatalytic, nonlinear, complex adaptive systems."[68]

Many believe that these systems—even life itself (remember the movie *Jurassic Park* and chaos theory?)—"arise and thrive on the edge of chaos with just enough order to give them pattern."[69]

Hock coined the term "chaord" to describe what he means by "any self-organizing, self-governing, adaptive, nonlinear, complex organism, organization, community, or system, whether physical, biological, or social, the behavior of which harmoniously blends characteristics of both chaos and order."[70] His new term combines portions of the words *chaos* and *order*.

For Hock, organizations are chaordic and hence require a new form of leadership. He observes that an organization harmoniously blends conflicting characteristics such as competition and cooperation or theoretical and experiential learning. In some ways, this complex or chaordic blending is reminiscent of the intentional choice fostered in Collins and Porras's *Built to Last*.[71] Avoid the "tyranny of the 'or.'" Instead, embrace the "genius of the 'and.'"

Collins and Porras stress that visionary companies avoid choosing between two apparent paradoxes (e.g., change *or* stability, low cost *or* high quality, and so forth). Instead, organizations that are built to last welcome two "seemingly contradictory forces or ideas at the same time." In other words, these organizations accept and tolerate Hock's theory of the chaord.

Leaders and Followers

Chaordic organizations require chaordic leadership. For Hock, this means a different understanding of the relationship between the leader and follower, yet another dichotomy.

Leaders and followers require each other to exist, and both presume choice. Any coercion is merely a form of manipulation. If a follower is coerced—even following willingly the dominance of the leader—then she is no longer a follower. Neither the follower nor the leader can be bound one to the other. Hock observes, "Where behavior is compelled, there you will find tyranny, however benign."[72] For Hock, the leader/follower relationship reflects, instead, induced behavior.

Everyone agrees that leadership is not always ethical, open, and constructive. Everyone seems to know a leader who induces destructive behavior, and does so through unethical and even corrupt ways. If you cannot find one such leader close to home today, just look at history. There you will find any number of examples of leaders and followers choosing to work together in ways harmful to others.

But surely when we think of leadership, we aspire to an ethical, constructive, open behavior that generates positive results for the good of many. This leadership requires leaders who are ethical and honest, trustworthy and open. Hock challenges us with the question: How do we make sure that our leaders are ethical, honest, trustworthy, and open? His answer is simple: Follow only those who are!

Hock reminds us all: "True leaders are those who epitomize the general sense of the community—who symbolize, legitimize, and strengthen behavior in accordance with the sense of the community—who enable its shared purpose, values, and beliefs to emerge and be transmitted. A true leader's behavior is induced by the behavior of every individual choosing where to be led. The important thing to remember is that true leadership and induced behavior have an inherent tendency to the good, while tyranny (dominator management) and compelled behavior have an inherent tendency to evil."[73]

Hock brings us back to the inextricable link between leader and follower, the partnership of the individual and the collective. Leadership is about our shared sense—shared between leader and follower—of our values and mission, vision and direction. As Hock says, followers lead by choosing whom to follow. Leaders lead with an understanding of and commitment to their followers.

In the deepest sense, distinction between leaders and followers is meaningless. In every moment of life, we are simultaneously leading and following. There is never a time when our knowledge, judgment, and wisdom are not more useful and applicable than that of another. There is never a time when the knowledge, judgment, and wisdom of another are not more useful and applicable than ours. At any time that "other" may be superior, subordinate, or peer.

From "The Art of Chaordic Leadership," by Dee Hock, *Leader to Leader* (Winter 2000), 24

What Chaordic Leaders Do

So what do chaordic leaders do? Hock proposes four things.

- First and most important, manage yourself. By this he means your own integrity, character, ethics, knowledge and wisdom, temperament, words, and acts.
- Second, manage those who have authority over you. Manage your own boss or supervisor or director or regulator—whomever—to ensure their consent and support. Without their consent and support, no leader can exercise his own judgment, follow his own conviction, innovate and enable others, or achieve results.
- Third, manage your peers. That's right, manage those over whom you have no authority and who have no authority over you. Manage these relationships well

so your associates—whether inside or outside the organization—respect and have confidence in you and your behavior, words, and deeds.

- And fourth, manage those who report to you. But Hock claims that if you manage yourself, your superiors, and your peers, there won't be enough time to manage your subordinates—and that's great! Hock summarizes in this way: "One need only select decent people, introduce them to the concept, induce them to practice it, and enjoy the process. If those over whom we have authority properly manage themselves, manage us, manage their peers, and replicate the process with those they employ, what is there to do but see they are properly recognized and rewarded—and stay out of their way?"[74]

Hock acknowledges the obvious question in his litany of whom leaders manage: How is it that we manage our superiors and peers? His answer: You cannot.

It is simply not possible to manage your superiors and peers. But you can understand them and inform them. You can motivate them and cause them to question. You can influence and persuade them. You can set an example. Hock even suggests that you can forgive them. And for Dee Hock, all this is, indeed, leading them.

And what about managing yourself? That is, perhaps, the easiest and hardest leadership task of all. But this is where each of us has the greatest power. Think about it. What prevents you from managing yourself? What prevents me?

To paraphrase Hock, surely there are no rules or regulations that can stop us. There is no hierarchy and there are no bosses that can prevent us from behaving in the way that we choose. Sure, others can make it difficult sometimes. But finally, each of us has the power.

No individual and no organization, short of killing us, can prevent such use of our energy, ability, and ingenuity. They may make it more difficult, but they can't prevent it. The real power is ours, not theirs, provided only that we can work our way around the killing.

From "The Art of Chaordic Leadership," by Dee Hock, *Leader to Leader* (Winter 2000), 23

Connective Leadership

Everyone talks about the increased interdependence inherent in the world of today and tomorrow. This interdependence is driven largely by technology, once television and now the Internet and social media. Everyone is connected to everything everywhere. The free flow of information and citizen communication makes everything more transparent—whether organizations want it so or not. It's easier for our constituents—whether employees, clients, donors, board members, or other volunteers—to watch what we say, what we actually do, and how well the two match.

All this is about access and alignment. And interdependence drives organizations into the continuum of collaboration—from communication and knowledge alliances to networking and coalitions, from collaboration and joint ventures to merger. But even with interdependence, diversity remains valuable. The best organizations foster both.

Jean Lipman-Blumen notes that diversity refers to the different characteristics of individuals, groups, and organizations. Diversity reflects "the human need for identity, diversity highlights everyone's uniqueness, underscoring differences and emphasizing independence and individualism. It is a force for social, economic, and cultural differentiation."[75]

These two—interdependence and diversity—distinguish what Lipman-Blumen calls the "connective era." She notes that "the importance of diversity and the inevitability of interdependence require a more fully developed leadership repertoire."[76] Connective leaders discern and understand the connections between diverse people, experiences, ideas, and organizations. These leaders perceive the overlap, reinforce the commonalities, and expand the common ground.

Lipman-Blumen notes that connective leaders "negotiate, persuade, and integrate antagonistic groups. They reach out to long-standing adversaries in order to accomplish mutual goals. . . . They construct and call upon social networks and multiple, shifting coalitions. They open these networks to colleagues. They seek active constituents, unshackled by orthodoxy, who can share the burdens of leadership but feel free not to support the leader's every issue."[77]

Leadership Strengths

In this connective era—balancing interdependence and diversity—Lipman-Blumen describes six important leadership strengths.

1. *Ethical political savvy.*
   Connective leaders possess lots of savvy to use everything possible to accomplish goals, including people and resources. And connective leaders use this "political savvy" in an ethical, altruistic, and transparent manner.
2. *Authenticity and accountability.*
   Authenticity refers to the leader's dedication to the group and the purposes of the group. Authenticity establishes the leader's credibility and reinforces the followers' faith. For Lipman-Blumen, authenticity helps the leader's constituents discern whether changes in behavior are due to waffling or due to an increased understanding of a situation.
   Accountability is authenticity's "twin imperative." To be accountable to others means that we explain our decisions and actions and accept our obligation to the others. Leaders accept their accountability, subjecting themselves to examination by their constituents. In the connective era—where everything is known and seen—connective leaders operate transparently, with maximum disclosure.
3. *Politics of commonalties.*
   In other words, the connective leader builds community. Strong community allows for the simultaneous flourishing of interdependence and diversity.
4. *Thinking long-term, acting short-term.*
   Building community is about keeping it all going. Regardless of today's issues and performance measures, leaders keep an eye on the future. Leaders make

decisions that are best for the future even when it means choosing against current demands.

Building community is also about ensuring a legacy for the future. That's why leaders put aside their own egos, surround themselves with the best people, and find the best people to replace them when necessary.

5. *Leadership through expectation.*

Connective leaders enable others. Lipman-Blumen notes that these leaders "stand back and rely upon the principle of reciprocation, whereby the gift of the leader's confidence is usually repaid by the constituent's outstanding performance."[78] Connective leaders encourage creativity and questioning, requiring only that their colleagues behave in ethical and legal ways.

6. *A quest for meaning.*

As a leader, you are measured by your ability to influence others, your ability to help others make a difference. Finally, that is your legacy. "In reconciling the forces of interdependence and diversity, [connective leaders] invite those around them to join their quest for greater meaning. By calling supporters to change the world for the better, connective leaders present constituents with elevating opportunities. They also stand as shining examples."[79]

Behavioral Foundations

Lipman-Blumen describes the behavioral foundations of connective leadership as three major sets of achieving styles: direct, relational, and instrumental. Each set has three broad strategies whereby an individual can accomplish her goals.[80] The best connective leaders choose between the various styles, personalized to the situation or circumstance.

1. *Achieving style: direct* (closely linked to diversity, the force of the individual):
   - Intrinsic: Individual derives satisfaction from mastering own tasks compared to internal standards of excellence.
   - Competitive: Individual derives satisfaction from outdoing others, comparing performance against external standards.
   - Power: Individual takes charge, and delegates to and coordinates others.
2. *Achieving style: relational* (closely linked to interdependence, working together):
   - Collaborative: Individual works with others, sharing responsibility for action and results.
   - Contributory: Individual works behind the scenes helping others to complete activities.
   - Vicarious: Individual derives satisfaction from facilitating, coaching, and observing the accomplishments of others.
3. *Achieving style: instrumental* (linked to political savvy):
   - Personal: Individual uses all her personal assets (intelligence, wit, personal background, etc.) to attract supporters.
   - Social: Individual creates social networks and uses these and others to accomplish shared goals.
   - Entrusting: Individual relies on others to enhance shared vision, doing so without supervision but with strong expectations for success.

Connective leaders understand and support this new era. They develop their leadership strengths and carefully use the achieving styles and strategies.

Is Charisma Essential to Leadership?

Absolutely not. Just read *Built to Last* for documented proof.

The dictionary defines *charisma* as "a personal magic of leadership arousing special popular loyalty or enthusiasm for a public figure; a specific magnetic charm or appeal." As usual, watch the morphing at www.visualthesaurus.com. But charisma does not guarantee substance, and leaders have substance. Take a look at those whom you would describe as charismatic. Are they necessarily good leaders or are they simply engaging and somehow magical?

Now take a look at the individuals you respect as leaders. Is it charisma that encourages you to follow these leaders or is it their ability to influence you with meaningful information? Is it charisma that inspires you or is it the leader's ability to communicate values and involve you in dialogue?

The quality of leaders matters less than the quality of citizens.

—George Scialabba, a book critic living in Cambridge, Massachusetts, whose reviews appear in such publications as the *Nation*, the *American Prospect*, and the *Boston Globe*

Consider this definition for leadership, modified from the U.S. Marine Corps manual (note there is no reference to charisma): Leadership is the art of influencing and directing people in such a way as to obtain their willing support, confidence, respect, and loyal cooperation to accomplish a mission.

P.S. Does Leadership Guarantee Success?

That depends on your definition of success. Winning? Money? Results? Recognition? Or do you subscribe to John Wooden's definition, included in Chapter 3: "Success is peace of mind, which is a direct result of self satisfaction in knowing you made the effort to do the best of which you are capable."

Apparently that's how Wooden coached, focusing on doing your best with no mention of winning. Wooden developed a pyramid of success.[81] Elements of his pyramid include: poise, confidence, condition, skills, team spirit, self-control, alertness, initiative, industriousness, friendship, loyalty, cooperation, and enthusiasm. He worked on his concept for 14 years and completed it in 1948, way before his basketball fame. In fact, his fame might more reasonably be called extraordinary respect and admiration beyond basketball, expanded to business and life philosophy.

So leaders are coaches, said before in this chapter. Leaders define success in broader terms than money and recognition. Leaders define winning and results differently, too—more like Wooden defines success. Here's a question to explore: Can leadership guarantee success when you define success so differently?

Summary

So there you have it—thoughts on leadership. Now it's up to you. Read and talk about leadership. Develop your own leadership. Help others develop their leadership.

With good leadership, you build a stronger organization. With expanded leadership, you can create a sustainable organization. Leadership is one of the key components of relationship within your organization.

And without leadership . . . are you slowly going out of business?

Never forget: Leadership is about more than your organization and its success, or even your own success. Think bigger and broader. Think about the local and global community.

And ask yourself this one, final question: "Should leaders wait to be invited?"

It was one of those cage-rattling moments that often happen in my classrooms at Saint Mary's University of Minnesota. This time, thanks to Ann Hermes, Mary Miller McCrae, Wendy Zufelt-Baxter, and Carolyn Egeberg, members of Cohort 15.

"Is part of our job as leaders to 'unblind' people? To reveal issues relevant to group effectiveness? To make the invisible visible—things like unearned privilege, unacknowledged group dynamics, elements in the room, and skeletons in the closet?

"Or is this appropriate only when invited?"

What was their response to this question they identified?

"Yes, the leader is responsible to 'unblind' others. Yes, the leader must reveal issues relevant to group effectiveness."

"Yes," these four said. "Leaders make the invisible visible, with or without invitation. Yes," they said, "even without invitation."

Yes, leaders must "unblind" people. Because the most essential and cage-rattling questions too often remain invisible. Because that which is invisible may be so secret and so scary that others will not or cannot take the risk.

Leaders take the risk. Leaders exist to take the risk for others.

CHAPTER 6

The Second Relationship—With Your Community

Ensuring Your Organization's Relevance through Strategic Planning

A company is not a machine but a living organism. Much like an individual, it can have a collective sense of identity and fundamental purpose. This is the organizational equivalent of self knowledge—a shared understanding of what the company stands for, where it's going, what kind of world it wants to live in, and most importantly, how it intends to make that world a reality.
—Ikujiro Nonaka, "The Knowledge Creating Company,"
Harvard Business Review (November–December 1991)

For a football team to function as an intelligent organism rather than as a group of individuals, the players need to take advantage of not only the fact that they have a stronger potential together than one by one, but also that they have different competencies and skills as individuals. This, in turn, requires that the players create shared mental models about football. To merge the different skills of all the players into an effective whole, they need to have exactly the same overall perception of what the game is all about—the non-negotiable set of rules for football.

—Karl-Henrik Robèrt, *The Natural Step: Simplicity without Reductionism*
(Stockholm: The Natural Step Environmental Institute)

Make Sure Your Organization Is Relevant to the Community

Your organization's relevance to the community significantly affects your ability to fundraise. More importantly, your organization's relevance to the community justifies your organization's existence. And the process of strategic planning defines—and can renew—your relevance.

Think of it this way: Your organization's internal relations—what I call the first relationship—provides the foundation for good fund development. Strategic planning—the second relationship—provides the framework for good fund development.

Strategic planning defines your relationship with the community and provides the frame for all other organizational activities. Just ask yourself: How can we raise money without knowing:

- Why our organization matters—and what results we produce that make a difference.
- Where we are going—and why that direction.
- How we will get there by doing what.
- How much it will cost.
- How all this fits in with community needs and priorities.
- How our organization fits in with other groups in the community.
- Who might be interested in the needs we meet and the results we produce.

An organization's strategic plan establishes direction. The written plan clarifies where the organization is going, how it will get there, and why gifts will help. The plan generally describes a vision for the future and a blueprint for action. With this delineation of vision, direction, and action, the fundraiser can seek charitable contributions.

But strategic planning is more than a written document and a road map. Effective strategic planning is a process that brings about organizational commitment and alignment, and produces organizational learning and change. The planning process is a way of thinking and acting. An organization that thinks strategically and acts accordingly is better positioned for everything, including fund development.

Effective strategic planning is designed to answer the big-picture questions, questions like:

- What are we doing now? Who are our customers? What do they value? What has been the outcome of our work?
- What is happening in the world outside our organization? What are the implications for the work that we do and might do, and how we do it?
- What needs are being met, and who is meeting these needs? How do we cooperate and collaborate with these organizations? What needs are not being met? Might we have the capability and wish to respond to any of these needs? Could we build alliances and collaborate to meet the needs?
- What is our unique contribution to the community—and why does this matter and to whom?
- What is our vision for the future? Will we change who we are? What is our business? Who will be our customers? What do they value? Who will be our collaborators? What knowledge alliances will we need?
- What will be the outcome of our work? How will we achieve this?
- How will we move from where we are today to our vision of the future? What are our strategies to move forward? How will we organize to do the work? Who will do what in what general time frames? How will we measure success?
- How much will all this cost, and how will we finance our endeavors?
- How will we ensure that we are accountable?

Strategic planning should also strengthen your fund development by:

- Assessing the productivity and effectiveness of fund development activities.
- Evaluating board, staff, and volunteer understanding of and performance in fund development.
- Developing and enhancing relationships with donors and prospects.
- Targeting areas of stakeholder interest.
- Identifying fund development themes.
- Increasing the organization's visibility.
- Building board and staff understanding of how the organization fits within the community and the fund development and volunteer marketplace.

Avoiding or Compromising Strategic Planning

Strategic planning—which includes strategic thinking and acting—is part of doing business. Actually, planning is the central business function from which all other functions evolve. Effective strategic planning produces learning and change.

Despite its obvious benefits, organizations don't always embrace the process. Some organizations avoid planning altogether. They claim:

- "There isn't enough time."
- "We are so busy (and threatened) that we must focus on the here and now."
- "We know who we are and our mission is clear. We don't need to do strategic planning."
- "We are a strong organization. Nothing is wrong. Not much has changed. We're headed in the right direction."

Many organizations try the quick version of planning. These groups acknowledge some need for a plan but deny the value of a planning process. For example, these organizations might:

- Conduct a one-day retreat with the board of directors and bang out a plan.
- Put together a small group of key leaders and let them recommend direction and action to the board.
- Expect staff to plan and present the plan for board review.

Some organizations focus on programs only when planning. These organizations look at mission but ignore the infrastructure—those critical supporting systems like management and governance, fund development, marketing and communications, physical plant, and information systems.

Don't kid yourself. Strategic planning is all about motion and change. Indeed, the best strategic planning teaches organizations and people to think and move continually.

Still others say that organizations should not do strategic planning. These individuals say that planning is too binding and inhibits thinking and acting. Instead, perpetual motion and quick change are best.

Certainly perpetual motion and well-thought-out change are essential in the world of yesterday, today, and tomorrow. But how do organizations develop this capacity and know which change to embrace? Organizations learn through ongoing and continual planning, thinking, and acting. This is a leadership attitude, a corporate culture, and a key component of your organization's internal systems and processes. Just look back at Chapter 3, "The First Relationship—Within Your Organization."

Planning for the Future While Operating Today

Strategic planning for the future is so important that every organization, no matter its size, experience, or longevity, can likely benefit.

However, planning for the future occurs in tandem with current operations. While you plan, you also carry out your business. Since planning is an ongoing process, your organization implements a plan and evaluates its progress while you prepare the plan for the next interval.

Expect that a comprehensive strategic planning process will require at least six months of concentrated effort. From the moment your organization launches the process to the time you adopt the plan, as much as a year could pass. The board of directors, chief executive officer, and key staff will all be involved. Other staff and key constituents also play a role.

Here are some cautions as you plan and operate simultaneously:

- Do not launch major new initiatives while you are planning. Instead, consider these initiatives as possible choices within the strategic planning process.
- If a unique opportunity arises and a decision cannot wait until the planning process is completed, assess the opportunity very carefully. While you may need to launch this new activity before the planning process is finished, apply the information you have already learned in the planning process.
- During the planning process, you may identify infrastructure issues that demand immediate attention. If immediate attention is necessary, refer these issues to the appropriate group (e.g., management or board) for action.

It's all very well planning what you will do in six months, what you will do in a year, but it's no good at all if you don't have a plan for tomorrow.

From *Wolf Hall: A Novel*, by Hilary Mantel (New York: Henry Holt, 2009)

What Makes Planning Work

There are many different versions of strategic long-range planning: standard tactics and cutting-edge techniques, bells and whistles, and assorted models with various components. The key is to tailor the process to meet your organization's needs and resources.

Nine factors that contribute to a viable planning process and meaningful plan are:

1. The right planning process tailor-made to your organization.
2. Involvement of those who will be affected by the plan.
3. Critical mass of leaders who support the planning process and will guide the resulting plan.
4. Accomplished manager for the planning process.
5. Commitment of time to carry out the process, balanced with adequate pace to maintain forward momentum.
6. Receptivity to new information and willingness to change.
7. Adequate and appropriate information upon which to make decisions.
8. Ongoing critical thinking and behavior.
9. Ability of your organization to dialogue, argue, decide, and then align.

Notice that items 6 to 9 are described as core components of your organization's internal relations in Chapter 3, "The First Relationship." Quite frankly, strategic planning is not particularly effective unless that first relationship—within your organization—is in place.

Everything in Chapter 3 relates to strategic planning—from values to participatory decision-making, from questioning to conversation, from consensus to change. Everything. And if your intent is to develop that first relationship through strategic planning, go for it. But be prepared for a difficult process.

Defining the Process and Benefits for Your Organization

Planning determines your direction and devises strategies to move you forward. Through planning, you clarify your values, test your mission, and articulate a vision—all powerful enough to engage the hearts and minds of all people within your organization. The process itself produces valuable dissonance, which forces individuals and groups to look into themselves. And those who are not engaged by the values, mission, and vision then leave.

The best strategic planning means systems thinking, individual and organization learning, and strategic action. To plan well, you see the whole and the interconnections of its parts. To survive, effective organizations learn. To progress, you act strategically. Again, look back at Chapter 3 for further discussion of systems thinking and learning organizations.

Good planning is both a process and a product, both an attitude and a behavior. The planning process is as important as the resulting plan, perhaps more important. The process informs the organization, builds investment, mobilizes participants, and leads change. The planning process must be sufficiently comprehensive while maintaining momentum to reach completion.

In this book, strategic, long-range, and business planning are synonymous. "Strategic" suggests the big picture and a flexibility and responsiveness to the environment. "Long-range" connotes a time frame of multiple years. "Business" outlines how the work will be implemented, financed, and evaluated.

Planning demands honest dialogue and difficult decision-making. This is tough stuff. The process identifies and challenges the most critical and sacred assumptions of the organization and its members, including the relevance of your mission. Good planning actually rewards individuals for raising difficult issues and asking hard questions.

Planning is the creative act of synthesizing experiences into a novel strategy.

From "The Rise and Fall of Strategic Planning," by Henry Mintzberg, *Harvard Business Review* (January–February 1994)

Decision-making relies on information gathered, insights provided from experience, and critical self-assessment. The organization explores different opportunities and examines the consequences of possible choices systemwide.

Strategic planning always involves those who will be affected by the plan. Whether they are clients, staff, volunteers, donors, or community leaders, these constituents have a stake in the decisions of the organization. That's why we call them stakeholders.

Strategic planning cannot really forecast the future. Oh, if only it could! But the world is too complex and uncertain. Instead, strategic planning tries first to understand multiple possible futures. Second, through planning, the organization learns how to respond robustly to different alternative futures. And third, through ongoing strategic thinking and planning, the organization builds its own capacity to adapt.

In summary, strategic planning makes sure that your organization clearly knows its shared purpose and destiny. *The Fifth Discipline Fieldbook: Strategies and Tools for Building a Learning Organization*[1] notes that shared purpose and destiny include vision, values, mission, and goals.

Think in these terms:

- Vision is an image of an organization's desired future. Vision describes where an organization wants to go and what it will look like when it arrives. Vision is tangible. Its sense of immediacy helps direct your organization and its members.
- Values indicate how an organization expects to get where it is going. Values describe how the organization intends to operate and behave. The *Fieldbook* describes values as: "If we act as we should, what would an observer see us doing? How would we be thinking?"

    Values really are the start of it all. Life starts with values: yours and those with whom you connect. Organizations start with values, articulated or not.

    A group of people—or even one person—starts out with a sense of what matters and why it matters and what can be done. Those basic beliefs, that fundamental philosophy, stimulate mission and vision. It's values that start organizations, certainly nonprofits and often for-profits, too.
- Mission or purpose describes what your organization is here to do. It is rare that an organization ever achieves its purpose.

    But how wonderful that would be, wouldn't it? To achieve one's purpose. To close the homeless shelter because there are no more homeless. To celebrate the end of the literacy center because everyone now can read.

- Goals[2] are "the milestones we expect to reach before too long."[3] They should be challenging, but at the same time realistic and achievable.

Is Your Organization Relevant?

You can't really answer that. Only the community can. That's what strategic planning will do for you.

First and foremost, effective strategic planning ensures your organization's relevance. Planning justifies your existence by defining your meaning to the community (I call that your relationship with the community) and by defining your position in the marketplace. Finally, the resulting long-range strategic plan provides the framework for your fund development.

Through effective planning, your organization reaches out to the community, examining its relevance to the community. Organization leaders forgo their own opinions and desires, turning first to the community.

Organization leaders are stewards, caretakers of the public trust. But too often, organization leaders focus on their own opinions, experiences, and desires. Instead, these leaders should be executing an objective planning process that turns to the community. These leaders are expected to assure the organization's relevancy rather than focus on the organization's desires, needs, and turf.

The process of planning makes your organization more effective and helps ensure your survival. Or the planning process shows you aren't relevant, aren't sustainable, and should close. That's an okay result, too. Now you can close carefully and graciously.

Strategic Planning at Royal Dutch Shell

Here's a wonderful example of effective strategic planning carried out by Royal Dutch Shell in the early 1980s. Because of this planning process, the company moved from the bottom of the seven major oil companies to become one of the top two. Arie de Geus, then head of Shell's planning, explained what happened.[4]

The planning team looked for businesses around the world that had survived over the long term. Only a few had survived more than the average of 30 to 50 years. Those companies that had lasted longer possessed four common attributes.

- First, the companies were sensitive to the world around them. Their leaders were aware and active in the world in which they lived. They were looking outward.

   Peter Drucker calls this external focus one of the basic rules. "Focus your people, and especially your executives, to be on the outside often enough to know what the institution exists for. There are no results inside an institution. There are only costs. Yet it is easy to become absorbed in the inside and to become insulated from reality. Effective [organizations] make sure that their people get out in the field and actually work there again and again."[5] See also

Chapter 3, which talks about external focus and its role in adaptive capacity and making change.

- Second, these long-lasting companies each had a sense of cohesion and company identity. Employees and management understood what the company stood for and what it did. People willingly committed to the company values.
- Third, these companies changed successfully by fully using decentralized systems and structures. Slowly, carefully, and incrementally, these companies diversified. They developed new portfolios of service and product in response to the changing world.

  The enduring companies had a high tolerance for pluralism and diversity, both inside and outside the company. According to de Geus, the surviving companies "accepted activities in the margin" and took risks.

- Fourth, the handful of companies that survived longer than average were conservative in their financing. They knew the value of dollars in hand: allowing flexibility and options. De Geus commented that a surviving company is in any business that allows it to survive. If an organization changes its portfolio, it scuttles assets and that's okay. Assets are expendable capital and profits are not a top priority.

Through strategic planning, Royal Dutch Shell learned what all organizations must learn, even nonprofits/NGOs.

- First, the world is complex, impermanent, and pluralistic. Because this is an unstable, uncertain, and uncontrollable environment, organizations must have high tolerance for openness and diversity to survive.

  Organizations that are centralized, controlled from the top, ignorant of the environment, and intolerant of diversity will not survive. They haven't survived in the past, they aren't surviving now, and they certainly won't survive in the future.

- Second, successful organizations understand that the purpose of any planning or plan is to achieve constructive change. Change is a prerequisite for success. The process of planning is the catalyst for change, altering the way an organization thinks about itself, its community, and the larger world.

The ability to learn faster than your competitors may be the only sustainable competitive advantage.

From "Planning as Learning," by Arie P. de Geus, *Harvard Business Review* (March–April 1988)

Strategic Planning Produces Learning, and Learning Produces Change

Change requires information, learning, and innovation. Innovation involves intuition, information, and creativity. Peter Drucker notes that successful innovation depends on seeing change as an opportunity rather than a threat. He goes on to observe that, when faced with change, one of the common mistakes is repairing the old rather than seeking the new.

It has been said that there is no such thing as a new idea; there are only old ideas that can be used in new contexts or configurations. Perhaps, then, organizational creativity identifies new contexts and configurations for the old ideas that add value to your organization.

High-level, effective, and continuous institutional learning produces organizational change. Philip J. Carroll, a former president and CEO of Shell Oil Company, calls learning "the fulcrum for change."[6] Arie de Geus notes that organizations learn as they make decisions because "people change their own mental models and build up a joint model as they talk."[7]

The problem, observes de Geus, is how slowly organizations learn. Too slowly, he claims, for a world where learning faster is an advantage. An organization's most relevant learning is done by those people with the power to act. And the purpose of planning, says de Geus, is to change the mental models of decision-makers, not to make plans.

This is really important: The purpose of planning is to cause people—especially organizational leaders—to change their own mental models. Remember mental models, those pesky but human assumptions we all have, often need, and too often embrace past the expiration date?

In that one little statement, de Geus reminds us that strategic planning is all about systems thinking and learning organization theories. Strategic planning is about helping people challenge their own assumptions and those of others—and that is critical thinking, discussed in Chapter 5.

Effective organizations produce change when they understand the environment and themselves. These organizations recognize and react to environmental change before they are in crisis.

Unfortunately, according to de Geus, it typically takes 12 to 18 months for an organization to act on information received. The organization learns, but with such delay that the learning may be useless. The thought arises: Is the organization slowly going out of business?

The challenge, then, is to accelerate learning by organizations. Strategic planning helps. Effective planning enhances organizational learning. Conversely, learning organizations do more effective strategic planning.

De Geus observes that the learning of the group is much harder to accomplish than that of its individual members. "The level of thinking that goes on in the management teams of most companies is considerably below the individual managers' capacities. In institutional learning situations, the learning level of the team is often the lowest common denominator."[8]

The process of planning produces commitment. Commitment is a personal choice and no one can demand it from another. Once made, commitment can be a powerful catalyst for change.

Effective planning mobilizes the enthusiasm, investment, and action of your board of directors, staff, volunteers, clients, and the community. When invited to participate in creating something one truly cares about, people are usually willing to change. It is said that to accomplish change, 17 percent of your staff must support the change effort and direction. Further, for every 100 employees, studies show that it requires 10 months for change to happen. See the results of effective planning, outlined in Exhibit 6.1.

Exhibit 6.1   Eight Key Results Produced by an Effective Strategic Planning Process

1. Determine shared vision and direction of your organization and define how to get there.
   - Test validity of your mission and perhaps recommend adjustments or major change.
   - Determine priorities and set limits.
   - Define strategies and measures.
2. Justify your organization's existence in the community and clarify your organization's position in the marketplace.
   - Assess community needs.
   - Identify responses to meet those needs and gaps in meeting those needs so that your organization can choose what it will be and do.
   - Examine institutional capacity and capability to meet the needs.
3. Identify stakeholders and build stronger relationships with them.
   - Identify new stakeholders.
   - Bring current stakeholders closer to the organization.
   - Build stakeholder understanding of community needs and your organization's response.
4. Build an aligned, cohesive organization.
   - Engage the hearts and minds of those closest to the organization.
   - Produce positive experiences for participants.
   - Foster shared vision, ownership, and teamwork.
   - Bring stakeholders closer together and give permission for others to move on.
   - Mobilize people for investment of time, money, and action.
   - Clarify roles and relationships and distribute workload.
   - Build cross-functional bridges.
5. Build a learning organization.
   - Encourage pluralism.
   - Develop individual and team skills.
   - Foster flexibility within a general direction.
   - Encourage critical thinking and creativity.
   - Enable the organization to use its strengths for comparative advantage and to mobilize against threats.
   - Develop capacity to detect and respond to changes in the internal and external environments.
   - Create a forum for conversation, dialogue, and improved decision-making.
6. Identify the cost of doing business and the resources available to do the work.
   - Justify fund development.
   - Create the case for support.

7. Define measures for success and set benchmarks for achievement.
   - Define accountability.
   - Outline measures for success, benchmarks of achievement, and the evaluation process.
   - Establish general time frames.
8. Produce the best planning process and written plan.
   - Annualize the plan, its priorities, financing, and benchmarks.
   - Guide annual work plans and budgeting for staff, board, and other volunteers.
   - Support staff and board performance assessment.

Components of the Written Plan

The process of planning produces a written document, the blueprint for organization direction and action. The strategic plan directs all other plans within the organization, including your financial plan (the budget) and your fund development plan. (For example, compare the Steel Yard's multiyear long-range strategic plan and its fund development plan, Appendices 6-M and 9-F.)

The plan serves as a key tool to assess institutional health and your relationship with the community. Progress of the strategic plan is the single most critical factor to evaluate the CEO's effectiveness. The strategic plan also helps define the performance goals and assessment of other staff—and the board of directors and its committees, as well.

Each plan has its own personality and format relevant to the particular organization. What should be in your written strategic plan? Here's one example:

- Statement of values and mission.
- Description of future vision.
- Goals (program and infrastructure) for the multiyear period (duration of plan).
- Indicators of success (sometimes called measures or critical success factors).
- Strategies or action steps to achieve the goals.
- General time frames and key assignments of responsibility.
- Multiyear financial projections and/or narrative explaining the financing approach.
- Process to monitor progress, evaluate performance, and extend the plan.

Your institution's strategic plan is critical to fund development effectiveness and success. Moreover, your strategic planning process is fundamental to a healthy and effective organization.

Of course, there are other ways to write your plan, a different table of contents, so to speak. For example, here are the five sections that Seth Godin wants in the "modern business plan":[9]

Part 1: Truth. "Describe the world as it is ... the market, the needs that already exist, the competitors ... technology standards, the way others have succeeded and failed in the past." And what makes the truth section even better? More specifics. More "ground knowledge." More "visceral stories." For Seth, the point of this section is "to be sure that you're clear about the way you see the world, and that you and I agree on your assumptions. This section isn't partisan, it takes no positions, it just states how things are."

Part 2: Assertions. Here's where you describe how you're going to change things. "This is the heart of the modern business plan. The only reason to launch a project is to change something, and I want to know what you're going to do and what impact it's going to have." Seth is smart. He doesn't have unreasonable expectations. In fact, he specifically says this section will be incorrect. "You will make assertions that won't pan out. You'll miss budgets and deadlines. . . . So the alternatives section tells me what you'll do if that happens."

Part 3: Alternatives. Think about this as the scenarios section. You project multiple scenarios and pick one or two. Or maybe you keep multiple scenarios in the plan. See scenario planning, Exhibit 6.2.

Part 4: People. You might think of this as the core competencies—the capacity and capability. Seth focuses on attitudes, abilities, and track record.

Part 5: Money. How much will the plan cost and how will you finance it? For nonprofits, think about revenue and charitable contributions. Seth suggests looking at cash flow, margins, and exit strategies.

Exhibit 6.2   Scenario Planning

Scenario planning is often useful, particularly in this rapidly changing world. People work together to create pictures (scenarios) of possible futures. The pictures are bound by predetermined forces—those things that are reasonably predictable—identified by the group. The group then introduces uncertainties into the pictures.

Scenarios are not predictions but "posit several potential futures, none of which will probably come to pass, but all of which make you more keenly aware of the forces acting on you in the present" (Peter Senge et al., *The Fifth Discipline Fieldbook: Strategies and Tools for Building a Learning Organization* [New York: Doubleday, 1994], 275). By creating these alternative futures, your organization examines its assumptions and the uncertainties of the environment. Scenario planning forces your organization to consider how it might respond to different futures. Then you test various strategy options against the scenarios of possible futures.

For example, did any organization doing strategic planning create a great recession scenario? Given the global economic crisis, will your organization use scenarios for its next strategic planning process?

Roles in the Planning Process

Three groups or individuals are critical to produce an effective planning process. These are:

1. Board of Directors: the body that decides the organization's future and approves the strategies to reach that future.

2. Staff: leaders in the planning process and essential partners to decisions for the future.
3. Planning process manager: staff person or consultant responsible for designing and coordinating the planning process.

And there's a fourth (but optional) group, a planning committee. Let's start with the planning committee. Then you can decide if you even want one.

Planning Committee

The planning committee oversees the planning process on behalf of the board. Key responsibilities are:

- Engage the board in the process of planning.
- Work with the organization's CEO and planning process manager to design the overall process, most particularly the information gathering and decision-making components.
- Identify strategic issues facing the organization.
- Identify areas of challenge and opportunity for the board.
- Identify and recruit volunteers to help with information gathering.
- Review research results.
- With the board, participate in the decision-making process.
- Help outline goals, action steps, indicators of success, and assignments of responsibility.
- Review the draft plan, adjust, and recommend to the board for action.

Put together the best planning committee by combining the right skills and behavior, experience, and diversity. Make sure all candidates possess the requisite skills and behavior. Seek experience and diversity in the committee's composition.

- *Skills and behavior.* Choose critical thinkers. These individuals see the big picture, ask the difficult questions, challenge the status quo, dialogue well, argue, create consensus, and seek change. Good committee members set aside their personal agendas and work to benefit the organization and the community.
- *Diversity.* Standard considerations include gender, generation, sexual orientation, race/ethnicity, socioeconomic status, and so forth. Your organization will need additional diversity. For example, depending on your mission and scope of service, you may need to be sensitive to geography, education, faith, and other factors.
- *Experience.* Recruit individuals both inside and outside the organization. Consider clients, donors, current and past trustees, key staff, community leaders, philanthropists, and representatives from other organizations.

Your organization's CEO serves as a member of the planning committee. She or he participates in all deliberations, offers insight and perspective, and provides significant leadership to develop future vision and goals.

Some committee members have extensive experience with your organization, knowing the history, service, and reasons for past decisions. For example, recruit current or past board members, major donors, clients, and so forth. These individuals know how to balance history and change. Others can be more distanced so they challenge your assumptions and offer new perspectives.

People external to your organization bring particular expertise and insights to your deliberations. Look for experts in your organization's particular field of endeavor, recruit a respected CEO from another nonprofit/NGO organization, and seek people of influence who work in key areas of the community. Invite someone you're considering as a future candidate for board membership.

Typically, a current board member chairs the planning committee. She or he is well respected within the board, and capable of commanding attention for the planning process. If you have a chair-elect or president-elect, this individual is often a good candidate to lead the planning committee because she will be motivated to move the plan forward during her tenure as chief volunteer officer.

Sometimes, the chair of the planning committee and the CEO invite other key staff to serve as members of the planning committee. However, avoid staff outnumbering volunteers.

Recruit as many people as you need to ensure the appropriate skills, behavior, experience, and diversity. Probably the minimal number is six members. That way, if a couple of members miss a meeting, there's still a meaningful group present. As many as a dozen members work well.

Prior to confirming any planning committee member, explain the role of the committee and the performance expectations of the committee member. Make sure that each candidate agrees to carry out this role, or select another candidate.

Planning committee members are expected to:

- Regularly attend planning committee meetings, estimated at no more than five or six sessions during a nine- to 12-month planning process.
- Review planning materials in advance and participate actively in conversation.
- Help design the information gathering/research component of the planning process.
- Identify key constituencies who might provide useful information for the planning process.
- Carry out portions of the research, in particular conduct key informant interviews.
- Make personal contact with board members regarding the planning process.
- Participate in the decision-making process (generally a planning retreat).
- For those committee members who also serve on the board, provide leadership to board discussion about planning.

DON'T USE A PLANNING COMMITTEE Yes, that's an option. A planning committee is *not* essential. To have or have not is a strategic decision. Neither way is preferable. It depends on your organization and the design of your planning process. Think carefully. Decide what's best for your organization.

Review the job description of the planning committee again. Really, it doesn't make many decisions. In fact, the planning committee doesn't make any decisions that actually require a committee. There's just not that much for a committee to do. You could choose to have staff, the planning process manager, and the board itself do whatever might typically be allocated to a planning committee.

In fact, committees—whether for planning or anything else—too often usurp the board's authority. Watch out for this error! For example, too much dialogue happens within the committee and too little dialogue happens with the board. The board just acts as a rubber stamp, albeit a careful one.

Here's an example of wrong (and dangerous) assumptions for a planning committee: Years ago, I served as the strategic planning consultant for a large nonprofit that operated throughout North America. As the board and I discussed the planning committee, lots of board members volunteered to serve. Lots! I was surprised and pleased—but then, fortunately, suspicious.

"Why," I asked, "do so many of you want to serve on this committee?" And several responded: "Because I want to promote my vision for this organization at the meetings." In other words, these avid volunteers expected to talk about vision at planning committee meetings. These board members expected to make big decisions and have loud voices with the small planning committee. And these board members assumed that this planning committee would recommend to the board.

My response to them: "Oh, my, the planning committee doesn't discuss vision. The planning committee doesn't discuss the future of the organization. Those conversations happen only when the full board is together—along with staff—during the decision-making process. The planning committee just attends to process."

Guess what? All of those volunteers withdrew their offers. Well, maybe not every one of them. But everyone was startled. I could see it in their faces: "You mean the committee doesn't guide—even control—the decision-making?"

No, committees do not talk about everything and promote their opinions and then deliver recommendations to the board. That's not good, not good at all! Read more in my blogs. Read more in the Free Download Library on my website. And I'll explore this more in my future book on boards and governance.

Board

The role of the board[10] is particularly critical in planning. The board examines the relevant information, talks about trends and implications, asks the challenging questions, and then determines the organization's direction. The planning committee does not exclude the board from this process. In fact, it's best if the planning committee doesn't talk much about trends, implications, questions, and so on. The board does all of this.

Remember, your board is legally and morally accountable for the health and effectiveness of the organization. The board has authority and responsibility only as a group. No single individual has more authority or voice than any other. No officer or committee can take away the board's responsibility to explore, examine, dialogue, argue, and decide.

As a group, the board is responsible to:

- Decide to launch a comprehensive strategic planning process.
- If desirable, retain consulting services.
- Identify strategic issues facing the organization.
- Identify key constituencies that might provide useful information to the planning process.
- Review and endorse the research outline for the planning process.

- Talk about the compiled information, trends, and implications.
- Serve as the focus for the decision-making process, determining such things as future direction and vision and key steps to achieve vision.
- Review and adopt the comprehensive written plan.
- Use the resulting plan as the basis for board, committee, and staff work.
- Regularly monitor progress of plan and evaluate performance.

As a member of the board, the individual trustee is expected to:

- Review planning materials.
- Regularly attend board meetings and participate in planning dialogue.
- Possibly help carry out portions of the information gathering—in particular, conduct key informant interviews.
- Provide information to the planning process by responding to surveys and other inquiries.
- Participate in the decision-making process (generally a planning retreat).
- Review the draft plan, discuss, and take action.
- Ensure that the planning process is appropriate and is implemented properly. Ensure that the resulting written plan is monitored regularly.

Staff

The institution's staff is accountable for the success or failure of the planning process and the plan's implementation. Staff advocate for strategic planning and encourage strategic thinking and acting.

The chief executive officer (CEO) provides overall leadership to the planning process. She or he must be committed to the process and welcome the opportunity for institutional self-assessment and external exploration. In partnership with the planning process manager, the CEO ensures that the most difficult questions are asked and explored, encourages innovation, and welcomes learning and change.

As the institution's leader, the CEO helps determine the organization's future vision, direction, and goals through the group process of planning. The CEO actually may have a vision for the organization's future, but tests the validity of that vision through the planning process. The most effective CEO understands that his vision is not what matters. Rather, it is the vision put together through group process that matters.

The CEO ensures that all constituencies participate in the planning process. As a partner to the planning process manager, the CEO:

- Keeps planning on track, moving forward with consistent momentum.
- Enables the planning committee, board, and staff to carry out the planning function.
- Ensures that adequate and appropriate information is gathered for decision-making.
- Integrates the planning process with other agency activities.
- Ensures the necessary administrative support for the process.

Review Chapter 5, "The Art of Leadership," to gain further perspective on the role of the CEO in this and other situations.

Various staff members help gather information to support the planning process. They provide internal institutional data regarding client service, financing, and so forth. Staff secure relevant printed information from various sources. Staff also provide information to the process when they are asked for their opinions through surveys and conversation.

Planning Process Manager

The planning process manager[11] acts as navigator for the planning process. She or he serves as staff and adviser. Serving as staff means that the planning process manager prepares meeting agendas and communications materials, ensures availability of advance materials, and prepares meeting summaries. Serving as adviser means designing and leading the planning process and providing expert counsel. Your planning process manager anticipates barriers in order to avoid them, and has sufficient expertise and experience to solve problems as they arise.

Generally, the planning process manager is one of three people: the CEO, another person on staff who is responsible for planning, or a consultant retained specifically for the planning process. Sometimes a professional planner volunteers time to act as the process manager.

Watch out. It can be difficult for a staff member to serve as the planning process manager, even if the staff person's position is planning. Staff members need to participate in the process, and it is difficult to participate while managing and facilitating. Also, staff members (particularly the CEO) may be seen as driving the process to their own conclusions rather than maintaining sufficient objectivity.

No matter who fulfills the function of planning process manager, the individual must be an experienced strategic planner. Strategic planning—just like financial management, fund development, or your specific service area—requires skills, knowledge, and experience.

Henry Mintzberg[12] describes planners (i.e., planning process managers) as analysts, strategy finders, and catalysts.

- As an analyst, the planner studies both hard and soft data and pursues tangible and intangible information.
- As strategy finders, planners can "snoop around places they might not normally visit to find patterns amid the noise of failed experiments, seemingly random activities, and messy learning."[13] In this way, the planner may identify new ways of doing business and find new information and strategies that can assist the strategic planning process.
- As a catalyst, the planner ensures that decision-makers pay attention to the information. Planners get the right people involved in planning, including those working on the line and in the field.

    Planners "encourage managers to think about the future in creative ways . . . [seeing] their job as getting others to question conventional wisdom and especially helping people out of conceptual ruts. . . ."[14] Planners provoke reaction by asking challenging questions and questioning organization and individual assumptions.

Because effective planning causes temporary dissonance within the group, the process is stressful and issues may be controversial. Your planning process manager must manage the process to produce positive experiences and best results.

Planning expertise is not sufficient. The individual also must understand group dynamics and conflict resolution, organizational development, and the differences and similarities between governance and management.

The best planning process manager for a nonprofit/NGO possesses the following attributes:

- Experience designing and managing planning processes for diverse organizations in various stages of evolution.
- Expertise in strategic planning, organizational development, governance, management, and fund development.
- Knowledge about standard and cutting-edge theories and strategies for planning and organizational development.
- Ability to tailor a process for your organization, given its personality, evolution, and needs.
- Ability to enable others to participate in the process.
- Competency as a group facilitator, stimulating creativity, critical thinking, conflict resolution, and consensus.
- Sufficient time to focus on your planning process.

If your planning process is not effective, examine the performance of your CEO and your planning process manager.

Sixteen key responsibilities of the planning process manager are:

1. Provide information, advice, and recommendations about the various planning techniques.
2. Based on standard principles and cutting-edge developments, tailor a planning process to best meet the organization's needs.
3. Ensure that the organization's planning process produces the eight key results of an effective planning process (Exhibit 6.3).
4. Engage the institution's leadership and stakeholders in the planning process.
5. Ensure that the institution adequately communicates with its key constituencies about the planning process.
6. With the agency's CEO, keep the process moving forward with sufficient momentum while balancing planning with other demands.
7. Anticipate challenges and opportunities that might arise during the planning process and, with the CEO (and possibly the planning committee), devise solutions.
8. Design the information-gathering process to secure adequate and appropriate data for decision-making.
9. Prepare any needed research instruments[15] (for example, surveys, focus group questions, and key informant questions).
10. Help the organization identify useful reports, studies, articles, and other resources to inform the planning process.
11. Prepare resource materials for the planning process, for example, a description of the planning process, calendar, interview, and focus group guides.
12. Train staff and volunteers to help conduct research.

Dotted line represents feedback loop and operates in all directions between all elements.

Clarify values

Always ask the cage-rattling questions.

Conduct situation analysis
(Environmental scan/SWOT analysis)

Where are we today?

Internal Strengths	Internal Weaknesses
External Opportunities	External Threats

Gather information

Community Needs Assessment

Competitors/Collaborators/ Knowledge Alliances

Customer Satisfaction

Institutional Capacity

Current and future trends in external environment

Continuously Improve quality

Discuss implications and make choices for future

Test mission

Articulate vision for future

Project

Income and Expense

Performance Measures

Accountabilities

Time Frames

Set multiyear goals and strategies to achieve vision

Program scope, delivery, and target audiences	Enhancements to institutional capacity

Monitor plan's progress, adjust, extend

Annualize the multiyear strategic plan

Set priorities each year and define results and benchmarks. Outline work plans and subplans and determine budget.

Carry out multiyear strategic plan and annual plans, striving toward your vision

Always ask the cage-rattling questions.

EXHIBIT 6.3 The Strategic Planning Process

13. Facilitate meetings and focus group sessions.
14. Help prepare the information gathered, analyze trends and themes, and then help identify implications for your organization.
15. Design the decision-making process, facilitate it, and prepare the summary of decisions made. Help board, planning committee, and staff create the plan.
    ▪ Define vision and future direction.
    ▪ Establish corporate goals and indicators of success.

- Outline strategies and action steps to achieve goals.
- Project income and expenses.
- Outline steps to monitor progress and evaluate performance.

16. Draft the written plan or serve as editor to a staff-drafted plan.

And sometimes the planning process manager helps the organization craft a communications document once the strategic plan is completed and adopted.

Using a Consultant as Your Planning Process Manager

Only your organization can decide if you should hire a consultant. This is a joint decision of the board and the CEO. Can you manage and guide the process on your own? Do you have an individual who can serve as the planning process manager? To decide, consider these questions:

- Is there an individual available—staff or volunteer—who has sufficient strategic planning expertise and experience?
- Can she or he anticipate problems in the planning process and intervene with solutions?
- Does this individual keep current on the trends and techniques in strategic planning?
- Does she or he have the respect and trust of your organization's leadership?
- Does she or he have the time to manage and guide this process?

Talk to other organizations in your community and industry. Did these organizations use a consultant? If yes, why? If no, why not? Would they use a consultant for their next planning process?

If you use a consultant, consider the following:

- *Hire a consultant at the start of the planning process.*

   If you bring in a consultant later, it's hard to adjust what your organization may have already done. (And adjustments are often necessary to ensure a good planning process.)
- *Anticipate the costs.*

   In addition to consulting fees, expenses may include such items as: printing and distributing surveys, photocopying and distributing meeting agendas and summaries, conducting data searches, purchasing relevant publications, hosting meetings and retreats, photocopying and distributing the resulting market research results and trend summaries, and printing and distributing the written plan. The consultant provides advice about these costs.
- *Negotiate the scope of service provided.*

   While all the tasks must be accomplished, you might limit the consultant's responsibilities to certain activities, thereby reducing your cost. While all the steps need to happen in some way, there are harmless shortcuts, modified approaches, and alternative methods. Personalization to your organization needn't compromise the integrity of the planning process.
- *Use a good process to select your consultant.*

   Seek the expertise, experience, and behaviors described in this chapter. Find an individual whom you can respect and trust. Involve your board in the selection of a planning consultant just as you would the selection of a fund development consultant.

Other thoughts about hiring a consultant:

- *You're not hiring a retreat facilitator.*

    You're hiring an expert in strategic planning—organizational development (including process design and management, individual and group behavior and dynamics); systems thinking and change; market research methodology and tools; and so on. And, yes, you do want a good facilitator, too.

- *As a nonprofit/NGO, you seek a consultant familiar with the sector in general.*

    But it doesn't matter whether the consultant has any familiarity with your particular mission (e.g., education or environment or healthcare). Your organization provides that expertise.

- *You're very fortunate if you select a strategic planning expert who is also knowledgeable about governance, management, fund development, and marketing/ communications.*

    Why? Because these issues always come up in any good strategic planning process. And how delightful if your planning consultant can provide insight and advice in these areas.

- *Finally, anytime you hire a consultant, you seek a trusted adviser.*[16]

    Yes, you want expertise and experience. But lots of people have that. You want more. You want someone you trust with the skeletons in your closet, your fears and weaknesses, your dreams and hopes. A counselor and coach. A mentor and teacher.

Remember, do not hire a consultant unless you need one. But if you need a consultant, hire one.

Principal Components of an Effective Strategic Planning Process

Six major components are essential to effective strategic planning:

1. Values clarification
2. Situation analysis
3. Information gathering
4. Decision-making
5. Writing the plan
6. Implementing and monitoring the plan

Use these six components to design a strategic planning process that is relevant for your organization. Tailor the process to your organization by considering such things as: your organization's age, size, and complexity; resources (staff, volunteers, consultants) available to devote to planning; and the internal and external environments.

Start with values, described in detail in Chapter 3. Values are critical to an effective strategic planning process, setting the foundation for the process and the ultimate results.

Remember, values are the standards that influence us as we make choices among alternative courses of action. Values are the manner by which we operate as an organization. Values guide our actions and judgments. When we state our values, others can decide if they wish to affiliate with us, living with us in the way we want to live.

The situation analysis, also called an environmental scan or SWOT analysis, examines where your organization is now. Look at your internal strengths and weaknesses (SW) and external opportunities and threats (OT). Strengths and weaknesses refer to those things that you can control, albeit with difficulty. Opportunities and threats transpire beyond your control, but you have to manage them.

At the start of the planning process, conduct the SWOT analysis through group dialogue with your agency's key leadership, both staff and board. Use the results gleaned to outline the information gathering required to support the planning process.

Information gathering provides you with qualitative and quantitative data upon which to base your decisions about the future. You put together important information about your organization—information about programs and services, clients, financing, management, governance, marketing, and so forth. You bring together external information that examines current and future trends relevant to your organization and its future. You might also conduct market research to provide additional important information.

With the results of your situation analysis and information gathering in hand, your organization makes decisions. Decisions like your vision for the future and your key corporate goals. You align your mission with your vision. You define measures for success and establish benchmarks for those measures.

Often, you make these decisions at a planning retreat. Board and staff gather together to review the gathered information and talk about the implications. Then you choose your organization's direction.

With these key decisions made, the organization's staff identifies strategies to achieve the goals. Staff members project time frames and financing for review by the planning committee.

The planning process manager often writes the plan, incorporating the general components outlined previously. The planning committee reviews the draft plan and presents it to the board for review and action.

The planning process does not stop once the plan is written. Implementing the plan involves both staff and board members. Implementation also includes monitoring the plan's progress, adjusting when necessary, evaluating overall performance, and launching the next planning process. (Exhibit 6.3 shows a diagram of the planning process.)

Carrying Out Your Strategic Planning Process

Now here's the detail: the six principal components of strategic planning expanded into 20 carefully laid-out steps, all building one upon the other. However, despite the sequential order, planning is not necessarily linear. You may conduct some steps simultaneously, modify the order, or merge some steps. But be cautious about eliminating any steps. See Exhibit 6.4 for the list of steps.

Exhibit 6.4   Twenty Critical Steps in Strategic Planning

1. Formally agree to do planning.
2. Get ready to plan.
3. Engage key stakeholders in the planning process.
4. Articulate (or review) values.
5. Launch the process with board, staff, and planning committee.
6. Design the planning process and outline the information-gathering phase.
7. Gather the information, including market research as necessary. Compile and analyze the information and prepare it for distribution.
8. Design the decision-making process, typically some form of retreat.
9. Conduct the decision-making process and summarize results. This is it. This is where you choose and when you decide the big things.
10. Review (and possibly adjust) mission. (Or this is the point where you decide to go out of business.)
11. Determine goals and strategies.
12. Identify core competencies and supporting structures.
13. Define measures for success.
14. Assign time frames and entities responsible for strategies or action steps.
15. Describe financing.
16. Outline process to annualize the plan, including defining benchmarks for measures.
17. Outline process to monitor progress of the plan, evaluate performance, and extend the plan for subsequent years.
18. Write the strategic plan. Review and adopt.
19. Translate the plan into organizational and personal commitment.
20. Implement the strategic plan and generate and implement the subplans. (For example, see Chapter 9, "Creating the Most Effective Fund Development Plan for Your Organization.")

1. Formally Agree to Do Planning

The board of directors formally agrees to do planning, often voting to confirm the decision. Before the vote, make sure the board understands—to some degree—the scope of the planning process, the principal components of the process, the various roles (including its own), the time and resources required, and the possible implications for changing the organization.

On the other hand, don't overwhelm the board with too much detail. And don't panic board members with too much talk about change. Let this understanding evolve through the planning process.

2. Get Ready to Plan

Recruit your planning process manager. If you decide to hire a consultant, make sure that several board members have an opportunity to participate in the interview process and help choose.

Determine the composition of the planning committee and identify candidates. (Or, with your planning process manager, decide you won't use a planning committee.) Discuss responsibilities and expectations with all candidates for the committee. Secure their commitment to carry out the job description before confirming their participation.

Effective strategic planning may cause some people to leave your organization, even board members. That's okay.

---

3. Engage Key Constituencies in the Planning Process

At the heart of strategic planning is a group of people building a shared vision that reflects their shared values. Those who will be affected by the plan participate in the planning process. That means just about everyone in your organization in some way![17]

For strategic planning to be effective, it must create "ongoing processes in which people at every level of the organization, in every role, can speak from the heart about what really matters to them and be heard—by senior management and each other. The quality of this process, especially the amount of openness and genuine caring, determines the quality and power of the results."[18]

Effective engagement produces one of two results, both of which are valuable and acceptable. Usually, engaging people well generates understanding and ownership, cohesion and alignment. Sometimes, engaging people shows those individuals that they no longer support the organization's direction. In these cases, an effective engagement process gives people permission to move away without anger or frustration.

There are two types of constituents, internal and external. Your internal constituencies include such groups as your customers (clients, audience members, service users, or whatever you call them); staff and board members; direct service, administrative, and fund development volunteers; and donors and funding sources. These stakeholders—another word for constituents—are closest to you.

Your external constituencies include such groups as elected and regulatory officials, community leaders and people of influence, and collegial organizations (cooperators, collaborators, competitors). These constituents are further removed but do have an effect on your organization.

There are three principal ways to engage your constituents in the planning process.

First, seek their opinions and perspective because this information is vital for your decision-making.

Second, keep your constituents informed about the planning process. Explain why your organization is planning and tell constituents about progress and decisions. Distribute a summary of the final plan to your constituencies and keep communicating once the plan is put in motion.

Third, some of your constituents actually participate in decision-making—for example, your board, planning committee, chief executive officer, and key staff.[19]

Involve staff in the planning process, whether you have two or 2,000 employees. These individuals are on the front lines, facing the challenges and testing ways to cope. Staff members learn while doing, thus providing valuable information and knowledge to the organization.

From a fundraiser's perspective, donor participation in planning is critical. Donors who understand and support your organization's vision and strategic direction will at least maintain their gifts and may well increase them. By helping to plan, other constituents may be inspired to become donors.

INVOLVING THE BOARD Sometimes it's difficult to engage the board in the planning process. Yet, in its governance capacity, the board is legally and morally accountable for your agency. As individuals and a group, the board must understand the information gathered, explore the trends and implications, create shared values and vision, evaluate mission, and determine future direction.

The first step, then, is to understand why it's sometimes difficult to engage the board and its individual members. What excuses—and they are excuses—have you heard? Not enough time? Too much to read? Expectations that the committee will do the work and recommend a plan?

No matter. You have to overcome these excuses. Use these strategies to engage your board—every single board member—in the planning process.

- Talk about the planning process and its progress at every board meeting and the meetings of your various committees. After all, planning and the resulting plan will affect everything and everyone.
- Give board members regular and timely updates about information secured through market research.
- Help the board talk about the implications of the information gathered to inform the planning process.
- Practice self-examination and world examination, critical thinking, and honest, forthright dialogue.
- Practice conflict resolution.
- As necessary, maintain personal contact with individual board members between meetings.
- And, if necessary, threaten them. Yes, threaten them. For example:
  - "The decision-making retreat is based on the information provided in advance. If you do not read the advance information, you will not be able to participate in the dialogue."
  - "Your voice is important to our future. If you do not come to the retreat, your voice will not be heard. And we will not revisit decisions made at the retreat."

In summary, see Chapter 3, "The First Relationship—Within Your Organization." If this isn't working, strategic planning won't work so well, either.

4. Articulate (or Review) Values

You may be tired of hearing about values. But they really are important. Shared values form the foundation for any group or organization. Healthy institutions are well aligned, displaying a cohesion between values and behaviors.

Conversation about values helps establish the context for the rest of the planning process. This conversation is interesting and often stimulating.

If your organization has not already articulated its values, do so at the start of the strategic planning process. (Look back at Chapter 3.) If your organization has articulated its shared values at some point in the past, then review your values during the planning process.

Consider these strategies:

- At the strategic planning kickoff with board and staff, clarify values through group dialogue.
- Before the kickoff, develop a survey that evaluates how well aligned your organization's actions and values are. Distribute the survey to all board members and staff. Tabulate the responses and present the results to all those who participated in the survey process.

    Review results with staff, board, and the planning committee. Identify any areas of conflict, and outline strategies to align articulated values and action.
- Talk about values in small group sessions with board members, staff, and other key constituents. Stimulate dialogue with these statements:
    - "Reflect on our organization's stated values. Discuss how well our actions reflect our values. Describe why and how our values and actions were particularly well aligned in certain situations. Discuss situations when our values and actions were not well aligned and how we could improve."
    - "Think about the operations and activities within our organization. Look also at the outside world. Are there other values we might wish to add or change at this time?"

See values statements in the strategic plans posted on this book's website. For more values statements, also see *Keep Your Donors* and visit www .simonejoyaux.com.

5. Launch the Process with Board, Staff, and Planning Committee

Launching your planning process is as important as any other campaign start. An effective kickoff strategy involves the board, staff, and planning committee coming together in an introductory work session. If your organization is small enough, gather everyone together at a regular board meeting or special meeting. If your organization is too large or geographically diffuse, meet via conference call or conduct separate work sessions with board and staff.

This introductory session (the kickoff) sets the stage for the entire planning process. By bringing together your key constituents, you commit to a process that engages many voices. The kickoff helps people understand the process and what will happen during the process.

Equally important, the kickoff generates preliminary information so the planning process manager and planning committee can develop the information-gathering outline. See the agenda for the Steel Yard's kickoff, Appendix 6-F, posted on this book's website.

Participants in the kickoff identify issues and opportunities by conducting the SWOT analysis, mentioned earlier in this chapter. Participants talk about internal strengths and weaknesses and external opportunities and threats. A colleague described this SWOT analysis as a "heartburn and champagne" conversation. But be careful: Distinguish between the internal and external. Too many people (and their organizations) confuse them.[20]

Internal strengths and weaknesses refer to things that your organization can control. Reflect on what you do well and consider how you might capitalize on this. Expand the conversation by describing when things were at their best and why. Next, consider areas that could use improvement, often called your organization's weaknesses. Don't be put off by the word. Discuss how your strengths might help you address your weaknesses.

External opportunities and threats refer to issues in the environment in which your organization operates. You cannot control the external environment but you must manage it well in order for your organization to flourish. Look at your community and the larger world. Identify the trends, events, and developments that affect your organization.

Invite kickoff participants to identify types of information that would inform the planning process (e.g., census data, community reports, useful articles, etc.). Ask kickoff participants to suggest organizations and individuals that might also provide important information.

Conducting the kickoff is also your first step in the information-gathering phase of the planning process. Prepare a summary of the kickoff, distribute it to participants, and use the results to create the information-gathering outline.

6. Design the Planning Process and Outline the Information-Gathering Phase

The planning process manager designs the overall planning process. At the start, she designs steps 1 to 7. She designs the final steps (8 to 18) later because they evolve from the information gathering and group dynamics observed during the planning process. And the final two steps, 19 and 20, focus on implementing the plan.

Good planning depends on the scope and quality of information on which your organization bases its decisions. Too little information compromises the quality of your plan. Too much information overwhelms decision-making and demands unnecessary effort. But with the right information, committed people usually make good decisions. The key is to secure the right information—and then have all those conversations described in Chapter 3.

Generally, the information-gathering phase for strategic planning requires three to six months. Actual time depends on the scope of your issues and the information necessary for decision-making.

The organization that starts out from the inside and then tries to find places to put its resources is going to fritter itself away. Above all, it's going to focus on yesterday. One looks to the outside for opportunity, for a need.

From *Managing the Non-Profit Organization: Principles and Practices*, by Peter F. Drucker (New York: HarperCollins, 1990), 34

The planning manager uses the results of the planning kickoff as the basis for drafting the information-gathering outline. This outline describes the information needed and how to obtain it. Once it is endorsed by the planning committee (if you have one), distribute the outline to the board and staff for their information.

Keep key constituencies—in particular, staff and board and committee members—informed of progress while you gather the information. Since this phase may take a long time, people who are not closely involved could feel that the planning process has lost momentum.

Your updates help constituents feel connected to the process. For example, you might carefully share limited findings without drawing conclusions or discussing implications. Remember, save extensive conversation until you've gathered all the information.

7. Gather, Compile, and Analyze the Information

Gather the information,[21] including market research as necessary; compile and analyze the information and prepare it for distribution. You put together internal information about your organization and its performance. You gather external information about what's happening in the world and in your field. And you might even conduct some market research.

In general, the information you'll put together falls into four categories, listed here. The first two categories are external; the last two are internal.

1. Community needs assessment.
2. Analysis of competitors, collaborators, and knowledge alliances.
3. Customer satisfaction review.
4. Assessment of institutional capacity.

There's so much information out there. That won't be your challenge. Your challenge is to pick the best information of most use to your organization. That's where strategic thinking comes in.

First, let's start small and closest to home. Look inside your organization. Put together the available internal information, all presented in an easy-to-understand format that explains trends and implications. This information highlights your performance, in essence, documenting your institutional capacity.

For example:

- Multiyear comparisons of your client participation, finances, donors, and other relevant quantitative data.
- Overview of your impact and results, how you achieve these, and commentary about client satisfaction.
- Overview of your collaborating partners and why they are valuable.

The staff compiles this information. It should be easy enough to do, as this is basic information required to run an organization. Such information should be readily available—and frequently used—in your ongoing operations. If you don't have some of the internal data, your strategic plan will undoubtedly include a goal and strategies to improve this for the future.

But that readily available internal information is only the tip of the iceberg for good strategic thinking and planning. Now turn your attention to market research.

What is market research? "The process of gathering, analyzing, and interpreting information about a market, about a product or service to be offered for sale in that market, and about the past, present, and future potential customers for the product or service; research into the characteristics, spending habits, location, and needs of your business's target market, the industry as a whole, and the particular competitors you face."[22]

That's a very good definition for what you need to do in good planning. Substitute clients, volunteers, and donors as appropriate. Think about alliances rather than competitors. And notice the external rather than internal focus.

Market research includes both primary and secondary sources. Primary data refers to that which must be developed for your planning process. Secondary data refers to information that already exists for some purpose other than your planning process.

Again, let's start with what's easiest: *secondary research*. Identify existing reports, studies, articles, and plans from your particular field of endeavor, the nonprofit/NGO sector itself, and the external environment in which you operate. Make sure you investigate such issues as economics, education, public policy, demographics and lifestyles, technology, and societal issues like employment, healthcare, safety, and security.

For example, check with your city or state planning departments. Look at service providers that often do community studies (e.g., community foundations, national and regional foundations, United Way, professional associations). Check out government resources like census data as well as local and national polling data. Visit research centers[23] for secondary research on various topics.

Here are some examples of secondary research compiled by various organizations:

As an organization committed to health and fitness, the YMCA reviewed the state of Rhode Island's plan to develop healthy Rhode Islanders. In its capacity as a human services provider, the Y examined basic human needs reports prepared by the local United Way.

The YMCA reviewed U.S. Census data for demographic information and state and federal sources for statistics of crime and violence, poverty, and families at risk. In order to assess its own institutional capacity, the YMCA used *Giving USA: The Annual Report on Philanthropy* and *Giving RI* along with financial and service information from comparable YMCAs nationwide.

The Audubon Society of Rhode Island (ASRI) reviewed environmental research reported in various trade publications. ASRI also looked at findings from *Giving USA: The Annual Report on Philanthropy*.

The local library would likely review the town's comprehensive plan and the state library's long-range plans. Libraries would review trends from pertinent library publications and connect with various library associations and service providers.

An arts organization might look at research and resources from Americans for the Arts, the National Endowment for the Arts, and state and local arts councils. A child development organization could review local and national findings on the status of children—for example, the Kids Count work initiated through the Annie E. Casey Foundation.

Participants at your organization's planning kickoff help you identify some secondary resources. Staff members identify more based on professional expertise, industry resources, and information searches.

Use Google. Ask your local librarian for qualified reference sources. Don't forget your planning process manager. Whether staff, volunteer, or professional consultant, this individual provides guidance and expertise to the information-gathering phase, including primary and secondary market research.

Primary research requires more time, more resources, and more expertise than does secondary research. Nonetheless, don't dismiss it.

For example, you can easily do a governance self-assessment to help evaluate institutional capacity. You can conduct key informant interviews and focus groups where you explore all of the four categories of information necessary for good strategic planning. You may conduct surveys. Board and planning committee members can actually help do the research by conducting key informant interviews and, if capable, facilitating focus groups. See the appendices posted on this book's website for examples of surveys, as well as focus group and key informant questions that address the four categories of information necessary for good strategic planning.

COMMUNITY NEEDS ASSESSMENT   Strategic planning does not begin with who you are and what you want to do. Rather, planning begins with who your community is and what it wants and needs. Your organization operates within a community, and planning clarifies how you fit in and meet the community's wants and needs.

The community needs assessment helps answer the questions posed at the start of this chapter in the section called "Make Sure Your Organization Is Relevant to the Community"—questions like: What is happening in the external environment? What are the community needs, and to what degree are these being met (or not met)? With this information in hand, your organization decides whether it wants to respond.

Beware! Do not ask people what your organization should do or what your role should be to meet community needs. Why? First, the question is premature. Second, don't ask what others think you should do, because you may not choose to do it. You may focus on another need. The community needs assessment will likely identify conflicting and competing needs. Your organization evaluates all the information together and discusses the implications before you make decisions. Furthermore, if you ask others what you should do and then you choose not to do it, you may alienate them rather than produce understanding and ownership.

Once you've put together all your information and your organization begins to make decisions, then you answer the question: "Might we have the capability and wish to respond to any of the needs identified during our market research? And if yes, what will we do and how?"

In today's environment organizations must move fast or die. No enterprise, large or small, private or public, can afford to be slow, inflexible, or insular.

From "Leadership in a Virtual World," by Deborah L. Duarte and Nancy Tennant Snyder, *Leader to Leader* (Spring 2000), 43

ANALYSIS OF COMPETITORS, COLLABORATORS, AND KNOWLEDGE ALLIANCES Many organizations spend too little time on this portion of information gathering. Narrowly focused on their own territory, often insular, these organizations are threatened by others in the marketplace.

As you examine the external environment and assess community needs, turn your attention to other organizations, whether for-profit, nonprofit/NGO, or government. You can learn a lot. Keep in mind: Your organization must move quickly and must be flexible. But your organization doesn't need to do everything on its own or by itself. As Duarte and Tennant Snyder note, "Leaders are seeing that it is no longer necessary—or desirable—for their organizations to own all the assets required to serve customers."[24] Instead, you can share resources and compensate for each other's gaps. Work with other organizations to achieve shared goals and meet community needs. Think in terms of network connectedness and interlocking webs of resources.

Based on your information gathering, you may decide to withdraw from a particular service and leave it to another organization. If you continue to provide the service, the research results should help you better differentiate yourself from the competition.[25] Or you may choose to expand a service area by collaborating with others to create a marketplace niche.

Certainly you will identify individuals and organizations with whom you should maintain relationships to exchange information. These knowledge alliances help your organization carry out its mission.

CUSTOMER SATISFACTION REVIEW Your organization has many constituents (i.e., customers). Find out how satisfied they are with your performance. In particular, speak with the clients who use your service and the volunteers and donors who give. Find out what they all value and why they choose to associate with your organization. Talk with your volunteers of time and donors of money, too.

A small aside: Too few organizations assess their donors' satisfaction. What a shame. You can learn so much. And what you learn can help you retain your donors. Read Adrian Sargeant's books and research for guidance about measuring donor satisfaction. See Appendix 6-E on this book's website, a member/donor survey for the Audubon Society of Rhode Island.

ASSESSMENT OF INSTITUTIONAL CAPACITY Institutional capacity refers to how well your organization's infrastructure operates and includes such elements as:

- Administration/management (staffing, technology, fiscal and personnel systems, and so forth).
- Governance.
- Program scope and service delivery.
- Human resources.
- Corporate culture (alignment of values and action, cultural diversity and sensitivity, group dynamics).
- Financing (revenue and charitable contributions).
- Marketing/communications and image.
- Facilities.

Think of this as your organization's performance review. You need to know how well your organization does its work and whether you have the skills (capability) and resources (capacity) to take on new endeavors or expand current activities.

To assess institutional capacity, evaluate such things as organizational design, governance and management, role delineation, information flow, allocation of resources, fund development, and marketing/communications.

Get opinions from volunteers and staff as well other stakeholders. Examine your organization's existing information such as donor and service statistics, trends in income and expense, and so forth. Plot relevant information over a multiyear period, analyzing trends and implications.

MARKET RESEARCH METHODS   There are lots of research methods. For primary research, use surveys (written, telephone, and intercept); focus groups; and personal interviews. Each is described in the following paragraphs.

Construct your research instruments to ensure useful and valid responses. Usually research instruments include questions about each of the market research components (community needs, customer satisfaction, institutional capacity, and collaborator/competitor/knowledge alliances).

It does not do to leave a live dragon out of your calculations, if you live near him.

—J. R. R. Tolkien (1920–1973), in *The Hobbit, or There and Back Again*

The Wethersfield (Connecticut) Library asked its patrons to complete a written survey. Patrons picked up the survey while visiting the library. See Appendix 6-D on this book's website for a copy of the library's survey.

The Audubon Society of Rhode Island (ASRI) mailed its strategic planning survey to all 3,000 donors and members. See this survey (Appendix 6-E) posted on this book's website. The ASRI survey is also included in *Keep Your Donors: The Guide to Better Communications and Stronger Relationships*.

Here's an absolute must for any strategic planning process: Conduct a governance self-assessment. In fact, your organization should conduct a governance self-assessment at least every two years—and some organizations do so annually.

See Appendix 6-A for a sample governance self-assessment.[26] Copy or modify this tool for your organization. Make sure that the key staff who work with the board also complete this survey. Compare the staff and board answers and note commonalties and differences. For more information about governance, visit www.simonejoyaux.com, click on Resources, and visit the Free Download Library.

Examine the effectiveness of management, too. Management refers to staff, as distinguished from governance, the work of the board of directors. You might conduct a survey of employees. If you're using a consultant, she could conduct a focus group with employees, examining such issues as:

- Adequacy of resources to carry out one's job (e.g., equipment, time, training, etc.).

- Effectiveness of communications from leadership, between departments, and so on.
- Opportunities for professional development and advancement.
- Supportive work environment and morale.

It's essential, of course, to protect the anonymity of staff and encourage their candor. Also, it's critical to direct the findings from the management research to management for improvement. The board does not get involved in fixing management issues. That's management work. However, the board may well expect updates from the CEO about the progress of change.

Key informant interviews and focus groups provide in-depth perspective for planning. This qualitative, anecdotal information offers useful insights. For example, you might conduct focus groups and interviews with donors, volunteers, clients, and other nonprofits.

Ask open-ended questions that focus on community needs and trends as well as your organization's image. Tailor some of the questions to a particular audience—for example, donors.

Sometimes you start with a longer list of questions to make sure that the conversation keeps going. Questions for focus groups and key informant interviews are often the same. The focus group facilitator prepares a summary of the focus group—and the interviewers do the same with the key informant interviews.

Use personal interviews with stakeholders who request privacy due to their positions or to the nature of their information, or who are unable to participate in a focus group. Conduct focus groups when it's appropriate and possible to bring together 10 to 15 people for a facilitated conversation with a competent facilitator. Often the synergy of the focus group offers unique insights and ideas for the organization. Interesting collaborations and knowledge alliances can also result from this group process.

You can use volunteers to conduct most key informant interviews. This saves money. And board members and planning committee members hear from key stakeholders firsthand. This helps engage volunteers in the planning process and builds their understanding of the issues facing the organization.

Sometimes the planning process manager facilitates the focus groups. In other cases, independent facilitators or volunteers may do so. You might provide the focus group summary to participants as a benefit for giving you their time. Remember, everyone is promised anonymity but not confidentiality. In other words, you share what is said but not who said what.

During its strategic planning process, the Audubon Society of Rhode Island (www.asri.org) conducted focus groups and key informant interviews. Environmental groups from throughout the state participated in focus groups, offering important insights and useful information for the planning process. Public and private school teachers responded to questions about the importance of environmental education and the quality of Audubon Society programs.

Volunteers, too, shared their observations about current service and future direction. Board members conducted key informant interviews with corporate and foundation funding sources, individual donors, and government representatives.

The Steel Yard (www.thesteelyard.org) also used focus groups to help inform its strategic planning process. Focus group participants included instructors and students as well as artists using the Steel Yard's facilities. Arts organizations and government representatives also participated.

The Women's Foundation of Southern Arizona conducted focus groups and personal interviews with donors, community leaders, grant recipients, and other nonprofit/NGO organizations.

See Appendix 6-B, posted on this book's website, for the focus group and key informant questions for both the Audubon Society and the Steel Yard. See Appendix 6-C for the questions used with the Women's Foundation of Southern Arizona.

Market research acts as a catalyst to help the organization think strategically.

COMPILING THE INFORMATION   Once you complete your research, compile the results. Review the findings from surveys. Analyze the notes from key informant interviews and focus groups. Review the highlights from your secondary research. Then the planning process manager identifies the trends and themes, and works with staff to prepare the information for advance distribution.

The information package is one of the most critical products in the planning process because it is used to make your decisions for the future. Equally important, the package serves as a valuable resource to staff and volunteers during implementation, after the planning process ends and you've adopted the plan.

Practically speaking, you might compile this information in a three-ring binder with separate sections on key topics (e.g., community needs assessment, services and client satisfaction, financing, management, governance, etc.). Sometimes you can create one electronic document that includes everything.

No matter how you organize your information or what you call it, this manual or document or notebook or package brings together all the internal and external information, all the primary and secondary research, into one place. Everything is there, without censoring or recommendations. No one prioritizes anything!

Once you've completed the information package, distribute it to everyone who will participate in the decision-making process. These individuals read the information, consider the possible implications for the organization, and participate in conversation about the trends and implications for the organization.

See this book's website for the table of contents of the Audubon Society's information package, and that of the United Way of Dutchess County, New York, Appendix 6-J.

OVERWHELMED YET?   Does every organization have to put together some information to support the planning process? Yes. That is not negotiable. Quality decision-making requires quality information.

Do you have to do all this market research? No.

Here's a modified approach. First, compile the internal information—for example, multiyear comparisons of financing, service statistics, and the like. Then prepare background papers to provide critical information for the planning process. Your staff writes background papers on specific topics.

What's a background paper? A narrative overview—including trends and implications—about areas of operation and community issues. For example:

- The homeless shelter writes three background papers.

    One paper describes the community need and community response, including highlights from a local report, roles of various providers and partners in the community, conversations with local government, and observations about future need. A second background paper describes the shelter's financing trends and their implications. The third background paper describes challenges facing the shelter, including staffing and facilities.

- The child development center writes three background papers.

    One paper describes the center's services and audience patterns. The second paper describes community need, changing demographics and the implications for enrollment, and the availability of other childcare services in the marketplace. The third background paper summarizes the financial history and projected financing changes for the childcare center.

In addition to background papers written by staff, include key articles and reports. For example, the homeless shelter might include an important article about homelessness published in a newsmagazine. The child development center may include an article published by the national lobbying body that promotes universal childcare. An arts organization might include an article about new trends in audience development. Any organization can find important articles about fund development and charitable giving (e.g., highlights from *Giving USA* at www.givingusa.org).

8. Design the Decision-Making Process, Typically Some Form of Retreat

Sometimes there might be talk about specific findings and their possible implications before the market research is finished. For example, the planning committee may engage the board of directors in conversation to build understanding prior to the retreat.

However, take care. Don't draw conclusions prior to completing all the market research and integrating the various findings. And talking too much with the board in advance excludes other constituents who should participate in decision-making.

Decision-making usually happens at a planning retreat. Groups go off together, away from regular interruptions, to deliberate and decide. Actual decisions depend on the information gathered as well as the experience and expertise of those attending the retreat. The board, as legal corporate entity, confirms these decisions by adopting the written strategic plan.

Your organization makes two levels of decisions during the decision-making phase of the strategic planning process:

- *First, your organization decides its overall direction.*

    This happens with everyone together, typically at a planning retreat. See step 9, "Conduct the Decision-Making Process," for further detail.

    This highest level of decision-making requires full dialogue with the board, planning committee, CEO, and key staff. The dialogue is based on the background information. Then, together, the group decides most broadly.

- *Second, the organization decides how it will get where it is going.*

    See step 11, "Determine Goals and Strategies," for further detail. Generally the staff, perhaps with participation of the planning committee (if you have one—and remember, you don't have to have one), outline the strategies to move the organization forward. Eventually, this is all woven together as the written plan, outlined in steps 12–17.

The effectiveness of the decision-making process depends on a combination of elements, specifically:

- *Participation of your institution's key leadership.*

  Those invited to help decide include the board, planning committee, and senior management staff. Attendance is considered mandatory—unless, of course, you absolutely cannot make it. And I mean absolutely cannot make it!

  For example, you already bought your vacation travel tickets and will be gone on the date selected. Or you're hospitalized.

  But if your kid has a soccer game, you don't go to the game—you go to the planning retreat. You hoped to go away that weekend—pick another weekend! It's your life partner's birthday, too bad—celebrate it some other time; go to the retreat.

  I'm really tired of board members who won't inconvenience themselves for the organization and the board work. Board members, collectively, are legally and morally accountable—liable!—for the health and effectiveness of the corporation. And by the way, if you aren't there, your voice won't be heard. We will *not* revisit our decisions later when you've reviewed the results of the planning retreat that you did not attend.

  What else contributes to the effectiveness of the planning retreat?

- *Equity in the decision-making setting.*

  Every invitee has equal voice in the dialogue. No individual, by virtue of position or behavior, has any more power than another. Although the board is the legal corporate entity, at the retreat everyone talks and everyone votes. And yes, that includes staff and others you invited to participate in the process.

- *Adequate time balanced with timely choosing.*

  Sometimes a single session of four to six hours suffices; sometimes a two-part retreat, four hours each in consecutive weeks, works. And there are other versions. Whatever your format, allocate sufficient time to accomplish your desired outcomes. The challenge is to ensure that decisions are made and sustained rather than delayed and revisited.

- *Ability to talk, argue, resolve conflict, and decide.*

  Deciding your organization's mission and direction for the future requires critical thinking and forthright conversation. This happens well when individuals display respect for one another, know how to listen, understand the difference between discussion and dialogue, and value constructive conflict for the understanding and synergy that it produces.

  To prepare for your retreat, review key sections of Chapter 3, focusing on group dynamics, conversation, and fighting well.

The planning process manager designs the decision-making retreat for review by the planning committee, if there is one. If there isn't a planning committee, the CEO and board chair can review the retreat agenda.

The retreat format depends on the nature of your organization and the issues you face. With the background information in hand, the process manager understands the scope of the issues facing the organization as well as the opportunities and challenges available within the community. By now, the planning process manager also has a feel for the organization's corporate culture, including its group dynamics.

The planning process manager considers many variables when designing the retreat. For example:

- How complex are the issues presented in the findings report? How can conversation be structured to bring the decision-makers to consensus?
- Which decisions of what scope should be made by which group (e.g., the planning committee, board, or staff)?
- What kind of small group and full group activities will help the decision-makers deliberate?
- What kind of facilitation techniques will work best?
- What particular group dynamics must be managed during the decision-making?

Make sure your retreat includes specific activities to encourage conversation and focus attention. Use various voting tactics to trigger decision-making and priority setting at various points. Use both full group and small group work in your planning retreat. Small group work produces a number of benefits; for example, it allows more intense focus on specific topics, better engages those who are not as comfortable in larger groups, and accomplishes more work in a shorter period of time. The small groups then report back to the larger group, inviting comment and creating consensus.

VARIOUS RETREAT FORMATS You could design your decision-making retreat by focusing on the key components of a written plan, outlined earlier in this chapter. You could design your decision-making process based on Seth Godin's sections in his modern business plan, also described earlier in this chapter.

Some decision-making retreats focus on strengths and weaknesses and opportunities and threats of program and infrastructure, described in Appendix 6-G, Retreat Format #1, posted on this book's website. The group uses the background information provided in advance, coupled with its own experience and wisdom, to select program areas for the length of the strategic plan. Participants define program goals.

In this retreat format, conversation focuses on such issues as:

- What the organization currently does well.
- What the unmet community needs are.
- Which audiences need which programs.
- Which organizations provide service within the marketplace.
- What capabilities the organization currently has or can develop to maintain and expand current programs and start up new programs.

Next, the group focuses on infrastructure. The advance background information results clearly state what areas require focus. This may involve adjustments in fund development, management and governance, human resources, marketing and communications, and so forth. The group decides which areas will be addressed during the course of this strategic plan. Then, as a final step in the retreat, the group identifies its key infrastructure goals.

Sometimes, organizations use the concept of visioning to make their decisions about the future, described in Appendix 6-G, Retreat Formats #2 and #3, posted on this book's website. Visioning is a lively process of sharing what people most care about in a way that creates enthusiasm and shared commitment, a collective sense of what matters to the organization and its participants.

An organization's vision is different from its mission or purpose. The dictionary defines *vision* as something seen in a dream or trance; an act or power of imagination; unusual discernment or foresight. Your organization's vision is a snapshot of your desired future. Vision tells what, not how. Peter Senge describes vision as a "sense of commonalty that permeates the organization and gives coherence to diverse activities."[27] People who share a vision are connected by a common aspiration.

Bryan Smith, in Senge et al.'s *The Fifth Discipline Fieldbook*,[28] describes five ways for building shared vision. These are telling, selling, testing, consulting, and co-creating.

1. *Telling*. Leadership decides the vision and informs the organization.
2. *Selling*. Leadership decides the vision but seeks organizational support before moving forward.
3. *Testing*. Leadership has an idea or two about the future and seeks the organization's reaction before making a decision.
4. *Consulting*. Leadership seeks creative input from various groups within the organization before determining vision.
5. *Co-creating*. Together, leadership and the various constituencies of the organization build a shared vision.

While the strategic planning process described in this chapter uses the co-creating method, your organization may be at a different stage of development. Attempting to use this method may stymie your planning process. If this is the case, use one of Smith's other methods for determining vision. Then, during the implementation of your strategic plan, you can build organizational capacity to use co-creating in your next planning interval. See *The Fifth Discipline Fieldbook* for tips about developing your vision through telling, selling, testing, consulting, and co-creating.

9. Conduct the Decision-Making Process and Summarize Results

This is it. This is where you choose and when you decide the big things. The purpose of the decision-making process is to determine who your organization is (its mission) and what your direction is (vision and goals) for the next three to five years.

Based on the background information and its implications, you discuss your organization's possible choices and the consequences of each choice. Then your organization picks its preferred consequences. Remember, there will always be consequences. You simply must choose the ones you prefer.

Planning means choosing—choosing among various consequences.

The planning process manager facilitates the retreat, ensuring that questions are asked and the status quo is questioned. The process manager keeps dialogue focused and moving. She or he summarizes key points, brings conversation to closure, helps the group reach consensus, and moves the group toward its final decisions.

Begin the decision-making process by affirming your values. Often this conversation happens at the planning retreat. But sometimes the values conversation happens elsewhere, in a different time frame.

Allocate time at the start of the retreat to talk about the information gathered. Invite questions to clarify the findings. Explore the trends and implications of the information. The more you talk, the clearer your choices are. No matter whether you have lots of choices or only a few, they are probably challenging and stressful.

Use questions to stimulate conversation and focus choices. For example:

- What are the changing needs, short-term and long-term, in the community? Which of these needs are of greatest interest to our organization? Consider such things as compatibility with current mission, organizational experience and capability, marketplace competition, and return on investment.
- Who are the primary and secondary customers seeking services to meet these needs? Which customers do we currently serve? How might we reach new audiences in need? Are there customers we no longer choose to serve?
- Which internal and external factors, both recent and anticipated, are most important to the health of our organization? Consider such things as: changes in the philanthropic sector and within our industry specifically, changes in our customer base and customer expectations, technology demands, and competitors entering and leaving the service arena.
- What are the major relationships our organization needs to operate well? Which collaborations should we develop to provide services, to fundraise, to train volunteers, to bulk order supplies? What kind of alliances should we maintain to secure the information and knowledge to do our business better?
- How must we change our services to meet the changing needs of current and future customers? How can we alter our service scope and delivery without harming the customer? How do we differentiate our programs and services from those of other organizations?

Raise the questions worth asking, presented throughout this text. Your organization will identify more. And please, ask the most cage-rattling questions. Here. Together. During the decision-making process.

Not all visions are equal. Visions, which tap into an organization's deeper sense of purpose, have unique power to engender aspiration and commitment. To be genuinely shared, such visions must emerge from many people reflecting on the organization's purpose.

From *The Fifth Discipline Fieldbook*, by Peter M. Senge et al. (New York: Doubleday, 1994), 299

At some point, conversation is finished and your organization must choose. It doesn't matter whether you define your direction (where you are going) or determine your vision (what you will look like). In fact, some organizations do both. And this shared vision or direction, or both, is the major outcome of the decision-making retreat.

The concept of shared vision or direction brings to mind the same concern as shared values: does "shared" encourage homogeneity and discourage pluralism and diversity? No.

Ikujiro Nonaka observes that "umbrella concepts and qualitative criteria"[29] are critical to produce a unified direction within all the group's individuals. Karl-Henrik Robèrt describes these as a set of nonnegotiable agreements that allow teams to function.[30]

Nonaka goes on to say that "a company's vision needs also to be open-ended, susceptible to a variety of different and even conflicting interpretations. . . . If a vision is too unambiguous . . . it becomes more akin to an order or an instruction. . . . A more equivocal vision gives [people] the freedom and autonomy to set their own goals."[31]

MORE PLANNING RETREATS   See Appendix 6-H on this book's website for the Steel Yard's planning retreat agenda. See Appendix 6-I for the United Way of Dutchess County (UWDC) retreat agenda. Compare the retreat designs. Both organizations began their strategic planning processes in late 2008, at the start of the global economic recession. For the United Way, strategic planning is a regular process. For the Steel Yard, this was the first time.

Facing the United Way: radical changes in the United Way movement itself, including challenges to workplace giving and an unevolved understanding of donor-centered fund development. Facing the Steel Yard: a young entrepreneurial organization confronting professionalization and the body of knowledge in governance and management, planning and fund development.

Both retreats began with a conversation about the background information gathered, the trends and implications. This introductory conversation established quality information as the basis for decision-making. Retreat participants asked questions and, together, identified what was most important to the organization's future.

For the United Way, this preliminary conversation produced an insightful set of external trends that participants believed would set the context for the next several years.

For example: the economy (increasing unemployment, financial and housing crises, unpredictability over the longer term); nonprofit sector (institutional distress, competition for gifts, mergers); government trends (election and subsequent implications, troubled finances and disinvestment in community services, increased scrutiny); technology (changes in customer service expectations, new technologies like cell phones, texting, social networking); demographic trends (aging population, baby boomers and the wealth transfer, fewer residents in Dutchess County, more commuting from home to job, second homes versus primary residences). And, of course, there were more external trends, and internal trends, too.

Next, the UWDC retreat participants defined their vision for the future in mission and program, and in infrastructure. And finally, retreat participants identified the key points of leverage to move forward toward future vision.

The Steel Yard planning retreat used questions posed by Jim Collins, Peter Drucker, and Jeff Bezos. Questions like:

- What results will we hold ourselves accountable for?
- What is our theory of change?
- What are we deeply passionate about?
- What can we be best in the world at?
- What do we do/should we do that makes the biggest impact on those we serve?
- What is the optimal organizational structure required to support this direction?
- What are the biggest points of leverage for change?
- What, if we can get it to work, will be big—big enough to be meaningful to the Steel Yard as a whole if we're successful?

In both cases—the United Way and the Steel Yard—retreat participants worked together as a full group, and worked in smaller groups reporting back to the larger group.

The Women's Foundation of Southern Arizona defined its vision in a day-long retreat, Appendix 6-K posted on this book's website. Notice the length of this vision statement. Compare this long vision to the vision statement of the Greater Providence YMCA, presented in its strategic plan (Appendix 6-O) on this book's website. Is a vision statement only a few sentences or brief paragraphs in length?

Forget any rules you've heard. What will best serve your organization? Distinguish between a long vision statement and the brief inspirational summary that describes your vision. You post the latter on the wall and publish it in newsletters and annual reports. But rarely do these brief paragraphs provide the richness and detail required to clearly describe your desired future.

Call it vision or direction, or something else entirely—your organization needs a description of sufficient detail that it is not subject to excessive interpretation. Why? Because this lengthy and comprehensive description provides the foundation for the strategic plan and serves as the basis for your future decision-making. Make sure you have the detail that you need.

The test of a vision is not the statement, but in the directional force it gives the organization.

From *The Fifth Discipline: The Art and Practice of the Learning Organization*, by Peter M. Senge (New York: Doubleday, 1990)

Your organization's vision may not be achievable during the three- to five-year time frame of your strategic plan. Indeed, your vision should be a stretch—and it might take decades to achieve. Your vision might actually last through several iterations of a strategic plan. But the goals and strategies may change every few years as you make progress, launch new strategic planning processes, and learn and change.

Your organization moves toward its vision by bridging the gap between current reality and desired future. Each subsequent multiyear strategic plan moves you closer to your vision of the future until you finally reach it and must create a new vision.

10. Review (and Possibly Adjust) Mission

(Or is this the point where you decide to go out of business?)

Mission describes your organization's purpose, the reason you exist. Your mission statement defines what specific role your organization takes to achieve the result you desire.

Effective strategic planning tests mission. A healthy organization continually evaluates whether its mission best serves changing community needs and reflects the organization's vision of the future.

You do not create a plan to meet your mission. Absolutely not! Remember, the process of strategic planning ensures your organization's relevance. And what you learn through the planning process may require that you change your mission in order to be relevant.

Once your organization defines its direction for the future, circle back to your mission. Ask yourselves, "Does our current mission statement reflect our direction and vision for the future that we decided during our planning process?"

To evaluate your mission statement, use the decisions made about vision and direction to answer these questions.

- What is your geographic catchment area?
- Who is your audience? To whom do you provide your activities and services?
- What is your desired outcome? That is, what do you want to achieve by investing resources to carry out your activities?
- What are the basic means to achieve your desired outcome? That is, what activities or services will you do to achieve your vision?

Compare your answers to your current mission statement. Are all these answers reflected in your mission statement? If there is alignment, your mission statement is still relevant. If not, adjust it.

Look at the mission again and again to think through whether it needs to be refocused because demographics change, because we should abandon something that produces no results and eats up resources, because we have accomplished an objective.

From *Managing the Non-Profit Organization: Principles and Practices*, by Peter F. Drucker (New York: HarperCollins, 1990), 33

You can evaluate your mission statement in a number of ways. For example:

- *Test mission at the decision-making retreat.*

    Once retreat attendees choose your organization's direction, then evaluate your mission. As a full group, answer the mission questions. Compare the group's responses to the current mission statement. If the group decides that adjustments must be made, assign the rewriting to staff. Staff then shares the revision with the planning committee and then the board.

Or have retreat attendees work in small groups to answer the mission questions and compare their team's answers to the current mission statement. Reconvene the full group and discuss findings. Then, if the full group decides that adjustments must be made, proceed as just described.

■ *Test mission with the planning committee.*

Following the retreat decisions, the planning committee evaluates the mission statement. The committee answers the mission questions and compares results to the current mission statement. If necessary, staff drafts an adjusted mission for review and action by the board.

Keep in mind: You may need to go out of business. Your planning process may determine that your organization is not sufficiently relevant to justify its existence, draining community resources. Furthermore, your planning process may demonstrate that mission adjustment or even dramatic change doesn't produce relevance, either.

It's okay. Deciding to go out of business may be the best decision. And then planning to go out of business well is the right thing to do.

11. Determine Goals and Strategies

With mission and vision in hand, it's time to delve deeper. Goals and strategies explain how you will move toward your vision. Goals and strategies focus on program and infrastructure.

Karl-Henrik Robèrt describes this process as forecasting and back casting. The group forecasts its vision and back casts how to achieve the vision. Then the organization's various parts draw conclusions specific to their areas of operation.

Develop goals that are both realistic and challenging. Make sure the goals are measurable or observable. Achieving them propels you in your desired direction, toward your vision.

Outline the general strategies (also called action steps or activities) you will use to achieve your goals. Strategy, as postulated by Kenneth R. Andrews in his classic book *The Concept of Corporate Strategy*, reflects "the match between what a company can do (organizational strengths and weaknesses) within the universe of what it might do (environmental opportunities and threats)."[32]

There is no best format for presenting your organization's goals for the strategic plan. There are no rules that demand that you include objectives for each goal and strategies to accomplish each objective. You may find objectives useful or you may not. You may or may not establish benchmarks. You may use the terms *strategies* and *action steps* interchangeably, or you may decide that action steps are more detailed and will be done annually in work plans.

Whichever you choose, at least include measurable or observable goals accompanied by strategic activities to achieve the goals. Whatever you choose, don't be too specific. Don't get caught with detailed objectives, too many strategies, lots of activities, or concrete action steps. A certain vagueness maintains your flexibility. As the plan proceeds, you develop annual activities that reflect the constantly changing environment.

Also, remember that action is short-term. Peter Drucker tells organizations to always ask: "Is this action step leading us toward our basic long-range goal, or is it going to sidetrack us, going to divert us, going to make us lose sight of what we are here to do?"[33]

Your organization needs to be results driven as you outline your activities. Ask yourself if you are getting sufficient return on your investment of time, money, and other resources. Ask yourself if you are allocating resources in the best way possible, using your organization's strengths, to meet your benchmarks and achieve your goals.

Everyone should recognize the goals because they are a natural outgrowth of the market research results and the chosen direction or vision. Ask the board to approve the goals before the plan is actually written. With this approval, the board authorizes the planning committee and staff to move forward with the next steps in the planning process. These incremental approvals help build understanding and ownership.

For example, the goals of the United Way of Dutchess County are expressed as four pillars of excellence: Meaningful community impact. Engaged community. Donor-centered fund development. Top-quality governance and management. See the full plan, Appendix 6-N, posted on this book's website. The goals of the YMCA of Greater Providence New Century Plan are: Family focus. Working with others. Quality improvement. See the full plan, Appendix 6-O, posted on this book's website. See Appendix 6-L, posted on this book's website, for the strategic plan of the Audubon Society of Rhode Island, listing all its goals.

See Exhibit 6.5 for the goals of the Steel Yard.

Exhibit 6.5   Steel Yard Goals

Program, Activities, and Space

Goal #1: Develop the site.
Goal #2: Strengthen programming and activities to fulfill mission and vision framework.

Building an Effective Organization

Goal #1: Get the right people on the bus.
Goal #2: Enhance financial sustainability.
Goal #3: Create the necessary systems and processes to assure excellence and adaptive capacity in all areas of operation.

Source: Courtesy of the Steel Yard, Providence, Rhode Island (www.thesteelyard.org).

---

12. Identify Core Competencies and Supporting Structures

With your vision, goals and strategies in hand, identify the core competencies that your organization will need to move forward. Consider the competencies required of staff as well as board and committees. Your organization may need to develop new competencies and strengthen others. Think about how you will make these changes. Does your organization need a comprehensive training program to develop the competencies required of board and staff? How will you introduce and manage the change? As architect Louis Sullivan said, form follows function. Now that you know your direction, design the best structure to support your forward movement. Perhaps your organization will abandon certain committees and institute new ones. Maybe you need to redefine committee and officer roles. Maybe the CEO will devise a new staffing structure, revise job descriptions, reorganize departments, eliminate some staff positions, and invent new ones.

13. Define Measures for Success

Hold your organization accountable for achieving its goals by defining measures that are quantifiable or, at least, observable. Measures describe how you will know if you have accomplished your goals. These measures should be both short-term and long-term, both qualitative and quantitative. Often it is easier to project quantitative targets over the shorter term.

Although general parameters for success may be defined at the retreat, staff often define measures later. Staff may involve the planning committee in preliminary discussion or may present a draft for committee conversation and review.

You might find it useful to present the measures, along with their relevant goals, to the board for conversation prior to drafting the complete plan. Do this as an incremental step in the strategic planning process. Once the board reviews and adjusts the measures, include these in the strategic plan.

See Exhibit 6.6 for an example of a goal, its strategies, and its measures for the Audubon Society. See this book's website for more examples of plans and measures.

Exhibit 6.6   Example of Audubon Society Goal and Its Strategies and Measures

Goal: Develop an environmentally literate and motivated local populace that supports and promotes sustainable living and stewardship of our natural resources.

Rhode Islanders recognize that everything is connected—from economic development to stewardship of natural resources. Young and old promote sustainable living.

Strategies:
A. Assure proper integration of educational focus with ASRI advocacy and conservation focuses. *(Ongoing)*
B. Design quality educational experiences relevant to our target audiences, and responsive to their changing finances. Specifically:
   ■ Provide authentic, investigative, hands-on learning experiences. *(Ongoing)*

(continued)

(Continued)

- Develop place-based educational experiences for use in urban, suburban, and rural schools, and ensure interface with RI curriculum standards. *(Ongoing)*
- Refine current programs to assure that they are place-linked and relevant. *(Initiate in 2007. Maintain thereafter.)*
- Develop public programs that educate, entertain, and motivate. *(Ongoing)*

C. Ensure teaching and learning excellence. *(Ongoing)*
D. Improve program quality on a continuous basis. *(Ongoing)*
E. Promote understanding of environmental issues and how these affect the local populace. *(Ongoing)*
F. Educate local constituencies so they can effectively solve local problems. *(Ongoing)*

Key performance measures (Performance outcomes will be developed annually.)
A. Program participation trends
B. Satisfaction rate
C. Repeat business
D. Environmental literacy trends
E. Advocacy participation trends

Source: Courtesy of the Audubon Society of Rhode Island, www.asri.org.

14. Assign Time Frames and Entities Responsible for Strategies

Accountability is more than just achieving measures. Accountability demands a time frame and requires assignments of responsibility.

An effective strategic plan includes an overall implementation calendar and a general description of which entity is responsible for which activity. Think in terms of quarters of the year for implementation. Don't get too specific projecting time frames for future years. See the sample strategic plans in the appendices posted on the website.

15. Describe Financing

Some organizations include multiyear financial projections as part of the strategic plan itself. Other organizations describe the overall cost analysis and financing strategy.

No matter your approach, the financial section of your strategic plan does not replace your annual budgeting process. Neither does the financial section guarantee income and expenses. The financial section should, however, establish parameters and demonstrate the viability of your goals.

While it isn't possible to estimate the cost or identify the income for all the activities in your plan, you can present general financial considerations. You can outline the process you will use to secure funding for a specific activity. Sometimes the strategic planning process establishes a new or extended set of guidelines for financial decision-making and planning.

Staff prepares the financial section of the strategic plan. The board's finance and fund development committees provide useful insights. Further, their understanding and support help build full board ownership. Use the multiyear strategic plan to establish your organization's annual priorities. These priorities provide the framework for the annual budgeting process. Use the strategic planning process to segue into the annual budgeting process. Staff and finance committee may use the strategic plan and its priorities to project income and expense for the first fiscal year of the strategic plan.

In each subsequent year of the strategic plan, host an annual retreat to prepare staff and finance committee for the new budget process by reviewing progress on the strategic plan and determining priorities for the new fiscal year. Then staff along with finance and fund development committees draft the annual budget and fund development plan. For more about fund development planning and plans, see Chapter 9.

16. Outline Process to Annualize the Plan, Including Defining Benchmarks for Measures

Your strategic plan sets the context and defines the parameters for a multiyear period. But what about this year and the next, each year of the multiyear plan? You know it's tough to project the focus for the years in your plan. Sure you try. But things change. Even the best strategic planning process can get stuck targeting what should happen in the third or fourth year of the plan—and sometimes year 2, too!

So break it down. I call this annualizing the multiyear plan. Each year, identify the priorities for that year. Based on those priorities, draft the budget for that year. Project the annual benchmarks for the measures outlined in the multiyear plan, but anchored in the previous year's performance, not some multiyear hoped-for estimates defined back when you first drafted the plan.

Here's more detail. And, remember: All this happens within the context of the multiyear strategic plan, and what's been happening both internally and externally.

First, a few months prior to the new fiscal year, host a planning retreat. Do this at an extended board meeting or at a special retreat.

Focus on progress to date. Review your results based on the measures you identified. Do another SWOT analysis. Bring in any new information that can help make quality decisions. Make sure you embrace the essential questions and cage-rattling ones, too.

After this review and conversation, identify the priorities for the new fiscal year. Yes, your goals will likely be the same. But different strategies may be a priority now.

Of course, use those priorities to draft the budget for the new fiscal year. Define the fiscal year benchmarks for your measures. Assign accountabilities and estimate time frames. And that's it: the annualization of your multiyear strategic plan.

17. Outline Process to Monitor Progress of the Plan, Evaluate Performance, and Extend the Plan for Subsequent Years

A viable plan requires a process for monitoring progress, evaluating overall performance, and extending the plan in subsequent years. This section of the plan describes the steps by which staff and volunteers gauge progress and performance.

Here, too, the plan proposes target dates or time frames. See examples in the strategic plans posted on the book's website.

Your strategic plan has a time limit, generally three to five years. Toward the end of the current plan, start the process of strategic planning for the next interval. Your current plan may briefly describe how you propose to extend the plan or launch another strategic planning process.

18. Write the Strategic Plan; Review and Adopt

Now put all the pieces together. Your written strategic plan is a living resource for your organization. It guides your organization's activities and decisions. Well-used, smudged, and dog-eared, the plan accompanies the board, committee members, and staff to meetings; sets the context for fund development; shapes annual budgeting; and helps evaluate staff and volunteer performance.

To be this useful, make sure your plan is user-friendly. Write clearly and organize well. Provide enough detail but not too much. See the four strategic plans posted on this book's website: Audubon Society of Rhode Island, Steel Yard, United Way of Dutchess County, and the YMCA of Greater Providence.

Often, the planning process manager writes the strategic plan, bringing together the various components in an organized fashion. The CEO reviews and edits the draft. Sometimes the organization writes the plan, and the planning process manager serves as guide and editor. This is a good way to save money if you're using a consultant as your process manager.

The CEO reviews the strategic plan before it goes to the planning committee for review and recommendation to the board. The planning committee recommends the plan to the board. Board discussion will likely be quite brief if board members have been engaged throughout the process and if you have done incremental approvals along the way.

19. Translate the Plan into Organizational and Personal Commitment

The most effective strategic planning process generates organizational commitment. The best process generates understanding and ownership, learning and change. The process produces alignment and commitment within the organization and its stakeholders.

Now step back a moment: The planning process began by securing the opinions and perspectives of individuals and organizations. Individuals worked together to produce a shared vision and strategies for your organization.

Once a shared vision has been developed, it is critical that all components of the [organization] be aligned to achieve the goals and objectives laid out in the plan.

From "The Power of Plan," by John F. Schlegal, in *Association Management* (Washington, DC: American Society of Association Executives, 1995)

Now return to the individual. How will each individual in your organization translate this shared plan into her or his personal commitment? What tasks are appropriate for each person? What kind of short- and long-term financial commitment will be forthcoming? How will each individual use the learning acquired during the planning process to strengthen personal performance?

For example, use a number of activities to translate the plan into personal commitment for board members.

- *First, return to the beginning, before board members become board members.*
  Many of your constituents are potential board members. Develop their understanding and commitment, for example, through the strategic planning process. Then, if you recruit these constituents, they already understand how your organization plans and what the vision is.
- *Second, based on the new vision and strategic plan, examine the roles and responsibilities and performance expectations of board members.*
  Make changes as necessary. When you interview candidates for board membership, discuss your values, current vision, and the strategic plan that takes you there.
  Explain how your organization uses planning to help produce learning. Evaluate the candidate's commitment to your vision and strategic plan before offering her or him a position on the board.
- *Third, make sure each incumbent participates in the planning process.*
  Ensure that each one supports the shared values, vision, and strategic plan. If a board member is not comfortable with the results of planning, then encourage him or her to resign from the board. If possible, keep the individual involved on a committee or in some manner.
- *Fourth, meet personally with each board member and negotiate his or her individual commitment to the vision and plan.*
  Naturally, this commitment includes task assignments, committee or team participation, financial investment, and assistance with fund development. Many organizations create a written contract, which is signed by each board member.
  Share the commitments with the entire board, except for the confidentiality of gift amounts. The full board should know what each of its members commits to the organization and hence to each other.

20. Implement the Strategic Plan and Generate and Implement the Subplans

Implementation should be the fun part—or at least the more fun part! (Yes, some of us find the planning process just as much fun.) But implementation is challenging, too. Your organization must keep the plan alive and the constituents engaged.

Moreover, the multiyear strategic plan serves as the framework for all other institutional plans—fund development, marketing to acquire clients, and so forth. See, for example, the integration of the Steel Yard's fund development plan and its strategic plan, both located on this book's website.

Keeping the Plan Alive

You've finished the planning process. Your organization has its plan.

Let's assume your planning process was effective. Your constituents participated actively and they own the resulting plan. Your organization is more cohesive than it has ever been, sharing a vision and excitement for the future.

Now you must implement the plan, keeping the vision alive and moving forward. This may be the hardest process you face. For many organizations the strategic plan generates significant change. In this situation, the organization must focus on the transition and change process. Don't just assume change will happen. Look back at Chapter 3, the sections on well-managed change and adaptive capacity.

Bring together organization leadership to discuss transition and change. In the context of the vision and strategic plan, outline what has to be done. Consider the barriers to change. Consider the resources that can overcome the barriers. Remember: You will not achieve your vision of the future if you end the process with the strategic plan. Your plan now serves as the starting point for the next process, that of transition and change. Plan this next process well, execute with care, and you will realize your vision.

As you implement your plan, focus first on your CEO. Your organization's CEO is responsible for ensuring institutional health, which includes achieving the organization's vision. In operational terms, this means that the CEO is principally responsible for ensuring progress of the plan. The CEO enables staff and volunteers to work together, moving the organization forward.

Achievement of vision and progress of the plan is a key component of the CEO's annual performance appraisal. In fact, strategic planning is part of the CEO's job description.[34]

The best way to keep your strategic plan alive and used: annualize it.

Use these strategies to help your organization keep its plan alive.

- *Follow the plan.* Carry out activities to reach your benchmarks and achieve your goals. Adhere to the time frames.
- *Create integrated subplans.* Use the strategic plan to develop other plans such as marketing and fund development. Construct the plans as a coordinated, integrated whole.
- *Annualize your strategic plan.* Translate your multiyear strategic plan into detailed annual work plans for board, committees, and staff. Use the strategic plan as the framework for annual budgeting.
- *Annually, conduct a planning retreat.* Review progress to date and make adjustments for the next year of the plan.
- *Hold each individual and all groups accountable.* Make sure that each committee, department, team, and individual regularly explores his, her, or their role and progress in achieving your organization's vision.
- Use the plan to set the context for deliberations, decision-making, and action. Make sure that leadership communicates the linkages (see Exhibit 6.7) among the planning process, plan, and current activities. Use the plan as a guideline for decisions.

Exhibit 6.7   Using Linkage Analysis

Linkage analysis is another way to structure decision-making conversations. This planning tool helps organizations recognize the various interrelationships that exist in current operations and identifies the interrelationships necessary to implement a new vision.

You create diagrams that describe your organization's internal and external relationships. Start with a question you want to answer or a goal you wish to achieve. The linkage diagrams document the factors that answer your questions or affect your goal. Discussion continues by constructing multiple levels of diagrams that pursue factors in greater depth.

Linkage analysis makes no assumptions. Participants put aside any preconceived notions. Whatever is important goes on the linkage chart. As dialogue proceeds, participants continually ask, "How will this item I add to the chart help us achieve 'substantial and sustainable strategic advantage'?" Link staff, board, team, and committee performance to the strategic plan. Translate the goals and benchmarks of the strategic plan into goals and responsibilities for departments, work teams, and individuals. Define key performance criteria in terms of progress of the plan.

Source: Kenneth I. Primozic, Edward A. Primozic, and Joe Leben, *Strategic Choices: Supremacy, Survival or Sayonara* (New York: McGraw-Hill, 1991).

- Reshape board and staff meeting agendas. Use the goals of the plan as the key elements for each agenda. Use the plan's benchmarks as the focus for leadership's dialogue.
- Regularly review and discuss progress of the plan. Provide written and oral updates. Discuss challenges and opportunities.
- Institutionalize internal and external assessment as part of operations.

  Alternate the assessment process yearly. One year, evaluate program and institutional capacity; the next year, assess community needs. Use the information for continuous quality improvement for your institution's operations. Also, use the information to make adjustments to the strategic plan.

  When it is time to update the strategic plan, your organization will have much of its market research completed.
- Maintain a planning committee or team that reports to the board. This group carries out many of the strategies suggested here.
- Remember that planning is learning. Create a learning organization. Then get ready to change—because planning is learning and learning is change.

Most importantly, the right attitude keeps the plan alive. Every choice, each decision, all actions evolve from organizational vision and the strategic plan.

Because planning is learning, organization leaders consistently and continually use the plan to frame all activities. These leaders keep the plan alive by asking the questions worth asking. A useful mantra for the individual and his or her group might be:

- How does what I am/we are doing relate to the vision and strategic plan?
- Are these activities the best use of my/our resources?
- What should I/we not do?
- What should I/we do next to make progress on the plan and move toward our vision?

Documenting and Communicating Your Planning Process and Plan

Documenting both the process and plan provides multiple benefits to your organization. For example:

Documentation serves as an important part of individual and organization learning. Documenting and communicating help keep the planning process and plan alive—and allow you to evaluate your processes and make improvements for the future. Also, you can use the wealth of information produced during the planning process to develop programs and other activities.

Ongoing communication enables your organization to build understanding and support for its processes, decisions, and direction. Throughout the planning process and the plan's implementation, communicate with your constituents. For example, tell them:

- Why your organization is planning and how planning will strengthen your service to the community.
- What the planning process looks like and why the process itself is so important.
- Why the stakeholders' participation in planning is critical.
- General findings and implications of the planning process.
- Key decisions of the planning process.
- How the organization will change.
- Progress of implementing the plan.

Evaluating Your Strategic Planning Process

Effective organizations regularly evaluate management and governance functions, including the process of strategic planning. Debrief when the planning process ends and use the evaluation results to improve the design of your next strategic planning process.

If you established a planning committee, it can lead this assessment. Certainly, each board committee (e.g., fund development, governance) uses the strategic plan and can assess performance in their respective spheres of work.

Conduct formal and informal conversations with constituencies that participated in the planning process. You could even conduct focus groups and surveys to help evaluate the planning process.

Consider the following issues as you evaluate the effectiveness of your planning process.

- Which constituencies were involved in what components of the planning process? How many, how often, and to what extent? What might you change in the next planning process?

- Was the market research—both internal and external—sufficient to help you ask the right questions and make the best decisions? What would you do differently in the next planning process?
- Were all parts of the organization—all functions and systems—involved in the planning process? How well did the process reach throughout the system?
- How did you use questioning and conversation during the process? Do you still do this? Did you ask the really cage-rattling questions? If so, what were the results? How involved were various constituencies in the asking process? How might you engage people differently in the next planning process?
- How well did you address issues of program and infrastructure?
- How engaged were your trustees and staff in the planning process? What was the level of understanding and enthusiasm for the process? What might you do in the future to enhance understanding and participation?
- How well did you maintain the momentum of planning while maintaining normal operations? Are there other strategies that would help you balance future planning and current implementation?
- How well did you inform constituents of the progress of planning? Was communication adequate? How might it be improved?
- Throughout the process, were there extensive formal and informal conversations about planning? How might you encourage even more conversation?
- How well did your decision-makers dialogue? How comfortable were they with disagreement and conflict resolution? How can you enhance this capability?
- Overall, how well did your organization and its individuals learn? Did planning produce learning? How can you enhance your organization's learning capacity?
- How excited are people about the resulting plan? To what extent are individuals, teams, departments, and committees using the plan? How well is your strategic plan integrated into the organization?

Challenges to Strategic Planning

Regular effective strategic planning by nonprofits/NGOs will produce healthier communities. Why? Because community needs assessments encourage organizations to be more responsive. Analysis of competitors, collaborators, and knowledge alliances can create integrated systems that provide better service by reducing duplication and producing areas of excellence. Examination of institutional capacity builds stronger, more stable organizations.

Yet, strategic planning is neither sufficiently regular nor adequately effective. Too often, the challenges overwhelm both process and results.

However, effective organizations anticipate and accommodate the challenges. These organizations—and their communities—benefit from strategic planning.

Committing Time

Often staff and board members are reluctant to commit sufficient time. Current demands are so overwhelming that considering the future is not possible.

This excuse reminds me of a colleague who could not attend a time management seminar—offered in our own facility at no charge—because she did not have the time. There is no response to this attitude. Either individuals and organizations eventually recognize their own folly or they do not.

Maintaining Momentum

Once embarked upon planning, some organizations cannot maintain enough momentum. Current reality interrupts so frequently that the planning process lingers, limping along beyond anyone's interest and out of step with the changing environment.

Often this happens because a staff person with too many other responsibilities acts as the planning process manager. Anticipate this problem in advance. It's easier to succeed if you take some responsibilities away from the staff person until the planning process is finished. Or get some additional help; maybe hire a consultant.

Narrowing the Scope of Planning

You compromise the planning process by narrowing its scope. Be inclusive rather than exclusive. For example, make sure you focus on program and infrastructure, project income and expense, and include your key stakeholders.

Succumbing to the Marketplace

Organizations are relevant when they are meaningful to the community. Fund development works when the organization meets the need of the donor and volunteer. But organizations can be too responsive, thereby compromising their values and vision.

For example:

■ *A donor offers a significant gift if your organization agrees to develop a specific program.*

The proposed program does not reflect your organization's vision and priorities at this time. Should your organization accept the donor's offer? No. Within your values, vision, mission, and priorities, you seek donors. You learn their interests and meet their needs if possible. Seeking funds happens within the framework of your values, vision, and mission.

■ *Though most organizations should alter their mission if so indicated by an effective strategic planning process, this is not appropriate for arts groups.*

An arts organization possesses an artistic vision. A theater's vision might be to produce contemporary and avant-garde work. Market research indicates that the community prefers lighthearted, classic comedy. Should the theater change its artistic vision? No. But it must either find an audience for the vision or choose to close.

"Marketing does not tell an artist how to create a work of art; rather, the role of marketing is to match the artist's creations and interpretations with an appropriate audience. . . . The belief that the consumer is [king or queen] . . . would be harmful if applied to the arts world. The artist, not the consumer, should have the final deciding vote."[35]

Issues Conspiracy

A group can compromise its own planning process through issues conspiracy. In this situation, group members recognize that the organization faces significant issues. The issues are stressful and controversial and may demand dramatic changes for the organization. Anxious about conflict and threatened by possible change, the group colludes to avoid discussion.

While issues conspiracy is dangerous to institutional health, planned delay can be appropriate. Some organizations are simply not prepared to discuss challenging issues. Group members may not have enough experience with conversation. They may be unable to share their opinions and concerns, afraid of disagreement, and uncomfortable resolving conflict.

If this is your situation, build in delay. Put the issues on the table but don't expect to resolve them by the end of the planning process. Describe the issues in the plan and outline a process whereby the organization learns to dialogue and address difficult issues. Establish goals that include discussion and resolution of the issues.

This intentional delay provides time for the organization to learn how to discuss and resolve difficult issues. The issues do not need to be resolved during the planning process itself.

Routine Instead of Visionary

Some individuals in your organization expect a creative, farseeing, and visionary strategic plan. However, the organization may not yet be ready for this. Your organization may need to address more routine issues before moving into a visionary phase. A less visionary plan may be the necessary bridge, preparing the organization for a more creative plan in subsequent years.

False Expectations

Some people expect to resolve all issues during the planning process so the resulting written plan has all the answers. This is not possible. The best plans contain some answers but not all. However, the best plans outline how the organization will address any outstanding issues during the course of the plan's implementation.

Balancing Flexibility and Inflexibility

Even though you have a plan, things change. Opportunities may arise that you wish to pursue. New challenges demand attention.

The plan is a road map to get to your destination, but you may detour along the way. Experienced and successful voyagers anticipate and accommodate these detours. Just remember, adding something new requires additional resources, or your organization will have to decide what to eliminate from the current plan.

Be careful. Don't be too flexible, though, because this suggests that you do not value the plan. Sometimes organizations use flexibility as an excuse to avoid their goals.

Changing Leadership

Some of your leadership will change during the plan's implementation and also during the planning process. Yet this change should have little effect in successful organizations.

A good plan, produced by an effective planning process, belongs to the entire institution and all its constituencies. When changes in position occur within the organization, they should be of little consequence to the plan. The new players helped design the plan or have been adequately oriented to understand and support the plan and its process.

Violating Integrity of the Process

After the decision-making retreat, someone questions the decisions made. Perhaps this person didn't attend the retreat and doesn't like the choices made. Maybe your most important donor heard about the decisions and has some comments.

You've seen this before. Maybe this happens at your board meetings where the absent people raise issues later. Or those who didn't agree with the decisions keep bringing up the issues at subsequent meetings.

Don't let this happen! Remember the old saying, "Those who show up decide." If you miss a meeting—albeit reluctantly—those present make decisions and the smart organization doesn't revisit those decisions. Effective organizations don't violate the integrity of the group who worked together, explored issues, and made decisions.

Think about this: Why is the absent voice more important than all those who were previously present? If you want to revisit the decisions, then you're obligated to bring back together all the people who participated in the decision-making previously. Really. And how is that good business?

Planning While Implementing

Henry Mintzberg postulates that traditional strategic planning behaves as if the world holds still while we plan. Then the world stays on the course we predicted while we implement the plan.

Naturally, as Mintzberg observes, this is absurd. Locally and globally, change is constant. True strategic planning does not rely on predictability. Rather, strategic thinking and action are part of strategic planning. Effective organizations balance planning while implementing another plan. These organizations embrace uncertainty and ambiguity, and effective strategic planning helps them do so.

Really Important Musings

And now some final thoughts, mini-musings that are really important.

Risk or Gamble

Was it National Public Radio or some article somewhere? I don't remember where, but I do remember what: There's a difference between a risk and a gamble; a really big difference.

A risk is something you can back out of.

A gamble ... no way out.

The military talks about risks and gambles regularly.

But how can we apply risks and gambles to the operation of the nonprofit/NGO sector? What is the application in your organization? How might we apply risks or gambles to strategic planning and decision-making?

For example:

- Use strategic planning processes to explore risks and gambles. Incorporate risk ratings for the strategies in your plans.
- Define criteria for risking and gambling. Then use these criteria to evaluate strategies. Keep the risky strategies and abandon the gambles.
- Define the moment when risks might cross the line into gambles. Pull the plug prior to crossing the line.
- Craft a series of questions—a checklist—to monitor risks. And don't forget to use the checklist.
- Create a risk rating system (e.g., based on points or percentages). Rate the risks you choose.
- Of course, host regular staff and board conversations to explore the concepts of risks and gambles. Build an organizational culture capable of exploring and examining, monitoring and measuring risk.

Taking Risks—and Failing

Gambles are bad. Risks are good if you can extricate yourself without too much damage. Risks are really good if you learn how to risk well. And risks are especially good if you succeed.

But wait: Risks are especially good if you succeed? That's not the message we want to embrace. By linking risk to success, we suggest that failure is bad. By linking risk to failure, we may be reluctant to risk often and sufficiently.

Pay attention to what Seth Godin says in his blog, "A Hierarchy of Failure Worth Following":[36]

Fail often: *Ideas that challenge the status quo. Proposals. Brainstorms. Concepts that open doors.*

Fail frequently: *Prototypes. Spreadsheets. Sample ads and copy.*

Fail occasionally: *Working mockups. Playtesting sessions. Board meetings.*

Fail rarely: *Interaction with small groups of actual users and customers.*

Fail never: *Keeping promises to our constituents.*

The thing is, in their rush to play it safe and then their urgency to salvage everything in the face of an emergency, most organizations do precisely the opposite. They throw their customers or their people under the bus ("we had no choice") but rarely take the proactive steps necessary to fail quietly, and often, in private, in advance, when there's still time to make things better.

Better to have a difficult conversation now than a failed customer interaction later.

Assuming Assumptions—or Questioning Them

See the many references to assumptions in Chapter 3. Read Chapter 3 again. Now review the section about leaders as critical thinkers in Chapter 5. This is really important. Actually, assumptions can be really dangerous, too.

What's an assumption? Something we take for granted, that we assume is true. Think generalizations, deeply held beliefs, images.

Learning organization theory calls these mental models, deeply ingrained in our minds. We draw conclusions based on our assumptions. These mental models influence our thinking, how we understand the world, and our actions.

The trouble is, these assumptions may not be true. Our mental models may stop us from learning and changing. Just remember what Admiral Thad W. Allen of the Coast Guard, national commander of the 2010 BP Gulf of Mexico oil spill, said when asked about BP's clean-up response: "I think they're adequate to the assumptions in the plans. I think you need to go back and question the assumptions."[37] Read that again. Admiral Allen didn't critique the actions steps outlined in the clean-up response. He critiqued the risk assessment that formed the basis for the plan. He expressed grave concern about the assumptions that BP used to make its decisions.

Critical thinking—and good planning and quality leadership and effective organizations—require that we suspend our assumptions, call them into question. We cannot get rid of our assumptions—nor would we want to, in many cases. But we can challenge our assumptions and those of others. Only then can we listen and learn—and change as necessary.

Think how you might use these questions:

- What assumptions stop our organization from learning and changing?
- What assumptions—if we don't explore them—might cause us to take risks that are really gambles?
- What are the big unforeseens—the unimaginable—that we assume will not happen?

Only the careless leave a possibility unattended due to assumptions.

From *Locked Rooms*, by Laurie R. King (New York: Bantam Books, 2010)

Organized Abandonment

Imagine: Your organization abandons a service or a program. Intentionally, in a well-organized and planned fashion, your organization stops that thing. Constructively and honorably, you put an end to it.

You had many meaningful conversations. You asked strategic and cage-rattling questions. You challenged people's assumptions. Perhaps you conducted research. You explored alternatives. You forecasted the future. You brainstormed the unforeseen.

Then—with careful planning and communication—you ended that service or program. Intentionally. In a well-organized and constructive fashion.

If you haven't done this yet, why not?

Anticipating the Unforeseen

How do we protect organizations from the unforeseen and the unexpected? By confronting the unforeseen and the unexpected. Good planning isn't just about forecasting. The best planning actually explores the unforeseen. Just imagine: What if banks and mortgage holders had envisioned what might possibly go wrong? What if governments had projected worst-case scenarios? Think about this: "You're waiting for something to happen, and you expect it to go one of two ways. But you're wrong because there's always a third way."[38]

There's always a third way. There's always something unforeseen.

But surely we can anticipate better. In strategic planning, organizations could create the worst-case scenarios. Actually, it's probably not that hard to do, given the actual examples we have.

We can ask ourselves:

- What could go wrong? How? Why?
- What might be the third way?
- What is the most unforeseeable thing we could imagine?
- What could be the next disaster like the 2010 Haiti earthquake or the Pakistan floods?
- What would it take to create disasters like the 2010 BP Gulf oil spill or the 2008–2009 global economic crisis?
- What would we do if our government eliminated the tax deductibility of charitable gifts?
- What if . . .

Think about this: "For the Americans and the British, a nuclear Iran represented a regional challenge; for Israel an existential threat."[39]

What if you designed your strategic planning process to ask: What are our challenges? What are our existential threats?

Or: What are the challenges facing our community—and how can our organization help the community respond? What are the existential threats to our community—and how can our organization help the community respond?

How do we make organizations listen to Cassandra? How do we ensure that all organizations develop Cassandra-like warning systems?

Now think about what Peter C. Goldmark Jr. said back in 1991:

You and I are constantly called upon to make assumptions about what the world will be like in five or ten years—and we guide our programs on the basis of these assumptions. The degree to which we are successfully clairvoyant will vary. But we all know what it is like not to be able to see ahead. And we all have had that queasy feeling that comes when we are surprised by something we should have known was coming all along.

Samuel Beckett caught that insight best. He penned one of the great, instructive thoughts of our time: "Everything will turn out all right—unless something unforeseen crops up."

That thought of Beckett's haunts me. If we remain . . . trapped in political gridlock, paralyzed in the face of challenge, it will not be because there were too many surprises. It will be because of what we can foresee but choose to ignore.[40]

Summary

Strategic planning ensures your relevance by defining and renewing your relationship with the community. And your relationship with the community is the second of four relationships that are essential to effective fund development.

Planning is an ongoing activity. Planning is also a well-devised campaign, on a broad scale, conducted to achieve an end. Effective planning is a process whereby an organization or group decides where it wishes to be in the future and how to reach that future. You map out modes of related action and invest and mobilize resources to attain your goals.

Strategic planning helps your organization accept ambiguity and uncertainty and develop a high tolerance for complexity, learning, and change. Planning focuses your organization's activities, determines priorities, and sets limits.

Strategic planning takes the long view. Your organization will likely decide things today whose effect will not be felt for five or even 10 years. The plan's time frame is generally three to five years, no longer because we live in such a swiftly changing world.

Your written plan answers the following questions.

The Questions You Ask	Your Answers Articulated as ...
Where is our organization going and why?	Values, mission, and vision
How will we get there?	Program and infrastructure goals and strategies
What is our blueprint for action?	Budget, time frames, and assignments of accountability
How will we know if we are on track?	Accountability and control (measures and benchmarks, process for monitoring progress)

CHAPTER 7

The Third Relationship—With Your Constituents

Nurturing Relationships to Build Loyalty

As the amount of inputs goes up, as the number of people and ideas that clamor for attention continue to increase, we do what people always do: we rely on the familiar, the trusted, and the personal. The experience I have with you as a customer or a friend is far more important than a few random bits flying by on the screen. The incredible surplus of digital data means that human actions, generosity, and sacrifice are more important than they ever were before.
—Seth Godin's blog, "The Blizzard of Noise (and the Good News),"
August 27, 2010, at www.sethgodin.com

Many of marketing's most severe critics give it more credit than it deserves. Marketing is not manipulation; it cannot make people buy things they do not desire. . . . As the legendary impresario, Sol Hurok, is reputed to have said, "If the people do not want to come, there is nothing you can do to stop them."
—Michael P. Mokwa, William M. Dawson, and E. Arthur Prieve,
Marketing the Arts (New York: Praeger Publishers, 1980, 5)

More Thinking Since the Previous Edition

In 1996 and 2000, I wrote the first and second editions of *Strategic Fund Development: Building Profitable Relationships That Last*. Then—and now—I proposed four relationships to build effective organizations and successful fund development programs. Within this premise, I defined the third relationship as the relationship with your constituents.

In the original editions, I wrote about *customer-centered*, but didn't yet use the term *donor-centered*. I demanded a focus on prospect and donor interests and emotions, motivations and aspirations.

In the original editions, this chapter focused on communicating and cultivating. I provided lots of tips and specific steps to develop your relationships with your constituents. But then. . . . Well, then came *Keep Your Donors*. Published in 2008 and co-authored with Tom Ahern—leading expert in donor communications—the book's subtitle pretty much tells the whole story: *The Guide to Better Communications and Stronger Relationships*.

Keep Your Donors actually is the expanded, comprehensive, detailed version of the third relationship. *Keep Your Donors* is the sequel to *Strategic Fund Development*. *Keep Your Donors* is the companion text to this chapter that you're starting right now.

I'm not rewriting *Keep Your Donors* in this chapter. I'm not including all of Tom Ahern's books in this chapter—but all of his books are important to nurturing the third relationship. So is his free e-news. For more, visit www.aherncomm.com.

I'm not citing all of Adrian Sargeant's research, past, current, and future. Read it yourself. Read Sargeant and Jay's *Building Donor Loyalty*. Read *Fundraising Principles and Practice* by Sargeant, Shang, and Associates.

Stay on top of the research about donors and fundraising. Read the research about similarities and differences in giving based on gender, generation, race/ethnicity/culture, and socioeconomic status. Read the research about solicitation strategies, social media, and response.

Pay lots of attention to psychology and neuroscience. Read the neuroscience marketing blog at www.neurosciencemarketing.com. Read Jeff Brooks's blog at www.futurefundraisingnow.com. Read books by the Heath brothers and Seth Godin. Read Lisa Sargent's donor loyalty blog at www.lisasargent.com.

I'll stop now. This is only the tip of the iceberg. Check my website, newsletter, and blogs for more ideas. Read as much as you can. Keep learning. It's up to you. This chapter—focusing on constituency development . . . nurturing relationships with your constituents (in particular your donors)—depends on all the books and blogs and research in the field.

Defining Constituency Development

First, review the various definitions in Chapter 1, explaining words like *constituent* and *stakeholder*, *predisposed* and *prospect*, *donor* and *customer*. That refresher will help guide you through this chapter.

Now, what is constituency development? The process of developing relationships with your constituents. Call it your relationship-building program. Call it the moves management process.[1] Or how about customer relationship management (CRM)?[2] All this means relationship building.

Constituency development means relationship building.

I used "constituency development" in the first two editions of this book. I used "relationship building" in *Keep Your Donors*. I'll use both those phrases in this third edition. (But I won't use "moves management" or "CRM." They focus too much on the organization and sound too ... I'm not sure what but I don't much like the feeling they give me.)

No matter what you call the process, keep in mind the following: This is a strategic process firmly rooted in customer centrism and donor centrism. Every organization in each sector needs such a program. Your constituency development program nurtures relationships. And relationships are critical to healthy and effective organizations.

Your constituency development program identifies and enables constituents to move through the various stages of relationships with your organization. Think of this as a continuum of relationships. Your process brings people (or businesses or ...) into the continuum. You hope the individual or business will move along the continuum from predisposed to constituent to prospect to engaged supporter.

Notice I say "engaged supporter" in this introductory section. But please remember, constituency development doesn't only focus on securing donors. The constituency development process applies to all relationship building that may produce any kind of engagement. For example, the constituency development process may result in more volunteers and new advocates. Your constituency development process may nurture relationships with other nonprofits/nongovernmental organizations (NGOs) that partner with your organization.

And remember, too, your hope (for whatever you hope for) is *not* what matters. What matters is the interest and decision of your constituents. That drives the process and the result.

Your Relations with Constituents

Strong relationships build strong organizations. And strong organizations build strong communities. Look back at Chapter 2 and Gardner's building community. Pay attention to civic engagement and social capital, civic capacity and civil society. Strong relationships are critical to effective and productive fund development. Nothing else matters as much. Strong relationships produce loyalty.

There it is, the really big concept: loyalty. That's what makes the world go 'round.

In all these cases, Dale Carnegie's famous quote drives achievement: "You'll have more fun and success when you stop trying to get what you want, and start helping other people get what they want."[3] What does Carnegie mean? Pay attention to others, first. Figure out their wants and needs. Help them achieve their goals.

For instance, focus on other organizations in your community, building robust partnerships to achieve results. Concentrate on your volunteers and donors, helping them fulfill their aspirations.

Put your constituents at the center of the relationship, not your organization. That's how you create community, extend your connections, and enlarge your base. Keep your constituents at the center, and that's how you grow a strong organization.

From a fund development perspective, constituency development benefits your organization by:

- Helping you understand constituent interests and disinterests, motivations and aspirations.
- Bringing your constituents closer to your organization.
- Allowing you to understand what to ask your constituents for.
- Bringing them closer so they are ready to be asked.
- Empowering them to fulfill themselves through you.

- Fostering loyalty among your constituents.
- Acquiring new constituents and moving them through the system of relations with your organization.

Certainly constituency development is not new to most organizations and fundraisers. But sadly, it's too often ignored. Or it's rather harshly compromised in the press for quick money. Irony of ironies: to compromise the very process that, when effectively done, dramatically affects donor loyalty and acquisition, too.

For fundraising, the constituency development approach—in the spirit of Dale Carnegie—reduces board member anxiety by paying attention to people, not money. Respect for constituency development makes fundraising seem less crass and mechanical, and more user-friendly.

Loyalty Makes the World Go 'Round

What is loyalty? Visit www.visualthesaurus.com again and watch the little diagram morph. Definitions include: Feelings of allegiance. The act of binding yourself—emotionally or intellectually—to a course of action. A strong positive emotion of regard and affection. The shifting words include things like commitment, dedication, faithful, and true.

Surely you want loyal constituents—every smart organization does. Surely you want loyal donors—every truly effective organization has them. Otherwise how would you survive and thrive?

What are the key drivers of loyalty, both for donors and for customers? Satisfaction, commitment, and trust. And satisfaction is the most significant. Research shows that very satisfied donors are twice as likely to give again. So all you have to do is keep them well satisfied. But satisfied with what? The quality of your service. And what is your service? Things like communications, acknowledgement and recognition, frequency of requests and type of requests, choice, and more.

How satisfied are your donors, and other constituents, too? How do you measure their perceptions so you can learn and make change? Yes, this takes work on your part. But the information and tools are readily available through existing research.

You want their loyalty and they want yours.

Research also tells us that loyalty requires trust. No surprise.

Yes, trust matters. One trusts, and the other is trusted. To be trusted, you must be trustworthy. And *you* means you and your organization.

There's lots of research on trust. Definitions vary. Apparently there's some confusion between trust and confidence. Regardless, I found this description of trust (from Charles H. Green[4]) useful:

- Credibility: the words we speak.
- Reliability: how we act.
- Intimacy: safety or security a person feels when entrusting someone with something.

- Self-orientation: are you focused on me or on yourself?
- Green proposed an equation to measure your Trust Quotient (TQ):

$$TQ = \frac{C + R + I}{S}$$

Increase your C (credibility), R (reliability), and I (intimacy) and then you increase trust in you and your organization.

What's your personal Trust Quotient? What's your organization's Trust Quotient? Talk about this with your staff and your fund development committee. Talk about this with your board of directors. And how about asking your various constituents?

Donor loyalty and customer loyalty are very similar. There's lots of research about customer loyalty—because that translates into lots of purchasing in the for-profit sector. In the nonprofit sector, the same kind of information can increase donor retention and promote loyalty.[5] So get to work.

Building Strong Relationships

The success of your organization depends on your ability to build relationships— strong, diverse, and loyal relationships. What do you have to do?

First, respect and understand the needs and motivations of your constituents. Second, meet those needs if they are in keeping with your values, mission, and vision. Third, engage your constituents in meaningful ways (meaningful to them). Fourth, communicate your programs and activities and their value to the constituents. Fifth, follow up to nurture the relationship.

When confronted with the concept of benefiting a constituent, charities usually think about the services provided to clients. Certainly you must benefit your clients, or your organization is irrelevant.

However, when seeking charitable gifts, you focus on the benefits to the donor and prospective donor. Often, donors of time and money do not use your services. These donors experience no direct benefit from your services. Instead, you identify how the prospect might benefit from giving a charitable contribution. This is more complex than determining the benefit of services to clients.

To successfully secure gifts, find the common bond between the needs and interests of your constituents—called prospects in this case—and the needs of your organization. Find the link between the prospective donor's motivation for giving and your organization's vision. Identify the mutually beneficial exchange. Now your organization is well positioned to ask and will more likely receive. Then you produce positive value for the prospect and your institution.

Strong relationships with your constituents require both a philosophical commitment and an adequate infrastructure—just like the other relationships described in this book. First you commit to respect the diverse interests, needs, and opinions of your constituents. You genuinely want to understand them better. Then your organization establishes the structures and systems to carry out the process of constituency development.

To survive and flourish, your organization requires lots of constituents in-volved in many supportive ways.

The biggest challenge is fulfillment—doing what you promised as an organization. And that means nurturing the relationships. Forever. In the case of fund development, you acquired me as a donor. This automatically constitutes a relationship between me and your organization. (Notice, "me" comes first.)

I know what a relationship is. It's two-way, mutually beneficial, and rewarding *to me!* This relationship is *not* just about you asking me for money and me giving it.

But all too often, you, the NGO, fail at your end of the bargain. You're in the fulfillment business, but you don't do it. I notice. And I may leave. I probably will. I likely already did. So did lots of others. Just look at the donor retention crisis running rampant around the world for the past decade or so.

For example, what's your transition rate from first gift to second gift? Research says that 8 out of 10 first-time donors don't give a second gift. If a for-profit business got a second piece of business from only 20 percent of its first-time customers, the company would close.[6]

What's your retention rate for donors who've given more than once? Some research says that retention rates are averaging about 50 percent. If a for-profit business had only a 50 percent customer retention rate, heads would roll. Think about your lapsed donors. What happened? How did you lose them? What's your organization's responsibility?

Identifying Your Constituents

A true constituent feels some level of association with your organization. The constituent feels part of you in some way. Being a constituent is about how I feel about you, not how you want me to feel. Don't presume that someone is your constituent because you want him to be. No organization has "everyone" or "the general public" as its constituency.

Neither should you presume that someone who is predisposed to your cause is your constituent. If someone is predisposed, she feels an affiliation with the cause, not yet an affiliation with your organization.

As noted earlier, a constituent can be a single entity—for example, a person, family, business, service group, or foundation. Constituency refers to a group of like persons or families, businesses or corporations, religious congregations, and so forth.

The single entities within a constituency (or constituent group) share common characteristics that your organization defines. To easily manage a constituency, the group must be fairly homogeneous.

You seek some exchange of value with these constituents. In a customer-centered and donor-centered organization, you focus on the value your constituents seek. This is a basic marketing relationship. For example:

- You want to recruit more clients and there are people out there looking for services. Can you meet their needs?
- You want more people to attend your theater's productions and they want entertainment. Can there be an exchange of value?

- You want new board members, and some people seek positions of influence in a highly respected organization. Others want to develop their resumes. Can there be an exchange of value between your organization and any of these candidates for board membership?
- You hope for a contribution and the donor seeks an organization to fulfill her aspirations.
- You seek investors and the donor wants to be remembered.
- Still others have benefited from your service and want to ensure your continuation. Can you and the constituent both benefit?

No matter what they seek or you seek, this chapter focuses on constituents, building profitable relationships that last. Constituency development is the process of moving people along the relationship continuum with your organization.

They are constituents because they so choose, not because you want them to be.

Maybe someone starts out as a customer (e.g., ticket buyer or student or counseling client or guest in your homeless shelter). Maybe the customer moves along the continuum, through your comprehensive relationship-building program, and becomes a volunteer or donor. Or someone moves along the continuum and becomes a vocal advocate on your behalf. Or an organization moves along the relationship continuum with your organization and becomes a collaborator to deliver services or eventually you merge.

It's Not What You're Selling That Counts

You have to focus on the constituent first. Just like Dale Carnegie said, "You'll have more fun and success when you stop trying to get what you want, and start helping other people get what they want." That's what the adjectives *customer-centered* and *donor-centered* mean.

What do your constituents want from you? Find out. Then meet them where they are and where they want to go. (But only, of course, if meeting their needs doesn't conflict with your organization's values, mission, and vision.) See Exhibit 7.1, about the Endowment Book of Life, for an inspiring example of understanding and meeting constituent needs—in this case, donors.

Exhibit 7.1   Meeting the Needs of Your Constituents

"I want to be remembered." These words represent a common wish that's shared by all of us. We wish to register our presence here in some imperishable way.

"I am a signer [of the Endowment Book of Life].... I cannot overstate the gratification I feel every time I realize that the names of my parents and of their

(continued)

(*Continued*)

parents can be preserved for centuries to come, along with the names of the family my wife and I have created.

"And to know that, along with these names, something of our story will be recorded. Not just who we were, but where we came from, what we accomplished, and what we believed in and stood for.

"All this will be set down and saved for our descendants. That is very satisfying to me." (So said Saul Tobin, quoted in *Promise*, the newsletter of the Jewish Community Foundation of Southern Arizona.)

For hundreds of Jews in southern Arizona, a simple signature bears witness to one's birthright. The signature honors the values and achievements of the signer, of his or her parents and grandparents, and the legacy of their culture.

Here's what happened:

In the Jewish community there were many stories to tell. These were told when people came together to socialize, work, and volunteer. Proud of their heritage as individuals, families, and Jews, they wanted to keep the stories alive forever.

The Jewish Community Foundation made all this possible with the Endowment Book of Life. On permanent display, this living document commemorates the history and continuity of the Jewish community in southern Arizona.

The Book of Life records the names of individuals and of families, and their histories. Each signer writes a brief personal statement about himself or herself, the family, and their philosophy.

This statement is entered into the Book of Life for posterity, as a gift for future generations. In addition to this paragraph, each signer is encouraged to write a page or more, which is kept on file as a record of his or her generation.

Everyone can sign the Book. There is no minimum gift, because that could exclude people. Carol Karsch, executive director of the Jewish Community Foundation, explains:

"In Judaism, giving of *tzedakah* (which translates into righteousness, not charity) is a mandate or law. And it is forbidden to exclude anyone from the privilege of fulfilling the law. Consequently, in Jewish tradition, even those whose sole support comes from the community are expected to take a portion of what they receive and donate it to others."

People from every walk of life and all economic means sign the Book of Life: individuals and families, small business owners, and retired people. Together they celebrate the Jewish tradition of *Chai*, the Hebrew word for "life," a commitment to one's legacy and to the future.

When you sign the Book of Life, you promise that you intend to provide some portion of your estate for the continuation of the Jewish community. Your signature indicates your future intent.

Annually, the Jewish Community Foundation hosts a Signers Night for the Book of Life. A special ceremony recognizes new signers and each receives a certificate, suitable for framing. This designated night allows prospective donors to look forward to a set time each year when they can see themselves as signers.

At some point in time, each signer takes action. You, the signer, arrange for your gift, choosing the giving method best for you. Volunteers from the

Foundation can offer advice and meet with you and your own financial and legal advisers. Signers can direct their gifts to the Foundation's unrestricted fund or to any one or more Jewish charities in southern Arizona.

Once a signer has taken the legal step to give, his or her name is added to the roster of the *Chayamim*, those who believe in the tradition of *Chai*, and inscribed on a plaque that is displayed with the Book of Life. The donor also receives a sterling silver replica of the *Chai* in the form of a lapel pin, charm, or pendant, handcrafted in Israel. Wearing this memento raises the consciousness of others by showing one's personal commitment.

Carol Karsch notes that the real recognition is intrinsic: the invitation to tell one's own story. Karsch says, "The opportunity to make a heartfelt personal statement is testimony to the 'why' of the legacy gift, whereas the endowment is the 'what.'"

The Foundation regularly communicates with its constituents about the Book of Life. For example:

- Printed materials describe the program.
- Newsletter articles and features in the *Arizona Jewish Post* honor signers and tell their stories.
- Volunteers invite people to participate in Signing Week.
- Special-recognition events commemorate signers and honor them when they make their gift.
- The Archive Committee helps signers record their family histories and narratives.
- Donors are also invited to place with the Foundation posthumous messages to loved ones or friends.

In addition to these special activities, the Book of Life is an integral part of other events and milestones for the Foundation and the Jewish community.

The Jewish Community Foundation understands its constituents well. The Book of Life commemorates the strength and vitality of hundreds of individuals and families. Each year, more people sign.

Think how each of these signers feels. They tell their own stories. They honor their birthright. Together, they build a legacy for future generations and challenge those who follow.

In this way, the Endowment Book of Life ensures the tradition of each individual, the family, and the Jewish people. Think how you would feel if your own favorite philanthropy offered you an opportunity that so well reflected your interests and aspirations.

Source: Developed by the Jewish Community Foundation of Southern Arizona, Tucson, Arizona.

What's your organization's donor-centric quotient? Compare your performance to the Donor-Centric Pledge[7] that Tom Ahern and I propose.

Let me repeat: It's not what you're selling that matters. It's what the constituent is buying that counts.

This marketing principle is critically important for constituency development. Effective organizations understand this. Effective organizations don't focus on themselves, proclaiming their good works and expecting someone, to give time and money.

Furthermore, these organizations know they will not survive by selling the "good of the community." Instead, effective organizations focus on the constituents' needs and interests. Effective organizations embrace customer centrism and honor donor centrism.

Beware! Do you think this way?

- "Our community wants a children's museum. Our organization has the skills and resources to help solve the problem or meet the community need. To do the good work that the community wants, our organization needs charitable contributions."
- "There are prospects out there in the community. Our organization targets those who seem to be interested in this issue or opportunity. All our organization has to do is tell the prospect about the community need or opportunity, then explain how good our organization is at meeting that need or opportunity. Certainly, the prospect will understand and then give."

Not good. Doesn't work. Misses the point. You're selling the community want or need and your organization's ability to respond. You have yet to consider the prospect. What is she or he buying?

Try this approach instead.

- The local manufacturing company wants employees who don't miss much work, arrive on time, and focus on work when at work.

  Your counseling organization teaches people how to manage their finances, solve family crises, and overcome drug and alcohol abuse. Can you convince the local manufacturing company that your services help employees fulfill the company's needs?
- A prospect wants to enhance her position with community leaders by volunteering for a worthy cause.

  Will affiliation with your recognized and respected organization help the prospect achieve her desire?
- Your AIDS organization knows a particularly affluent individual whose life partner died from the disease. Yet the prospect doesn't volunteer or give to the cause.

  Perhaps he's never been asked. (Remember, the biggest reason anyone gives is because he's asked.) Maybe he fears the stigma and doesn't wish to associate himself with HIV/AIDS. Perhaps an anonymous gift might be appropriate.

  But maybe he isn't interested in the cause. Maybe he gives money to other causes. Just because his partner died of HIV/AIDS doesn't mean he wants to invest in that issue.

Remember the story of my dad's death in Exhibit 2.3? Papa Georges died of cancer. But I don't give to fight cancer.

- Consider your relationship to a board member, one of your most important constituents. You want her to help fundraise. You want her to see how easy fund development is, so you provide useful tips, support materials, and training. Unfortunately, she doesn't make her calls.

You remind her, but still no action. Why not? Why isn't she performing when you gave her all the tools?

Perhaps it is because you decided what she needed. You tried selling her easy fund development. Maybe she wasn't buying that. So the exchange didn't work.

What was she buying? Who knows? Ask her. Perhaps she was buying companionship and a fundraising partner would help. Perhaps she was buying time and you could have scheduled the appointments for her.

Your organization needs to know what the prospect is buying. You best figure it out before you try to sell the wrong thing. Don't waste the prospect's time. Don't waste your organization's time.

What's in It for Me?

Think about your own giving. Why *do* you invest more in one institution than another? Don't just say, "I believe in the cause." Really think about why you give a gift of time or money to a specific institution. You're interested in some things, not in others. You're motivated by certain feelings. You want to accomplish specific things.

You might want something to change in your community. Or in the world. You want to make some kind of difference. You want your investment of time or money to matter. *You* want to matter. So you pick an organization that helps you accomplish all that. You pick an organization that helps you achieve your desires. The organization is the means by which you make the difference you want to make.

Now think about this: You give *through* an organization, not *to* an organization. The organization is a means to an end, the means through which you achieve your desires. Ask yourself again: Which of your needs is met by the organizations you give through?

Next, focus on your organization and its various constituencies. Ask yourself why each of your various constituencies participates in your organization.

Fundraisers, of course, focus on donors. And as fundraisers hurry to the campaign goal, they often don't really know enough about their prospects and donors. This is true of both small organizations and large ones. Let me give you one quick example. My life partner and I give to a French immersion school, preschool through eighth grade. Yet we do not have children. Why in the world do we give? Well, we have our reasons. And it's your job to figure out what they are.

Focus on your constituents, their interests and disinterests. Pay attention to the basic human motivations as well as changing demographics and lifestyle patterns. Inform yourself about philanthropic trends. Review the research about giving by different populations. Look at the research about relationship building and fundraising strategies.

> *Marketing is the voluntary and purposive process of developing, facilitating, and executing exchanges to satisfy human wants and desires.*
>
> From *Marketing the Arts*, by Michael P. Mokwa, William M. Dawson, and E. Arthur Prieve (New York: Praeger Publishers, 1980), 15

Understanding Marketing

What is constituency development but marketing? Relationship marketing.

The American Marketing Association defines marketing as "the activity, set of institutions, and processes for creating, communicating, delivering, and exchanging offerings that have value for customers, clients, partners, and society at large."[8] Marketing is not selling. "Here's my product, will you buy it?" That's selling. Marketing starts with a blank page. "Who are you? What are you interested in? What do you want or need?" Then you create a product to suit.

As Ken Burnett wrote when introducing the term "relationship fundraising," it is "an approach to the marketing of a cause which centres not around raising money but on developing to its full potential the unique and special relationship that exists between a charity and its supporter."[9]

Ken[10] went on to state:

> *Whatever strategies and techniques are employed to boost funds, the overriding consideration in relationship fundraising is to care for and develop that special bond and not to do anything that might damage or jeopardise it. In relationship fundraising every activity of the organization is therefore geared towards making donors feel important, valued, and considered. In this way relationship fundraising will ensure more funds per donor in the long term.*[11]

Yes, customer-centered and donor-centered are the most productive way to perform. And as far as I'm concerned, it's the moral way to behave. This customer-centric and donor-centric approach then produces loyalty. And loyalty makes the world go 'round, your organization included. Better yet, the most loyal donors become part of your tribe, in the Seth Godin sense of tribe. Read more in the section entitled "What Donors Want," later in this chapter.

Marketing (and fundraising) aren't tawdry, sleazy, arm-twisting, hard-sell gimmicks that disrespect and annoy. Nope. As Philip Kotler says, "Marketing is a way to harmonize the needs and wants of the outside world with the purposes and the resources and objectives of the institution."[12]

Marketing is strategic. Marketing focuses on the why, the context, the meaning. All the rest are marketing tools. Public relations. Advertising. Communications. These are the techniques. Without the strategic understanding, both traditional marketers and fundraisers are merely technicians.

Marketing relies on the concept of mutually beneficial exchange. Various constituencies (e.g., clients, donors, and volunteers) are involved in an exchange with your organization. You and they each receive something from the exchange. This concept is the foundation of any relationship.

The marketing exchange process contains four conditions.

1. There are at least two parties.
2. Each can offer something that the other perceives to be a benefit.
3. Each party is capable of communication and delivery.
4. Each is free to accept or reject the offer.

The four relationships presented in this book depend on marketing. Marketing principles help your organization strengthen its internal relations. Marketing helps your organization remain relevant, given community needs and interests. Through marketing, you develop strong relationships with your various constituencies.

Marketing is an essential part of effective organizations, part of your corporate culture and systems. Capable organizations articulate marketing as a value and see marketing as a management activity. As a value, marketing means your constituents are at the center of your organization. Here come those adjectives again, customer-centered and donor-centered. Let's just say "constituent-centered" and be done with it, eh?

Marketing mandates a sensitivity to and understanding of others. You are sensitive to their needs, interests, and aspirations. You learn and understand "what I am buying" rather than relying on "what you are selling."

As a management activity, marketing forms the basis for other activities such as strategic planning, board recruitment, client service, fund development, constituent relations, and volunteer enabling. You incorporate marketing into all the management activities of your organization.

Effective marketing segments your constituencies into manageable, distinct subgroups, each of which has something in common. Then you target those you want to reach. Marketing positions your organization to meet the target group's needs and helps you communicate in ways that reach your target audiences. To do this work, you need systems that can:

- Determine the target group's interests and commonalities.
- Decide how they will best receive information and devise responsive communications activities.
- Anticipate the role they want with your organization.
- Evaluate when and who should make the request for participation.

Market segmentation is a clinical name for one of the richest opportunities that new technology has afforded us. We are able to gather information on customers and actually determine more about what they want. This allows us to increasingly delight the customer, and it also gives employees opportunities to target offers that are relevant, thereby increasing the feeling of service and reducing the sense of selling.

From *Clicks and Mortar: Passion Driven Growth in an Internet Driven World*, by David S. Pottruck and Terry Pearce (San Francisco: Jossey-Bass, 2000), 258

Relationships Rule—In Fact, They're Now Assets

By now, I expect you have "drunk the Kool-Aid" or maybe you're bored. No matter. I assume that you believe in customer centrism and donor centrism. You're even willing to say "constituent-centered."

You embrace relationship marketing and relationship fundraising. You're continuing to read this chapter because you want to build a constituency development process and program that effectively nurtures relationships.

You're committed to all this because you realize that honest and genuine relationships rule. You believe that the effectiveness of your organization depends on the strength and diversity of your relationships. You believe that the wealth of your organization depends on the quality of your diverse relationships. And you know that "wealth" is not just money. With all that in mind, I think you'll like this quote a lot. Just change "customer" to "constituency": "The wealth embedded in customer relationships is now more important than the capital contained in land, plant, buildings, and even bank accounts. Relationships are now assets."[13]

The authors of this quote talk about the expectations in today's world—in particular, the expectations of electronic commerce. Specifically, the need for immediacy, interaction, transparency, and the required alignment between promises and action. And that means a whole lot of work.

Think about it: So much information about the unique needs and personal tastes of so many different individuals and groups. So much customization for so many different individuals and groups. So much intensive and personalized service for so many different individuals and groups. What does this describe but constituency development?

The chant of the Industrial Revolution was that of the manufacturer who said, "This is what I make—won't you please buy it?" The call of the Information Age is the consumer asking, "This is what I want—won't you please make it?"[14] The Industrial Revolution is past; so, apparently, is the Industrial Age.

Marketing should always be about your customers, whether they are clients, donors, volunteers, or partners. History tells us that was the case in the really olden days. But mass production changed that. Sadly, in the Industrial Age, organizations changed their focus from customers to products. Now we've changed back. Have we ever!

Marketing isn't about making and pushing products. Neither is fund development. Relationship marketing and relationship fundraising are about knowing, respecting, and satisfying the needs of your constituents, whether customers or donors. It's about what I'm buying, not what you're selling. "[O]ne requires only efficiency, the other requires relationship skills," say Pottruck and Pearce in *Clicks and Mortar*.[15]

Remember the earlier comments about fulfillment? You are in the business of fulfillment. In marketing this is called delivering on the offer. When you consistently deliver on the offer, you build your reputation. Pottruck and Pearce call this "building reputation one experience at a time" and note that an organization can eventually "convert that reputation into a promise that is broader than any one offer. It is the brand, the family name."

The authors go on to say that this reputation—or "broad guarantee of character"—is not made just to the customer but is also made within the organization, to the self and to the others. This fulfillment is external, as in constituency development, the third relationship in an effective organization. And this fulfillment is also internal, as in the first relationship, within the organization. The authors conclude by noting that the way an organization delivers on its offer—fulfilling its internal and external promise—is the organization's legacy.

Now it's time to talk a bit about branding. And please don't think that branding is your print image or your website or your tagline or those great messages someone invented for you. Your constituents brand you. (Think of calves and branding irons. Those little guys get branded; they don't brand themselves.) You get branded through your behavior. You get branded through your performance. How is that working for you?

Imagine getting branded as "the best place to give money" or "the greatest place to volunteer" or "the place where my gift makes the biggest difference." What brand image do you want? What brand image do you have now?

Ultimately, branding is about your values. Your values help create your brand and you must be true to these values and, hence, to your brand. See how this played out for Bruce Springsteen and Chrysler in Exhibit 7.2.

Exhibit 7.2   Branding—Chrysler and Bruce Springsteen

Here's a great story about the branding of Chrysler and the brand identity of Bruce Springsteen. It's a story about consistency in values and reputation management.

Years ago, Chrysler asked for permission to use Springsteen's "Born in the USA" as the theme song for the company's massive advertising campaign. Chrysler had identified its values as passionate, hardworking, everyman, stubborn, open-hearted, American, brave, down to earth, battered but not broken, home grown, and proud.

For Chrysler, "Born in the USA" captured this spirit and would be like the company with a strong image and reputation consistent with its desired brand identity.

And what did Springsteen say? No. Why? Because Bruce Springsteen has a brand identity himself. His brand identity is reflected in his core values, which include independence, integrity, and "it's not about money."

Sure, the values of Springsteen and Chrysler matched when it came to independence and perhaps integrity, too. But aligning his song with making money for the car manufacturer did not match Springsteen's value of "it's not about money." To remain true to his own integrity—one of his core

(continued)

(Continued)

values—Springsteen could not allow his brand to be identified with the Chrysler brand.

Just remember, part of branding is managing your own identity, which is your reputation. Always be true to who you are as a brand.

Source: From a presentation by Lee Gustafson, Holland Mark Edmund Ingalls, Boston, Massachusetts, at the April 1999 conference of the Yankee Chapter of the International Association of Business Communicators.

As noted in *Clicks and Mortar*, "A company's brand is the symbol of promises and expectations."[16] The authors go on to say, "Brand building is grounded in the day-to-day work of people who care. Building brand is a step-by-step, moment-by-moment process of service."[17]

So what's the ultimate goal of relationship marketing and relationship fundraising? Perhaps finding clients and donors who respond to your compelling offers. Definitely fostering relationships that produce loyalty. And doing all this in a customer-focused, donor-centered manner . . . because that's the only way this works.

Engaging Your Constituents

Constituency development can prepare your constituents to be asked for something. With further relationship building, you increase the likelihood that your constituents might say yes to your requests.

Call this the engagement process, part of relationship marketing and relationship fundraising. Engagement is essential when trying to construct any mutually beneficial exchange, whether with a client, donor, or volunteer. Engagement is essential when building relationships. So, of course, fund development depends on the engagement process, too.

All engagement processes include a phase of gaining attention and building awareness, and end with a call to action. Gaining attention and building interest involve a mix of emotion and intellect. Nothing happens at this time. The constituent doesn't take action at this time.

Next, you stimulate desire and request action. This is the pivotal step—and 99 percent of this is emotion. Oops. Change that to 100 percent. Yes, indeed, neuroscience now proves that all human decisions are triggered by emotions.[18] As neurologist and author Donald B. Calne notes, "The essential difference between emotion and reason is that emotion leads to action, while reason leads to conclusions."[19]

Consider these two traditional engagement processes, AIDA and ACCA.

- *AIDA (Attention, Interest, Desire, and Action)*
  First you gain the constituent's attention and create (or capitalize upon) an interest in the product your organization offers. Next, turn that interest into a strong desire for the product. Once there is desire, you ask the constituent to act. Remember, acting may mean buying the service or giving money or time.

■ *ACCA (Awareness, Comprehension, Conviction, and Action)*

Make the constituent aware of the product. Develop the constituent's understanding (comprehension) of what the product is and how it will benefit him or her. Remember, the product might be giving money, and the benefit to the prospective donor might be visibility within the community.

Your activities must move the constituent from an understanding of the product to conviction about the product's value to her or him. The final step is when the constituent acts—for example, giving money or volunteering time.

Robert W. Bly,[20] one of the gurus of good writing, introduced another asking process:

■ Get attention.
■ Satisfy the need.
■ Prove your superiority and reliability.
■ Ask for the order.

Bly describes these as: Get the constituent's attention by focusing on the single most important benefit to that constituent. Show the constituent that she needs the product by explaining how it will help her. Satisfy the constituent's need by explaining how the product will help her. Prove your superiority and reliability by telling your own success stories. Ask for the order by requesting that the constituent participate.

In turn, David R. Dunlop[21] proposed a six-step fund development sequence, adapted from G. T. Smith and H. J. Seymour. Dunlop's steps are:

1. Information
2. Awareness
3. Knowledge
4. Caring
5. Involvement
6. Commitment

Contemporary models for donor behavior and decision-making offer more important insights to fundraisers. Explore these as a framework for relationship building and the engagement process. See, for example, the comprehensive analysis and explanation in *Fundraising Principles and Practice*:[22]

■ The Individual Giving Model shows several psychological processes that can affect gift decisions. These include attention, perception, emotion, knowledge, attitudes, and decision-making.

See Figure 4.2 in *Fundraising Principles and Practice*, along with a detailed description. As noted in the textbook, this is a process model, outlining the stages and processes donors go through while making a giving decision.

■ The Sargeant and Woodliffe Model of Giving Behavior is a content model, sequentially presenting the psychological processes that a person goes through when choosing to give.

Elements of this model include: external influences, individual characteristics, perceptual reaction, processing determinants, motives and inhibitors, outputs, and feedback. See Figure 4.7 in *Fundraising Principles and Practice.*

- The Social Giving Model documents the individual's sense of self—her thoughts and beliefs about who she is. People act in ways consistent with this self-concept. Fundraisers then work to enrich the donors' giving experience.

Take a look at Figure 5.1 in *Fundraising Principles and Practice.* You'll see things like the social environment (e.g., history, philosophy, literature, religion, economy, culture, and policy), and the social environment (e.g., social categories, groups, significant others, acquaintances, strangers, networks, etc.).

Absorb this information from *Fundraising Principles and Practice.* Use this research and tools to enhance your constituency development program. Apply these sequences—and combinations thereof—to better understand what's happening and your role in facilitating what's happening.

In summary, use engagement processes to focus your constituency development. Decide which engagement sequence (or combination thereof) best describes how you will get your constituents ready to be asked. Devise strategies for each phase in your engagement process. Use the process to help explain constituency development to your staff and volunteers. Make sure they understand that each step is essential.

What Donors Want

Now let's focus specifically on donors. Remember, your organization is the means to achieve the donor's end. Here are some key things to think about. Do all donors want all this all the time? Of course not. But those who do—are they still waiting for you to catch up?

To Be Heard

Giving is a way of being heard. Giving amplifies and empowers voices.

Giving is an act of civic engagement, a public statement of interest and commitment. Giving should be a democratizing act in our society.

Giving tells you, the organization, what's important to me, the donor. Are you listening? What stories do your donors tell about themselves? What emotions do you hear? What feelings do you understand?

To Tell Their Stories

Sure, this sounds like "being heard." But there's another angle: Donors may actually want to tell their philanthropic stories. Yet so few donors are ever asked.

Do you collect donor stories? Do you interview donors and retell their stories in your newsletters, in your annual reports, on your website, and at your fundraising events and cultivation gatherings?

I expect you to collect donor stories. I expect you to retell your donors' stories. The retelling validates donor voices, acknowledges their investment, and honors their commitment. And I suspect your donors expect you to do this, too—even if they're not conscious of this expectation.

And here's a final thought: Lots of donors want a conversation with you. Do you engage your donors in conversation?

To Realize Their Dreams Through Your Organization

Remember, donors give *through* your organization, not *to* your organization. Donors give to achieve their aspirations. Donors give to live out their values. Donors expect to realize their dreams through your organization. If that doesn't happen through your organization, the donor will give elsewhere. Here's another angle: Do donors also *negotiate* their dreams through your organization? Maybe *negotiating* is about finding the balance between donor-centered and mission-centered.

Certainly *negotiating* reflects the conversation with a donor who plans to invest what is a significant gift for her. She isn't just "sending something in." She's talking with you. Together, the donor and the organization's representative are negotiating the fulfillment of the donor's dreams.

To Join a Fight

Are you inviting your donors to a fight? A fight they can help win? A fight that makes a difference?

You know what's even better than a fight? A whole movement. All those people connected, working together, seeking something better. All those people believing.

Through their giving, donors want to win some of the fights, sometimes. Donors even hope to win the whole war, because of their gifts. Now that's impact.

To Be Part of a Tribe

A movement works because it's a tribe. "Tribes are about faith—about belief in an idea and in a community. And they are grounded in respect and admiration for the leader of the tribe and for the other members as well."[23]

People want to be part of something. People look for connection and meaning and change. In fact, Seth Godin says, "caring is the key emotion at the center of the tribe. Tribe members care what happens, to their goals and to one another."[24]

It only takes two things to turn a group into a tribe: a shared interest and a way to communicate. The tribal leader helps "increase the effectiveness of the tribe and its members by: transforming the shared interest into a passionate goal and desire for change; providing tools to allow members to tighten their communications; and, leveraging the tribe to allow it to grow and gain new members."[25]

To Be Flattered

Flattery really works.[26] And surely donors deserve to be flattered for their investment of time, service, and money.

Research shows that "even when people perceive that flattery is insincere, that flattery can still leave a lasting and positive impression of the flatterer." Of course, ethical marketers—and that means fundraisers, too—use flattery honestly.

To Matter

Everyone wants to matter. Everyone wants respect and to be seen as valuable and important. Giving is one way to matter.

But organizations often don't adequately communicate that to their donors. It's a fairly simple equation, but organizations and their fundraisers and communicators lose track too often.

So here's the key point: The difference that the gift makes (impact) = the value of the donor. But for donors to clearly understand this—that they matter—the organization must clearly communicate this sequence, this string of consequences, as it were:

- I give a gift. You tell me the impact of my gift, the results produced by my gift.
- Because of your communication, I understand that my gift made a difference.
- Because I now know that my gift made a difference, I understand that my gift matters.
- Because I now know for sure that my gift matters, then I know that I matter.
- Now I understand. My gift means that I, personally, matter. I, the donor, have value.

You are obligated to communicate all this to me. And absent any of these incremental moments—this sequence, this string of consequences—I won't understand. I won't make the link. I will not see the equation, the all-important equation: My gift matters; hence I matter.

What Donors Want Might Not Be What You Want

Thanks to marvelous Jeff Brooks (www.futurefundraisingnow.com) for this wake-up call to all of us:

"What donors want from life: it's likely not what you want."[27]

Your donors are likely different than you: different generation, gender, ethnicity, interests, experiences. Different.

What you want—what you think and believe and feel in the fundraising office—might actually conflict with your donors' wants. Consider these research findings:

- Boomers (your prime prospect and donor market) define happiness as peacefulness.
- Twenty-, thirty-, and forty-somethings equate happiness with excitement.

Young fundraisers want to create excitement, things like: "excessively vibrant and youthful-looking design; advertising-style hype; constantly changing messaging." And that's exactly what the older prospects and donors do *not* want.

Jeff notes: "The young fundraisers are not only wrongly assuming that 'excitement' will be a good way to motivate their older donors to give. They're also seeking more excitement for themselves by jazzing up and frequently changing their fundraising."

Jeff warns us that this behavior is a very big and an all-too-common mistake. Instead, "Remember who your donors are. And remember the ways they are different from you."

Challenges to Constituency Development

You don't think this is going to be easy, do you? Constituency development is hard work. Building all these relationships requires capacity (resources) and capability (expertise).

Even experienced development officers need to think more about the process and tasks of constituency development. But they often don't, no more than their less experienced counterparts.

In conversations with fundraisers around the world, even the most experienced professionals make the following comments:

- "I don't have enough time to focus on these relationship steps. I'm too busy balancing this year's budget."
- "I can't spend this kind of time or money on any but the largest donors. I just do an annual letter and a few newsletters to small donors."
- "For acquisition, my agency just sends solicitation letters to selected lists. We don't do any advance cultivation or much qualifying. There's no time or money."

Stop it! Really. This is madness leading to failure—or at best very weak success. Fundraisers need to help their organizations change this dynamic. So let's examine the challenges right now, up front. I don't want you to be distracted by these thoughts as you go forward in this book. Instead, I want you so inspired to do the right things that you'll work even harder to overcome the challenges.

The process of constituency development is challenging, even when you're committed to it. Be prepared. Anticipate these challenges. Then it's easier to overcome them so your organization can proceed and succeed.

Start here: Ask yourselves, staff and board together:

- "How can we make the constituency development process practical and manageable?"
- "How will we allocate resources?"
- "What is a good return on investment?"
- "When will we actually ask for something?"
- "How do we set priorities?"

Challenge 1: Getting Everyone to Value Constituency Development

The process of constituency development—relationship building—belongs to everyone in your organization, not just development staff and fundraising volunteers.

Make constituency development part of your corporate culture and a requirement of individual performance. Build a constituent-centered organization, which includes customer-centered and donor-centered.

Challenge 2: Finding Time

Actually, this is about *making* the time. If you overcome the first challenge, you'll make the time because you choose to do so. Or you won't because you don't.

How do your staff and volunteers currently use their time? What is really important? Choose your priorities. And, make constituency development a priority if you want your organization to survive (and thrive) into the future. Allocate your time differently. Change the way you do business.

Challenge 3: Using Research

Fact: Research is valuable and can help you work smarter and better. So first, your organization must value research and use it.

To generate contributions, pay attention to the research in philanthropy and fundraising, and in tangential or applicable fields. Read trade publications to learn about current research. Then read the actual research and figure out the implications for your organization and use accordingly.

Conducting research within your own organization can be overwhelming. But it's necessary. You can do some of this at low cost and with modest human resources. And, if you have the financial resources, outsource some of this work. Increase the value of your research by working across organizational functions, addressing client needs, your strategic planning, and fund development. Select employees to share research functions throughout the organization. Involve someone from your program and fund development areas. See more about research later in this chapter.

Challenge 4: Treating Major Donors Differently

Fundraisers usually direct most of their time and effort to major donors, giving proportionately less attention to smaller donors. This is all fine and good, but only up to a point.

Be careful. Too much of this exclusionary attitude and you will almost certainly overlook (or lose) your most loyal donors and their future gifts. For example, how about loyalty and lifetime value (LTV)? I've given you $50 per year for 10 years. My LTV is $500 now and I'm not dying anytime soon, so that increases my LTV. And, because of my loyalty, I'm a good prospect for a bequest. What does *major donor* mean anyway? You know I'm going to start ranting now.[28] The donor defines what is a major gift, not your organization. Sure, you have to allocate resources and consider return on investment. Just be careful.

Most people define *major* according to organization standards. A small grassroots organization might define a major donor as one who gives $100. A hospital probably defines a major donor as someone who gives more than $10,000. For a recent capital campaign, an Ivy League university defined its major donors as those who gave $100,000 or more.

This approach focuses on the institution and its wants and needs, with little sensitivity to the donor's perspective. Certainly you need some mechanism to allocate organization resources. However, the donor defines what a major gift is based on his or her own circumstance. If you forget this, you are likely to harm the relationship.

Try a different approach to allocating your resources. Focus on the outcome(s) you want from constituency development. The gift amount is only one dimension. Consider other outcomes. First, loyalty. Then things like: first-time gift; increased gift; multiple gifts in one year; help fundraise as well as give money. Estimate the likelihood of achieving your desired outcome. Allocate your resources based on the combination of desired outcome and likelihood of achievement.

Challenge 5: Contacting Your Constituents a Lot but Not Too Much

Find the balance between too little contact and too much. Don't overwhelm your constituents with too much contact. On the other hand, make sure you contact them enough so they feel well informed and engaged. Remember, absence does *not* make the heart grow fonder!

So what's enough but not too much? That's a judgment call that you make for each constituent or constituency. You identify which activities will most effectively move the constituent along the continuum.

But keep in mind: Too often nonprofits/NGOs don't communicate enough. For example, four to six donor newsletters per year is good; fewer is not so good. Communicating with donors once per month is just fine; that's not too much. Among those 12 contacts per year, include your solicitation, your newsletter, your program announcements, your e-blasts, and so forth.

We know for sure that more relationship building is required. It's the only answer to poor donor retention rates and increasing loyalty. We know pretty much for sure that organizations aren't doing relationship building all that well.

Challenge 6: Asking for Participation without Developing Relationships

Without constituency development, you have only vague knowledge about and little relationship with those you want to approach. But the truth is, in fundraising, sometimes you solicit a gift without adequate constituency development.

For example, many organizations conduct acquisition campaigns by mail or telephone. Interested recipients give and then you cultivate relationships. You have raised some money while introducing yourself.

Just remember: Most of the letters are thrown away or the calls refused. There is no substitute for constituency development. The ideal fund development program would use constituency development 100 percent of the time.

Challenge 7: Welcoming Diversity

This is more than mere tolerance. This is not merely accepting. Effective organizations and good people actually welcome—proactively seek and embrace—diversity.

Constituency development works only if it is sensitive and tailor-made to the targeted constituencies. In our pluralistic world, this means your constituency development must be sensitive to diversity, which, at the least, includes gender, generation, culture and ethnicity, socioeconomics, sexual orientation, faith, physical challenge—and any other differences.

Our world is full of glass ceilings that limit the access by people of color, women, gays and lesbians, those who are poor, and those who experience some form of physical challenge. While we make some strides, we have not overcome prejudice nor broken through all the ceilings.

Ironically, changing demographics increases the numbers of women and people of color. Economists say that early in the twenty-first century, there may be no more middle class in the United States, only the wealthy and the poor. Is it the same in other countries?

To survive, your organization must welcome and encourage diversity—and in turn be respected and trusted by diverse people. To be morally viable, your organization will have to embrace pluralism. Effective organizations will seek, not just embrace, diversity. Successful constituency development tactics will reflect different cultural traditions, languages, and lifestyles.

By the way: Do you actually think those who've been excluded will give to you if you continue excluding them? Not likely.

Challenge 8: Compromising Organizational Values

Ah yes, values again. Sometimes organizations worry that focusing on benefits to the donor will compromise mission. Organizations see themselves following donor desires rather than the organization's own vision and strategic plan.

Don't do it. Constituency development does not mean compromising your organization's values or vision. Don't cater to a donor's whim if it conflicts with your organization. But don't push your organization's needs with no consideration for the donor's interests.

Once you understand what will benefit the donor, find the intersection with your organization's needs. If that is not possible, explain why to the donor. Based on what you understand about the donor and his or her wants and needs, try to change the donor's mind. If that isn't possible, don't make the ask. Don't accept the gift if offered.

Challenge 9: Misrepresenting Intentions

Make sure your staff, volunteers, and constituents clearly understand that this is a professional relationship with the organization. Don't let constituents misinterpret your intentions.

Volunteers are sometimes concerned about this. They worry that constituents may think that the organization's representatives are offering personal friendship. Sometimes staff cross the line into friendship.

Take care and don't confuse the relationships. When you speak personally with a constituent, make sure the context is that of the organization. Focus on the constituent's relationship to the organization, not to any single individual.

Challenge 10: Competing with Other Organizations

You already encountered my rant about this in Chapter 1. I'll say again: I think competition for philanthropic gifts is a myth fostered by organizations that do not know how to develop the four relationships described in this book. Competition suggests that there are limited dollars instead of donors who would give more and people who might give but have not been asked.

Certainly there is congestion in the marketplace. There are lots of fundraising messages out there. But effective organizations distinguish themselves to their targeted constituents. These organizations assure their relevancy to the community. Then they focus on constituency development. If you develop relationships well, your committed constituents will give to you. They will give again and again. Many will give more and more.

An organization cannot take donors away from another organization. Donors choose to go away. Donors always have a choice. They leave an organization because of what the organization does—or doesn't do.

Many donors and prospects are swiftly outpacing nonprofit/NGO organizations. These constituents expect their needs to be understood and met. They expect a lot of other things like meeting community need and quality and collaboration. Organizations need to pay attention to all these expectations.

Nonprofit/NGO organizations and their fundraisers had best catch up and get ahead or risk that donors will go elsewhere. There's choice—on the part of donors about who they do business with and on the part of organizations about how they do business. There is no real competition. There's only congestion, which nonprofit/NGO organizations can overcome.

Challenge 11: Universalizing Your Own Passion

Remember my mention of this in Chapter 1, in the section entitled "Basic Principles of Fund Development." I know. You're convinced that your cause is worthy and that your organization is essential. That's great. But not everyone else *is* convinced and lots of people are *not interested in being convinced.*

That's right. As a donor, I'm simply not interested in lots of causes. Remember my dad's fund? I appreciate the fact that the American Cancer Society exists. I respect its work and am pleased that there are many who give to this cause. However, I'm not interested. Nope. Not interested. Period. Not at all. And please don't waste your breath trying to convince me.

Beware. Is your organization universalizing its own passion by pursuing those who are not predisposed, or those who appeared to be predisposed but upon further interaction keep displaying a distinct lack of interest? Are you one of those fundraisers who keeps saying, "But if I could get her alone for 15 minutes I could convince her"?

How dare you? That's just plain arrogant and even patronizing. Don't universalize your own passion to those who do not care. It's okay not to care about you. We care about something else.

Challenge 12: Trespassing on Personal and Professional Relationships

Back again to Chapter 1 and the basic principles. Nonetheless, this is worth repeating: Don't trespass. And don't ask others to do so. Just stop it. Stop the madness!

Too often, fundraisers pressure their board members and fundraising volunteers to "reach out to your friends and neighbors and colleagues." Furthermore, fundraisers exhort their board members and other volunteers to "use your personal and professional contacts to get gifts."

Stop right there. What about the match of interest between the friend or colleague and the organization and cause? This is about commitment to a cause, respect for an organization, and building relationships. This is not about robbing family piggybanks and exchanging favors in order to raise money.

Stop the bottom-line and short-term thinking. What should you ask your board members and volunteers to do? Ask them to look at their personal and professional contacts and decide if any of those contacts might be predisposed to the cause or to the organization. Ask your board members and volunteers to reach out to those who may be predisposed and explore the possibility of a mutually beneficial exchange.

Give your board members and volunteers permission to ignore the contacts who are not predisposed. Encourage your board members to turn to others and find out if they are predisposed.

And what about those who are predisposed? Once your board members and volunteers have confirmed this predisposition, build a relationship. Engage your board members and volunteers in the process of building these relationships. And only then do you talk about solicitation.

Challenge 13: Just Do It

This is one of those bottom-line moments: Despite all the challenges, just do it. In the end, you have to do it. No more planning. No more ready and aim. Now fire. Execute.

Make constituency development part of your ongoing operations by creating the necessary management systems and using them. Regularly evaluate the effectiveness of your systems and alter them as necessary. Your shared values will support your management systems.

One Final Thought

Every organization wants more constituents. Every organization wants increased donor loyalty, increased gifts from current donors, and new donors.

Just because you want it doesn't mean it will happen. Your cause may not generate more constituents. Your organization—no matter how effectively you work—may not acquire more donors. Maybe you have to merge. Or close.

Roles in the Constituency Development Process

Relationship building must be a central value of your nonprofit/NGO. Make sure to integrate constituency development throughout the organization. Involve board members, staff, and other volunteers.

The development officer leads the process of constituency development. Aware of the four key relationships, the fundraiser always reaches beyond fund development and includes the chief executive, staff, and volunteers in the process. The chief development officer makes sure that the entire organization understands the importance of relationship building.

Together, the chief executive officer and the board of directors are responsible for the health of the organization. The chief executive and board make sure that the organization values marketing as a philosophy and uses marketing as a management tool. These leaders ensure that there is adequate infrastructure to support constituency development. They ensure that there are sufficient constituents to support the organization—as clients, donors, and volunteers, partner organizations, and so forth. Or, the CEO and board recognize the organization cannot survive and must take other steps.

Involve the Board and Individual Board Members

See Chapter 9 for details about the role of the board and the individual board member. Download Appendix 9-C, "Key Roles in Fund Development," from this book's website. Use the handout to direct conversation with your board, committee, and board members.

The board—as the corporate governing body—must ensure the organization's capacity and capability to do relationship building. Together, the chief executive officer and the chief development officer make sure that the board understands.

Individual board members take on relationship-building roles. Individual board members host cultivation gatherings, and schmooze guests at agency programs and fundraising events. In partnership with staff, individual board members meet personally with donors and prospects to nurture the relationship.

Start with good ideas for relationship building. Then figure out who can help execute, whether staff or board member. Don't get distracted by "board member." Think, instead, which person could help implement this strategy.

Engage the Staff

Include customer-centered and donor-centered behavior in the job description for every single staff position in your organization. Hold staff accountable for these behaviors.

Provide orientation and training about how to operate as a customer-centered and donor-centered organization. Regularly strategize about relationship building.

Create Affinity Teams

Look at the target audiences you hope to reach. Create affinity teams to support constituency development for a specific audience. From the target group, recruit a few individuals who are predisposed to your organization. Ask them to join your affinity team.

Explain your organization's values and philosophy up front, so team members understand and are supportive. Make sure there are no values conflicts between your organization and affinity team members.

With the affinity team, set realistic goals for building relationships with the targeted constituents. Make sure your goals are not related to money alone. Remember, a donor is more important than a donation. A focus on constituent needs will capture their interests; a focus on money will turn them off.

Use the affinity team to devise the constituency development plan for that targeted group. The plan includes communications and cultivation strategies.

Use the affinity team to monitor progress and measure effectiveness. Ask these volunteers to help carry out the strategies.

The Process of Constituency Development

Don't focus on donors only. Think about your clients and your volunteers, too. Think about those who might be advocates and partners. All of these are your constituencies.

Retention comes first; that's loyalty. Then acquisition. Keep your customers, partners, and donors. Then find new ones to add to your tribe. Honestly. Think this way and you'll focus better and more effectively. You'll be more successful.

Your goal is to find those who can fulfill their aspirations by giving through your organization.

Imagine this: Your organization successfully designs and implements ongoing systems and activities that foster loyalty. Your organization uses the engagement scenarios and marketing approach described here to design its relationship-building activities.

Just imagine: Your organization successfully designs and implements ongoing systems and activities that actually enable people (and businesses, and other organizations, etc.) to self-identify as predisposed and then reach out and engage in your organization. Through top-notch constituency development, you build profitable relationships that last.

So you want specifics on how to do this? Think of this as a virtuous circle, continually reinforcing itself. Use the steps in Exhibit 7.3 to help guide your organization's planning and execution. Use this relationship-building process for a single constituent or for a constituency.

Exhibit 7.3   Steps in the Process of Constituency Development

Organize your constituency development with these eight steps. All steps matter in the process of relationship building.

1. Identify the predisposed.
2. Get to know the predisposed well enough to either qualify them as a prospect, or determine they are not interested and hence not a prospect. If they're not interested, you move on and they move on.
3. Identify their interests and disinterests. Understand their emotions, and their motivations and aspirations.
4. Identify the mutually beneficial exchange, what you have in common. Define this commonality.

5. Nurture the relationship to develop commitment. This includes communications and cultivation.

These first five steps apply to any relationship. And the relationship is the result. In some cases, however, you'll want to make a request of some form. Perhaps to join the board or serve on a committee. Maybe to invest financially or to lobby for a particular public policy.

6. Evaluate interest and readiness for the request. If yes, design the request. If the prospect is not ready for this step, continue relationship building.

7. Ask. This is the inviting moment. Thank the prospect. And continue relationship building.

8. Monitor progress. Measure results.

Step 1 initiates the relationship-building process: finding those who might be interested. From a fund development perspective, this begins the acquisition process. Once you have qualified prospects, your process is no longer so linear. Steps 3 through 8 become a virtuous circle. Each action builds upon and generates another action, producing a mutually reinforcing cycle.

You may move through some steps more quickly than others. Sometimes you'll collapse some of the steps into each other. But be careful: Don't enter the process midstream. The whole point of the process is to properly cultivate before making any request. Constituency development is not always a linear process. It is, however, a progressive process.

Really, that's it. In the proverbial nutshell: Identify and qualify them. Get to know them. Nurture the relationship through communications and cultivation. Move constituents along the continuum, engaging them more and more. Eventually, evaluate their interest and readiness to be asked for something. Then ask. Ask again. Continue nurturing the relationship.

But do remember—I've said it before and I'll keep saying it: Occasionally, the constituency development process doesn't work. They simply are not sufficiently interested for any ask. When this is the case, accept it and move on.

Start with Your Constituents

The easiest and fastest route to success is to start with those who already care about you. For fundraisers, that's your donors and prospects.

Your first task is to strengthen relationships with your constituents so they move through the relationship continuum. You get to know them better and better. You identify the potential dimensions of the relationship. You define the mutually beneficial exchange. You nurture the relationship between them and your nonprofit/NGO through communications and cultivation.

Identifying the Predisposed

Bear in mind that it's harder to find new constituents than it is to enrich relationships with current constituents. You have to identify individuals or businesses or groups that might be predisposed to your cause.

Then you design ways to introduce them to the cause and clearly explain your organization's role in the cause. Next they have to confirm their interest. Only if they confirm their interest, do you consider them qualified as constituents—and for fund development, qualified as prospects.

This is lots of work, and particularly challenging to do. But once you've done all the work you can with your constituents, most organizations begin looking for those who might be predisposed. In fund development, this is the acquisition process as opposed to the retention process. Be cautious when identifying the predisposed. It's too easy to assume that someone is interested when she or he actually isn't. Don't overestimate.

Asking or Inviting

Ready to be asked. Ready to respond. It's just that simple and complex. Through the constituency development process, you evaluate the constituent's interest and readiness for a deeper relationship—for example, a request of some sort. As appropriate, you design the ask and you ask. Depending on the answer, you decide your next steps.

Now Comes the Fun Part

I wonder, is the process of constituency development—building those relationships—even more important in fund development? After all, fundraisers are asking prospects for gifts. This isn't a traditional customer relationship where the constituent gets a tangible benefit. Organizations are asking for a financial investment that produces impact—but often at arm's length from the donor.

I think donor-centered—and all that entails—is at least as important to fund development as customer-centered is to marketing and sales. So let's start with the most important part: nurturing relationships to retain your current donors.

Remember, loyalty depends on a donor-centered organization that engages in a donor-centered relationship-building process. And that means you have to know your donors (and prospects) at some level.

The rest of this chapter is devoted to the key elements of donor-centered relationship building, with a bit at the end about asking. The key elements of relationship building are: getting to know your donors and prospects, and building relationships through communications and cultivation. This is the heart of the constituency development process.

And this is the fun part, too. Honest. Relationship building is fun.

Getting to Know Your Donors and Prospects

Let's talk about getting to know your donors and prospective donors. And you can apply this to other constituents, too, as appropriate.

First, how well do you know your donors—or any other constituents? Probably not as well as you should and could. Getting to know them means understanding them well enough to create that mutually beneficial exchange.

Nonprofits/NGOs certainly need to know as much about their donors and prospective donors as marketers know about their customers, actually more. I know we mostly don't know that much. But at least let's try.

To start, please don't let your mind race to prospect research. Instead, think about getting to know someone because you are genuinely interested. Please care enough to want to find out their interests and disinterests, their motivations and aspirations. This is about them, not about money for your organization. That's what true relationship building is.

You need to know your prospects and donors well enough to nurture loyalty. Eventually, you need to know them well enough to design the appropriate ask, if that is your intention.

What kind of information is useful to gather? Ultimately, you decide. Find the balance between too much and too little information. Decide how you will use the information and why it is meaningful. Decide how you will manage the resulting information. Then devise methods to secure the information. Decide when and how to involve which staff and volunteers in the information-gathering work.

Start by asking:

- What do we want to know about our donors and prospects? How will this information add value in our relationship-building program?
- What is the minimal information required to maintain only the most cursory relationship?
- What is necessary to cultivate the relationship further?
- What is essential to engage the donor or prospect in our organization?

The effective fund development function regularly uses both formal and informal means to learn more about its donors and prospective donors. The fundraiser encourages the entire institution to reach out and get to know its constituents better. And the fundraiser makes sure to gather all the information and manage it well.

For effective constituency development, you need two kinds of information. First, you need specific information about a targeted constituent (single entity) or targeted constituency (fairly homogeneous group). Second, you need to know the general trends and patterns of your various constituencies and other audiences predisposed to your organization.

Some information must be attached to the individual donor or prospect. Other information can be generalized to a homogeneous group (e.g., baby boomers, Millennials, women donors). If you wish a closer relationship, you need specific information about the specific donor or prospect.

Generally, you seek demographic and psychographic information[29] about your donors and prospects. Demographics refers to the characteristics of a group, such as size, growth, and distribution, and the vital statistics of individuals like age, gender, marital status, family size, education, income, occupation, and geographic location. Psychographics describes the lifestyle characteristics of a group or individual, including their activities and behavioral and personal traits. Psychographic indicators cover one's interests and values, hopes and fears, aspirations and needs.

Pay attention to societal trends, too. Learn how your donors and prospective donors fit in with these trends—for example, social networking, workplace, and so forth. Read sector research. For example, learn about the implications of gender, generation, and race/ethnicity in philanthropy. Read research beyond the nonprofit/NGO sector. All this can help you better understand some of your constituents. Use this information to help develop questions that will engage donors and prospects and create lively conversations. Use this information to help you decide what research your organization needs to do with its own donors.

All information gathering should lead to one thing: the process and practice of taking the donor's view in cultivating the philanthropy partnership with the organization.

From *Achieving Excellence in Fund Raising*, by Henry Rosso and Sherree Parris Nudd (San Francisco: Jossey-Bass, 1991), 184

Your organization may also conduct some research itself, for example through focus groups, surveys, and interviews. Before you start researching, decide what you want to know and why. Figure out how you will use the information and why it is meaningful.

Yes, conducting your own research takes time and can cost money. But don't let that stop you. For example, recruit marketing students from colleges and universities. The student receives practical experience and a grade. You get a motivated worker who often uses the resources of his or her professors. You might secure pro bono services from a market research firm.

Of course, the best way to get information about your constituents is to ask them. Engage them in conversations both formally (a specific meeting) or informally (while attending a program or event). Have lunch with a board member. Speak with volunteer while she's working with you. Meet with committees and clients. Mingle with guests at special events.

Use these opportunities more effectively. For example, train board members to schmooze, engage in conversation, and provide you with the resulting information. Assign board members and staff to speak with specific constituents at special events and programs.

The fundraiser, chief executive, and other key staff should contact different constituents regularly. Several times a week, eat breakfast or lunch with a constituent. Daily, contact someone to get to know him or her better.

By the way, the process of getting to know your donors and prospects better actually cultivates the relationship. Donors and prospects—everyone—likes to be asked their opinion. Everyone wants to offer advice and perspective and insight. Whether it's a focus group, survey, or personal interview—you get a double benefit: much-needed information and a great relationship-building strategy.

And finally, it's your job to create more extensive conversation between your constituents and organization. Ask specific questions. Pursue issues your donors and prospective donors bring up. Listen to what people say and don't say. Remember relevant information gleaned during conversation and record it later. Write down anecdotes and note your impressions. (But be discreet. Prospect and donor records are not all that confidential. The donor can ask to see the information. The solicitor certainly will.)

Do not misrepresent your intentions. Do not pretend to be a personal friend offering privacy and confidentiality. This is a professional exchange and should be considered so. Behave ethically and professionally and there will be no confusion.

With this information in hand, get to know your donors and prospects better. Gather more specific information about their personal interests and activities. Explore what their philanthropic behaviors say about their interests and aspirations. Find out why your donors affiliate with your cause and your organization.

Look at Chapter 6, the strategic planning section of this book, for more information about market research methods and tools. For questions to ask donors, see all the research in the field. Use the questions relevant to your organization. One of my favorite sources for good questions is *Building Donor Loyalty* by Sargeant and Jay. I also like the questions asked by the Russ Reid Company in its research *Heart of the Donor*. For good conversation with donors, see the questions in *Keep Your Donors*. See also the donor questions posted at www.simonejoyaux.com.

Relationship Building through Communications

Communication is central to developing relationships. Communication is two-way, otherwise it isn't communication. You transmit your ideas, information, and feelings to others; they share the same with you. You seek information and perspective from others, valuing their input; they do the same with you.

Communication implies understanding on the part of the person you are communicating with. Communication is information received and, hopefully, acted upon. The effectiveness of communication can be evaluated only after the fact. If the recipient of the communication acts in the way you intended, there was communication. If not, there was only information.

Through communication, you invite people into your organization. You invite them to use your service, to give you time or money. You position your organization by communicating your distinct niche within the community.

Communication is more than a fundraising brochure, your newsletter, the annual report, or posters for an event. Communication includes things like: your conversation at board meetings; the structure and content of formal meetings and informal gatherings; casual conversations with colleagues, clients, and donors; gossip and official memoranda. Effective communication translates information into knowledge and knowledge into learning. And learning produces change. Effective communication helps build a strong organization.

Fund Development Must Communicate Better

Upstairs in his office, Tom is ranting and raving. Soon he'll visit my office and continue the tirade. "How can fundraising communication be so bad when it is so important?"

How, indeed?

How do organizations expect to nurture relationships with their constituents when the communications violate best practice? Why do bosses and boards stick their noses in when they don't know the body of knowledge?

Fund development produces far too much mediocre communication. And there's no excuse. There are enough books and articles, blogs and e-news out there that tell us what to do, how to do it, and why we must do it that way.

Fund development produces far too much very bad communication. And there's no excuse. There's substantial and substantive research that tells us how people think and decide, why they do what they do, and what triggers their action.

There's no excuse for this bad work we do. No excuse.

What Effective Communication Does

Effective communication does four things:

1. Grabs attention: Is tailored to your target constituency.
2. Stirs interest: Motivates your constituency to take the action you request.
3. Builds conviction and desire: Promises a desired benefit to the constituency if they take action.
4. Calls the constituent to action: Tells the constituency what to do to act.

Or, to paraphrase Jerry Weissman: Key messages must move the uninformed audience to understand, the dubious to believe, and the resistant to act in a particular way.[30]

Who Is in Charge of Donor Communications?

That's the question: Who is in charge? And the answer is: The development officer. Is that you? Are you the professional fundraiser? Even if your organization has marketing and public relations (PR) staff, the development professional is still in charge of donor communications. The fundraising professional knows the body of knowledge. The fundraiser's job is to ensure that donor communications follow the research and follow the rules.

Tell that to your boss. Have him call me if he's got a problem with this. Too often, the marketing/communications staff are not experts in donor-centered communications. Too often, the marketing/communications staff only know about corporate communications. Now you're in trouble. Unless they listen to you.

Corporate Communications Are Not Fundraising Communications

Corporations do lots of that image and reputation sort of stuff. They pour lots of money into it. I suppose, if you had lots of money, you could do that, too. But even if you had lots of money, why would you want to do this general, institutional promotion thing that isn't measurable and doesn't elicit action?

Corporate communications and fundraising communications are not the same. Thanks to Tom Ahern[31] for this explanation: What you *need*—to spur giving and to bring new people into your organization's family on a regular basis—are marketing materials. Corporate communications and marketing communications are separate pursuits with dissimilar goals.

MARKETING IS ABOUT ACTION NOW Corporate communications are soft-sell PR activities, meant to burnish image and reputation. Annual reports from publicly traded companies, for example, are corporate communications. Their primary goal, aside from meeting Securities and Exchange Commission (SEC) obligations, is to impress upon the audience the stability and sheer magnificence of a company. They lean on fancy-pants graphic design and bold assertions to do the trick.

Corporate communications talk about how wonderful the corporation is. That's good in corporate communications. Good corporate communications talk about the organization's mission and vision in glowing, lofty, credible terms.

Marketing communications are different, though. Completely, utterly different. Marketing communications are action oriented. They are single-minded. They sell hard (though, for a nonprofit organization's audience, pleasantly so). The goal: to persuade a specific target audience to do something *right now*. If nothing happens, the communication is a failure. If response happens, it's a success. Measuring the effectiveness of marketing materials is easy: Response rates tell the tale.

Corporate communications, on the other hand, do not require action today. Sure, they hope something positive will happen ultimately. But they're not in a frantic panic about it. If nothing happens immediately, okay. Because response is not the point of the exercise, the effectiveness of corporate communications is notoriously difficult to measure.

Unmeasured communications inevitably squander resources (time, money, hope). An ineffective program can linger for years unchallenged. An example is "building image." Unfortunately, you can never say whether this kind of advertising works. This doesn't produce, for example, new donors.

"Image" advertising versus "response" advertising neatly illustrates the difference between corporate communications and marketing communications.

AND IT'S ABOUT MAKING THE CUSTOMER THE HERO—FOREVER Another shining distinction between corporate communications and marketing communications is the value placed on the reader's time and interests.

Marketers treat the reader as sacred—and a squirmy beast, eager to escape. Corporate communications treat the reader as a foregone conclusion, like students in a college classroom. Corporate communications lecture. They make points. They explain at length. They unashamedly use insider language (a.k.a., jargon that insiders understand and outsiders can only guess at).

All fundraising copy should sound like someone talking.

From *Tiny Essentials of Writing for Fundraising*, by George Smith (Melrand, France: White Lion Press Limited, 2003), 37

Writing for donors and prospective donors must (at a minimum):

- Entertain them.
- Interest them.
- Gratify them emotionally.

- Exalt them (this is what donor-centricity is all about).
- Make clear offers.
- Exhort people to act now—and make action quick and easy.

That last is key. The worst and first enemy in marketing—and donor—communications is inertia. Getting *anyone* to do *anything* is hard, even when they are predisposed. The only safe attitude I know is this: Assume no one will respond to your communications; now what can you do to improve on that?

The good news is this: Shifting your communications from a corporate orientation to a marketing orientation can be done pretty much in a blink. It does not require special talents, just different methods and different language.

Beware of the Public Relations Mistake

Organizations assume good public relations will make them famous and lead people to give. The exact opposite is true. Good public relations requires immense effort and may lead to no gifts at all.

Let's define public relations as building your organization's image and reputation. Image and reputation are important to fund development. Think of this as credibility and trust.

To achieve this goal, commonly used public relations strategies include media coverage and special events. You release information to the media and you do special events. You put these out into the community and hope. You hope the media will present the information. You hope people will notice, think well of you, and remember you.

But you have almost no control. There is no call to action in public relations. You cannot guide the response or measure the effectiveness. (By the way, the same holds true of advertising. The greatest ad agencies in the world tell you that they cannot measure the effectiveness of advertising.)

You cannot control media coverage unless you buy it. Standard media releases written by organizations are notoriously poor communications, often overlooked by editors and reporters. (What works better is a personalized, well-written letter explaining the newsworthiness of your story to the particular media outlet. Better yet, first have a personal conversation with the media representative. Follow up with a letter, fact sheet, and release.)

Special events require even more effort and, often, a significant financial investment. But these events are not as important as the accumulation of printed material and dialogue that you use in fund development.

Avoid Another Mistake . . . the Focus on Visibility

You already read about visibility in Chapter 1. I don't need to rant much more. Just remember Simone and the NCAA basketball championship and the World Cup, described in Exhibit 1.2

Keep this in mind: Increased media coverage and community visibility do not produce more charitable contributions. Donor-centered communications—directed to your donors and qualified prospects—can increase donor retention and acquire donors.

Just because your organization receives lots of media coverage doesn't mean that anyone will pay attention. Remember, people pay attention to what interests them. Those who aren't interested in your organization or your cause won't read the article about you. They won't listen to the broadcast about you.

Target your audiences instead. Then develop your own communications directed to the target audiences. You'll get a better return on your investment of resources.

Sure, media coverage has value. It's great when someone says something nice about you. You can use it as testimony in your own communication. You can copy a news article and distribute it to the targeted audiences you want to read it. Your volunteers like media coverage, too. It makes them feel secure. Media coverage gives an external seal of approval.

What Can You Do?

Spend most of your time on the communication you can control. Focus most of your effort on communications directed at your targeted constituents. Remember, communication is information received and acted upon. Communication is targeted, controlled, and measurable.

Because effective communication is essential to effective fund development, each fundraiser needs to know the basics. Even if you hire professional copywriters and speechwriters, improve your own communications skills. Every leader—especially fundraisers—needs to communicate well.

In practice, communicating well often means learning to write more persuasively since 98 percent of the content of your organization is conveyed in written form. Communicating well means understanding readability—and, apparently, most graphic designers don't!

Read the experts. Have an expert critique your work repeatedly. And practice, practice, practice. (By the way, writers say there is no such thing as writer's block. Just keep writing.)

Successfully Reaching Your Target Audience

Successful communications depend on your organization's understanding of the group with which you wish to communicate. Tailor your communications for the audience. You need to know their interests and you need to understand how they best receive communication. (But don't panic. You needn't produce a different newsletter for each of your donor audiences. You needn't write a different solicitation letter for each group.) To penetrate your target audience, your communications messages must:

- Clearly state benefits to the audience.
- Translate information into language and images that the audience will recognize.

- Deliver information through means used by the target audience.
- Reflect the values of your organization.

Start by reviewing the section entitled "Understanding Marketing" earlier in this chapter. Remember to focus on benefits, not features, described later in this chapter. Repeat your mantra, "It's not what I'm selling; it's what they're buying."

Next, read the research: research that documents what donors want to know; information about personality types and donor motivations; and so forth. Use all that to help you tailor and target.

You will not, in many cases, know the actual recipient of your communications. But you should know enough about him or her to create a picture in your mind. Communicate with that picture of a real person.

To paraphrase Robert Bly: Successful cultivators empathize with their constituents. Effective cultivators do not launch into some pitch that talks about the organization and its activities. Instead, effective cultivators try to understand the constituent's needs, mood, personality, and prejudices. By mirroring the constituent's thoughts and feelings, effective cultivators "break down resistance ... establish trust and credibility, and highlight only those benefits that are of interest" to the constituent.[32]

Beware the onset of the institutional voice. It drives people off. Do you begin your case statements and direct-mail letters by talking about your organization and all the great things it has done? The "we do this" style is the single best indication that an organization is not oriented toward the constituent.

When communicating, review the following checklist:

- Will the recipient of my communication understand what I am saying (or writing or showing)?
- Will she or he understand the insider language or examples or images that I might use?
- Am I personalizing my communication to the recipient's interests?
- Have I clearly explained benefits to the recipient?
- Is my communication clear and to the point?
- If I were the recipient of this communication, would I be interested?

How to Influence People

The art of influencing can be counterintuitive. For instance, the threat of loss is more motivating than the promise of gain. So says the research of Robert B. Cialdini[33] in his theory of scarcity.

Cialdini's experiments in social psychology produced critical theories applicable to constituency development and to your communications. He defines six "weapons of influence" to persuade people to act: reciprocation, commitment and consistency, social proof, authority, liking, and scarcity.

1. *Reciprocation.* People tend to return a favor. For example, think about free product samples. Or how about those free address labels and coins included in direct-mail letters?

This sure sounds familiar to fundraisers. Ask your board members to use their personal and professional connections to secure gifts. You know, the reciprocal exchange of favors. Don't worry that your board member will have to return the favor to everyone he has asked. Don't worry that without the same people negotiating the deals, reciprocity might not be sustained.

On the other hand, the generalized concept of reciprocity that's essential to social capital—described in Chapter 2—has people feeling an obligation to community. People step up because they recognize their interdependence with others.

2. *Commitment and Consistency.* If people commit, orally or in writing, to an idea or goal, they are more likely to honor that commitment.

This sounds pretty good: People honor their commitments. Even if you change elements of the offer, people stick with you. On the other hand, we label this "cognitive dissonance" when people stick to a decision that has turned sour, that conflicts with their better judgment.

For fund development, this weapon of influence might mean that with only a little effort, organizations can keep donors because they've committed. Imagine the result if organizations put in great effort?

3. *Social Proof.* People will do things that they see other people doing.

This is a bit like conformity, sort of like follow the leader, and lots like join with others. In Cialdini's experiments, one or more people would look up into the sky; then bystanders did; then so many people did that traffic stopped. Take a look at the Asch experiments, for example.

In constituency development, this could be an affinity group of baby boomer women putting together a giving circle. This might be your invitation to join a tribe.

4. *Authority.* People will tend to obey authority figures, even if they are asked to perform objectionable acts.

Check out the Milgram experiments in the early 1960s. Think of the My Lai massacre and Abu Ghraib torture and prisoner abuse.

In the good sense, perhaps this, like social proof, is when your well-respected colleague asks you for a gift. Or when your boss encourages all employees to give.

5. *Liking.* People are easily persuaded by other people whom they like.

Think of those house parties—hosted by a neighbor—selling jewelry, cosmetics, and Tupperware. Think of kids going door-to-door selling candy and magazine subscriptions.

This persuasive tactic also has its negative aspects—for example, the stereotype of physical attractiveness and the biases favoring more attractive people.

6. *Scarcity.* Perceived scarcity will generate demand. For example: Making offers available for a "limited time only" encourages sales. Telling donors that without their support the theater company cannot produce a full season elicits just such support.

Here's a Surprise: Negative Is Better Than Positive

Negative information is better received than positive. So says research from the Institute of Cognitive Neuroscience at University College London, www.icn.ucl.ac.uk.

Why? Because human beings process negative emotions more easily than positive ones. That's biology. "Oh my gosh! Watch out! That huge lion is rushing toward you!"

Here's how researchers explain this: "People can perceive the emotional value of subliminal messages...and [people] are much more attuned to negative words.... [T]here are evolutionary advantages to responding rapidly to emotional information."[34] Emotional messaging works. This shouldn't surprise you. Remember, emotions are the key decision-makers. Review the basic principles in Chapter 1.

Rational messaging actually hurts. Okay, that might be a bit surprising—but it's true. Advertising campaigns with purely emotional content performed about twice as well as those with rational content only, 31 percent compared to 16 percent. The emotional advertising campaigns even outperformed those with both rational and emotional content, 31 percent compared to 26 percent. It turns out that the human brain can process emotional input without cognitive processing or even cognitive awareness. We feel without thinking![35]

Still More Surprises

This probably won't surprise you: People prefer to think about easy things than about hard things. When things are made easy to think about, people like that, too. In summary, easy = true![36]

Cognitive fluency, a hot topic in psychology now, describes how easy it is to think about something. Fluency affects any situation where we evaluate information—for example, our voting, buying, and giving decisions.

Cognitive fluency also means something is likely familiar to us. Biologically, we have an instinctive preference for familiarity. Familiar means safe; unfamiliar, well, that's the big lion running toward you again.

People are very sensitive to the experience of ease or difficulty.

—Norbert Schwartz, researcher in social psychology and consumer psychology, and professor at the University of Michigan; quoted by Drake Bennett in his article "Easy = True," January 31, 2010, www.boston.com

---

The human preference for fluency is an "adaptive shortcut." It's faster to think through something, to make a decision. And fluency's opposite, "disfluency," causes alarm.

Practically speaking, here's what this means:

- When something is harder to read, we transfer that difficulty to the topic we're reading about.

    For example, the researchers reported that poor legibility describing an exercise regimen made readers thing the exercise program itself was more difficult. Worse, poor legibility in a questionnaire made readers respond less honestly than a more legible version.

- Auditory cues contribute to fluency.

    For example, rhyming, repetition, and catchy phrases are easier. And people interpret them as "inherently truer."

- And here's an easy = true example that I just had to include: Stock shares in companies with easy-to-pronounce names outperform those with hard-to-pronounce names. How strange is that?!

Disfluency may be just as interesting, at the right time and in the right situation. Because disfluency causes discomfort, people might think more carefully. Researchers found that disfluency caused people to think more abstractly. Sometimes, disfluency makes a product more interesting. Sometimes less familiarity suggests greater innovation.

Isn't the human brain fascinating?

Maybe disfluency means cage-rattling questions? Maybe disfluency is essential for critical thinking and challenging assumptions? Maybe the balance of fluency and disfluency help produce learning and change?

Read the full article for more examples—examples of how cognitive fluency affects self-confidence and personal relationships. Read the full article and think about how this affects your communications—your vocabulary and the reading level, the images and metaphors you use.

Make Sure They Hear You

First, make sure they *want* to hear from you. That's the permission marketing thing back in Chapter 1. Here's a great example of permission marketing, from the Chico's catalog I received in the mail: "Thank you for inviting us into your home. Stop by ours soon."

Now, back to making sure they hear you. Your job is to anticipate and overcome their barriers.

Recognize the Volume of Information They Receive

What can I say? Any statistics I use will be out-of-date by the time you read this page. You know how much information you receive. You know how many messages hit you daily. And your organization is part of that deluge overwhelming recipients.

What's the answer? There are several. For example: Make sure that whoever receives your communications gave you permission. Make sure your communications adhere to the body of knowledge. Make sure your communications are donor-centered.

Overcome the Inertia of Your Constituents

Inertia is your biggest challenge, says Tom Ahern. Stand in awe of inertia!

People do things quite reluctantly and often have trouble committing. That's human nature, and it is a very powerful obstacle. You have to overcome people's tendency to do nothing. Even self-interest alone may not be enough to yank people from their inertia.

Kurt Lewin[37] addresses inertia in his concept of force field analysis. To move someone from inertia to action, change must occur. Lewin views change as the result of a struggle between forces that seek to upset the status quo and forces that want to maintain the status quo.

"Driving forces" move a situation toward change. Think about driving forces as the motivation someone has to take a particular action. On the other side, "restraining forces" block the change. These are the barriers that stop someone from taking a particular action. Remember, if the restraining forces are stronger than the driving forces, change will not happen.

Practice this yourself. For example, think about someone who is trying to learn to read. Ask yourself: What are the reasons this person would like to read? What are the individual's personal motivations? What might stop the individual from learning? Take a look at the following ideas:

Driving Forces	Restraining Forces
Can't complete an employment application.	No childcare during scheduled classes.
Can't use road signs to get somewhere.	Expense of classes.
Read a bedtime story to my child.	No transportation to get to the class.

Apply this to fund development. Identify the reasons why people will not respond to your face-to-face solicitation, your telephone call, or your letter. Identify the restraining forces and attack them directly. Respond to the objections before prospects raise them. And remember: Different people will experience different driving and restraining forces.

Remember inertia. In force field analysis, the prospect is always ready to do nothing. If you don't make a case against the restraining forces, the prospect will choose inertia.

Different constituents will experience different driving and restraining forces. Focus on your targeted constituents and their respective needs.

Attack the restraining forces! Diminish and eliminate as many as possible. If a driving force is "end world hunger," a restraining force might be the fear that "my own few dollars won't do much good."

Identify the driving forces. Use them. But be careful about reinforcing the driving forces. Studies indicate that strengthening the driving forces may actually increase resistance!

Target the Personality Types

Not everyone hears and learns in the same way. In fact, everyone has a preference for how they like to take in information. Psychologists have identified four distinct learning styles. Personalize your communications to these styles.

1. The expressive loves new stuff and is easily bored. Tell him or her about your new and exciting activities. Use bold statements and keep it lively.

   Example: "I'll learn a bunch of new insights and skills. Who knows what will happen? Could be great! I don't want to miss something that could be important."

2. The analytical craves facts and more facts and has trouble deciding. She or he expects documentation and statistical evidence like charts and lots of data.

   Example: "I'm not sure. But maybe this guy has something to say. He sounds qualified. I have my doubts, but you never know."

3. The bottom-liners want you to jump to the chase and they'll decide instantly. They appreciate summaries and want brevity.

   Example: "I want to do my job right the first time. Tell me how."

4. The amiable values relationships above all and wants you to be a friend. Use "you" a lot and create warm-hearted pictures. Talk about an ongoing relationship by asking him or her to "stay in touch."

   Example: "I'll be around lots of people I like and respect. I'll get to exchange stories and ideas with them. Maybe even make some new friends."

These personality types are evenly distributed among all target audiences. In a random sampling of any group, each of the four styles is represented by 25 percent of the group.

Your communications must have something for everyone. Just imagine sending a dry, lengthy memo full of facts and figures. Only the analytical type would read it and you would miss 75 percent of the audience. Worse yet, you reached the 25 percent who have trouble deciding.

Some portion of your communication must respond to each of the personality types. Reach these different audiences through different facts and stories presented by your face-to-face solicitors. Make sure articles in your newsletters capture the attention of each learning style. When you make a presentation, pay equal attention to the expressives, analyticals, bottom-liners, and amiables.

Talk about Benefits, Not Features

Don't keep talking about features in your brochures and case statements. Features only describe what you do. Features don't focus on the constituent's needs or interests. Features don't explain how the constituent will be better off. Features are lifeless; benefits add the life.

Talk about benefits. Benefits explain why the features provide something useful to the person participating.

As Kotler and Andreason note,

People—at least those who are mentally competent—behave in ways that they perceive will leave them better off than if they behaved in some other fashion. Since every action implies perceived costs (if only some anxiety about not taking an alternative action), it follows that people act in certain ways because they perceive the ratio of the benefits to costs to be better than for any alternative.[38]

Features tell, benefits sell. Always translate features into benefits. The translation is easy. Pretend you are the constituent and ask yourself, "What's in it for me?" Remember, "What's in it for me?" is always a heart issue for the constituent.

Unfortunately, organizations mostly describe themselves and their activities in terms of features. A literacy center talks about teaching women to read and write. The homeless shelter describes its food and overnight program. The independent school describes its art curriculum for students in kindergarten through high school.

Remember to write about benefits, not features. Benefits directly address the reader's self-interest. It is by expressing features as benefits that you speak most powerfully to specific target audiences.

—Tom Ahern, ABC, Ahern Communications, Ink. (www.aherncomm.com) (Yes, Ink., not Inc.)

But effective organizations communicate their features as benefits to a specific constituency. These organizations know that constituents buy benefits, not features.

The benefits for clients are often easiest to identify. For example: If the feature of the literacy center is teaching women to read and write, one benefit might be that the women can find job opportunities by reading want ads. Another benefit might be that the women can spend meaningful time with their children by reading a story together. The benefit of a shelter's food and overnight program is saving people from starving and freezing.

The benefits to a prospective donor are usually harder to determine, and depend on the prospect's interests and motivations.

- If your business gives to a literacy center, perhaps the benefit is more job applicants who can read and write. As an avid reader yourself, you may want everyone to experience the joy of reading.
- As a parent, you give to your child's school because the K–12 arts curriculum teaches your child to solve problems better through creativity and self-discipline.
- As an artist, you give to the school because you want future audiences for the arts. You believe the school's arts program will help young children grow up loving the arts.

To sharpen your skills, use a common object and translate its features into benefits for the user. For example, differentiate between the features and benefits of a car. Conduct the same exercise with a program or service of your organization. List the features directed at a specific audience. Then outline the benefits as you see them. Test your ideas by asking your clients' opinions. See the example in Exhibit 7.4, "Features and Benefits."

Exhibit 7.4   Features and Benefits

Features and benefits of a workshop on fund development:

Features	Benefits
Cost is $25 per person or $40 for two people from the same agency.	Reduced price makes it easy to bring more than one person from your agency.
Workshop content includes basic principles of fundraising.	Key tips to help you raise more money.
Located at the Holiday Inn.	Location is easily accessible off major highways, just 15 minutes from anywhere in the metropolitan area.

More examples of features translated into benefits:

Features	Benefits
Learn to read.	Read your child a bedtime story.
Attention welfare recipients: Enroll in a one-year computer training class.	Attention welfare recipients: One phone call could help you earn $50,000 a year!
Enjoy the benefits of your own private library. Join the athenaeum now.	Tired of the chaos at home? Enjoy your own quiet, private reading room. Join the athenaeum now.

Try this: Describe the benefits of serving as a board member. Remember, this means the benefits to the board member, not to your organization. First, list the features of serving as a board member. Then ask your board members what the benefits are for each of the features.

Now look at fund development. Identify the benefits to donors and donor prospects. The best way is to ask them. Call a few on the telephone. Meet them for breakfast or lunch. Conduct a focus group with targeted donors. Do the same with volunteers. Hold a similar discussion with the development committee and board.

Write Better, Lots Better

You must learn to write better. You cannot always hire a professional writer. You have to write, too.

Written materials are your organization's most used communications strategy. Many of your constituents—and probably most of your donors—will have no other connection with you except through the communications you send.

Good writing produces action. Do not compose a scholarly paper. Don't follow the rigid rules of grammar. Don't show that you're sophisticated or erudite. None of this is good communications. See Exhibit 7.5 for some quick tips to write better.

Exhibit 7.5   You Can (and Must) Write Better

Use these 12 tips whether you're writing a letter, advertisement, brochure, or some other copy. Keep in mind that most of these hints are applicable to speaking, too.

1. The reader (or listener) is most important. Focus on the benefits to that person. Use "you" lots.
2. Hit hard right away. Create interest and drama immediately when you write or speak.
3. Catchy phrases without a call to action won't motivate anyone.
4. Don't bury the important stuff. Target what is most important to the particular audience. Repeat it. As copywriters say: "Tell them what you're going to tell them. Tell them again. And then tell them what you told them."
5. Keep it simple.
   - Write and tell in small, manageable bits.
   - Avoid long paragraphs. One-sentence (even one-word) paragraphs are good.
   - Avoid compound sentences. Stick to 16 to 20 words or fewer.
   - Vary sentence and paragraph length so reading isn't dull.
   - Don't use extra words that waste the reader's time and use up space you could use for something else.
   - Use simple words like *building* rather than *edifice* and *words* rather than *vocabulary*.
   - Don't use technical jargon unless absolutely necessary. Make sure there is no easier way to say it. Don't use a technical term unless at least 95 percent of your audience will get it.
6. Use emotions. Remember, all human decisions are triggered by emotions.
7. Tell stories.
8. Don't use sexist language. There is no excuse.
9. Write in a conversational tone.
   - Use colloquial expressions like *kids* instead of *children*.
   - Use action verbs whenever possible.
   - Start your sentences with conjunctions to help your writing flow. Just like you would talk.
   - And end your sentences with a preposition. A rigid grammarian might say no. But rigid grammarians make dull writers. You know what I'm talking about.
   - Use sentence fragments. Same reasons.

10. Pay particular attention to your headlines and subheads, whether in newsletters, annual reports, posters, brochures, or direct-mail letters. Why? Because busy people scan. And what they scan are headlines, subheads, captions, opening sentences, and so on. Studies prove that 85 percent of people read the headline only. So a good headline grabs the reader's attention (if they're interested!) and tells a complete message. A good headline communicates the benefit to the reader and creates excitement. The headline also draws the reader into the copy.

11. Make your text easy to skim. Create ways for the reader's eye to move into the text. Use bullets, subheads, numbers, underlines, boldface, and boxed text. But don't go crazy.

12. Always use a P.S. in letters. Readers look at the signature after they look at the salutation. (Of course, they had to open the envelope first!) And the P.S. is right after the signature. It's a great spot for important info.

Source: Copyright © Tom Ahern, ABC, Ahern Communications, Ink. (www.ahern comm.com).

USE THE INVERTED PYRAMID STYLE Journalists structure their stories using inverted pyramids. In an inverted pyramid: first, describe the result; next, describe the reasons for the result; at the end, explain the context or background from which the result emerged.

This approach lets the reader get to the point of the story immediately. That's why good news writing seems so vivid and filled with significance. This writing style works well if you're speaking, writing any letter, creating a fundraising case statement, or developing a foundation or corporate proposal.

Read about the Three Little Pigs in Exhibit 7.6.

Exhibit 7.6 Visit the Pyramids . . . and Get to the Point

Here's the story of the Three Little Pigs, as told in the inverted pyramid style:

A wooden home in Fayetteville was reduced to matchsticks last night when a long-standing feud between a wolf and a family of bachelor pigs erupted into violence. Experts say feuds of this kind are a "predictable occurrence between natural enemies" and that the pigs should have built out of bricks.

The inverted pyramid always works the same way: first, there's the outcome ("home reduced to matchsticks"); then there are the reasons behind the outcome ("a long-standing feud"); finally, there's the background behind the reasons ("natural enemies").

It's called an inverted pyramid because it makes its point first, then builds toward the base.

(continued)

(Continued)

Which is exactly the opposite of how most people learn to write. In school, we're taught to build our case from the ground up.

Don't do it! You'll lose the reader. Put the key points first. Put the background in the background.

Source: Copyright © Tom Ahern, ABC, Ahern Communications, Ink. (www.ahern comm.com).

USE STATISTICS SPARINGLY   Generally, numbers are not very persuasive because intellectual arguments are the weakest and emotional arguments are the strongest. And remember those personality types, too. How many actually like statistics?

USE "YOU" LOTS   "You" is the most powerful word in the English language. (And I suspect that the version of "you" in any language is also powerful.) So use it lots and lots. Definitely avoid the institutional "we." Do not fall back on: "We at the theater company offer the best acting." "Our programs protect hundreds of women from domestic violence." "Please give us a contribution to help our good work."

Do you use "you" often enough? Examine the way you communicate. Do you describe the community problem and your organization's solution? Does your letter or conversation eloquently explain how your organization benefits those served?

Well, that's not enough. What about me, the listener? Sadly, fundraisers persist in talking about the organization's need, the organization's services, and the needs of the clients. You keep forgetting me. How do I feel as your potential donor? How will giving to your organization match my interests and fulfill my needs?

THE RIGHT WORDS DO MATTER—SO DOES SENTENCE CONSTRUCTION   Avoid complexity in your writing. Sure, communicate complex thoughts, but do so simply. Stick to active, not passive, sentences. Active does and passive is done to. Active sentences seem clear, direct, and forceful. How does the Bible start? "In the beginning, God created the heavens and the earth." Or there's the passive version: "In the beginning, the heavens and earth were created by God." Tangled, weak, and confused are what passive and convoluted sentences (like this one in which you are trapped) tend to be thought of.

Be vivid and bold. Use powerful words. For example, use "car," not automobile; use "kids," not children. Do what Jeff Brooks recommends in his blog: Ask yourself, "How would the *National Enquirer* write this?" Because the *Enquirer* knows the value of "the amazing, the lurid, the outrageous, the unexpected."

Are you ready for this kind of writing? Is your boss? How about the program staff and the board? According to Roy Williams,

Words are electric; they should be chosen for the emotional voltage they carry. Weak and predictable words cause grand ideas to appear so dull that they fade into the darkness of oblivion. But powerful words in unusual combinations brightly illuminate the mind. If a sentence does not shock a little, it carries no emotional voltage. When the hearer is not jolted, you can be sure he is not involved.[39]

WRITE AT THE EIGHTH GRADE READING LEVEL   News reporters write at an eighth grade level and so should you. See Exhibit 7.7.

Exhibit 7.7   Write at the Eighth Grade Level to Guarantee Understanding

Eighth-grade-level writing is not writing down; it's writing simple. Use short sentences and short paragraphs. Use clear, jargon-free language.

Newspapers write at the eighth grade level. You can write about anything—including atomic physics—at the eighth grade level. Check grade level in your word processing program.

Eighth-grade-level writing is transparent to most people. They understand the author's meaning immediately, at a glance.

Check out the grade levels of your favorite authors. You might find that today's most popular novelists write at the fourth and fifth grade levels. Fundraisers are storytellers, too. Learn from the best-selling storytellers in the culture: Write for quick and easy comprehension.

FYI: You've just read four paragraphs written at the seventh grade level.

Source: Copyright © Tom Ahern, ABC, Ahern Communications, Ink. (www.ahern comm.com).

It's easier for your readers to quickly scan and comprehend. They need not expend undue effort at understanding. The harder it is to read (above the eighth grade level), the more effort it requires. This is true for even the most sophisticated and intelligent reader.

When the reader spends too much time figuring out the communication, there is no time to act. If understanding requires too much effort, the reader may delay reading until later, perhaps too late. Or the reader may simply throw away the communication. In an oral presentation, the listener just tunes out.

Use the grammar check in your word processing program. This tool will automatically check your readability grade level and point out stylistic weaknesses like the passive voice.

PUT THE IMPORTANT STUFF FIRST   Put the important stuff first in your communication. Make it easy for the reader to find the important stuff. People won't read everything, so make sure that they read what's most important. Background belongs in the background, not at the start. Remember the *Three Little Pigs* and the pyramid style of writing.

FIX YOUR HEADLINES   Headlines are critical. Readers use the headlines to determine if they want to read the story. (And most of the time people read only the headlines and never read the story!)

"Real headlines work for a living, and their job is to explain the story clearly. Cute, vague, or lazy headlines leave readers cold. *Literally!!* A good headline warms up readers, easing them into the story in small, incremental steps." So says Tom Ahern.

Take a look at the headlines in the *Wall Street Journal*. This well-written publication uses a sequence of steps to warm up readers: an "eyebrow" (a few words of teaser above the headline), the headline itself, a "deck" (subhead) beneath the headline, and an evocative lead sentence. These four items function *as one unit* to move the reader quickly from disinterest to high interest.

Everything is a tale. What we believe, what we know. What we remember, even what we dream. Everything is a story, a narrative, a sequence of events with characters communicating emotional content. We only accept as true what can be narrated.

From *The Angel's Game*, by Carlos Ruiz Zafón (New York: Anchor Books/Random House, 2009)

TELL STORIES   You are a storyteller. You tell stories most every day of your life. A story is an account of an event: Something happened to somebody.

What makes a good story? Conflict and resolution. Characters we relate to somehow. Sufficient emotion that we want to laugh or cry or yell. Enough detail that we can "see" the story unfold. And so the story unfolds. There's a beginning, middle, and end. There's no mandatory length. Some stories are short. Some are long.

Stories—both oral and written—engage readers and listeners. But there's more. Brain scans now prove that stories can synchronize brains. Researchers at Princeton University found that "when two people communicate, neural activity over wide regions of their brains becomes almost synchronous, with the listener's brain activity patterns mirroring those sweeping through the speaker's brain."[40] This synchronization happens only if the listener really listens and understands. What helps the listener pay attention and understand: an engaging story. And brain synchronization may result from other conversations, too, not just storytelling.

So what happens with this synchronization? Good things like stronger relationships, deeper commitment—and maybe even more investment.

Beware of Creativity

Here's what famous ad man David Ogilvy said: "I do not regard advertising as entertainment or an art form, but as a medium of information. When I write an advertisement, I don't want you to tell me that you find it 'creative.' I want you to find it so interesting that you *buy the product*. When Aeschines spoke, they said 'How well he speaks.' But when Demosthenes spoke, they said 'Let us march against Philip.'"[41]

Use pro bono marketing and public relations with a few reservations in mind. Certainly these individuals or firms may donate their time because they care about your cause. For sure, they donate because they expect creative freedom.

But sometimes—perhaps too often—their creativity does not produce effective communication. Set the ground rules. You need effective communication. Remember that communication is the goal, not cute copywriting or glorious design or stunning video.

I'll turn this point over to Jeff Brooks, one of my favorite bloggers (www.futurefundraisingnow.com). Periodically, Jeff blogs about "stupid nonprofit ads." You'll learn by reading his critiques and examining the ads. Make sure you check in with Jeff's blogs before using any marketing or PR professionals.

The whole point of marketing is to bring in customers. So no matter how pretty or clever, it ain't creative if it doesn't do that.

From *Clicks and Mortar: Passion Driven Growth in an Internet Driven Age*, by David S. Pottruck and Terry Pearce (San Francisco: Jossey-Bass, 2000), 235

Call Your Constituents to Action

Action is the goal. Always include a call to action in your communication. The call to action tells people what to do. And it helps them overcome their natural inertia.

The call to action is the interactive portion of your communication. The call to action tells the constituent what to do. A good call to action has all or some of the following characteristics.

- It is specific. "Saving the world" is too general. "Put food in the bellies of the kids in Momo's African village" is much better. The constituent can see how her money will work.
- The call to action is introduced early and repeated. Ask early and ask often.
- A good call to action clearly states why your organization is an answer for an obvious problem or want. Your communication makes sure that the problem or want is obvious and pressing enough. Unless the constituent accepts the problem, he will not act.
- The call to action explains why the constituent will feel better by acting. You want the constituent to respond to your communication by thinking "Oh, this is awful (or wonderful)! What can I do to help?"

  Think about the biggest emotional issue associated with the problem or opportunity. For instance, if your organization provides volunteer caregivers to visit the elderly, the emotional issue might be "ending the fear and loneliness that are caused by isolation."
- Your call to action envisions a better future as a direct result of obeying the call to action. The constituent receives his reward and experiences a benefit just by acting.
- The call to action conveys urgency. "Act now before it's too late. Act now before another day goes by."
- You clearly communicate to the constituent that she is the right person to act. There should be no doubt in her mind that you mean her.
- Finally, make the call to action fun or satisfying to participate in. Your reply device is as important as anything else in the communications. In fact, many professional direct mail creators feel that the reply card may be the most important piece in the communications package.

Exploit "communication opportunity zones." Covers, envelopes, captions, headlines: places where the eye falls almost involuntarily and where you can stick your message.

—Tom Ahern, ABC, Ahern Communications, Ink. (www.aherncomm.com)

When you fundraise, the call to action is your request for a specific gift. When you recruit volunteers, the call to action is the invitation to join the committee or take on the particular task.

But what happens before you ask? What kind of call to action could you use that doesn't involve a financial contribution? Try some of these:

- Ask people to sign a petition or contact an elected official about some issue.
- Invite people to join your organization in a protest.
- Provide a response card in your newsletter that:
  - Invites their comment on a particular article in the newsletter.
  - Offers them additional information.
  - Requests ideas for future articles.
  - Offers them volunteer opportunities.
  - Invites them to a focus group to share their opinions and perspectives.
  - Asks them to select their areas of interest so you can send them specific information.
  - Asks them for demographic and lifestyle information so you can design activities targeted to their interests.

Make Sure They Can Read You

Back upstairs, in Tom Ahern's office: He's arguing with a designer. I hear Tom gritting his teeth. The last statement before the hang-up: "You won't design anything for any client of mine again."

Design and layout are essential elements of communication. What's the purpose of design and layout? Okay, pretty is part of it. Sure, good photos help illustrate the story.

But what's the most important purpose of design and layout? To help the viewer read the text. Layout and design can bring the reader in or keep her out. Keep her out? Yes, indeed. Eye motion studies tell us this. And Australian Curt Wheildon gives us invaluable data about readability.

Ironically, many designers don't know about readability. Apparently, readability is not a major part of the curriculum in graphic design school. Wow. How strange is that?

Design elements that superficially look attractive may actually undermine good communication. For example, italics, all caps, reversed type, and small type are hard to read. Make sure your designer follows the basic rules of good communication.

HELP YOUR READERS NAVIGATE THE PAGE   To quickly navigate a page, the eye needs many aids and landmarks. By the way, people start with skimming. Maybe after some skimming, they'll read. So your design and layout must be skim-worthy.

Here are a few rules that will improve the readability of your printed material.

- Always indent paragraphs.
- Double space between paragraphs.
- Include a few bullets and underlines.
- Use ragged right margins; do not justify.
- Select a serif typeface.
- Use initial capital letters; do not use all caps except for one to three words.
- Avoid colored type on colored backgrounds.
- Write short paragraphs (one to three sentences at most) and short sentences.
- Avoid small type (that usually means anything less than 12-point type).

So what's the big deal, you ask?

Imagine a page of all-over gray text with justified right and left margins, lengthy paragraphs, and sans-serif type. Take away the landmarks and the eye gets lost. Browsing is tough. The result? Frustration, wasted time, lower comprehension. Worse yet, your reader might well throw it away without ever reading your call to action!

Look at your recent publications. Which of these design no-no's did you use? Test your most important communications before using them. Invite some insiders and outsiders to review them. Get the reaction of your targeted audiences. And this is a great relationship-building strategy, too. You involve your constituents in a meaningful way. You get vital perspective and they appreciate the invitation.

Building Relationships through Cultivation

Of course, effective communications helps cultivate relationships. Together, cultivation and communications nurture relationships, producing loyalty.

But when I say "cultivation," I mean actions that engage the constituent/donor/prospect. Actions that engage people beyond reading your vastly improved communications.

My go-to-source, www.visualthesaurus.com, defines cultivation as: the process of fostering the growth of something. The morphing diagram includes words like: development, growing and growth, maturation. Now apply some of the definitions for growing plants: the process of an organism growing organically; an unfolding of events that enables an organism to gradually change from a simple to a more complex level. That's right on target for cultivating relationships.

More simply stated, the *AFP Fundraising Dictionary* says "to engage and maintain the interest and involvement of." A good, traditional definition for fundraisers; but not as interesting or as motivating as the words from www.visualthesaurus.com.

You develop and improve a relationship by getting to know your constituents and using selective cultivation techniques. You pay attention to, seek acquaintance with, and court friendship. This means a friendship with your organization, not a personal relationship with an individual.

Cultivation helps move people from interest to engagement. Engagement is a mutual state, shared between the organization and its constituent. When engaged, a constituent is ready to be asked. When engaged enough, a constituent is more likely to respond well to your request.

Cultivation is more than an invitation to a party, membership in a gift club, or participation on an advisory board. Cultivation requires a careful blend of activities tailored to the interests and needs of the targeted constituent or constituencies.

There are many different cultivation strategies. Your institution decides what is most appropriate. What you choose to do depends on two things: the interests and needs of your constituents, and the values, vision, and resources of your organization.

Beware of Entropy

Cultivation is an ongoing necessity because relationships just tend to run down. Who knew? This entropy is the natural tendency of relationships, says Richard A. Edwards.[42] Without adequate care, your constituents become inactive and passive. Consider how similar this is to inertia, discussed in the communications section. Effective communications and cultivation overcome both inertia and entropy. That's how you keep relationships and build loyalty.

Return on Investment

The central question is: Will your return on investment be sufficient? You need to decide where you will invest your relationship-building time.

For example, you might willingly devote 12 months and lots of volunteer and staff time to understand the wants and needs of an individual from whom you seek a financial contribution that is large for your organization. You might invest lots of time to understand the wants and needs of 100 upwardly mobile young women because you hope to engage 10 of them in your organization as future leaders and donors.

On the other hand, you might not invest many resources getting to know 500 donors who consistently give less than $100 to your organization. You just want enough information to maintain and modestly increase their participation.

- Your organization decides how much time and money you can spend cultivating which prospects to justify the resources you allocate. To answer this, explore the following questions: What are your cultivation goals for the particular prospect or group of prospects? What are the outcomes you desire? What measures best evaluate these results?
- What actions must your organization take to produce your desired results?
- What is a good use of your organization's resources? How will you justify the commitment of volunteer and staff time and financial resources? How will your relationship-building program benefit your organization in the short, medium, or long term?
- How long can you cultivate and how much can you invest before you must realize benefits to the organization?
- Do you have sufficient volunteers and staff to carry out your strategies?
- Is your organizational infrastructure (values and systems) adequate to support the cultivation strategies without hurting the institution?
- Will you be able to sustain the cultivation process, providing appropriate follow-up with prospects so they are not abandoned?

Yes, your organization makes these decisions regularly. That's your job. But be careful. Don't measure your return on investment based on money only. Remember loyalty and lifetime value. Remember that the donor decides what constitutes a major gift.

Ensuring the Infrastructure to Do This Work

Good infrastructure helps you do this work. You need core systems and procedures and the values to support them. Develop the best systems and procedures for your organization without creating a bureaucracy. Include things like:

- An organized way to think about the constituency development process.
- Goals, strategies, and measures to propose results and monitor progress.
- Specific tools to implement the process.
- Board and staff conversation to help guide and do the work.
- Job descriptions and task assignments for individuals, committees, and teams.
- Written constituency development plan with measurable goals, strategies, time frames, and assignments.
- Recordkeeping to track communications and cultivation activities and record constituent response.

Try the systems and procedures suggested throughout the chapters in this book. Look back at Chapter 3, which discusses your internal relations. Look at Chapter 6, which describes systems and procedures for strategic planning. Keep track of what happens when you cultivate the constituent. Record how she reacted. Jot down comments about his interests. Conduct formal debriefing sessions with volunteers and staff. Use this information for subsequent relationship-building strategies. Use this to inform the design of any request you plan to make.

Make sure you regularly assess your cultivation activities. Find out if your constituents appreciate the activities. Compare the results of the cultivation to your established goals.

Many fundraising books and publications offer useful tips about managing information and keeping track of constituency development activities. Also check with other development professionals to see how they do it.

Wrap it all up in a plan. Your constituency development plan is part of your written fund development plan. A written plan helps you focus. Remember that the process of developing the plan is as important as the resulting plan. Review Chapter 6 (on strategic planning) and Chapter 9 (on fund development planning) to ensure the optimum process.

DEFINING MOVES MANAGEMENT, A TOOL YOU CAN USE Some fundraisers use moves management as the infrastructure to coordinate the cultivation process. G. T. (Buck) Smith developed the concept to measure the progress of major gift fund development. Smith recognized that a series of activities (which he called initiatives or moves) is necessary to build a relationship with a donor. Each move involves six steps:[43]

1. Reviewing the prospect's relationship with your organization.
2. Planning the right initiative to strengthen the prospect's awareness, knowledge, interest, caring, involvement, and commitment.

3. Coordinating the planned initiative with volunteer and staff leaders (called primes and secondaries).
4. Carrying out the initiative.
5. Evaluating the initiative.
6. Documenting and discussing the results of the initiative.

Volunteers and staff carry out the initiatives. These individuals meet regularly to discuss strategy, plot next steps, and discuss progress. Staff maintain comprehensive records of each initiative. Records document the prospect's reaction and progress of the cultivation.

Specific people, called primes and secondaries, are responsible and accountable for the cultivation process. Each prospect has one prime who is charged with managing the moves related to that prospect. The prime develops, coordinates, implements, documents, monitors progress, and evaluates the fundraising initiatives with a specific prospect. Additional individuals, the secondaries, help plot strategy, develop and carry out initiatives, and monitor progress.

Nurturing any relationship requires frequency, continuity, and personalization. Moves management maintains that each major gift prospect requires at least one initiative per month. This management strategy has calculated the optimum number of initiatives, and hence prospects, any single staff person can handle per year.[44]

As in all fund development, you personalize some of the moves to the particular prospect. Other moves are common to all prospects within the organization.

Moves management may give you ideas for managing cultivation. But make sure you focus on your constituents, not your organization and its moves. If the donor or prospective donor is at the center of the process, then the question is: Is one initiative per month too much, too little, or just right to strengthen the relationship with that particular prospect?

Make sure the actual initiatives focus on the prospect rather than on your organization. Personalize your activities to the needs and interests of your prospects.

Defining Results, Setting Goals, and Identifying Measures

Some say successful cultivation is easy to measure: It produces a "yes" to your organization's request. I'm not a fan of this easy answer anymore. Certainly by now, you recognize my belief that relationships add more value than finally saying "yes" to some request your organization makes.

Whether you're moving to "yes"—or you believe that relationships add value beyond "Yes, I'll give money"—goals and measures are still good. Consider the following:

- What signs do you seek to validate the quality of the relationship?
- What are your incremental measures along the continuum to your desired result?
- What do you want to happen by the end of each separate cultivation activity?

Establish a realistic, measurable, and meaningful goal for each cultivation activity. Think about what you want your constituent to do at the end of the cultivation activity. Do this by focusing on the constituent.

Describe the best outcome, the result you're hoping for. Describe what would be points of progress toward achieving that result. Of course, aim for the optimum. But recognize that steps toward that achievement are likely and acceptable.

Define time frames to accomplish your goals. Estimate the amount of time required to carry out each cultivation activity. Anticipate the time span to carry out each step in the constituency development process for a particular constituent or constituency. Establish target dates to evaluate progress on a span of activities or step(s) in constituency development.

IDENTIFYING MEASURES How do you measure results? Counting the money, right? Counting the number of donors, too?

But how do you measure the quality of your relationships? How do you measure the effectiveness of your relationship-building program?

First, measure loyalty. For example, what are your retention rates—for your donors and volunteers, for your clients, for all your relationships? Measure the life-time value (LTV) of your relationships. And LTV doesn't mean money only.

How else can you measure relationships? Acquisition and attrition rates. Frequency of engagement. Number and types of complaints—and compliments, too.

Most importantly, measure the satisfaction from the constituent's perspective. How satisfied are your various constituents (e.g., donors and volunteers, clients, collaborating organizations)?

From the donor perspective, try these measures:

- Satisfaction with your organization's execution of its mission.
- Satisfaction with your customer service—and not just from the development office.
- Satisfaction with your organization's communications.
- Satisfaction with your organization's relationship-building strategies.
- Satisfaction with your donor acknowledgment and recognition activities.

And how about this: How often the donor feels wowed by your organization? Ask yourself: How many times has your organization "wowed" or "aha-ed" the donor?[45] More importantly, how would your donors respond to this question?

Remember: Start from the donor's perspective! How satisfied is she with the relationship? How does she describe her relationship with your organization? How satisfied is she that giving through your organization achieves her desires?

Now identify measures that can evaluate the effectiveness of what your organization does to nurture relationships. These are your inputs, so to speak. Measure how effective and efficient your various inputs are. For example, consider these:

- Frequency and regularity of outreach to donors to nurture the relationship, not ask for a gift.
- Adherence to body of knowledge for a quality donor-centered newsletter.
- Quantity and quality of information (in your files) about your donors.
- Level of personalization in communications and cultivation.
- Participation of board members in relationship building.

Look at Appendices 9-D and 9-E on this book's website. Both display measures for fundraising plans, including measures for relationship building. Look at *Keep Your Donors*, Chapter 24, devoted to measuring relationships. To evaluate your donor-centered newsletter, visit www.aherncomm.com for information about Tom Ahern's communications audit and his books, tips, and tools.

Nurturing Relationships by Doing Business Well

The cultivation process includes two distinct—and equally important—tracks. The first track is carrying out your standard business operations that support ongoing effective relationships; that's the focus of this section. The second track is conducting special activities designed to nurture relationships; more on that later, in the section entitled "Creating Extraordinary Experiences."

You cannot have one track without the other track. Do business well and you develop and strengthen relationships. Do business poorly and you threaten all your relationships.

Look at your standard business activities. Explore how these activities help you enhance or hinder relationships. Consider every area of operation, for example, strategic planning (described as your relationship with your community) and the internal functioning of your organization (described as your internal relations). Both are critical to effective fund development. Also critical is communications, presented here as a strategy to strengthen relationships. Consider other areas of operation. For example, providing quality service is your most important business activity. Continuous quality improvement helps you sustain and build relationships. Remember that quality is in the eye of the beholder. "It's not what you're selling that counts. It's what I'm buying that matters." Whether I am a client, donor, or volunteer, meet my expectations and I'll compliment your quality.

Direct exposure to your organization is critical for building relationships. As part of your business, you regularly interact with various constituents. Some use your service and others provide you with service. Constituents visit your offices and attend special events. Your constituents interact with your staff and volunteers by telephone and in person, at your agency, and elsewhere in the community.

Every contact a constituent has with your organization affects the relationship. Consider how these situations would affect your constituent's relationship with your organization:

- Clients are pleased with the quality of your programs.
- A volunteer slips on your icy sidewalk.
- A caller is stuck on telephone hold too long.
- A prospective donor receives useful information in a timely and friendly manner.
- My thank-you letter says "Dear Ms. Joyaux," when I know the signer well.

Enabling volunteers is another standard business activity that helps you cultivate relationships. This book describes enabling as the fourth relationship that is critical to effective fund development. See Chapter 8.

Always remember: Your organization's standard business activities lay the foundation for all your relationships. Keep the foundation solid and then develop activities especially for cultivation.

When I say "cultivation," I want you to think "creating extraordinary experiences."

Creating Extraordinary Experiences

Now think about the second track, donor-centered cultivation activities designed to nurture relationships and build loyalty. But not just any activities. Instead, create extraordinary experiences. Your donors deserve no less. And in this day and age, your donors may expect no less.

Pay attention to that last sentence. In this day and age, customers expect great customer service and unique experiences. Places like Amazon.com give customers quick response, interesting choices, speedy service, customer reviews, and recommendations personalized to your interests. Apple Computer gives customers extraordinary design, geniuses to solve problems, unique products, and a shared experience that rivals any tribe anywhere ever. Now that's loyalty!

Do you really think your donors will accept poor customer service, the poor customer service provided by so many NGOs? And if you provide good customer service—which is expected as the minimum—how will you distinguish yourself? How will you actively engage donor interests? How will you entice donors to commit more and more deeply?

Create extraordinary experiences. That's the answer.

Of course, some of your cultivation strategies will be rather tame, sort of typical, good and solid standbys. That's fine. But some, some must be extraordinary.

For example, how about inviting loyal donors—remember, loyalty first—to help the zookeeper feed the animals? Yes, zoos do this. They figure out how to ensure the safety of the donor and the animal. Wouldn't that be an amazing experience?

Consider this idea from Rhode Island's International Institute, committed to providing high-quality education, legal, and social services to immigrants and refugees: Invite a donor to join the welcoming committee at the airport, picking up that refugee family. Perhaps the donor gets to give the stuffed bear to the young child in the family.

Or think about this: An older woman reads stories—in English—to young children whose first language is not English. For the woman, she's reliving story time with her own kids. Every time she talks about this experience, her eyes light up.

Your donors will appreciate these extraordinary experiences. And so will your staff and board members. Cultivation—designing and delivering it—can be fun and rewarding for staff and fundraising volunteers, too. For many, cultivation is much more enjoyable than asking for the gift. No surprise there, eh?!

Our job is to give the client not what he wants but what he never dreamed that he wanted; and when he gets it, he recognizes it as something he wanted all the time.

—Sir Denys Lasdun, architect (1914–2001)

See Appendix 7-A on this book's website for lots of cultivation ideas. See Ken Burnett's *The Zen of Fundraising: 89 Timeless Ideas to Strengthen and Develop Your Donor Relationships* (San Francisco: Jossey-Bass, 2006). See also *Keep Your Donors: The Guide to Better Communications and Stronger Relationships* (Hoboken: John Wiley & Sons, 2008).

Three Types of Cultivation Activities

Group your specific cultivation activities into three categories:

1. Activities directed to all your constituents.
2. Activities designed for selected constituencies.
3. Activities personalized for a single constituent.

First, design cultivation activities for use with all your constituents. Don't segment your publics or target particular audiences. Devise generic cultivation activities. These activities directed to all constituents include your gift acknowledgment letter—and the welcome package[46] sent to all first-time donors. Of course, all constituents receive your donor-centered newsletter.

Second, add to your generic cultivation activities by focusing on specific groups of constituents. Segment your constituents into subgroups that share specific commonalties. Design cultivation activities to match the interests and needs of each subgroup. David Dunlop calls these background activities.[47] Although they affect individual prospects, the activities are actually designed for a particular market segment or subgroup.

Proceed with constituency development and you will identify single entities that warrant more personalized attention. Perhaps you wish to further cultivate an individual or family, a business, or service group members. Now launch the third category of cultivation activities. Develop a personal cultivation plan for selected individual constituents. For this business or individual, design specific initiatives that supplement the generic activities. In moves management, Dunlop calls these foreground activities, specific personalized initiatives for a selected prospect or donor.

Of course, all this cultivation depends upon judgment. Use good judgment. Be discreet. Carefully balance organization cultivation with personal relationships. For example, is a birthday card from your organization a good idea or a presumption of familiarity that may be resented?

Creating a Loyalty Program

I'll say it again: Fund development is all about donor loyalty. Relationship building is the strategy to nurture loyalty. So how about developing a loyalty program for your loyal donors?

You've likely experienced loyalty programs (e.g., frequent-flier miles and discount coupons). But what would you offer for donor loyalty?

Hopefully, not just gifts or gimmicks. Instead, how about special recognition for cumulative gifts in a 12-month period and consistent giving over multiple years? Maybe your loyalty program could include a regular insider update or invitations to special programs.

Talk with some of your loyal donors. Ask for their advice. What would they appreciate and enjoy? What would wow them?

Research other loyalty programs. Find out what works and why. Examine what doesn't work and why. Do whatever it takes. But definitely invent your own loyalty program.

Using Affinity Programs

Maybe affinity programs would be useful in your organization. Affinity programs are not gift clubs, which focus on philanthropy. Neither are these affinity teams recruited to help you develop relationships, discussed earlier in this chapter.

Affinity programs sponsor activities that revolve around the interests of the targeted constituency. Participation in the program may well include a financial contribution at a particular level. However, the program focuses on the constituent's interests.

Which constituency(ies) would you focus on for affinity programs? Consider professions or cultural background. Look at demographics and lifestyles. Perhaps you want an affinity program for women in philanthropy or Millennials. Maybe you want to reach out to the gay and lesbian community or Latino families. See Exhibit 7.8 for tips about how to start your own affinity program.

Exhibit 7.8   Creating an Affinity Program

What if you created an affinity program for each of your primary constituent groups? That's probably not possible. Devise only as many as you can manage well. But start one, soon. Evaluate its success and effectiveness. Then consider staring another.

Try the following 12 steps:

1. Identify a constituency that you want to cultivate.
2. Examine the group's demographics and psychographics. Identify various interests of the group that your organization might be able to support through an affinity program.
3. Compare these interests to your organization's values and vision. Proceed only if there is a good match between the constituency's interests and aspirations and your organization's values and vision. Identify any areas of possible conflict and decide how you will address these.
4. Consider the resources of your organization. Decide how you will support an affinity program, and outline general guidelines and boundaries.

(*continued*)

(Continued)

5. Identify a handful of individuals from the constituency who might serve as an initial brainstorming group. Meet with them to find out whether they might be interested in an affinity program and what they might propose as the focus. Share the values of your organization. Make sure you communicate any guidelines or boundaries that are necessary. Do this well, without alienating the people you're trying to cultivate.

6. If the response is positive, identify people from the brainstorming group who will serve as an initial steering committee. With the steering committee, design an activity or event targeted at the particular constituency. Evaluate the success of the activity or event. Talk with attendees to determine the extent of their interest in further activities. Host another activity, designed with the steering committee. Evaluate again.

7. Based on attendee response from the initial activities, determine whether it's appropriate to develop the affinity program. If yes, outline your next steps.

8. Make sure that the steering committee has enough committed people to sustain the affinity program. Make sure that the steering committee will help lead the affinity program, reaching out to the constituency to secure participation.

9. Use all the evaluation results and help the steering committee decide the focus of the affinity program. Expand the steering committee with new people who attended the preliminary activities.

10. With the steering committee, outline how the affinity program will operate (e.g., planning and promoting activities, relationship with your organization's staff, marketing plan, composition of the steering committee, member recruitment, ongoing evaluation, etc.). Consider the timing and frequency of the affinity program activities, minimum donations to join, and so forth.

11. Launch the affinity program. Plan the first series of activities for the affinity program. Extend invitations to join.

12. Monitor and evaluate.

Engaging in Conversation to Nurture Relationships

Conversation is a core business practice. So say the systems thinkers and learning organization theorists. But conversation is more than that. Conversation is at the center of what it means to be human. We talk together to obtain information and to better understand feelings and aspirations. We talk to hear and understand, to be heard and understood. We talk to share. We share our hopes and dreams.

These days, conversation is not just oral, but also written. Just think about all that social networking stuff. Think, too, about the implications of technology and conversation. For example, read Maggie Jackson's book *Distracted: The Erosion of Attention and the Coming Dark Age.*[48] This amazing book reports on important research—research that has big implications for relationship building.

As I mentioned earlier in this book, Distracted *is one of the most important books I've read in years. Read, too,* The Hidden Brain *and* The Art of Choosing, *also mentioned previously. Together, these three books strike at the heart of constituency development: relationship building for our organizations and with our donors.*

In *Keep Your Donors*, I devote an entire chapter to conversation with donors. Since then, I've discovered a lovely little book about conversation by Theodore Zeldin: *Conversation: How Talk Can Change Our Lives.*[49]

Zeldin talks about the importance of conversation—and the importance of talking about conversation so we can have better conversations. He talks about how conversation changes from era to era, how to save family conversation from boredom, what technology does to conversation, and how conversation encourages the meeting of minds. He talks about how the conversation of love is changing, and conversation in the workplace.

And most especially—to me—Zeldin talks about how true and meaningful conversation can change people. Zeldin encourages us to enter into conversation with a "willingness to emerge a slightly different person." This kind of conversation, he says, is "always an experiment, whose results are never guaranteed. It involves risk. It's an adventure in which we agree to cook the world together and make it taste less bitter."[50]

Just as conversation can change the individual, Zeldin reminds us that truly meaningful conversations can change the world. It is through conversation that laws changed and revolutions started. And you and I should know, it's through conversations that philanthropy grows.

Zeldin describes conversation as a "meeting of the minds with different memories and habits."[51] And to paraphrase Zeldin, when these minds meet, they exchange more than facts. The conversation transforms and reshapes. The conversationalists connect to new topics and explore new feelings. "Conversation doesn't just reshuffle the cards: it creates new cards."[52]

Here's something else that Zeldin notes: "The ideals of conversation remained masculine, until women changed the subject."[53] By talking about emotions, women helped improve the way we interact across gender. And eventually, racist and sexist talk began to diminish.

The powerful have always known that they are threatened by conversation. For most of history, the world has been governed by the conversation of intimidation or evasion.

From *Conversation: How Talk Can Change Our Lives,* by Theodore Zeldin (Mahwah, NJ: HiddenSpring, 2000), 7

I urge you to read this book. I urge you to think long and hard about the value of conversation in our organizations, in our politics, in our relationships.

Just imagine, asks Zeldin, what "if conversation were to become the most important kind of interaction, and the main agent of change?"[54]

Remember earlier in this chapter, the section called "What Donors Want." I think a whole lot of your donors want conversation. They want to talk with you. They may want to talk with other donors. Maybe they feel the absence of true and meaningful conversations in their lives.

So go forth. Have conversations with your various constituents. Talk with your donors of time and money. Collect their stories. Listen to their feelings and aspirations. Talk together to share and learn and build community. Talk together for change.

Asking for a Gift

Asking for a gift is one of the best cultivation strategies, as long as you don't ask prematurely. Don't focus on the request. Focus on the prospect. Remember this is constituent-focused and donor-centered philanthropy. Your organization is not at the center.

Create a dialogue, not a monologue. Don't just talk about your organization. Listen to what the constituent says. Watch how he or she reacts. Use this opportunity to create meaningful conversation. Don't be forced or artificial; just talk. Get to know the person even better. Create a bond, one of respect and trust.

Picking Your Cultivators

Many of your cultivation activities do not involve any single person (called a cultivator or relationship builder) to do the work. Rather, the organization carries out generic activities accomplished through mailings, events, and so forth. Through standard business operations, all employees and volunteers make sure they do business in a quality manner and behave in ways that are warm, welcoming, and supportive.

In other situations, a specific individual or multiple individuals help carry out specific cultivation activities with the constituent or donor. At this point, you must pick the right cultivator for each.

Sometimes this person may be a board member or fellow donor, a staff person or user of your service. Often you use a combination of many people. To pick the right cultivator(s), ask yourself:

- Does this particular cultivation activity require someone who knows the prospect well?
- What kind of person will the prospect feel most comfortable with?
- Which constituents and prospects will our cultivators feel most comfortable with?
- What advantage or disadvantage is there to involving someone new, not well known, or unknown to the prospect?

You will find someone who knows your donor or prospect. This is the concept of six degrees of separation.[55] Carefully track relationships and you will find someone who knows the person you want to contact. Moreover, during the "getting to know them" phase, you will develop more contacts.

If you must, do cold calls during the early phases of the constituency development process. If you are unable to find someone who will introduce you or make the connection, do it yourself. Invite the constituent to a meeting even if no one knows her well. Recruit the constituent to participate in an activity even if you don't know him. Just introduce yourself. The constituent will respond if she or he is interested in getting to know your organization better.

A Side Step: The Asking Part

Constituency development is about participation in your organization. By enhancing and extending constituent relations, your organization can generate more clients. You can effectively advocate for public policy and develop a stronger board. You can secure more volunteers, particularly for fund development. And you can also raise more money.

In earlier editions of this book, I said that the process of constituency development has, as its end result, the request. The request might be to join a committee or to serve on the board, to purchase the organization's service, or to cast a certain vote on public policy. You also ask for a charitable contribution, the focus of this section.

In *Keep Your Donors*, I changed my mind, or expanded my thinking. For me, the process of constituency development—relationship building—begins and ends with the meaningful relationship. That is the purpose and the end, a quality relationship.

I know that fundraisers will freak out at that thought. As will their bosses and boards. So, okay. I'll talk about asking[56] now—and asking for a financial investment, too.

In general, this section relates to personal, face-to-face requests. Not street fundraising. Not direct mail. I believe that every organization needs to engage in personal, face-to-face solicitation as part of its fund development to support annual operations and the core program.

When you believe the prospect is ready to be asked, you still have two steps to complete before asking: first, evaluate the readiness to be asked; and second, design the ask, also called the invitation. In addition to this chapter, use the tool "Evaluating Interest, Readiness, and Capacity—and Designing the Ask," in the Free Download Library at www.simonejoyaux.com. Also see handouts to help with personal face-to-face solicitation.

Evaluating Readiness to Be Asked

The prospect is ready when there is an optimum intersection of interest, readiness, and capacity. Asking prematurely is a waste of your organization's time. More importantly, asking prematurely is a waste of the prospect's time—and possibly insulting, too.

Furthermore, no one likes to be asked at a level so far beyond her means that she feels awkward. But asking too low—when she keeps signaling how much she likes your cause/organization—is equally bad.

These inappropriate requests show you're not paying attention. And that means you aren't donor-centered. Any request—including a financial request—is most effective when interest, readiness, and capacity all line up.

Sometimes a particular situation arises that suggests you may not be able to wait for the optimum alignment of interest, readiness, and capacity. Perhaps the prospect's financial situation signals asking earlier. Your organization judges each situation on its own merit. But do be careful.

Let's start with *interest*, the most critical element. Interest refers to a feeling of curiosity or attentiveness. Interested people are involved and concerned. In constituency development, interest means that the prospect is attentive to, involved in, and concerned about the cause and your organization's response. Interest also signifies something that is of advantage, profit, or benefit to the interested individual. For fund development, this means that the prospect sees how her gift will benefit her. This applies at the readiness stage.

Next comes *readiness*. Readiness indicates being prepared for action, likely, or liable to act in a particular manner. For constituency development, readiness means that the prospect is prepared in mind and heart and likely to act in the manner you seek. The prospect also sees how her gift will benefit her by meeting her needs and fulfilling her aspirations.

At the end, look at *capacity*. Capacity refers to the ability or aptitude to do something. Capacity also means the maximum output or production. From a constituency development perspective, capacity refers to the prospect's wherewithal to do what you ask. This could be time or money or something else altogether.

Keep in mind: A prospect can be interested in your cause but not engaged enough in your organization to be asked for something. A prospect may be ready to be asked but not have the capacity currently to give. A prospect may have the capacity to give $10,000 but isn't sufficiently interested at this time. And may never be interested anyway.

Another example: I may be interested in the cause and your organization. I willingly learn more about your activities. With your organization's help, I begin to see how my interests and needs can be fulfilled by participating in your organization. I begin to see ways that I could volunteer time or give money to a project. But I am not yet ready to be asked. Perhaps I do not have the capacity at this time. Maybe I must finish other commitments first. Perhaps you have not offered me the right project.

Managing the Prospect Evaluation Process

From one perspective, a prospect is someone who has not yet been asked. From another perspective, each time you plan to ask a current donor for a gift, she or he is considered a prospect.

A prospect—whether a donor being asked again or someone who has not yet been asked—is ready to be asked for a gift of time or money when there is an optimum intersection of interest, readiness, and capacity. If the prospect is not yet ready to be asked, continue the relationship-building process.

To evaluate whether you should ask yet, conduct a confidential screening session. Some fundraisers call this a rating session. I don't much like the term *rating*.

Gather together people who know most about the prospects you plan to evaluate. Evaluate interest first; then evaluate readiness. If the combined rating for interest and readiness is sufficiently high, discuss capacity.

Then review the results of interest, readiness, and capacity. Decide if it is time to ask. If your answer is "yes," then design the ask. If the answer is "not yet," then identify additional cultivation strategies that will move the prospect into the asking mode.

To help you evaluate, consider the prospect's relationship with your organization. Develop screening scales to standardize your evaluation. Make sure you document your deliberations and keep the information on file.

You may evaluate single prospects (perhaps an individual or a family or a business) or a group of like prospects (possibly 100 young families who share common demographic and lifestyle characteristics).

It's easier to evaluate a single entity. However, it's also important to evaluate the interest, readiness, and capacity of a group of similar prospects (e.g., a constituency). To evaluate a constituency, prescreen all the individuals within the group. Decide if all members of the group continue to share the same characteristics and remain at the same approximate stage in the constituency development process. Pull out those who do not meet these two criteria. Put them in a more appropriate group or treat them individually. Now return to the remaining homogeneous group and evaluate the group's interest, readiness, and capacity.

Using Scales to Evaluate Interest and Readiness

Examine the versions of scales presented here, each more complex but more useful than the prior one. There's nothing scientific or particularly sophisticated about these. Just tools that you might find useful. As necessary, modify the scales to best meet your needs.

VERSION 1   Use a 10-point scale with 1 being low and 10 being high. Define what you mean by low and high as well as a midpoint. This helps staff and volunteers assign points to each prospect.

First, evaluate interest using the 10-point scale; then evaluate readiness. The best rating is a combined 20 points. If the rating is 15 points or less, cultivate more. Talk a lot about those prospects who receive 17 to 19 points. Maybe some of these prospects need more cultivation. Perhaps others could actually be asked. Together, staff and volunteers decide what to do, when, and how.

VERSION 2   Create a point scale with descriptive statements. Descriptive phrases help evaluators think more deeply to better assign points to the prospect. For example, the following model uses five points as the optimum number to indicate interest. The key is to provide examples that demonstrate where the prospect fits on the scale.

1. Not very interested in your organization but interested in the cause.
2. Interested in the cause and somewhat interested in your organization.
3. Interested in the cause and increasingly interested in your organization.
4. Very interested in both the cause and your organization.
5. Extremely interested in both the cause and your organization.

You can use a similar model to evaluate readiness.

1. Not at all ready to be solicited.
2. Somewhat ready to be solicited.
3. More ready than not.
4. Moderately ready.
5. Very ready to be solicited.

The scales in version 2 likely provide more clarity than the simple point system described in version 1. However, the descriptions are not particularly distinctive. Attendees at your screening session still have to define what "somewhat ready to be solicited" actually means.

VERSION 3   Although more complex, it is more effective to combine a point system with substantive descriptions. You develop statements that describe degrees of interest within your organization. In the scenario presented here, the optimum points for interest and readiness are eight each for a total of 16.

The first scale describes the prospect's interest.

1. Predisposed to your organization: knows someone in the organization or is familiar with the organization.
2. Predisposed to the cause: has given time or money to similar causes.
3. Client of your organization or has family member who is client.
4. Minimally involved in your organization: is using/has used the organization's services; has given a modest gift once or twice. (You establish a range to define "modest" for your organization.)
5. Moderately involved in your organization: regularly gives a modest gift to the organization. (You define "modest" as well as "regularly"; e.g., annually for five years.)
6. Regularly involved in your organization, loyal: has given steadily over a consistent period of time; periodically increases contributions and may give to special projects as well as annual operations.
7. Very involved in your organization, loyal: periodically increases contributions and gives to special projects as well as core programs and annual operations.
8. Highly engaged in your organization, loyal: has given steadily over a consistent period of time, periodically increasing and diversifying gifts; volunteers advice, counsel, and/or time.

Using this model, a scale to describe readiness might look like this:

1. Is familiar with the cause.
2. Is regularly informed about your organization's activities, mission, and vision through newsletters and other communications vehicles.
3. Has attended a special event and/or responded to a modest call to action in your newsletter or some other communications vehicle.
4. Has offered advice and opinion, formally through a survey, focus group, brainstorming session, or personal meeting.
5. Serves on a committee, team, or task force.

6. Regularly offers advice and opinion and participates in organization activities.
7. Talks with you about her capacity and level of interest.
8. Talks with your organization about how and what he wants to give.

Assessing Capacity

Once you have finished evaluating interest and readiness, review the total points for each prospect.

Begin discussing capacity for prospects whose combined interest and readiness totals 75 to 80 percent of the maximum possible points. For prospects whose combined rating is less than 75 percent, continue cultivation. Decide what specific steps need to be taken to move the prospect forward. (Why these particular percentages? Because I think caution is important; no other reason. Establish your own benchmark—but be cautious. Don't overestimate someone's interest!)

For capacity, create actual request levels or ranges. Devise different capacity scenarios for different targeted groups. For one group, you might create a capacity table for gifts of $50 to $500. You have decided that this range best fits their available resources. For another group, your gift requests might start at $1,000 or $100,000.

Depending on your organization's relationships, some of your financial scenarios might look like this:

Capacity Code Sample Request Amounts

Capacity Code	Sample Request Amount	Sample Request Amount
A	$ 50–99	$1,000–1,999
B	$100–199	$2,000–2,999
C	$200–299	$3,000–3,999
D	$300–399	$4,000–4,999
E	$400–500	$5,000–6,000

If you seek a volunteer commitment, your scenario might look like this:

Capacity Code Request

Capacity Code	Request
A	Work alone on a single, short-term task.
B	Work on an ad hoc task force.
C	Serve on a committee (one- to two-year term).
D	Serve on the board.

A CAVEAT ABOUT CAPACITY Evaluating a prospect's capacity to give does not depend solely on his or her financial resources. Commitments are equally important. And you may not be able to identify all the commitments that a prospect has.

Commitments can include such things as:

- Payment of pledges to other nonprofit/NGO organizations.
- Education or healthcare commitments for family members.
- Gifts and loans to family and friends.

Some professionals say that if you examine the income statistics of a population, you can estimate the fair share that your organization should get in philanthropic gifts. Some say that you can estimate how much a cultivated, motivated, and effectively solicited prospect will give based on annual income and net worth.

I disagree. Why? Because neither of these suppositions seems to consider the fundamental characteristics of the philanthropic process:

- The other commitments of the audience.
- Their specific interests (and disinterests).
- Your organization's level of donor centrism.
- How well you develop relationships.
- How relevant your particular organization is to community need.
- How well you communicate with those predisposed to your organization.

Designing the Ask

You're extending an invitation, an invitation for the prospect to engage. Personalize the request to the best of your ability.

Use all the information you've gathered. Look at what you know about the prospect. Consider the results of your cultivation strategies. Review the debriefing notes from each cultivation activity. Talk to your cultivators. Talk with staff and volunteers.

Keep the donor or prospective donor at the center. Devise your request around his or her interests, motivations and aspirations, readiness, and capacity.

- How will giving benefit the prospect, given his or her interests, needs, and motivations?
- What is the appropriate focus (or project) that would be most appropriate to this prospect, given his or her interests, needs, and motivations?
- Who is the best solicitor or team of solicitors?
- Given the prospect's capacity and level of interest and readiness, what is the appropriate request amount?
- What is the best way to structure the ask—outright request for the amount, specific intervals within a range, costs for particular projects?
- When is the best time?
- What is the best approach: personal face-to-face, mail, telephone?
- What is the actual request scenario? What will be communicated and how?

Finalize your invitation for the prospect. Outline content for your conversation with the prospect. Pinpoint the key points of your conversation. Include questions you will ask the prospect. Create silent spaces so the prospect can talk—and make sure you listen. Anticipate potential barriers that the prospect might raise—and figure out how you will answer.

Think about the donor or prospect again. Keep in mind the emotional triggers. Figure out what stories to tell. Figure out which questions to ask to deepen the conversation.

If you're soliciting as a team, decide who will say what in the conversation. Practice. Create a natural flow. Figure out how to close the conversation.

Timing the Ask

Often we ask too early. We ask before the prospect is ready to be asked.

For example: The nominating committee invites a business leader to join the board, but she is only vaguely aware of your mission. Your organization asks her for a first gift, yet she barely knows about your service. You ask a donor for an increase, but he is not yet sufficiently interested or involved.

Repairing the damage of a premature ask requires great effort. Trying to overturn an answer of "no" demands extraordinary cultivation.

Instead, prepare the constituent. The purpose of constituency development is to get the constituent ready to be asked: whether to give money or time, serve as a board member, purchase a service, or lobby on your behalf.

Asking—Offering the Invitation

Okay. There you are, with the prospect. So ask. Invite the prospect to give. Invite the donor to give again.

If the prospect or donor gives, acknowledge and keep nurturing the relationship. Remember, asking and receiving is only a point in the virtuous circle of constituency development/relationship building.

If the prospect or donor refuses, acknowledge. And then determine if you should continue the virtuous circle of constituency development/relationship building.

Assess the effectiveness of your relationship-building strategies. Pay attention to what the donor or prospect says. Maybe you continue relationship building. Maybe not. Maybe they're just not that interested in you.

Summary

Constituency development is the third of four relationships that are critical to effective and productive fund development. Constituency development refers to donors as well as clients and volunteers, and other constituencies. Only by developing strong and effective long-term relationships will your organization have sufficient constituents to survive and thrive in the future.

You need many diverse constituents who will use your services, speak well of you, serve on your board and committees, help you fundraise, give charitable contributions, and open doors to new donors.

To develop these relationships, your organization has to benefit the constituent in a customer-centered, donor-centered, constituent-centered way. Then she or he may be willing to help you.

Unfortunately, constituency development receives little time and attention in many organizations, particularly those fighting for survival.

Too frequently, we ask people for money before they are ready to give. We ask current donors to increase their gifts before these donors are ready to give more. We invite people to join our boards before they are comfortable with our institutions. We even set the future direction of our organizations without engaging constituents in the dialogue.

Constituency development produces loyalty. Otherwise, why bother?

And what is the result in each of these situations? The organization does not meet the needs of the constituent, and the constituent does not meet the organization's needs. There is no mutually beneficial exchange.

Successful organizations embrace Dale Carnegie's mantra: "You'll have more fun and success when you stop trying to get what you want, and start helping other people get what they want."

Effective organizations create processes to develop relationships so organizations get to know their constituents, understand their interests and disinterests, and recognize their motivations and aspirations.

Successful organizations use constituency development to become more personal. They develop carefully crafted cultivation strategies tailored to the particular constituency. These organizations describe their activities in terms of benefit to the constituent. They communicate in ways that make it easy for the constituent to receive the message. These organizations "throw away the cookie cutter and start monogramming."[57]

Always remember: Different people care about different causes. Your challenge is to find those that care about your issues and then develop a meaningful relationship with them—meaningful to the constituent as well as to your organization.

I cannot resist closing with Seth Godin:

Loyalty is what we call it when someone refuses a momentarily better option.

If your offering is always better, you don't have loyal customers, you have smart ones. . . .

Loyal customers understand that there's always something better out there, but they're not so interested in looking.

Loyalty can be rewarded, but loyalty usually comes from within, from a story we like to tell ourselves. . . .

Loyalty isn't forever. Sometimes, the world changes significantly and even though the loyal partner/customer likes that label, it gets so difficult to stick that he switches. . . .

Rewarding loyalty for loyalty's sake—not by paying people for sticking it out so the offering ends up being more attractive—is not an obvious path, but it's a worthwhile one. Tell a story that appeals to loyalists. Treat different customers differently, and reserve your highest level of respect for those that stand by you.[58]

CHAPTER 8

The Fourth Relationship—With Your Volunteers

Enabling Them to Take Meaningful Action on Behalf of Your Organization

Hoarding power produces a powerless organization. Stripped of power, people look for ways to fight back: sabotage, passive resistance, withdrawal, or angry militancy. Giving power liberates energy for more productive use. When people feel a sense of efficacy and an ability to influence their world, they seek to be productive. They direct their energy and intelligence toward making a contribution rather than obstructing progress.

—Lee G. Bolman and Terrence E. Deal, *Leading with Soul: An Uncommon Journey of Spirit* (San Francisco: Jossey-Bass, 1995), 107

To what extent are the professionals in the independent sector becoming alienated from the volunteers? . . . I worry most about the growing lack of mutual understanding and deep sense of common values between . . . professionals and . . . volunteers.

A volunteer who works at a botanical garden says that she resents being given the scut work, relegated to it by paid staff. "That isn't what I volunteered for," she says.

More ominous, of course, are the comments that denigrate the competence, dedication, and value of the volunteers. "If it weren't for the alumni, I'd love alumni work." A certain amount of that kind of talk . . . is exasperation and not cynicism, and shouldn't be taken seriously. But all of us have also detected at times a different and more troubling tone of contempt in such remarks.

—Robert L. Payton, *Philanthropy: Voluntary Action for the Public Good* (New York: American Council on Education/Macmillan Publishing, 1988), 78–79

Enabling Your Volunteers

Enabling volunteers is the final one of the four relationships critical to a healthy organization and effective fund development. It is last but definitely not least.

Your relationship with volunteers enables them to take meaningful action on behalf of your organization.

There are several predictable benefits if you enable your volunteers well: Enabling your volunteers (or staff for that matter) helps your organization achieve its goals. When you enable, your volunteers can do what is necessary to help your organization. And when you enable well, you will likely raise more money.

Volunteers are critically important to nonprofit/NGO organizations. Whether individuals serve as board members, do clerical work, solicit gifts, or provide direct service, they make a difference in your organization. Volunteers contribute the "voluntary action for the common good," which is the hallmark of philanthropy. Volunteers justify your organization as philanthropy and extend your reach, capacity, and capability.

I first conceived of this concept in my role as a fundraiser. I was trying to figure out how to manage volunteers well—and was dissatisfied with what I read about working with volunteers. So my concept of enabling focused, first, on volunteers in fund development. But enabling is equally important for governance.

Look in the mirror, Ms. CEO and Mr. Executive Director. If your board isn't as effective as it must be, look in the mirror. Part of your job is to enable the board and its committees and members to be effective.

Fundraisers know how important volunteers are to support effective fund development. No matter how many fundraising staff your organization has, they cannot substitute for volunteers.

Nevertheless, volunteers often frustrate fundraisers. How often have you heard (or said) these phrases?

- "My board members just don't understand fundraising."
- "My volunteer solicitors procrastinate. Why won't they just finish their calls?"
- "My volunteers will do anything but fundraise."

Get a group of fundraising professionals together and they talk about their volunteers. Fundraisers complain about their boards and talk about how to get fundraising volunteers to do their jobs.

And it's not just the fundraisers who wrestle with volunteers. Just watch CEOs struggle as volunteers cross the line into management. Listen to the gasp from the marketing office when a volunteer speaks to the media.

Staff expect volunteers to understand their roles, respect staff authority and competency, and perform appropriately. We urge our volunteers to use their skills on behalf of our organizations. But often, the results aren't so satisfactory. Staff are not pleased.

Volunteerism is a hot topic in most nonprofits/NGOs. It's a continued focus for research and writing in the field. Certainly volunteerism is a hallmark of philanthropy.

Yet, volunteerism is also a challenging function within an organization, raising as many questions as opportunities. For example, do you talk about volunteerism at your organization? Has your organization defined its values and philosophy about volunteerism? Have you identified your volunteer needs and skills? See Appendix 8-C, "Questions of Meaning about Volunteerism," posted on this book's website.

One of the most significant questions about volunteerism is: What are we as staff doing to help our volunteers? Follow-up questions include: Are we doing enough? Are we doing the right things? For example, do we honor their roles and recognize their rights? Do we respect their interests and seek out their abilities?

Consider this: If your volunteers are not as effective as you want them to be, examine yourself first. Usually, volunteers are only as effective as we enable them to be. Their failure is too frequently ours. By the way, staff needs to be enabled too. While this book focuses on enabling volunteers, the concepts and functions can be applied to staff as well.

Concept of Enabling

Enabling is the process of empowering others. Enabling means giving people the wherewithal, opportunity, and adequate power to act. Synonyms for enable include invest, endow, and authorize. Synonyms for power include ability, influence, capability, and authority. When you empower someone, you distribute and share your own power. Power shared is power multiplied.

If someone has power, she or he has the authority to make decisions. Equally important, she or he has the right (and safety) to voice opinions, even if these opinions conflict with those of the boss.

Enabling depends on reciprocity, relating, and connecting. Enabling encourages participation, shares responsibility and authority, enhances the self-worth of others, and energizes everyone in the organization.

Enabling produces the optimum performance from individuals or groups. And there's another result: Enabling allows your volunteers to succeed, using their own power. The advantage? They may well volunteer for you again.

Usually staff want volunteers to perform a specific task competently, efficiently, and in a timely fashion. Fundraisers, for instance, may want their volunteers to plan a special event and sell tickets to it, cultivate relationships, and solicit major gifts.

Tasks are important. But they are only part of the system. The best staff also want their volunteers to participate in process, ask challenging questions, think critically, and help make key decisions. Effective staffs want their volunteers to be so invested that they insist on dialogue, not just discussion. (See the distinction described in Chapter 3.) These volunteers may disagree and argue about complex issues. And the best staff is pleased.

Enabling helps others exercise their potential and power.

Enabling Is Good

Some people mistake enabling for caretaking or suspect it will end up being patriarchal and patronizing. Enabling is even considered manipulative. In social service circles, the word *enabler* can be a pejorative term, meaning co-conspirator or co-dependent.

True enabling is none of these. Rather, enabling is a value-driven philosophy that invests influence and responsibility in all parties. Enabling empowers individuals, groups, and the organization itself. Read Exhibit 8.1, "A Theater Tale," which demonstrates the positive results of enabling.

Exhibit 8.1   A Theater Tale

"Invite the actors," said one volunteer at the theater. "They'll have fun, and our guests will be thrilled."

"We could use the theater's props and costumes to help decorate the space," suggested another.

"Let's use the stage for the event," added the next volunteer.

Whenever I sat down with special event volunteers at the theater, I worried. I enjoyed their enthusiasm but I feared their desires.

I understood the expectations of our volunteers. But meeting all their expectations simply wasn't possible.

Most of the actors did not enjoy being on parade. Usually, they were rehearsing or performing anyway. Props and costumes were precious and expensive. A set was always on stage, filling the space. Or we were taking one set down and putting another up.

But what could I say to the volunteers? My alternatives were either to say "no" or to be a good enabler.

"No" made volunteers feel unsupported and unappreciated. The theater looked bad, and volunteers quit in frustration. So I had to meet the needs of the volunteers and the theater.

The most important thing I learned was to anticipate. I knew what the volunteers would ask. I even understood why. All I had to do was explain first. Set the context and build understanding so they would rarely ask for what the theater could not give.

No rules. No bold statement of procedures. Instead, orchestrate a friendly dialogue about what it was like to operate a theater. Give volunteers insight before they made suggestions or demands. Share with our volunteers the needs of the actors, the stress of the technical crew, union restrictions, whatever. Talk about what we could do within those confines.

And I had to do all this before the volunteers suggested or asked for something that would require a "no" response.

I had to make the volunteers part of the inner circle, with special information and knowledge. Then the volunteers understood what was possible and what was not. Soon our volunteers were explaining theater operations and realistic expectations to newcomers!

Enabling worked. I did not wait until they asked. I did not withhold information. I did not say "no." I enabled. And we were all happier and more successful.

Enabling Depends on Two Other Relationships

Successful enabling relies directly on two of the relationships discussed earlier in this book: the relationship within your organization and the relationship with your constituents. These two relationships are particularly entwined with enabling. But there's more.

Review the eight components of your organization's internal relations, described in Chapter 3: shared values, art of leadership, commitment to process, learning organization, ongoing conversation, participatory decision-making, well-managed change (including adaptive capacity), and culture of philanthropy. Then refer back to Chapter 7, the third relationship—with your constituents. Enabling is a prerequisite for all eight of the components in your organization's internal relationship. All these components depend on good enabling to work well.

First, think about the first two components—values and leadership. First, leadership is enabling, and enabling is a core component and competency of leadership. Review Chapter 5, which focuses on leadership, its functions, and its obligations.

Second, think about values: Sharing values with those you enable can enhance the enabling process. When individuals who work together share values, these individuals are working within a common framework. Certainly your board—a particularly critical group—must share the values of the organization, as should those whom you hire as staff.

However, not everyone will share your values—and such an expectation is unreasonable. That's why enabling requires that you, the enabler, respect and be sensitive to the diverse opinions and experiences of others. You will likely work with volunteers who do not necessarily share all the values of your organization. (And donors who give but for motivations that may not match your organization's values.)

Nonetheless, these individuals may offer you valuable service and support. Neither their values, motivations, nor behaviors harm your organization. Undoubtedly you welcome many of these volunteers and donors now.

Now consider your relationship with constituents, described in Chapter 7. Think about the steps necessary for nurturing relationships. Think about getting to know your constituents so you understand and meet their needs. Consider how you engage your constituents in meaningful ways.

The relationship-building process creates a mutually beneficial exchange. And one exchange happens when a constituent gives to your organization because your organization is the mechanism to fulfill the constituent's aspirations. The gift can be many things—for example, money, service on the board or a committee, advice, or political advocacy on your behalf.

In many ways, enabling is the same process as relationship building. You get to know your volunteers, understanding their interests and concerns. You help volunteers overcome their concerns by eliminating barriers and providing support.

The ultimate exchange happens when the volunteer fulfills his or her aspirations through your organization, while successfully carrying out activities on behalf of your organization. And this happens because of your effective enabling. The process of enabling creates a successful use of volunteer resources for your organization.

Enabling Means Stewardship and Partnership

The enabler helps people and groups work together so your organization is more likely to achieve its goals. Enablers make sure people have the resources and authority to influence the system. The enabler helps develop the capacity of others.

To be successful, everyone needs to feel responsible. Everyone in the group (or organization) has to own the goals and strategies to achieve the goals. The enabler helps build this ownership.

Partnership does not do away with hierarchy and we still need bosses. Stewardship is the willingness to hold power, without using reward and punishment and directive authority, to get things done.

From *Stewardship: Choosing Service over Self-Interest*, by Peter Block (San Francisco: Berrett-Koehler, 1993), 31

Peter Block's concept of stewardship helps explain enabling. Block describes stewardship as "operating in service, rather than in control, of those around us."[1] Block goes on to say that authentic service requires four elements. Note how well these elements fit with the eight components that make your organization's internal relationship strong.

1. Power is shared and balanced.
2. People are, first, committed to the larger community.
3. Everyone helps define purpose and decides organizational culture.
4. Rewards are balanced and distributed equitably.

Stewardship includes partnership. Block observes that partners are connected in a way that the power between them is "roughly balanced." He describes four requirements for partnership, also reminiscent of the infrastructure that enhances the relationship within your organization. These partnership requirements are:

1. Exchange of purpose
2. The right to say no
3. Joint accountability
4. Absolute honesty

First, partners define purpose and values together. People at all levels talk with each other, sharing conversations and decision-making. People may disagree at times, but together they learn for the good of the organization and themselves.

Second, each partner can say no. As Block observes, "If we cannot say no, then saying yes has no meaning." Wow. That's an extraordinarily important and powerful statement.

Yes, there may be someone who has higher authority when you say no. Even though this individual may be able to tell you what to do, you can still say no. Block reminds us that partnership doesn't mean you necessarily get what you want.

But you never lose your right to speak. Enablers create a safe environment so people can disagree and even say no.

Third, everyone is responsible. Partners have joint accountability for outcomes. Partners know that together they created the current situation and can change it. Enablers help people see their roles, capabilities, and influence.

Fourth, absolute honesty is essential. Block describes not telling the truth as an act of betrayal. An omission is equally unacceptable. Enablers tell the truth and make sure that there is no retribution when others speak honestly, too.

Doesn't all this sound a lot like leadership? And learning organization theory, too?

Benefits of Enabling

Enabling may be the single most important contributor to improving your organization's fund development performance. Enabling certainly is the primary factor in a healthy relationship between governance and management.

The thing is, people are loyal to your organization's mission, not to fund development. So it can take lots of work to get them to help fundraise. Enabling does this.

Enabling holds multiple benefits for your organization. First, enable your volunteers and they will do tasks well, including fund development activities. Second, enable your volunteers and they will feel successful and important to your organization. Third, enable your volunteers and they will stick with you longer.

If your volunteers have good experiences, they are more likely to continue volunteering and to volunteer more. They will likely give you money and even increase their gifts. Equally important, satisfied volunteers will tell others about how great your organization is, thus encouraging more gifts of time and money.

Enabling can do more. It will:

- Engage volunteers in the meaning of your organization rather than the tasks and mechanics alone.
- Develop stronger relationships between your organization and its volunteers.
- Enhance the quality of your organization's decision-making.

Preventive Measure

Enabling is *the* strategy to enhance volunteer performance. When incorporated into the way you do business, enabling anticipates potential problems and prevents them from occurring. Effective enabling makes the system work. Look back at Exhibit 8.1, "A Theater Tale." I anticipated what the volunteers might say. I enabled well, thus preventing the problems from arising.

Once you understand the barriers, enabling will get you beyond them.

—Cohort 9, Master's Program in Philanthropy and Fund Development, Saint Mary's University of Minnesota

Intervention Strategy

Enabling is an excellent intervention strategy. Once there is a mess—big or small—turn the situation around by using the enabling functions. Enabling can solve the mess that resulted because enabling wasn't used in the first place. It's a neat little circle. Enabling is both an anticipatory/preventive strategy and a reactive/intervention strategy.

When you use the enabling functions as an intervention strategy, consider the following five steps:

1. Carefully examine the situation, its full scope and all its dimensions.
2. Analyze what happened and is happening. Identify what caused the problem and continues to cause the problem. Describe how the situation got to this point. Make sure that you clarify your own assumptions and then question them. Do the same with the assumptions of others involved.
3. Focus on the barriers that arose. Consider process and task issues.
4. As appropriate, engage others in a conversation about the situation. Learn together.
5. Then, using the enabling functions, outline how you would now intervene.

Take a look at Appendix 8-A, "Passionate Board Member Running Wild—a Real Life Story with an Enabling Response," on this book's website.

Really Big Problem

Sometimes—despite every effort—enabling will not solve the problem. Perhaps the individual or group is too dysfunctional. Perhaps individual egos will not tolerate enabling and so will not change, even for the good of the organization.

In this situation, use the enabling functions to co-opt the individual or group. If that doesn't work, use the enabling functions to contain and neutralize the problem people. Enable others in the organization to help you contain and neutralize—but only through appropriate use of the enabling functions. Remember that the end never justifies the means. You still must act ethically.

Finally, what if containment doesn't work? What if the volunteer is harming the organization? What would you do if a staff person were harming the organization—and the person refused to change despite your great enabling? Hopefully, you would pick the good of the organization, the good of the group, over the individual. You would fire the person.

So what do you do with a volunteer who is harming the organization and will not change? Enhance his or her attrition. Take a look at enabling function #18 in Exhibit 8.2, the final act of a consummate enabler.

Raising More Money

Enable volunteers and you will likely raise more money. Enabling makes the whole fund development process work better. Think about it.

- Does your fundraising goal result from the difference between expenses and revenue without considering the available prospects?

- Do your volunteers propose fundraising activities without understanding the costs and benefits?
- Is your organization cultivating too few donors and soliciting only a handful of prospects?

Enabling can fix these problems. With enabling, volunteers can help establish a viable fund development plan that reflects the resources of your organization. How?

Staff communicates appropriate information, both qualitative and quantitative, about fundraising productivity and solicitation strategies. Staff talks with volunteers about the implications of the information, the trends, possible choices, and consequences.

Then together—volunteers and staff (Block's partners)—establish realistic goals. Together, volunteers and staff determine the best mix of effective relationship-building and solicitation strategies and tactics. See Chapter 9, creating a fund development plan that produces ownership and results.

The process of enabling ensures that you have more volunteers helping with relationship building and asking. More relationship building produces more loyalty. More people asking produces more gifts. And enabling helps volunteers become less uncomfortable with all this work and provides them with tools to do the work better.

The Right Thing to Do

There is another reason to enable. It's the right thing to do, ethically and morally.

Enabling is good for your volunteers, staff, and the organization. The concept of enabling volunteers is inextricably entwined with voluntary association and volunteer leadership. Even if there were no tangible benefits, enabling would be worthwhile because it links organizations more closely to their volunteers.

Please don't minimize doing the right thing. The end doesn't justify the means. Doing the right thing is important. Really important.

The best enabling isn't even noticeable.

Enabling Functions

Enabling is much more than managing volunteers. Enabling is a leadership concept. Enablers, like leaders, carry out very specific functions. Indeed, many of the leadership functions (and attitude and skills) described in Chapter 5 lay the foundation for enabling. Furthermore, enabling is one of the major responsibilities of a leader.

By now I hope you're pretty excited to know what these functions are. Be prepared: Enabling has many facets, 19 as of this writing. In the first edition of *Strategic Fund Development*, there were only 16. But my colleagues in the classrooms at Saint Mary's University keep adding more. Thank you! See the complete list in Exhibit 8.2.

Exhibit 8.2   The 19 Principal Functions of Enabling

Each of these functions is related to the others. Without one, the others will not work.

1. Transmit the organization's values.
2. Engage volunteers in the meaning of your organization.
3. Articulate expectations and clarify roles and relationships.
4. Respect and use the skills, expertise, experience, and insights of volunteers.
5. Engage volunteers in process as well as tasks.
6. Provide direction and resources. Explain why, not just how. Identify and remove barriers, and help develop skills.
7. Coach and mentor people to succeed.
8. Transmit the body of knowledge and best practice, helping others anticipate next practice. (And this includes helping people distinguish between unqualified personal opinion and the body of knowledge.)
9. Communicate. And help transform information into knowledge and learning.
10. Encourage people to question organizational and personal assumptions and ask strategic and cage-rattling questions.
11. Engage people in meaningful conversation that produces learning and change.
12. Ensure quality decision-making.
13. Anticipate conflicts and facilitate resolutions.
14. Encourage volunteers to use their power, practice their authority, and accept their responsibility.
15. Model behavior.
16. Manage.
17. Create opportunities and strategies to buy more time to think things through.
18. Enhance attrition (and facilitate thank and release, if necessary).
19. Monitor, evaluate, and enhance enabling.

1. Transmit the Organization's Values

If an organization honors enabling, core values will reflect this. So too will the corporate culture. Remember, values describe an organization's philosophical approach to its work, the way the organization relates to its various constituencies, and how it carries out its work. See Chapter 3 for a detailed description of values.

Enablers make sure that volunteers understand the organization's values and how these values affect programs and operations. Enablers help synchronize volunteer behavior with organizational values—but only to the degree necessary. Remember: Not all volunteers will share your organization's values and that's okay. Synchronicity is necessary only to the degree that there is no apparent conflict. Alignment is not required except in certain situations, as previously discussed.

If an organization has not yet articulated its values, enablers make sure this happens. As organizational development specialists, enablers respect the importance of values clarification, particularly within the board and staff, and within the fund development function.

Enabling engages your board members in the meaning of the organization so its fate belongs to them.

---

2. Engage Volunteers in the Meaning of Your Organization

Tell stories. Share experiences. Have conversations.

Volunteer understanding of and personal experience with your mission and program validate the time and energy spent with the complex issues and endless tasks of your organization. Engaging volunteers in the heart and soul of the institution helps maintain interest in governance and fund development, both challenging areas of endeavor.

Keep the following two points in mind. First, the tasks and mechanics of one organization look pretty much like any other. So does its fund development. It's the meaning that is different. Enabling shows (and explains) the meaning unique to your organization.

Second, your volunteers (and staff) may feel that fund development is taking over the organization. Sometimes it seems that the board and its members do nothing but talk about money and fundraise. This is an unhappy state of affairs. Stuck in fund development, volunteers get increasingly frustrated and disinterested.

- It's very easy to focus on fund development and the tasks and mechanics of an organization. Sometimes the link to meaning is forgotten or assumed without adequate conversation. Do you find yourself in these situations? A board discusses finances instead of their effect on programs and constituents.
- Individual board members pore over the giving history of prospects rather than exploring prospect interests and aspirations.
- Staff report the results of fundraising solicitations without discussing the trends and explaining the implications for future solicitation activities.

It's up to the staff to make sure the organization avoids this disconnect between meaning and activities. The staff shows volunteers how fund development fits into the organizational and community system. The staff—remember that's both employees and consultants—helps volunteers understand the meaning behind tasks and mechanics. Through enabling, the staff links these operations to the meaning of the organization and the strategic nature of its choices.

You use the enabling functions to help your volunteers feel more connected to your organization. When volunteers understand and participate in the meaning of the organization, they feel a sense of ownership. Then they work better, give more time, and may give more money.

What at one time would have been termed "manipulating" to me is now more appropriately viewed as utilizing the principal functions of enabling. With the best of intentions and with a clear understanding of my organization's purposes and values, this can be a positive thing.

—Stacey Vanden Heuvel, Cohort 9, Master of Arts Program in Philanthropy and Development, Saint Mary's University of Minnesota

---

3. Articulate Expectations and Clarify Roles and Relationships

The enabler clearly differentiates between staff and volunteer roles. Equally important, the enabler helps volunteers and staff create a shared vision of roles and expectations.

This function means more than writing and distributing job descriptions. Certainly a written job description is essential in many situations. But what precedes the written document?

- The enabler must have the knowledge to clearly differentiate between staff and volunteer roles, and the skill to negotiate these potentially treacherous waters.
- The enabler must value the process of articulating roles and expectations rather than merely announcing them.
- The enabler must garner volunteer support for the process of clarifying roles and relationships, and the benefit of such work.
- The enabler must determine when negotiation of roles and expectations is acceptable and when not.

Naturally, the big question is, which roles belong to whom? Both for-profit and nonprofit/NGO practice and literature offer good guidelines. The enabler works with volunteers and staff to adapt these guidelines for his or her own organization and each specific circumstance. For example, see Appendix 9-C, "Key Roles in Fund Development," on this book's website. See the Free Download Library at www.simonejoyaux.com for information about management and governance, distinctions and limitations.

Authority—who has it and who doesn't—can be troublesome and stressful. For example, you can't give a person responsibility for something without giving them authority, too. You don't want to stifle initiative by disempowering.

Some volunteers (e.g., the board) already have authority. To ensure that the board and its members appropriately exercise their authority, an enabler must understand the difference between governance and management.

The competent enabler knows that the distinction between governance and management is not always clear-cut. She can judge when a decision is hers to make or whether it belongs to the volunteers. The enabler also knows when and how to negotiate these judgments with volunteers. And the enabler empowers the board to fulfill its authority.

Articulating expectations and clarifying roles and relationships helps get the work done. Each individual focuses on his task. Each group carries out its responsibility. All see how their respective roles fit into the overall picture, working together for the common good.

This enabling function does more than help get the work done. A member of Cohort 9 (Philanthropy and Development Program at Saint Mary's University of Minnesota) observed that a job description conveys how important the person is. Extend this thought to the function of articulating expectations and clarifying roles and relationships. Through this enabling function, you convey how important the volunteer is to the organization's efforts.

Finally, this enabling function helps set boundaries. Boundaries—also called limitations of authority—are an important element in both the social and work context. Boundaries provide guideposts to help people make judgments. Often boundaries help people feel more comfortable. The challenge, of course, is to ensure that boundaries are neither too limiting nor overly bureaucratic. Boundaries should facilitate roles and relationships, not inhibit questioning, initiative, creativity, and participation.

4. Respect and Use the Skills, Expertise, Experience, and Insights of Volunteers

The experienced enabler personally cares about the success and satisfaction of his or her volunteers. The enabler commits to fulfilling volunteer needs as fully as possible. The accomplished enabler makes volunteers into heroes.

People give their time and money to meet their personal needs and fulfill their own aspirations. Your organization is the conduit to achieve their desires. And these donors—of time or money—want to feel special and useful while contributing. They want to perform well and make a valuable contribution.

Enablers know that successful volunteer placement appropriately balances the volunteer's interests, knowledge, and skills with the organization's needs and the nature of the volunteer activity. Enablers assure this successful placement by understanding the interests and disinterests, skills and expectations, and concerns of their volunteers.

Enablers figure out what their volunteers know. Enablers recognize the scope of knowledge and the degree of skills possessed by their volunteers. With this perspective in hand, enablers work with the volunteers to identify the appropriate activity or role. Then enablers are ready to carry out the sixth enabling function, providing direction, resources, and skill development.

Enablers explore the interests and disinterests, motivations and aspirations of their volunteers, without making value judgments. Sometimes the volunteer's motivations may not be aligned with the organization. Yet, the volunteer wants to participate. The consummate enabler will try his best to negotiate a mutually beneficial exchange between the organization and the volunteer. If this match is not possible, the enabler will help the volunteer understand why, while maintaining the volunteer's integrity and sense of pride. Great enablers even suggest alternative organizations and opportunities for the volunteer (and for donors of money, too).

5. Engage Volunteers in Process as Well as Tasks

Fund development involves more than tasks; it requires process, too. Volunteers need to be involved in both. And enablers make sure that involvement happens.

Think of a task as a defined activity with a beginning, middle, and end. Think of process as a course or method of operation, a series of continuous actions that bring about a particular result.

Process is nonlinear, sometimes cumbersome, always time-consuming, and usually messy. Just take a look at all the other chapters in this book—all involving process and mess.

Process involves a lot of thinking and talking and exploring. To be effective, process involves lots of different people, all stakeholders in the outcome and owners of how to get there.

In her book *Our Wildest Dreams: Women Entrepreneurs Making Money, Having Fun, Doing Good*, Joline Godfrey notes that comfort with complexity often extends to comfort with process. Naturally, the reverse is true. Those who are not comfortable with complexity are not comfortable with process. They feel out of control—and feeling out of control for some feels like losing power.

For others, feeling out of control is empowering. Godfrey observes, "To relate, to be connected, one must pay attention, and paying attention is what process is all about. If comfort with complexity is the ability to hold and deal with conflicting problems all at once, comfort with process is a tolerance for the gradual unfolding of surprise."[2]

Enablers engage volunteers in all three forms of process, described by Godfrey as creative, group, and operational.

- The creative process means brainstorming, getting input and reactions from stakeholders, encouraging questioning and conversation, and welcoming heated discussion. "This is the difference between wanting a slick new brochure and understanding that the way you get that brochure will affect everything from employee relationships, vendor success and motivation, the quality of the finished product, and customer satisfaction."[3]
- Group process empowers others to participate in decision-making. This is the difference between "a staff meeting in which the leader talks, gives orders, and sticks strictly to the agenda, and one in which there is time and room to explore issues that are new, troubling, or confusing—or just time to share, brainstorm, or laugh."[4]
- Operational process means taking care of the systems, policies, and procedures that make things happen in a reliable, efficient, and quality manner. This dimension of process also balances the needs of the system and the needs of the system's people.

Enablers know which process and which tasks are appropriate for volunteers in general, and which volunteer (or group of volunteers) in particular. Enablers understand that volunteers are not merely extra bodies to carry out assigned tasks.

A focus on tasks may not keep the most experienced and talented volunteers involved for long. These individuals need to understand why, not just how. These volunteers want to discuss strategy and help make critical decisions. If you relegate these volunteers to tasks alone, they may lose interest in your organization. Sure, they may continue giving a financial contribution. But a limited or poor volunteer experience will probably not produce increased gifts, repeat volunteering, or good referrals.

Enablers are comfortable with complexity and welcome process.

Here are some tips for involving volunteers in process:

- At a board meeting, spend 15 minutes brainstorming the case for support. See the Free Download Library at www.simonejoyaux.com.
- In the appropriate setting with the appropriate volunteers, brainstorm any of the "Questions of Meaning about Volunteerism," Appendix 8-C on this book's website.
- With board members, talk about questions for building an effective board (Appendix 3-A on this book's website). Look at the strategic and cage-rattling questions sprinkled throughout this book, and engage volunteers in conversation.
- Conduct the complain and whine session described in Chapter 9. Do it with the board. Do it with your fund development committee. Conduct a session with some fundraising volunteers, too.
- With the development committee, brainstorm reasons why donors like recognition. Test these ideas in focus groups with donors. Or convene a focus group of donors to brainstorm how to improve your donor recognition program.

Before you initiate any process, decide how you will make it effective. Take a look at Chapter 3, the internal relationship. Take a look at Chapter 6, on strategic planning. Remember that good process demands outcome. Don't be a process abuser, one who uses process to placate people, to delay decision-making, and to avoid outcome.

When you use process, you owe people the following:

- Explain the purpose of the process, the desired outcome and how you plan to use the information.
- Describe how the process will work, how the session will be managed, and the ground rules for making the process work.
- Summarize the results of the process and outline the next steps.
- Use the resulting information and validate people's participation.

6. Provide Direction and Resources. Explain Why, Not Just How. Identify and Remove Barriers, and Help Develop Skills.

Enablers provide direction and describe the specific tasks necessary to complete the work. Enablers provide appropriate and adequate resources, be it clerical support, telephone numbers, or answers to questions, or. . . .

Equally important, enablers ensure that volunteers understand why something is being done as well as what is being done and how to do it. Without an understanding of why, a task may seem senseless or unclear.

The same holds true for understanding the connection between the big picture and the tasks. The enabler describes the big picture and then translates that into action steps and manageable tasks.

Enablers remove barriers that stop volunteers from succeeding. Enablers cannot always make the work easy. But they do make it interesting, challenging, and dynamic.

Also, many tasks require special skills. Your volunteers may need training to develop these skills. Acting as a teacher, the enabler provides the training, both formally and informally.

7. Coach and Mentor People to Succeed

A good enabler is both a coach and a mentor. And, there's a distinction between the two.

Coaching in business refers to the process of strengthening work behavior—for example, teamwork, communication, and leadership. The coach needn't have expertise in the particular work knowledge (e.g., fund development). Coaching happens one-on-one or in groups. Midlevel and senior-level employees coach other employees. Staff members coach volunteers.

A coach is someone who can give correction without causing resentment.

—John Wooden, American basketball coach, author, and lecturer

---

Mentoring, on the other hand, means a more experienced individual shares advice with a less experienced partner. For example, you mentor a professional fundraiser or a volunteer in fund development.

One definition of mentoring is "a process for the informal transmission of knowledge, social capital, and the psychosocial support perceived by the recipient as relevant to work, career, or professional development; mentoring entails informal communication, usually face-to-face and during a sustained period of time, between a person who is perceived to have greater relevant knowledge, wisdom, or experience (the mentor) and a person who is perceived to have less (the protégé)."[5]

Enablers coach and mentor for success. As effective leaders, enablers also allow for failure. Enablers know that success depends on taking reasonable risk, thus supporting potential failure. Enablers allow for failure because we tried, not because we did nothing. Enablers build trust within staff and volunteers.

Enablers don't abandon volunteers to their own devices. For example, once an assignment is made, the staff stays in touch. Volunteers receive ongoing contact and support. Sometimes the staff offers advice to help volunteers complete tasks successfully. Sometimes the staff helps volunteers brainstorm solutions to situations. Other times, the staff joins volunteers in a task or process. Staff may just call to say hello, thanking volunteers for their efforts. No matter what, enablers help their volunteers succeed. A wise student in the Saint Mary's University Philanthropy and

Development Program noted: an important part of enabling is to uphold a volunteer's integrity and self-respect whenever possible.

Faced with a difficult volunteer, the enabler strives for a respectful resolution. Confronted with harmful volunteer actions, the enabler tries to protect the volunteer.

And what happens if the situation between the volunteer and the organization becomes dysfunctional? So dysfunctional that the volunteer is harming your organization? Then the enabler enhances attrition, with the volunteer's integrity and self-respect still intact. See enabling function #18.

8. Transmit the Body of Knowledge and Best Practice, Helping Others Anticipate Next Practice

(And this includes helping people distinguish between unqualified personal opinion and the body of knowledge.)

There is a body of knowledge and best practice in fund development. The same holds true for other areas of nonprofit/NGO work. It's way past time that board members and executive directors recognize this.

Unqualified personal opinions from well-intentioned board members and ill-informed CEOs waste precious time. These unnecessary distractions compromise an organization's limited resources.

That's where the enabler steps in. The best enablers help others acknowledge that there is a body of knowledge and there are best practices. Effective enablers use all the other enabling functions to make sure that the body of knowledge and best practice provide the foundation and framework for the organization's work.

Moreover, enablers understand that bad practices in other organizations confuse board members. Enablers anticipate the barriers that board members and the CEO use to avoid reality, whether this avoidance is conscious or unconscious.

To enable well, you'd best be an expert in your field. And you must stay an expert. Enablers stay current through continuing education, reading, research, and hands-on work.

As a development officer, position yourself as the critical resource in fund development. If you're the CEO, position yourself as the expert in governance. Even better—in both jobs—position yourself as an organizational development specialist.[6]

True enablers—real professionals—embrace research. They read the reports on sector research and read the original research. "So what?" enablers ask themselves. "What are the implications of this research for my organization? How can I use this research to make forward progress in my organization?"

It's up to you. Acquire and maintain the expertise. Stay on top of the research. Only then can you demonstrate your expertise and experience. Only then can you position yourself as the expert reliable resource.

Don't get behind. The information is out there, qualified information from recognized experts: more books and articles, more research, and more training. You have no excuse. Take the initiative.

Communicate the body of knowledge and best practices to your volunteers. Don't overwhelm them. Find the right path at the right time in the right way.

Don't let those with less (or no) expertise deny the body of knowledge with their unqualified opinion. It's up to you!

People must take responsibility for informing their bosses and colleagues, and above all, for educating them. And then all members of the non-profit institution—paid staff and volunteers—need to take the responsibility for making themselves understood.

From *Managing the Non-Profit Organization: Principles and Practices,* by Peter F. Drucker (New York: HarperCollins, 1990), 89

---

9. Communicate and Help Transform Information into Knowledge and Learning

Communication, which includes helping people transform information into knowledge and learning, is essential to effective enabling. Max DePree notes that good communication has a number of obligations.

We must understand that access to pertinent information is essential to getting a job done. The right to know is basic. Moreover, it is better to err on the side of sharing too much information rather than risk leaving someone in the dark. Information is power, but it is pointless power if hoarded. Power must be shared for an organization or a relationship to work.[7]

Read that quotation again: "The right to know is basic."

The right to know is basic: not just to get a job done but also to make good decisions, to feel safe, to feel included, to generate initiative and innovation, to create effective organizations and effective communities. Is that the way your organization behaves?

Yes, pertinent information is important. But information is just information. Data. Just the starting point.

Actually, information isn't even the starting point. The starting point was when your organization decided why it needed certain formation. Add to that, why your organization decided that the analysis of the information would help achieve results.

Peter Drucker notes the importance of building your organization around information and communication rather than hierarchy. He observes that every individual within the organization is responsible for information. Better yet, every individual is responsible for providing information and helping others translate the information into knowledge and learning.[8]

To paraphrase and expand upon Drucker, you assume responsibility for communication by continually asking yourself:

- What information do I need to do my job—from whom, in what detail, when and how often, and in what manner?
- What information do I owe others so that they can do their jobs, in what form and detail, when and how often?

- What do I need to do (with what help from whom) to understand the information given to me?
- How can I ensure that the information I communicate is understandable and useful and results in learning?

Enablers know that people need knowledge, not information. Enablers take three critical steps:

1. Disclose all necessary information.
2. Translate the information.
3. Help transform information into knowledge and learning.

With good enabling, individuals in the organization can then exercise their own curiosity, judgment, and authority and make responsible and informed decisions.

DISCLOSE ALL NECESSARY INFORMATION   First, the enabler discloses all the necessary information. Because knowledge is power, full disclosure is critical if you want to enable well. The more transparency the better.

But this doesn't always happen. Staff members (and volunteers) think carefully about whom they will tell about what. Sometimes this is done to retain power. Sometimes this is done to protect people. But the result is the same—disempowerment.

Peter Block observes that full disclosure is a basic difference between partnership and patriarchy. He goes on to say that when we don't tell a partner the truth, we are betraying him or her. And staff and volunteers are partners in the nonprofit/NGO organization.[9]

For people to contribute effectively to their organization, they need to know the truth about what is happening. Clearly this does require some discretion. Not everyone needs to know everything. But err on the side of inclusion and fuller disclosure rather than exclusion and limited information.

Regina Herzlinger of the Harvard Business School talks about full disclosure as a strategy for enhancing performance. She describes how nonprofit/NGOs can "boost public confidence in vital institutions and thereby broaden their financial base."[10]

Disclosure can also increase confidence internally and bring more wisdom to tackle tough issues. Consider how you would use Herzlinger's four questions to enable increased knowledge and learning within your organization:

1. "Are the organization's goals consistent with its financial resources?"
2. "Is the organization practicing intergenerational equity?"
3. "Are the sources and uses of funds appropriately matched?" Herzlinger notes that "variable revenues" such as grants should not fund ongoing expenses like salaries.
4. "Is the organization sustainable?"[11]

TRANSLATE THE INFORMATION   Part of disclosure is translating the information, explaining its meaning and implications. Remember, information is just raw data, useless without its current and potential meanings. Keep in mind, however, that translating information does not mean controlling the receiver's interpretation.

As Debashis Chatterjee notes:

Whereas knowledge is the gathering of information, learning is the development of creative intelligence to transform this information into action. Knowledge deals with the what *of reality; learning deals with the* how *of it. Knowledge is merely classification of information; learning is the ability to draw the energy out of this information into the arena of action. Leaders integrate the* what *of knowledge with the* how *of learning. There is total integration between knowledge and action.*[12]

Jay Lorsch describes the need to transform information when he writes about the chief executive officer (CEO) and board.

Directors may obtain any data they want, but such information must be converted into useful knowledge through the prism of a broader understanding of the company and its markets and operations—information that inevitably must come from management at board meetings. . . . Superior knowledge about such matters provides even the most well-intentioned CEO with a real power advantage over . . . directors.[13]

HELP TRANSFORM INFORMATION INTO KNOWLEDGE AND LEARNING   The enabler helps transform information into knowledge and learning. The enabler does this by encouraging dialogue that investigates the information and its meanings. As the authors of *Framebreak: The Radical Redesign of American Business* note that "the right information conveyed at the right time to the right people is what enables effective decision-making in an organization."[14]

FIVE PROPERTIES OF EFFECTIVE COMMUNICATIONS   Martha Golensky[15] describes five properties that contribute to effective communication:

1. Frequency: how often communication is received.
2. Timeliness: when it is transmitted.
3. Comprehensiveness: how complete it is.
4. Specificity: how detailed it is.
5. Directional flow: who originates it.

The competent enabler knows what information volunteers need from whom in order to make which decisions. The enabler provides information appropriate to the situation, to the individuals involved, and to their roles and responsibilities, and based on the boundaries.

The enabler figures out which things key people have to hear immediately, which items are just "for your information," and which items are of no interest. The enabler does not censor information; neither does she waste people's time with items of no interest.

Good enablers pay lots of attention to *how* they communicate. These enablers ensure that the receiver actually hears and understands the communication.

Effective enablers recognize that the means of communication are as important as the content. They know that different people hear best in different ways. Effective enablers also respect the power of words, and take special care with language and its meaning.

Yes, an enabler must understand and do all this. An enabler is a good communicator, able to transmit information and help transform that information into knowledge and learning. The enabler seeks information, asks for opinion, listens to interests and concerns, and hears what is hard to discern. In summary, the enabler ensures ongoing conversation.

10. Encourage People to Question Organizational and Personal Assumptions and Ask Strategic and Cage-Rattling Questions

This enabling function depends on good conversation, a core business practice. And meaningful conversation—enabling function #11—is essential to effective organizations. You've certainly heard that before in this book!

Look back at Chapter 3, the relationship within your organization. Focus again on learning organization theory, which includes questioning assumptions, and asking the essential and cage-rattling questions.

Think about *metanoia*, a Greek word meaning changing one's mind. To paraphrase Peter Senge, learning organization theorist: *metanoia* means truly understanding the deeper meaning of learning. And what is true learning but a fundamental shift or change in the mind?

Enablers encourage people to ask questions and challenge the way things are always done." The enabler creates an environment where this is accepted and expected practice.

The confident enabler accepts questions as part of healthy dialogue. She or he does not consider questions to be criticisms or accusations. The consummate enabler welcomes this challenge on the part of volunteers and believes that the best solutions, plans, and outcomes result from this curiosity and interest. But more than accepting questions, the enabler encourages them. The enabler actually instigates questioning at every opportunity. The enabler knows that the functions of communications and questioning work to produce good decision-making and quality decisions. The enabler uses ongoing conversation to help people question. See Chapter 3 for a detailed discussion of ongoing conversation and asking the right questions. See this book's website for stimulating questions related to volunteerism (Appendix 8-C) and questions about building a board (Appendix 3-C).

11. Engage People in Meaningful Conversation That Produces Learning and Change

By now, you might find another reference to "conversation" frustrating or boring. But wait!

Meaningful conversation is critical if you want to produce learning and change. And good enablers—effective leaders—know that learning and change are essential to remain relevant, vibrant, and sustainable.

In fact, how can you carry out most—even all—of the enabling functions without conversation? Good questions stimulate good conversation.

Good questions, coupled with conversation, help people analyze and translate information, interpret meaning, explore challenges and opportunities, anticipate and manage risks, build ownership and understanding, learn and make decisions. And all that nurtures creativity and stimulates innovation so you can make change.

12. Ensure Quality Decision-Making

Okay. You've got the picture by now:

Information translated into trends and implications → transformed into knowledge → stimulated by questions → generates conversation → produces learning → makes decisions → creates change.

Of course, this isn't linear. There are tons of feedback loops and intersections and interchanges and collisions. One of these days, I hope to draw a picture to represent all this.

Quality decision-making, presented more fully in Chapter 3, is critical to organizational health and effective fund development. And enabling assures effective group decision-making. Enablers help volunteers use their expertise to add value to the decision-making process. The enabler fosters open dialogue—even debate—so the best decisions result.

Enablers set the context for decision-making and facilitate dialogue. At different levels within the organization, volunteers make tactical and strategic decisions. In order to make these decisions well, volunteers need the following from staff:

- Context of this issue relative to mission, direction, and past decisions.
- Appropriate and sufficient information; possible and likely implications of the information.
- Possible choices, and consequences of those choices.
- Why this falls within the volunteer rather than staff purview.

When setting the context, the enabler encourages conversation. Volunteers are repeatedly asked to add their own observations, suggest more implications, and identify other choices and consequences.

13. Anticipate Conflicts and Facilitate Resolution

Inevitably, conflict happens. But conflict is valuable when the process of its resolution builds understanding and mutual respect.

Enablers recognize the benefits of disagreement and conflict and use them. Rather than avoid conflict, enablers anticipate the situation. They help clarify the nature of the conflict and then they facilitate resolution. Sometimes enablers stimulate conflicts. Look back at Chapter 3 and the *Harvard Business Review* article about fighting good fights.

As Peter Drucker observes, important decisions are risky and, hence, should be controversial. The dissent and disagreement found in controversy can resolve conflict. "Because it is essential in an effective discussion to understand what it is really about, there has to be dissent and disagreement."[16]

Naturally, enablers create a safe and risk-free environment. That's what good leaders do. In this environment, conflict and its resolution are not threatening.

14. Encourage Volunteers to Use Their Power, Practice Their Authority, and Accept Their Responsibility

This is the enabling function most often resisted by staff. Some staff members believe that only the select few should exercise power. These power hoarders insist that power is territorial and has boundaries. This narrow view fails to recognize that sharing power causes a dramatic increase in power for all concerned.

The enabler encourages volunteers to use their power and authority and accept their responsibility. An enabler makes it possible and practicable for individuals and groups to carry out their rights, authorities, and responsibilities.

Enablers help groups function well—for example, the board and its committees. As noted in Chapter 3, effective groups depend on sufficient cohesion (but not too much). The enabler helps the group build this solidarity by doing the following:

- Encouraging free communication between volunteers when they are together as a group or talking one-on-one.
- Making sure all members of the group have the same translated information.
- Remaining loyal to the group rather than to its individual members.

Psychologist Robert Coles advises board members, fundraising volunteers, and other volunteers to be "stubbornly curious." Coles says, "We [volunteers] must watch for signs of conformity, a behavior that limits the possibilities of our own independence and personal initiative as philanthropists."[17] He observes that it's easy for volunteers to avoid asking questions and hard for volunteers to suggest something new. Yet, as Coles notes, a key role of volunteers is to "shake up the organization."

Accountability is a big part of this enabling function. As an enabler, your job is to encourage volunteers to accept their responsibility. But without authority too, how can they be accountable? And that is one of the biggest challenges working with individuals or groups. How do you ensure that an individual—whether volunteer or staff member—is accountable? How do you ensure that the group—whether it is the development committee or the board—is accountable?

Sure, you can enable all you want. You can carry out these various functions. But accountability is a reciprocal act. The other—individual or group—must accept the responsibility and act accountably.

Lighting another candle doesn't diminish yours. It increases the illumination.

When was the last time your board of directors discussed *how* it would hold its individual members accountable for their performance expectations? Does your board regularly discuss *how* it holds itself accountable for carrying out due diligence, for executing corporate governance?

The board of directors is legally and morally accountable for the health of the organization. But what does this mean in practical terms? As an enabler, you help individuals and groups to hold themselves accountable. You are responsible for facilitating conversations about accountability and helping to design and implement systems, policies, and procedures for assuring accountability.

Then, as an enabler, you help determine and implement the consequences when people and groups do not act accountably. The bottom line: An effective enabler is accountable for effective enabling.

15. Model Behavior

One of the best ways to enable others is through one's own acts and behaviors. As leaders know, one's own behavior begets the behavior in others.

Using all the enabling functions provides a good model for others. The enabler's own behavior shows volunteers how to communicate well, how to help make decisions, and how to carry out specific tasks well. By sharing information, knowledge, and power, the enabler encourages others to do so.

For enablers, teaching other staff how to enable is a critical aspect of modeling behavior. As an enabler, you want other staff to enable well, thus producing benefit to the organization. In addition to transmitting information about enabling and helping others learn the functions, you regularly demonstrate appropriate enabling behavior.

16. Manage

Someone's got to do it and that may as well be you.

Enabling requires efficient administrative skills, an attention to detail, the ability to balance competing demands, and a thorough knowledge of the particular topic (for example, fund development or governance) for which you are providing the enabling.

Enablers coordinate and integrate many tasks and processes with lots of volunteers. Enablers make sure that volunteers don't step on each other's toes but rather complement one another's activities.

Just watch www.visualthesaurus.com morph the definition of "manage": One node of the diagram says supervise, superintend, and oversee. Another node says wangle, finagle, and do. Yet another says wield, bring off, and pull off.

Management texts frequently define management as the process of getting work done through people. These texts define distinct but interrelated activities such as coordinating, planning, organizing, and controlling. (And yes, some texts include leading as part of managing.)

Many thinkers distinguish between managing and leading. For example, Charles Handy says that "leadership focuses on doing the right things; management focuses on doing things right. Leadership makes sure the ladders we are climbing are leaning against the right wall; management makes sure we are climbing the ladders in the most efficient ways possible."[18]

Is managing the same as leading? Not in this description of enabling functions. However, effective enablers—*and* effective leaders—manage. Enablers and leaders do not absolve themselves of the skills required of managers and the responsibility for managing. Just look back at Chapter 5, focused on leadership.

17. Create Opportunities/Strategies to Buy More Time to Think Things Through

Thanks to Cohort 14 at Saint Mary's University of Minnesota for this idea: Maybe you haven't yet figured out what's going on and how to proceed. You don't know which enabling functions to use. Sometimes you just need more time. So good enablers know how to buy that time.

How can you buy time? Send the volunteer on vacation? Go on vacation yourself? Say you're sick? Quit returning phone calls? Probably none of these is particularly useful, despite any attraction the vacation idea holds.

So, look back at the previous enabling functions. Are there any opportunities there to delay, to buy more time to think things through? Might it be useful to step back and articulate roles? Offer some form of training? Suggest some articles to read? Define again the purpose of the particular process, task, activity, or enterprise?

Perhaps you might suggest the need to conduct a bit of research to find comparable experiences or activities in other organizations? Perhaps you explain that something else has come up that must take priority, without insulting the volunteer(s) or the project. Maybe you recommend a hiatus—a bit of time to take a deep breath and reflect. This needn't look like a weakness or like disorganization.

And if there's high trust between staff and volunteers, then you might say, "I'm uncomfortable. My instincts tell me to stop for a bit."

This enabling function means you really have to think quickly on your feet—even more quickly than other enabling functions. You have to see that you cannot see—acknowledge to yourself that you need extra time to figure things out. And decide how to buy that time with the volunteers.

18. Enhance Attrition (and Facilitate Thank and Release, If Necessary)

Enablers enhance attrition. They don't fire. They enhance attrition and the volunteer leaves with his or her integrity and self-respect intact. And your organization still has a friend.

Let's face it. The fact is, sometimes nothing works. You're a great enabler. You enable as a preventive measure. You use enabling as an intervention strategy, too. You continually monitor your performance as an enabler and you tweak and tweak. You successfully enable any number of individual volunteers and groups.

But there is that one individual. No matter what you do, it doesn't work. The individual is harming the organization. Others realize this, too. (And if it were a staff person, she or he would be fired. But this is a volunteer, perhaps even a board member. People complain, but the organization tolerates the behavior because "he is a volunteer.")

When no other enabling is successful, the best enablers turn to this 18th enabling function: enhance attrition. The best enablers figure out how to encourage the volunteer to step away from the activity, or even from the organization.

Is this hard to do? Sure. Is it impossible? No way. Over and over effective enablers enhance the attrition of volunteers. It may take months or even years. The question is: How long can your organization bear the harm that is being done? And the subquestions are: How quickly can we enhance attrition? Or do we actually have to revert to firing? (Firing is confrontational. Firing rarely allows the volunteer to leave with integrity and self-respect.)

Review all the enabling functions. Use them to help the volunteer realize that she does not have the resources (whether it be skills, time, or whatever) to do the job at hand. Use the enabling functions to help the volunteer realize that her skills would be put to better use in another situation.

Try any ethical strategy that you can. Your job is to get the volunteer to opt out, to choose to move on without losing face.

You may be surprised at how easy this often is. Sometimes volunteers already feel uncomfortable or awkward. They are waiting for an excuse or the opportunity to gracefully depart without looking like a failure, without appearing to cop out. As an enabler, you help them do so.

But what if . . . What if the volunteer does not accept the excuse or take the opportunity? Use enabling as an intervention strategy. Enable others within the organization to help you co-opt the individual, discouraging him or her from staying. For example, with board members, involve the board chair and the governance committee. With a problematic fundraising volunteer, get the chair of the fund development committee to handle the situation.

Shocking? Hardly. What's best for your organization? You are accountable. As a staff person, you are morally liable for the health of the organization. (And the board is both morally and legally liable.) Are you actually going to allow a volunteer to harm the organization? What does this say to the community, to your clients and donors, to the other volunteers?

Enablers are strategists, not technicians. That's the toughest thing about enabling. There aren't any technical tools to help. All you have are attitude, skills, and functions.

But what if . . . What if enhancing attrition doesn't work? Well, then, it's time for thank and release, a more gracious phrase than "fire" or "terminate." Whether board member or other volunteer, the person doesn't get to stay on. Effective organizations don't wait around until the board member's term ends and then just avoid renominating the individual. When enhancing attrition doesn't work, the best organizations thank and release.

However, the staff doesn't thank and release a board member—just like the staff doesn't enhance the attrition of a nonperforming board member. The staff enables the governance committee to enhance attrition or to thank and release.

19. Monitor, Evaluate, and Enhance Enabling

Enabling is a fluid process that benefits from continuous monitoring, regular evaluation, and ongoing enhancement. As a strategy of leadership, organizational development, and change, enabling is constantly examined and refined.

Enablers know this. They incorporate both internal and external monitoring, evaluation, and enhancement. Enablers monitor and evaluate their own performance of the enabling functions and then adjust. Enablers invite colleagues to provide feedback. Enablers also engage in conversation with those whom they are enabling.

Part of enabling is talking with volunteers: "How is it going?" "Are you satisfied with your experience?" "How might we better meet your needs?" These are questions that monitor, evaluate, and enhance enabling.

Attitudes, Skills, and Behaviors of Enablers

So how do you carry out these functions? What are the attitudes, skills, and behaviors you need? See the list in Exhibit 8.3.

Exhibit 8.3   Attitudes and Skills of Enablers

Attitudes of Enablers

They:

1. Respect and trust others.
2. Are trustworthy themselves.
3. Are comfortable with diversity and complexity.
4. Welcome divergent opinions.
5. Question their own assumptions (and expect others to question them, too).
6. Are flexible and comfortable with change.
7. Commit to process as well as outcome.
8. Appreciate conversation and disagreement.
9. Share responsibility for success.
10. Acknowledge responsibility for failure.
11. Balance personal ego with the egos of others.
12. Persevere.
13. Are patient.

Skills of Enablers

They are:

1. Organizational development specialists.
2. Proficient teachers and learners.
3. Effective communicators (listening, observing, informing, and helping to transform information into knowledge and learning).
4. Critical thinkers (anticipating problems, identifying solutions, and redirecting volunteer energies).
5. Strategists (analyzing situations, identifying barriers and opportunities, capitalizing on strengths, and ensuring action and results).
6. Comfortable with conflict, and resolve conflict through shared power with as many individuals as possible.
7. Effective motivators and can focus and manage people.

An effective enabler is a person with the willingness and ability to lead and influence others and the assets to do so. Individuals who enable well possess three assets: the right attitude, the necessary skills, and adequate knowledge. Combined, these help the enabler move the institution forward.

The enabler helps others be the best they can be. The enabler empowers others so that power is shared, process and tasks accomplished, and the philanthropic need met.

The enabler understands the four relationships presented in this book. The enabler knows how critical these relationships are for effective organizations and productive fund development.

The enabler uses relationship building to better understand his or her volunteers. This awareness helps the enabler make sure enabling functions are sensitive to diversity, particularly those of universal concern—gender, generation, ethnicity, sexual orientation, socioeconomic status, faith, physical ability, and so forth.

Enablers use the eight core components that contribute to the organization's effective internal relations: shared values, art of leadership, commitment to process, learning organization, ongoing conversation, participatory decision-making, well-managed change, and culture of philanthropy.

The enabler leads, facilitates, guides, and manages. As a leader, the enabler influences conduct, takes the initiative, and sets an example. As a facilitator, the enabler works with others to determine direction, set standards, identify issues, and encourage resolution. As a guide, the enabler goes ahead to show the way. As a manager, the enabler coordinates activities, explains and gives instructions, and makes tasks easier and more convenient for others to do.

The Enabler's Attitude and Behavior

Attitude refers to a state of mind, behavior, or conduct that reflects a person's values and opinions. Like values, attitude cannot be acquired through training. People choose their attitude and values through self-examination, personal experience, and thought.

My good friend Doris raises an interesting point: Do we really care what a person's attitude is as long as his behavior is appropriate? In some ways, I agree. It's hard to know the secret heart of an individual, her attitude. And we don't actually hold people accountable for their attitude—we hold people accountable for the way they behave.

But behavior reflects attitude. And if people fake the behavior because their attitude is different, I suspect others eventually know.

A true enabler believes that enabling is the consummate artistry leadership and essential to the philanthropic process. The enabler is committed to ensuring that his or her institution embraces enabling as an essential aspect of corporate culture and organizational systems.

The enabler believes that enabling will work. She or he is patient, helpful, encouraging, and hopeful. The enabler is upbeat and acts as a cheerleader. Despite periodic setbacks and frustration, enablers have confidence in their volunteers.

Typically, enablers are generous in attitude and behavior: They share responsibility for success and balance their personal egos with those of others.

Enablers are trustworthy, and respect and trust others. Enablers, like leaders, value process as well as outcome. They welcome different opinions and differences of opinion. Both enablers and leaders acknowledge failure and still persevere. They are open and flexible.

The Enabler's Knowledge

Knowledge refers to a deep and extensive learning, a certainty, and a conviction. Knowledge is more than the accumulation of facts. Knowledge means understanding the information, perceiving relationships, elaborating concepts, and translating information to application. Knowledge means formulating principles and evaluating. Knowledge is acquired through experience, practical ability, and skill.

On the one hand, the enabling functions represent the knowledge you need to better engage and manage volunteers, strengthen fund development, and assure good governance. These same functions help build a competent and innovative staff.

On the other hand, the enabler needs additional knowledge to carry out the enabling functions. The best enablers learn key management theories to improve enabling. The following are of particular benefit to enablers:

- Organizational development theory, including process, facilitation, and group dynamics.
- Systems thinking and learning organization theory.
- Leadership theory.
- Conversation and decision-making processes.
- Change management.
- Marketing and constituency development.

This sounds a lot like an organizational development specialist, doesn't it? And enabling sounds a lot like leadership, too. Look back at Chapters 4 and 5.

To successfully enable fund development volunteers, the enabler also knows things like:

- Role of volunteers and staff in fund development.
- Differences and similarities between governance and management.
- Philanthropic theory.
- Fund development principles and practices.
- Fundraising strategies and techniques.
- Process and task opportunities for fund development volunteers.

The Enabler's Skills

Skill means proficiency or technical ability and is demonstrated by ease or expertness in performance and application. Skills help a person translate his or her attitude into behavior. The professional acquires skills through self-assessment, experiential learning, training, and study.

Enablers know what organizational development is, as described in this book. And enablers have the skills to do this work. Enablers are skilled leaders and managers and learners. Enablers are good communicators and effective teachers.

Enablers adeptly resolve conflict by sharing power. They anticipate potential problems and identify possible solutions. Enablers are good at focusing and, if need be, redirecting volunteer energies. Great people managers, enablers also manage systems, processes, and tasks well.

Effective enablers possess the executive competencies and knowledge described in Chapter 4, summarized as: commitment to results, business savvy, leading change, and motivating.

Compare the enabler's attitude and skills in Exhibit 8.3 to the 10 essentials of good people management, quoted here from Kay Sprinkel Grace by Henry Rosso in *Achieving Excellence in Fundraising*.[19]

1. Respect for one's self and others.
2. Open communication.
3. Confidence in one's own abilities to manage and lead.
4. Personal and professional goals that are clear and achievable.
5. Belief in the organization's goals and the importance of seeing them accomplished.
6. Trust in others.
7. Ability to delegate, reward, and provide feedback.
8. A belief that "systems liberate"—that people function best in a structure that systematizes routine tasks and encourages creative approaches to tasks that are new and unusual.
9. Consistency, including standards and expectations that are broadly communicated and understood.
10. Accessibility.

The Challenge of Enabling

"Leadership requires major expenditures of effort and energy—more than most people care to make." So says John Gardner in his book *On Leadership*.[20] Enabling requires this same level of effort and energy.

Good enabling can produce immediate, albeit somewhat limited, results. However, the most dramatic and protracted benefits require the cumulative effect of long-term effort and energy.

Staff must be convinced of the value of empowered volunteers. If staff members resist, they don't enable and the organization doesn't move forward.

Enabling is one of the most critical functions within a philanthropic organization. This holds true for all philanthropic organizations of any size or type.

As such, enabling is an essential role of the chief executive and development officer. Through enabling, the staff/volunteer relationship works. Without enabling, dysfunction reigns.

For professionals in the philanthropic sector, the challenge is to create an organizational culture in which volunteers are enabled well. If there are no professional employees, volunteers perform the staff function of enabling. And in good governance, a board chair is a good enabler, not one of the all-too-common rogues (rogue like an elephant rampaging around!).

Sometimes we professionals succeed in creating this culture. But often we don't. Fundraisers and chief executives still complain about their volunteers, particularly boards and fundraising volunteers. Many volunteers seem only modestly pleased with their own efforts and experiences with nonprofit/NGO organizations.

Why is it so difficult to create the culture of enabling? There are five principal factors:

1. Interdependence of volunteers and staff
2. Organizational life cycles
3. Corporate culture
4. Staff capability and power
5. Staff conflict

Interdependence of Volunteers and Staff

Take a look at any philanthropic organization. Immediately you see the paradoxical position of volunteers. The volunteer serves at the top and bottom of the organization. Also, the volunteer is neither paid nor made to work for the organization. One moment, the volunteer is the authority; at another time, staff is. For example:

- The board of directors hires the CEO, evaluating his or her performance and, if necessary, firing him or her. Yet, the CEO is the principal enabler of the board.
- The development officer must lead, guide, and facilitate the efforts of fundraising volunteers. However, the development officer supervises board members when they're fundraising. Often that's awkward.
- The staff directs and supervises the clerical and service volunteers, but has difficulty dismissing them.

The question arises: Who is boss? Rarely is there a definitive answer. It depends on situation and circumstance. And generally, if there is effective enabling by staff, the question does not arise.

This is the complex and intrinsically conflicted relationship at the core of philanthropic organizations. This relationship demands effective enabling—but also makes enabling difficult.

USING RULES AND JUDGMENT   To address this inherent conflict, both volunteers and staff seek rules. We seek industry standards that describe volunteer and staff roles and relationships.

We write policies and procedures. We rationally define responsibilities for the chief executive, boards, officers, and committees. We clearly outline the reporting structure.

All this helps. But it's not the whole answer.

Judgment is as important as rules. Despite role delineation and defined lines of authority, all organizations face various situations. These situations demand judgment rather than rules.

The best rules, the clearest roles, and the tightest policies and procedures cannot respond to every issue. Judgment is necessary, and good enablers have it. Enablers know when to involve volunteers more, despite conventional standards. Enablers know that roles may change, depending on the particular situation or its possible implications.

RECOGNIZING AUTHORITY   Authority is spread throughout your organization, between staff and volunteers. Different degrees of prerogative are exercised in different situations, depending on various situations.

The fact is, the board of directors is legally and morally accountable to the community: those who are served, those who give, and those who regulate and legislate. Volunteers are the acknowledged stewards of the public trust. By virtue of position, theirs is the inherent and inherited authority.

The staff receives its authority from the volunteers. The board confers authority on the staff through acts of hiring and delegation. More specifically, the board of directors hires the CEO, thus conferring management and operational authority. The CEO then confers authority on staff through hiring.

But the staff also possesses moral authority. As philanthropic professionals, staff members act as stewards, too.

And the staff possesses the most control. As day-to-day implementers of mission and program, staff members act as the institution's gatekeepers. Staff holds the information and regulates access. Staff sets context and manage activities.

In summary, staff either empowers or disempowers. Or does neither, in some sort of passive approach. And sins of omission are as great as sins of commission.

ENABLING THE MOST RESPONSIBLE VOLUNTEERS   Enabling is most difficult with volunteers who have the most responsibility (and authority) in an organization. Generally, this includes board members and committee members. Trouble arises with fundraising volunteers, too, because they're often board members.

Some volunteers—because of their capability—give significant input and hold major responsibility. Some volunteers possess legal and/or moral responsibility because of their position within your organization, for example, your board members. (In actuality, individual board members—including the board chair—have no authority by virtue of position. Corporate governance is a collective act. Only the board, as a group, has authority—and only when it meets. Learn more about governance and you can better enable board members in both fund development and governance. See governance resources in the Free Download Library at www.simonejoyaux .com.)

You choose to bring these individuals into your organization because of their expertise, experience, and insights. With their attributes, knowledge, and skills, these volunteers can be particularly beneficial to your organization.

Yet, because of their capability, these volunteers can also be difficult to enable. Still others hold an organization hostage due to their gifts of time or money—or some other form of privilege and power.[21]

These volunteers usually exercise initiative and critical thinking professionally and personally. They expect to do the same when volunteering.

This can cause confusion, stepping on toes, and conflict. (But actually, all this experience and expertise—of both staff and volunteers—is wildly exciting, deeply rewarding, and extremely beneficial to your organization.)

In response to this situation, some staff try to limit volunteer access and input. This frustrates the volunteers and they will ultimately abandon your organization.

On the other hand, if the staff welcomes volunteers into the organization and enables them well, volunteers add value. Competently enabled volunteers carry out the specific tasks you want done, do them well, and do them in a timely fashion. In addition, well-enabled volunteers help your organization remain relevant and healthy. These volunteers will ask strategic questions, challenge the status quo, and consider things critically.

Organizational Life Cycles

Organizations evolve through life cycles. These can be summarized as: emerging, maturing, institutionalizing. Different organizations spend different lengths of time in each cycle. Organizations may return to an earlier cycle and then move forward again. When an organization is emerging, it usually has few staff members. Traditional distinctions between governance and management do not adequately reflect practical reality. Volunteers often serve as governors, administrators, service providers, and fundraisers. Some volunteers do more than one of these functions at the same time.

Lines of demarcation blur. Wearing so many hats, volunteers often confuse their roles. For example, when a board member volunteers professional advice about renovations, she isn't acting in a governance capacity. If a board member reviews brochure copy, he is a volunteer reporting to the staff person responsible.

As an organization matures, professional staff may increase. The organization begins to differentiate between the roles of its volunteers and staff. A formalized structure typically results.

Further maturation often produces more staff. As the organization moves into the institutionalizing cycle, volunteer roles are more clearly delineated.

Distinctions between governance and management are clearer, too. As boards try to focus on governance, they sometimes lose close contact with the mission and program of the organization. The same may happen as committees move from implementation to policy and as the staff encourages volunteers to focus more on fundraising.

Moving through the life cycles causes lots of change for staff and volunteers. Each group may need to adjust attitude and develop new skills as the organization evolves.

Sometimes the staff and volunteers for one life cycle are neither comfortable nor skilled for another cycle. If they cannot change their attitude and learn new skills, effective organizations encourage these staff people and volunteers to move into more appropriate positions or to move on. Then the organizations recruit the appropriate volunteers and staff.

Organizations seem to be most vulnerable during the emerging and institutionalizing years. For emerging organizations, the concept of enabling is rarely understood. Practical matters usually supersede strategic thinking about organizational development.

At this time, staff may not understand the theory or possess the skills, knowledge, or experience to operate as enablers. Nonetheless, enabling is very important at this juncture. Exposing people to the theory and functions of enabling will help.

Even in more established institutions, people often don't pay enough attention to enabling. During the institutionalizing phase, the staff absorbs more responsibility, sometimes leaving volunteers behind. For example:

- The development officer writes the fund development plan with no input from volunteers and gives the committee a draft to review, edit, and approve.
- The chief executive avoids in-depth discussion of strategic issues with the board and merely encourages them to approve recommendations.

Now a great danger arises, one that is inexcusable. Some staff members abandon enabling. Some volunteers accept this. Both staff and volunteers are responsible. Whether staff ceases enabling willfully or unknowingly, the harm is equal and the action unconscionable.

What is the harm? When a board does not adequately exercise its governance function, those trustees may be legally and morally vulnerable. If poorly enabled, volunteers lose interest and move away, taking their gifts of time and money with them. Without voluntary action, access to constituent insights decreases, community credibility lessens, and charitable contributions shrink.

Make enabling a value of your organization and a responsibility of management.

Corporate Culture

Corporate culture, discussed in Chapter 3, describes the way an organization arranges the interaction of its participants. This arrangement may be intentional, designed and documented through values, systems, and procedures. Or this arrangement may be unwritten and unnegotiated tradition. It's "just the way we do things."

Concepts of voluntary leadership, moral accountability, philanthropic steward-ship, and interrelationship with community help define corporate culture in non-profits/NGOs. So does the relationship of volunteers and staff.

In effective nonprofits/NGOs, enabling is a central element of corporate culture. When your organization respects the volunteer role, you have the attitude necessary to comprehend enabling. Then your staff can acquire the knowledge and use the skills necessary to enable well.

The individuals and groups in your organization make the corporate culture. Either they value enabling and then this attitude pervades your organization—or they don't and it doesn't. Either they try to modify behavior accordingly and you see it in the interchanges of staff with staff, staff with volunteer, and volunteer with volunteer—or you don't.

Staff Capability to Enable

Capability includes willingness and commitment as well as ability. Staff who are enablers possess the right attitude, knowledge, and skills.

Sometimes I think that the staff's capability to enable volunteers is likely the most critical factor affecting overall institutional health and fundraising productivity.

Why do I say this? Because institutional health is a lot about governance. Yet too many boards are inadequately enabled and hence inappropriately involved. Why? Because money is money. Yet too few volunteers are adequately enabled and hence don't help with fund development. Obviously, institutional health and fundraising productivity directly link to your organization's capacity to serve. So there you have it: Sometimes I think the staff ability to enable might be your organization's most critical factor. And if your organization lacks capable enablers, you organization makes very little progress.

Unfortunately, many professionals—both staff and consultants—don't understand their enabling responsibility. Or else they avoid it. For example, to improve fund development, they seek better solicitation strategies rather than enabling volunteers.

Not surprisingly, these same professionals complain that their fellow employees don't always understand fund development. Of greatest concern to fundraisers are the chief executive and financial officers. It is essential that these individuals understand fund development.

To achieve this end, some fundraisers suggest that the fundraising profession develop training materials and resources directed to these staff members. But this is a very, very small part of the solution. More appropriately, the organization's fundraiser must enable the staff. That's how the best learning will happen. It is the fundraiser's responsibility to enable the chief executive and other staff as well as volunteers.

We know, intellectually and empirically, that partnership and participation are the ... strategies that create high-performance [organizations].

From *Stewardship: Choosing Service over Self-Interest*, by Peter Block (San Francisco: Berrett-Koehler, 1993), 10

Initially, enabling may be compared to the personnel function of a supervisor, a theory familiar to nonprofit/NGO professionals. The effective supervisor develops the effectiveness of his or her employee through such activities as: encouraging; supporting; motivating; appraising; directing; and facilitating problem solving, decision-making, and independence.

Unfortunately, this function is more complex when one is enabling volunteers. There is only a moral imperative, little actual authority, on the part of staff. This paradoxical relationship between staff and volunteer demands an accomplished enabler.

Staff and Power

Abuse of power is the major barrier that limits enabling. When staff act as power holders, they are neither enablers nor leaders. For some, this abuse is intentional. For others it is unintentional. Unfortunately, the result is the same: poorly enabled volunteers, a less-than-effective organization, and ineffective fund development.

Some staff members don't want to share power so they don't enable their volunteers . Instead of enabling, these staff members focus on their own vision, their own goals, and their own authority. These staff members are busy exercising control to ensure the outcomes they wish and prohibit those they do not wish. These individuals will likely never accept enabling.

Other staff members don't understand empowerment. The concept of enabling is foreign to them. These professionals hold power loosely and get by as best they can. They will likely consider enabling if it is explained to them.

There is a third group. These individuals know things aren't working well even if they aren't sure why. These individuals are ready to explore enabling.

Staff Conflict

What happens if you want to enable but your boss doesn't? Can you enable without the boss's permission? The first answer is, yes. You do lots of work without your boss's direct permission. As Nike says, "just do it." For example: Start talking about enabling with the development committee as one of the key strategies in a good fund development program. Get the buy-in of the development committee chair and committee members. Start an advocacy campaign with other staff, one-on-one, one person at a time.

The second answer is, enable your boss to understand how beneficial enabling is. Remember it's not what you're selling but what your boss is buying that counts. Figure out what your boss is buying. Use the enabling functions to convince your boss that enabling volunteers will meet his or her needs.

But what happens if your boss actually prohibits your use of certain enabling functions? It could happen. So, if you've already starting enabling, then talk about results. Tell your boss what enabling has produced and why it is beneficial. That may reassure him or her.

If you've already started enabling your volunteers, they will expect you to continue doing so. Even if they don't say this out loud, they will actually *feel* different if you stop enabling. They will likely express frustration or discomfort even if they cannot define why. Once enabled, volunteers balk when they no longer experience the same level and type of interchange with you. Report this volunteer dissatisfaction to your boss. Help her or him see the value of reverting to the old way, and that's enabling!

You can back down somewhat on the degree within a particular enabling function. Your boss may feel more comfortable and learn to value the results.

Try to enable others in the organization—staff and volunteers—to get your boss to see the light. Be very careful doing this. Try to co-opt your boss without behaving inappropriately. Of course, you cannot criticize your boss. You cannot pit yourself or your volunteers against your boss. But it might be possible to engage others sufficiently in enabling that they actually help convert or co-opt your boss.

What if none of this works? Your boss doesn't endorse the enabling functions. You cannot enable him or her to value this way of doing business. Your boss is abdicating his or her responsibility and you don't like it.

Remember enabling function #18? Perhaps it's time to enhance your own attrition. You face the ultimate dilemma: Do you want to continue working somewhere that does not share your values, that does not work to its optimum capacity?

Do you want to work with people who do not share your beliefs in leadership and management? Now it's your decision.

Also consider the opposite. You don't want to enable. It's too much work and too frustrating. It's easier to do it yourself. Your boss encourages you to enable but you simply don't devote adequate time and attention. Now your boss thinks about enhancing your attrition. Or else your boss just plain fires you. Are you ready for that?

The Biggest Challenge Facing Nonprofits/NGOs

Engaging volunteers in appropriate and meaningful ways may be the biggest challenge faced by nonprofit/NGO organizations. And enabling itself is the way to answer the challenge.

The big question is: What are the meaningful and appropriate activities volunteers can do? Philanthropic organizations continually wrestle with this. Often staff and volunteers disagree about what is meaningful and appropriate involvement. Through enabling, your volunteers and staff decide together.

Keep in mind that meaningful involvement depends on the individual's needs and interests. Is your organization volunteer-centered, donor-centered, customer-centered, and mission- and client-centered? These are not mutually exclusive. You and your organization must embrace all of these centrisms.

Enabling your volunteers helps engage them in meaningful and appropriate ways.

Now we're back to the process of constituency development. But of course, the involvement also has to be useful to the organization. This need for a mutually beneficial exchange confronts the organization as it develops relationships with its constituents. Balancing constituent and organization needs is part of the challenge of constituency development.

Appropriate involvement also has multiple dimensions. Aside from the legal requirements for the appropriate involvement of boards (which staff and volunteers sometimes interpret differently), the rest is up for grabs. Sure, there are industry standards that describe best practice, but best practice is situational. Staff and volunteers translate the standards for their own organization.

Appropriate involvement often depends on the number of professional staff members available to carry out key organization functions. Staff capability often affects how involved volunteers get and in what areas. Appropriate involvement also depends on the organization's culture and its maturation.

The more professional staff you have, the more the volunteer jobs change. Volunteers no longer do so much management. Indeed, they may rarely hear discussion of management functions like marketing, public relations, and program development. The staff even identifies strategic issues and forecasts trends and their implications while volunteers are left to focus on results and overall institutional health.

Sometimes this changed focus causes volunteers to move farther and farther away from the organization. Boards seem to do more routine business with less strategic dialogue. And that's too bad. The board only needs a few committees to help it do governance work. And that's good. The old committees that intruded in management, stepping on staff toes, are gone. That's good, too. And the staff just wants volunteers to fundraise. But that's bad.

Now there's potential for trouble. We weaken the philanthropic sector if our volunteers become disengaged or relegated to limited mechanical tasks, routine activities, or one single area of endeavor, like fund development. On the other hand, we thwart staff if volunteers intrude inappropriately.

The solution is for staff, in partnership with volunteers, to figure out how to engage appropriately. There's lots of material available. Don't just look at resources in the philanthropic sector. Look at evolving business theory in the for-profit sector.

For example, consider how you can focus your board members on policy, institutional health, and results rather than operations. What kinds of board committees would you establish to help the board do this work? How would you design board meetings to ask essential and cage-rattling questions, and to engage in meaningful conversation? How would you enable board meetings to keep conversation within appropriate boundaries?

For example, explore how you can best use volunteer expertise to help with such management things as copywriting, event design, administrative assistance, and so forth. How will you set boundaries and explain staff authority? What kind of supervision do the volunteers need?

In summary, keep asking yourself how to engage volunteers in meaningful and appropriate ways. Get the opinions of your volunteers and staff. Talk to colleagues in other organizations. Explore management theories. Test your ideas and then improve them.

All the while, make sure you enable your volunteers well. Carry out the 19 enabling functions described in this chapter and you'll engage your volunteers meaningfully and appropriately.

Strengthen Enabling

Unfortunately, there are all too few accomplished enablers. Instead, organizations employ very good technicians who don't use enabling.

The thing is, it's easier to do the work yourself than enable others. Enabling requires enormous amounts of energy, unlimited patience, and deeply held values, which buoy you when the hassles are huge.

Furthermore, the nonprofit/NGO sector does not yet focus enough on enabling. There is little evidence that professionals gather together to analyze enabling functions, explore the skills and knowledge, and discuss successful and unsuccessful experiences. It's difficult to find documented models of success or analyses of failures.

Fundraisers talk in generalities about volunteers—but don't talk explicitly about these functions. Job descriptions mention volunteer management—but don't actually understand the scope. Performance appraisals hold employees accountable for effective volunteers—but don't provide tangible feedback about how to do the work.

Chief executive officers and fundraisers must be good enablers.

This must change. It can, and it is changing to some degree. The nonprofit/NGO sector focuses more on leadership, and enabling is leadership. More publications, more continuing education, and more sector leaders promote appropriate for-profit business theory and discourage the tactic-dominant focus.

Still, more needs to be done. Will you help?

Action Steps for Your Organization

It's time that institutions demand proficient enablers. Institutions should include an understanding of and capability to enable as part of job descriptions, hiring decisions, and performance appraisals. This is particularly important for the chief executive and development officers, as well as most consulting relationships.

Your organization can incorporate enabling into its operation and immediately see some improvement. Try these seven ideas.

1. *Adopt enabling as an organizational value.*

   Talk with staff and volunteers about what enabling means and how it affects individual and group behavior and organizational systems. Remember that enabling is a natural outgrowth of such values as respect for and sensitivity to others, understanding the needs and interests of volunteers, and honoring marketing and the basic premise of constituency development.

2. *Make enabling a hiring criterion.*

   Acknowledge that enabling is one of the competencies required by your CEO and fundraiser at least. Start with your CEO. If she doesn't know how to enable, get her help fast. Make sure that she selects fundraisers who are good enablers.

   Use the interview process to ask questions that help you discern competency in this area. When checking references, ask how well the applicant carries out the enabling functions.

3. *Make enabling a performance expectation.*

   Incorporate enabling as a function in key staff job descriptions. Use the performance appraisal process to assess an employee's effectiveness at enabling.

   Make sure the board evaluates the CEO's effectiveness as an enabler. Make sure that the CEO evaluates the fundraiser's enabling performance.

4. *Expect your leaders to help employees develop and enhance their enabling skills.*

   Make sure your leaders model, coach, and mentor proper enabling behavior. Provide professional development opportunities to support enabling.

5. *Create a shared vision and benchmarks for strengthening enabling.*

   Identify situations that would benefit from enabling as an intervention. Talk about how enabling might have prevented a situation from arising.

6. *Make enabling a focus of management dialogue.*

   Design formal and informal opportunities for staff to explore enabling and to problem solve. For example, staff may:

   - Analyze specific situations, identifying why enabling did or did not work and how it might be improved.
   - Discuss the enabling functions and brainstorm specific ways to carry out the functions.
   - Consider particular individuals and their interests and barriers, and decide how staff might better enable these volunteers.

- Observe each other's enabling behavior and coach one another to strengthen performance.
- Develop benchmarks to appraise performance.
- Identify resources (e.g., printed materials, workshops, etc.) that can help staff develop their enabling skills.

7. *Include enabling in your governance dialogues.*

Talk about the philosophy and practice of enabling. Get volunteer input about enabling effectiveness.

Challenge to the Professional and the Profession

It's up to you and me. We professionals must direct our attention to enabling. We can help develop enablers, just as leaders develop leaders.

First, we develop our own individual proficiency. We model this behavior to others and pass along the values and philosophy. We make sure that volunteers, organizations, and other professionals understand the benefits of enabling.

Second, working through the profession, we insist that enabling be developed as a core competency. Then we help the profession figure out how to develop this competency in its leaders.

We make sure that the profession studies, talks, and writes about enabling. We teach those skills that are teachable and help develop the attitudes and behaviors that are not teachable. We help people develop enabling skills by doing such things as:

- Defining the functions of enabling.
- Describing the attitude an enabler has.
- Identifying skills that support enabling.
- Stimulating the professional's thinking.
- Encouraging self-examination.
- Creating opportunities for practice.
- Modeling appropriate behavior.
- Observing the professional's behavior, coaching, and providing feedback.

Personal Action Steps for You

As a professional, you can enhance your own capacity for enabling by taking the following four steps.

1. Evaluate your own understanding of enabling, its functions, attitude, and skills.
2. Assess your own effectiveness as an enabler. Then ask someone you trust and respect to evaluate your enabling. See Appendix 8-B, "Assess Your Performance as an Enabler," on this book's website.
3. Talk about enabling with colleagues and learn together. Discuss situations and help each other use the enabling functions as a preventive measure and an intervention.
4. Recruit a personal observer, someone who works closely with you. Ask this individual to watch your actions and comment on your enabling performance.

As a professional, you can enhance your organization's capacity for enabling. Indeed, you must. What to do and what it means is the focus of this chapter. Enough said.

Moreover, as a professional, you can enhance the profession. Talk about enabling with your colleagues, particularly those in fund development or those who are CEOs. Help them see the meaning and value to them and the benefit to their organizations.

Outline ways you can help each other develop this competency. Insist that professional associations talk about enabling, organizational development, and leadership. Demand continuing education opportunities that go beyond training in fund development.

Be Patient during the Transition and Stick to It

With a little bit of effort, you'll see some immediate gain. But long-term significant improvement requires lots of effort, more time, and infinite patience.

If enabling is not yet part of your organization's culture and behavior, this will be a new way of doing business. When you start something new, there are always some rough spots, even a little chaos.

That's to be expected. You'll stumble along the way, but just be patient and persevere. Change is tough. People will be tempted to return to the old way of doing things. Look back at Chapter 3, your organization's internal relations. Review the section about well-managed change, one of the key components for an effective infrastructure.

Remember the benefits of enabling. This is a new way of relating to each other. Talk about the philosophy and practice the functions. Give each other feedback.

Summary

Quit trying to find new ideas in philanthropy and fund development. Start by understanding and embracing the fundamentals and doing the basics better. And enabling is one of the basics, just like leadership is.

What happens if you don't enable? Here are just a few results.

- There is too much work for staff, particularly in fund development.
- You create disenfranchised volunteers who may reduce (or not increase) their monetary contributions.
- There are fewer knowledgeable people out in the community advocating for your constituents, your programs, and your support.
- There is less information and perspective (hence diversity) coming into your organization.

Lack of enabling produces role confusion. Without enabling, the lines between governance and management blur and the door opens for micromanaging by the board. Lack of enabling reduces your organization's capacity to make sound judgments and good decisions.

On the other hand, lots of wonderful things happen if you do enable your volunteers. For example:

- More people know about your organization and advocate on its behalf.
- Volunteers engage in the meaning and processes of your organization as well as its activities.
- The best volunteers stay with your organization and add value to your activities.
- You make better decisions with diverse inputs.
- More volunteers help nurture relationships and build donor loyalty.
- More volunteers participate in solicitation, securing more donors and gifts.

Through enabling, you provide adequate power, means, and opportunity to ensure an effective organization. And effective organizations help build a healthy community. Enabling enhances the volunteer experience. And proud volunteers help make organizations more attractive.

Enabling is leadership and management. Enablers are philosophers and strategists. They possess assets and skills that they hone to carry out functions that they can define.

Consider this. If you are not a good enabler, should you be a chief executive or fundraiser? I don't think so.

Entr'acte

Bridging the Gap

That's it: the four relationships necessary to build a successful organization and an effective fund development program.

So why isn't the book finished?

Because when I wrote the second edition, people were clamoring for me to write up my successful workshop on creating an effective fund development plan. I did so. And it seemed a shame to eliminate that chapter from this third edition.

Since I chose to keep the chapter about fund development planning, obviously I had to review it. And then add to it. So that's Chapter 9 in this edition.

Then I figured a postscript about creating the best fund development program was important. This book isn't about the basic principles and best practice of fund development, but they certainly deserve a mention.

So here I am, in this entr'acte. And here you are. Read on if you wish.

Creating the Most Effective Fund Development Program

Lots to know. More to learn from ongoing research. Things like donor centrism and donor-centered communications, solicitation strategies, gift management, prospect research, ethics, and lots more. All those domains of fundraising practice listed in Exhibit 4.1, from CFRE International.

For a comprehensive overview of fundraising, get your own copy of *Fundraising Principles and Practice* by Sargeant, Shang, and Associates (San Francisco: Jossey-Bass, 2010). This textbook synthesizes best practice and academic research. The book includes dozens of real-life examples and dozens and dozens of figures and tables documenting research and providing essential information to support our work. You'll want this in your library immediately. Even the most experienced fundraisers will learn from this book.

And that's not all. Check out the excellent work of leading practitioners in the field of fund development. I'm looking at the authors on my bookshelf—people like Mal Warwick, Kay Sprinkel Grace, Ted Hart, Jim Greenfield, Ken Burnett, Kim Klein, Laura Fredricks, Tom Ahern, and more. Check the CFRE International booklist. Check the AFP International bookstore.

Still, there's more. Don't just read fundraising materials. I make that point throughout this book. Read about organizational development to help you build the best fund development program. Read the great books on communications and business management. Read about society and its changes. Keep exploring.

Read the good blogs to get that extra kick, to stay on top of what's happening. Subscribe to the good newsletters and archive the useful tips. In fact, the good bloggers and newsletters regularly refer us to other good blogs and good newsletters. There's a collection of good to great out there, all reinforcing each other.

It's your job. You're the leader. Ensure you create the most effective fund development program because you're prepared, because you use the body of knowledge and research in fund development—and the bodies of knowledge and research in other critical fields

So that's my entr'acte: moving from the four relationships—the intent of this book—to my thoughts about creating the best fund development plan.

Read on.

CHAPTER 9

Creating the Most Effective Fund Development Plan for Your Organization

A Plan That Produces Ownership and Results

Leaders who engage their groups . . . may enjoy higher levels of morale, employee motivation, and loyalty. . . . Involvement, attention, and a willingness to listen, to reflect, and to be moved are all indications of respect.

It is our deepest desires that provide us with the strength and the willingness to attend to the tedium of process when we otherwise would turn off the light, close down the meeting, or just lose interest. When people follow their hearts, they equip themselves to grapple with process.

—Joline Godfrey, *Our Wildest Dreams: Women Entrepreneurs*
Making Money, Having Fun, Doing Good
(New York: HarperCollins, 1993), 19–20

The Most Effective Fund Development Program

Fund development is not a separate and independent activity that can be pulled out whenever there is need, focused on by only a few, and ignored the rest of the time. Instead, fund development is an ongoing, rewarding (but invasive) process that engages all staff and every board member in some way.

Fund development affects everything your organization does, from board and staff recruitment to client service to communications. (However, this does *not* mean that the only qualification for board membership is the ability to raise money.)

Fund development depends on the four relationships described in this book. And your fund development program relies on your organization's ability to develop and nurture these relationships.

Effective fund development produces more than money. Effective organizations understand that fund development goals and strategies focus on things other than money. For example: creating a culture of philanthropy, building stronger relationships, helping board members feel comfortable with fund development, understanding the interests of donors and prospective donors so the organization can ask for a gift, and so forth.

No matter what you want to raise money for, you must pay attention to process. Process means examining fund development and organizational development issues together in one system. The process requires a commitment of time and energy on the part of the organization's staff and volunteers. Direct participation (asking questions, discussing, deciding) by key leadership is essential to build understanding and ownership.

None of this should be a surprise if you've read the previous chapters in this book. For example, pay particular attention to Chapter 3, "The First Relationship—Within Your Organization." Reread everything about values and leadership, systems thinking and learning organization theory, participatory decision-making and group dynamics. Read about adaptive capacity and well-managed change. Without all this, you won't build a strong fund development program. Are you ready to tell your organization that?

What do you think about as you create an effective fund development program? First, think about philanthropy and community. Always think about the four relationships described in this book. Of course, think about fund development principles and practice. Take a look at Appendix 9-A on this book's website, "Creating the Most Effective Fund Development Program for Your Organization." You know how complex and extensive good fund development is.

How does all this hang together? What's the framework for managing and implementing the development program: your organization's fund development plan. In many ways, the fund development plan summarizes the key components of your overall development program—with a focus on what you want to emphasize at a particular time.

Your Fund Development Plan and the Planning Process

What is a fund development plan? It's closely partnered with your institution's multiyear strategic plan.[1] In fact, your fund development plan is one of those subplans mentioned as the final step in the strategic planning process described in Chapter 6. Your organization's strategic plan provides the framework and foundation for your organization's work. Then you create a fund development plan—guided by the organization's strategic plan—to secure the financing to support the strategic plan.

The fund development plan describes the highlights of your fund development program.

Your fund development plan belongs to the organization, not to the development operation or to the development staff. Just like the institutional strategic plan and the budget, the fund development plan is a board policy.

You use the four relationships to create and implement both your fund development plan and your fund development program. And creating your fund development plan is a major way to nurture the four relationships. Just like the strategic plan, the fund development plan belongs to the entire institution. Just like strategic planning, you involve board and staff in the fund development planning process. Just like strategic planning, the board endorses or formally adopts the fund development plan.

In large institutions (e.g., universities and healthcare systems) the board of directors may not actually adopt the kind of fund development plan described in this chapter. However, despite institutional size, the board must understand the institution's financing, both revenue and charitable contributions. When adopting the budget, the board should endorse or adopt the fund development strategy. It's not enough that the board of directors—the legal corporate entity—see a budget that summarizes charitable contributions. The board has to understand how to raise the money and board members have to accept their obligation to participate.

The development planning process helps produce the optimum development program. If you already operate a development program (and most organizations do in some manner), then the ongoing development planning process strengthens your development program.

Who is responsible for all this? The development operation. The development operation is accountable for creating a development program that is based on the four relationships *and* reflects the principles of fund development. Just look back at Chapter 4, "The Fund Development Professional," and Chapter 5, "The Art of Leadership."

Defining the Process and Benefits for Your Organization

Like institutional strategic planning, good fund development planning is a process that builds organization-wide understanding of and ownership for—in this case—philanthropy and fund development. Like the process of institutional planning, the best fund development planning process generates learning and change, and produces alignment and shared accountability. Just like institutional strategic planning, good development planning also produces results (e.g., a written plan).

Effective fund development planning depends on the same principles and process as institutional strategic planning. In fact, reread Chapter 6 and just substitute "fund development planning" for "organizational strategic planning."

No matter what kind of planning, both process and results (e.g., the written plan) are important.

In summary, the most effective fund development planning process accomplishes the following:

- Engages key stakeholders in order to gather quality information, build understanding, and enhance ownership.
- Assesses the return on investment—productivity and effectiveness—of fund development activities.
- Assesses the internal and external environments, responds to the challenges, and capitalizes on the opportunities.

- Ensures that volunteers (board members and other fund development volunteers) understand the most critical principles of philanthropy and fund development.
- Assures volunteer acceptance of the body of knowledge and best practices rather than personal opinions.
- Articulates the case for support and key messages for donors and prospects.
- Enhances the organization's position in the philanthropic marketplace.
- Develops volunteer skills.
- Reaffirms values, vision, and direction.
- Sets goals and strategies and tests their feasibility.
- Defines measures and benchmarks.

Typically, implementation of the fund development program and plan produces the following benefits when done well:

- Donor-centered organization.
- Stronger and deeper relationships.
- More volunteers to help nurture relationships and solicit gifts.
- Better use of volunteers and more satisfied volunteers.
- Growing understanding of what works and why, and what doesn't work and why.
- Meaningful criteria to measure success.
- Specific relationship-building and solicitation strategies that specific volunteers have agreed to implement.
- Institutionalization of development within the board.
- More loyal donors and more money.

Avoiding or Compromising Fund Development Planning

Despite its obvious benefits, not everyone embraces the process. Sound familiar? The same holds true for institutional strategic planning.

Some people want to jump to the bottom line: "Forget process—just write a plan!" Don't go there. Remember that the end does not justify the means. Process is as important as outcome. Your job is to enable others to understand the value. Often development staff members don't want to do process. "There isn't enough time!" you cry. Or "Volunteers don't understand and I'll just draft it myself." If that's you, read Chapter 8 on enabling again.

Development planning depends on enabling.

Ask yourself why you do not choose to enable your board, other volunteers, and staff. The first three relationships described in this book depend on your ability to enable. Effective and productive fund development requires your enabling. Creating a fund development plan that produces ownership and results requires enabling. So get over it. Realize the importance of enabling. Learn it and do it.

Maybe it's your volunteers and your CEO who don't want to do process. Enable them to see the benefit. Or start the process yourself. You don't need their permission to plan. Simply begin the process and they will likely follow along. And if they don't, maybe you need to find another job. Perhaps people in your organization think that a fund development plan is a few pages listing solicitation activities and a timetable. Wrong! You know better than that. Convince your colleagues that fund development is more than just asking for money, more than a calendar with assignments.

Maybe your organization will have trouble with development planning because the internal relationship is not strong enough. Review Chapter 3 again, "The First Relationship—Within Your Organization." Focus on your accountability as an organizational development specialist, described in Chapter 4—"The Fund Development Professional." Help fix what's broken. Only then can fund development succeed.

The bottom line? Do what it takes. Don't avoid or compromise your planning.

Planning for the Future While Operating Today

Planning for the future occurs in tandem with current operations. While you plan, you also carry out your current business. You have a fund development plan right now. Maybe it's written and maybe it's only in your head—but you're doing something. So carry out your current plan while you devise your new plan.

As you implement your current activities, evaluate results. As you complete each fund development activity, evaluate its results in order to make decisions for the next year and the new plan. For example: Compare results to goals, and current results to prior years. Analyze return on investment and productivity. Compare cost to dollars raised. Contrast your results to standards in the industry. Search the body of knowledge and best practice for standards relevant to your organization. Don't rely on one source only. Don't focus on your own particular mission niche, either.

Always remember, data alone isn't useful. With your evaluation results in hand, analyze the trends and talk about the implications. What do these results mean for your organization? What should you do differently next year? What do you recommend for the next plan?

Make sure that you conduct this evaluation—and the ensuing strategic conversation—with leadership. Specifically, debrief and evaluate with staff (including the CEO), and with the fund development committee and the board. This evaluation and conversation develop volunteer and staff understanding and promote best practice. This process makes sure that you hear their perspective and input. You learn about their concerns and identify their barriers. Together you make decisions for next year's plan.

Keep a record of the results, trends, and implications. Document the conversation and recommendations. Record the decisions made. Then file it all for use later when you create the next fund development plan.

Our Really Big Fundraising Mistake

Before we go much further, let's confront the devil. In the press for money, too many fundraisers and their organizations make bad choices about fund development. Really bad choices. Moreover, these bad choices are often uninformed, having little to do with the body of knowledge, research, or best practice. And there's no excuse for this mistake. None whatsoever.

For example:

- Fundraisers and their organizations give lip service to donor centrism but fail to demonstrate it in attitude and behaviors, strategies and tactics.
- We act like giving is a financial transaction rather than a personal act and choice.
- We treat donors like interchangeable bank accounts anonymously standing in a queue at the automatic teller machine.
- We expect our board members to trespass on their personal and professional connections to get money and convince those connections to be interested, despite any indications to the contrary.
- Fundraisers and their organizations focus on solicitation strategies rather than relationship-building programs.
- We think relationship building is just a few outreach strategies tossed out at our convenience.
- We concentrate on major gifts from the affluent, ignoring how disrespectful and hurtful this is to others, and ultimately to our organizations, too.
- We target major gifts and major donors too often, oblivious to years of loyalty from other donors.

You know the phrase "you reap what you sow." That's what's happening. Over and over.

These bad choices produce lousy donor retention rates, devalue loyalty, and disregard lifetime value. These bad choices alienate board members who might, otherwise, successfully help. These bad choices compromise the quality of our fund development programs. These bad choices reduce the effectiveness of our fund development activities. These bad choices reinforce a sense of entitlement and an arrogance that disgraces the importance of the nonprofit/NGO sector.

And if you must have an easily grasped bottom line to convince your board and CEO: These bad choices reduce the money raised. Yes, it's true. Your organization will raise less money. How ironic. How embarrassing.

This really big mistake reminds me of Albert Einstein's comment: "The definition of insanity is doing the same thing over and over again and expecting different results."

"Stop the madness!" says colleague Sheila Appel.[2] Thanks, Sheila. That's my new battle cry. Stop the insanity. Face the truth. Stop the madness. Fix what needs to be fixed. Fix the four relationships described in this book. Use the body of knowledge to fix your fund development. Fix all this and you can respect yourself in the morning, afternoon, and evening. Fix all this and others will respect you, including your donors and volunteers. And back to that bottom line: Fix all this and you'll raise more money and keep donors loyal.

Corollary to the Really Big Mistake

The boss and the board reject the body of knowledge. Yes, there it is. The ugly truth. We do so much poor fund development. And it's hard to fix because the boss and board won't listen to qualified fundraisers following the body of knowledge.

I say again: Stop the madness! You won't get a different result if you repeat the same mistakes—or different versions of the same mistakes. Stop it.

Look back at Chapter 4, focused on the fundraising professional. There is a body of knowledge. Serving on bunches of boards does *not* mean that your board members know the body of knowledge. Operating as the CEO of the biggest and best company doesn't mean you know best practice in fund development.

Photocopy this section and give it to your boss and board. Yes, have the courage to tell them they are wrong. Hey, bosses and board members: Pay attention to qualified fundraisers. Pay attention to the body of knowledge, research, and best practice. Stop the personal opinions. Hey, fundraisers: Make sure you know the body of knowledge and have the research and best practice to back you up. Regularly share tidbits of sector research with your boss and board members. Regularly share comments from good blogs and publications. All of you, bosses, board members, and fundraisers: Don't compound the really big mistake by rejecting facts.

Involving the Board and Individual Board Members

The best development professionals work hard to involve the board of directors, the governing body. The best development professionals work just as hard to involve each individual board member. This is my job and yours. That's why we have to be good enablers, described in Chapter 8.

Please, you're not trying to make fundraising fun. Most board members won't find this fun. Don't set unrealistic expectations. Don't make them suspicious with such a silly statement. All you're trying to do is make it "less worse." You're helping the board and its members understand that this is corporate accountability and a moral and ethical expectation. It's okay if board members are reluctant, as long as they do it.

Sadly, because of "our really big fundraising mistake" and the "corollary to the really big mistake," we've taken the honor out of philanthropy and fund development. By making philanthropy a transaction, we insult. By making fund development a graceless hard-core car sale, we scare people.

Stop focusing on money each time you talk with the board and try to involve individual board members. Stop the madness! Instead, try these strategies to build understanding and ownership, and reduce discomfort. Try these strategies to involve them in the deeper meaning, and foster their respect and admiration.

- Talk about customer-centered; that will resonate with your board of directors and its members. Then draw the link to donor-centered. Invite their experiences (both good and bad). Talk about research. Brainstorm strategies and tactics your organization might introduce.
- Invite board members to share their stories about why they give to your organization. Encourage them to share their emotions. Then "heartstorm"[3] key messages for your case.
- Ask the board what kinds of gifts the organization should not accept. Invent some scenarios and talk them through. Fine-tune the conversation into a policy for board approval.
- Invite board members to share their philanthropic stories with each other. Ask them to help interview donors to collect their stories.

- At a board meeting, compare your organization's performance to the Joyaux-Ahern Donor-Centric Pledge[4]—and talk about how to make improvements.
- With the fund development committee, identify the internal strengths and weaknesses of your organization's relationship-building program. Talk about the results with the board of directors.
- At each board meeting, briefly explain a bit of information from recent sector research. Depending on the available time, talk about the implications for your organization.

Here's another idea, one of my favorites: Conduct a complain and whine session. At a board meeting, ask everyone to share his or her worst experiences as a donor or as a fundraising volunteer. This is a tell-all session. Staff (including development staff) likely have had some bad experiences, too. Share them!

First, complaining and whining can be amusing—and certainly releases tension. Second, listen well to these bad and ugly tales. In my experience, almost all of the tales result from actions that no organization should do. Take this opportunity to promise better performance by your organization. This reassures board members and staff. Donors and prospects would be pleased, too. You could even tell donors and prospects how you plan to behave. And for the few items that are, well, just reality and unavoidable (like calling when someone is eating, because everyone eats at different times)—explain how your organization will handle this as appropriately as possible.

There are so many ways to engage your board and individual board members. There are so many ways to reduce anxiety and make all this "less worse." All this is enabling. You can engage each individual board member in specific work for philanthropy and development, in fact, you must. Remember, fund development is *not* just asking for money. Your board members can make thank-you calls to donors. Your board members can help you nurture relationships at fundraising events and programs, through personal meetings. Your board members can serve on committees and task forces that focus on strategy.

It's up to you, the development professional. Polish up your enabling skills. Look in the mirror. Then go out and do it.[5]

Roles in Fund Development Planning and Execution

You'll recognize some of the roles and positions. They're similar to the roles in strategic planning, Chapter 6. You, the fundraising staff, have to understand this first. So does your CEO. Then you can work on your board chair, your board and committees, and your individual board members.

ROLE OF THE BOARD   First, the board of directors—as the governing entity—is accountable for the health and effectiveness of the corporation. Yes, you've heard that before but it bears repeating . . . over and over and . . . And the process of corporate governance is a group activity. Corporate governance is, essentially, the process of due diligence. All governance conversations and decisions belong with the board.

Of course, the staff is talking about all these same issues, making the management decisions, and implementing them. The staff provides the most in-depth body of knowledge and best practice. The staff helps identify the governance issues and enables the board to talk and decide accordingly. Think of this as checks and balances. Management and governance move back and forth on a continuum, addressing the same or highly similar issues. Where on the continuum defines which is management or governance?

The board establishes committees (e.g., fund development) to help the board carry out its governance accountabilities. For example, when it comes to money, the corporate governance responsibility is to ensure that there is money and that it is well managed, appropriately spent, and so forth. Both finance and fund development committees help the board of directors ensure all this. And the board and its committees do this in partnership with the staff, and effectively enabled by the staff.

The board is the final decision-maker for corporate governance issues. Make sure that the board participates in strategic conversation and decision-making regarding fund development. Sometimes these conversations help the board and its members learn. Sometimes these conversations share ideas. Sometimes these conversations produce governance decisions. See Key Roles in Fund Development posted on this book's website.

ROLE OF THE FUND DEVELOPMENT COMMITTEE   In summary, the purpose of the Fund Development Committee is to help the board carry out its due diligence function related to assuring fiscal health through philanthropy and fund development. The committee partners with staff to institutionalize the philanthropic process within the board and its individual members, assuring a donor-centered organization.

The Fund Development Committee is not *responsible for raising the money.*

Just like any other committee of the board—that is, a committee that helps the board fulfill its corporate governance accountabilities—the Fund Development Committee works as a group and focuses on governance only. This committee—like all other governing committees—cannot usurp the authority of the board. And this committee does not engage in or direct management. See Appendix 9-B on this book's website, "Job Description of the Fund Development Committee," for the scope of work. Review the "Key Roles in Fund Development" (Appendix 9-C on this book's website) to see how all the roles fit together.

Here in the Fund Development Committee is where board conversation starts and gathers momentum. Usually staff members talk a lot before an issue goes to the Fund Development Committee. They then share trends and preliminary implications with the committee. Staff always brings governance issues to the committee, or directly to the board if unable to meet with the committee in advance.

The committee probes, explores, and may come to some conclusions. Sometimes the committee makes recommendations to the board. But most importantly, the committee presents strategic issues to the board and engages the board in meaningful discussion and decision-making. If you don't have a Fund Development Committee, establish one now. Start its work with the fund development planning process.

ROLE OF THE DEVELOPMENT STAFF   Actually, this is the easiest part. See Chapter 4, "The Fund Development Professional," and Chapter 5, "The Art of Leadership." Read the job description of the chief development officer in Appendix 4-A, posted on this book's website.

Now the board of directors, its committee, and the individual board members just need to stay out of management work. Yes, that's hard because board and committee members know all about management and darn little about good governance. But the staff must effectively enable the board and its committees to move into the appropriate points on that continuum, focusing on corporate governance, not management. That requires the body of knowledge in governance and very, very good judgment—an obligation of staff.

Remember the process manager for institutional strategic planning? For fund development, the process manager is the chief development officer. If you don't have development staff, then it's the CEO because she serves as chief development officer. The process manager designs and manages the fund development planning process. The process manager typically writes the plan. (But for heaven's sake don't draft something for committee review without prior conversations!)

ROLE OF THE INDIVIDUAL BOARD MEMBER   Here's where the trouble usually starts. Too often, board members do not understand their roles as part of the board. Most often, board members don't recognize that corporate governance is a group process and the individual board member has a voice only as part of the group. That means, for example, the chair of the fund development committee and the chair of the board have *no* authority by virtue of their positions.

Unfortunately, staff members often don't understand these distinctions, either. So the staff doesn't enable appropriately or effectively. There's no excuse for this lapse in staff accountability. Key staff (e.g., the CEO and the chief development officer) are expected to be organizational development specialists, and must understand all this process and enabling work.

But it can get worse. Here goes: Most organizations expect their individual board members to help carry out fund development activities (e.g., relationship building and soliciting). That's not governance work. Now the board members are really confused. And the staff members who don't understand the differences, and don't enable effectively, anyway, are unable to prevent this mess or intervene thereafter.

What to do with this mess? Clean it up! Or make it not happen in the first place. That's your job, Mr. or Ms. Development Officer. Translate board work into individual board member action. Yes, the board of directors functions as a collective, and so do its governing committees. But the development operation requires that each individual board member do specific work.

Staff works with each individual board member. Secure his or her commitment to carry out a portion of the development plan. Do remember, however, not all board members will help solicit gifts. That's okay. Fund development includes many components. Engage your board members in the right components for them and for the organization. That's part of your job as an enabler.

See Exhibit 9.1, my expectations of board members in your philanthropy and fund development program. Visit the Free Download Library at www.simonejoyaux.com to see all my expectations of board members. See

Appendix 9-E on this book's website for the menu of choices offered to board members in the Women's Fund of Rhode Island fund development plan.

Exhibit 9.1   Performance Expectations for Individual Board Members

I believe in board-adopted performance expectations—applicable to all board members regardless of gender, generation, socioeconomic status, and so forth.

I believe that only one small portion of the performance expectations focuses on philanthropy and fund development. Board member performance expectations include much more than fund development, much more! See the entire list in the Free Download Library at www.simonejoyaux.com.

I believe that organizations must secure commitment to performance expectations prior to nominating anyone to the board. I expect organizations to enforce these performance expectations through the board chair and governance committee.

And I believe that board members should resign if unable to fulfill these expectations. Hey, you nonperforming board members: Don't hold the board of directors hostage. Don't make the organization have to ask you to resign.

So here are my expectations in philanthropy and fund development. Every single board member will help support the charitable contributions operation of the organization. Specifically, every single board member will:

- Reach into diverse communities and help identify and cultivate relationships to support the organization as donors, volunteers, and advocates.
- Give an annual financial contribution to the best of personal ability.
- Consider this organization one of your top two or three charitable commitments.[a]
- Participate in fund development by taking on various tasks tailored to your comfort and skills.[b]

[a]Several of my clients suggested this expectation. Do you want to find out that one of your board members doesn't love you nearly as much as he loves another board he serves on?

[b]Every year the staff and development committee help board members select what they'll do from a menu of choices.

ROLE OF OTHER STAFF IN THE ORGANIZATION   You're building a culture of philanthropy, so you need to engage staff within the organization. Involve development staff in the planning process. Involve other staff as well, but in lesser ways. (Remember they do have their own jobs.) Staff members have ideas. They have concerns that you must overcome. And the program staff lives the stories that you tell in fund development.

ROLE OF OTHER VOLUNTEERS   Great planning processes engage other fund development volunteers, not just those who serve on the board of directors. All board committees can (and I think, should) include nonboard members. Also, a really great development planning process engages donors, prospects, and even the predisposed.

Review Chapter 7, on constituency development. You'll find lots of tips about engaging donors, prospects, and the predisposed. Some of that work affects the development planning process.

The Written Fund Development Plan

It's easier to carry out the process if you have some idea of what the result might look like. What do you want in your written fund development? Remember, this is a strategic plan that the board typically sees, talks about, and endorses. This is not your detailed operating plan. Make sure you find the right balance between sufficient strategic direction and too much operational detail.

The fund development plan is a written document, used regularly by staff, the development committee, and the board of directors. Like the organization's strategic plan, the development plan sets direction, defines boundaries, and guides action.

Keep your fund development plan close at hand. Monitor progress, report on achievements, and develop interventions as necessary.

Decide the content areas of your fund development plan by facilitating a conversation with the development committee. This helps them accept the complexity, scope, and length of the resulting plan. Engage staff colleagues. Also talk briefly with the board about the scope and content of the plan.

Staff decides the format of the plan. Typically, plans include narrative sections as well as an outline of action steps/strategies and financial information. Review the common components, described in detail here. See Exhibit 9.2 for a summary. *Note:* This is neither an all-inclusive nor a requisite list. Invent what works for you. But make sure you keep key elements like relationship building and solicitation strategies, measures, assignments of accountability, and some form of calendar or timetable.

Exhibit 9.2   Contents of the Fund Development Plan

This is just one example. The table of contents of your plan may look very different. That's okay. Personalize your plan to your organization. But remember this:

- A fund development plan is not merely a list of strategies plugged into a calendar.

- Like any good plan, this plan is a stand-alone document easily understood by any reader.
- The plan is a tool for staff and board, defining general direction and outlining specific actions.

In this list, which elements are most important? Items 3 and 4, 5 and 6, 9 and 10, and 11 and 13. The rest are pretty much optional and depend on your chosen approach.

1. Organization mission and values.
2. Mission, vision, and values for fund development.
3. Strategic goals.
4. Financial goals.
5. Relationship-building strategies (cultivation and communication).
6. Solicitation strategies.
7. Retention, acquisition, and upgrading strategies.
8. Case for support—key messages.
9. Measures and benchmarks.
10. Assignments of responsibility.
11. Timetable/calendar.
12. Resources/way of working.
13. Monitoring progress and evaluating performance.

1. *Organization mission and values.*

What a great way to start your fund development plan—reiterate your mission. Consider also reprinting your values and even your vision if it's short enough.

2. *Mission, vision, and values for fund development.*

How about creating a mission, vision, and values statement for your fund development operation? Remember that your values might include the Donor Bill of Rights and a code of ethics and standards of professional practice. Naturally, you follow the organization's mission and values.

3. *Strategic goals.*

Call these whatever you wish. Just remember, these are not financial. These goals focus on such issues as: improving board recruitment so that everyone understands his or her obligation to fund development, assuring quality information for decision-making by enhanced fund development reports or a new database, strengthening board understanding of the body of knowledge and best practice through training, launching a strategic planning process to assure the organization's relevance (thus justifying fundraising), and so forth.

4. *Financial goals.*

Summarize the charitable revenue goals presented in your budget. Include financial goals for each solicitation strategy.

5. *Relationship-building strategies.*

Relationship building is the core of your development program and process, and a critical component of your written plan. Relationship building nurtures donor loyalty, ensuring profitable relationships that last. Relationship building includes donor-centered communications and donor-centered cultivation strategies.

You could organize this section by communications and cultivation strategies, or by retention and acquisition strategies. Maybe you'll focus on the target audience.

Entire books deal with this central element of fund development. For extensive detail and examples, see *Keep Your Donors: The Guide to Better Communications and Stronger Relationships*, by Ahern and Joyaux. Visit our respective websites for suggestions of other books, publications, blogs, and more that will help you with relationship building.

6. *Solicitation strategies.*

All too often, this is the only element included in fund development plans. This section outlines how you will ask for money—for example, personal face-to-face solicitation, direct mail, a special event, foundation proposals, and so forth. Usually each solicitation strategy is targeted to a particular audience.

7. *Retention, acquisition, and upgrading strategies.*

Some plans include a separate section to describe these activities. In other cases, relationship building and solicitation strategies can be described as retention, acquisition, or upgrading activities.

8. *Case for support.*

You might choose to present key messages from your case for support in your plan. Sometimes plans include fund development themes targeted to certain audiences or used with specific solicitation strategies.

9. *Measures[6] and benchmarks.*

Measures state what's important. Pick your measures carefully. In this book, benchmarks refer to the results you've targeted for your measures. For more information about measures and benchmarks, see the separate section later in this chapter.

10. *Assignments of responsibility.*

Make sure you distinguish between the responsibilities of staff and volunteers. Get each board member to take on a particular responsibility. You can even stipulate board member names in the appropriate section of the plan.

11. *Timetable/calendar.*

Decide if your plan is for the fiscal year or for multiple fiscal years. Like multiyear strategic planning, you can write a multiyear strategic fund development plan. Then annualize the plan for the specific fiscal year, stipulating benchmarks for each measure.

Outline the general time frames for the major activities. Remember that this is a strategic fund development plan, and does not include your complete operational detail. The operational detail belongs to the staff, not the board.

12. *Resources/way of working.*

Describe the resources required to do the work. This would include your budget. You might describe the hiring of a new staff person or use of a consultant. Sometimes organizations include key job descriptions in this section, in order to clarify the roles of the board of directors, development committee, development officer, and individual board members.

Be careful. This section can get too operational, inviting the board into nongovernance (and hence inappropriate) areas.

13. *Monitoring progress and evaluating performance.*

Describe how you will monitor performance. What will staff do, when, and how? What is the role of the development committee and the board? You might describe the key types of reports that you will provide for strategic discussion and decision-making.

Remember, monitor and evaluate the plan as you implement it. The staff prepares assorted fund development reports, trend analyses, and overviews of implications. The quality of information that you prepare is critical to help volunteers talk strategically and make appropriate decisions. Engage your development committee in the discussion. Make sure that the board of directors also participates in the process of monitoring and evaluating. And reserve the governance decisions for the board of directors.

In the Plan but Not about Money

Over and over I remind people that there's lots of stuff in the plan that doesn't focus on money. Lots of the plan focuses on organizational development, all that stuff in Chapters 3, 4, and 5.

What organizational development issues need to be included in your fund development plan? Review the following goals and strategies taken from various fund development plans, across diverse types and sizes of organizations.

- *Goal:* Professionalize the process of fund development within the institution.
  Strategies:
  - Put in place the appropriate systems, policies, and procedures to support a comprehensive development program.
  - Provide training and coaching for staff.
  - Establish a board-level strategic fund development committee.
  - Appoint ad hoc task forces to work on specific projects, reporting to staff and the fund development committee.
  - Set up a management information system that maintains quality information about donors and prospects.
  - Build a culture of philanthropy throughout the organization.
- *Goal:* Assure quality information to support strategic conversation and decision-making.
  Strategies:
  - Optimize use of a management information system to collect information about donors and prospects.
  - Prepare fund development reports that analyze trends and implications.
  - Engage staff, committees, and board in strategic conversations.

- *Goal:* Improve board support for philanthropy and fund development.
    Strategies:
    - Adopt policies defining the role of the board (governance) and performance expectations of board members, including specifics related to fund development.
    - Ensure that screening interviews with candidates clearly communicate the philanthropy and fund development expectations of board members, along with other performance expectations.
    - Provide training opportunities for board members to expand their familiarity with fund development and reduce their anxiety.
    - Strengthen staff's capacity to enable board members to participate in fund development.

Sample Plans

THE STEEL YARD (www.thesteelyard.org)   The Steel Yard's fund development plan was a critical part of its multiyear capacity-building consultancy. The consultancy began with a governance assessment and improvements, followed by strategic planning. With the strategic plan in hand, the Yard developed its comprehensive fund development plan. See the complete plan, Appendix 9-F, posted on this book's website.

The Steel Yard's fund development plan begins with definitions, establishing a framework for this entrepreneurial organization. The next section firmly links the fund development plan to the strategic plan.

In a section entitled "Creating the fund development plan," the Yard outlines its overall approach to fund development.

- Fund development must be both realistic and manageable—otherwise, frustration results. Obvious, but good to state and then honor.
- The Steel Yard pays attention to return on investment and uses the body of knowledge and best practice to determine ROI.
- The Yard relies on dialogue with key parties (e.g., staff, fund development committee, and board) throughout the year to build understanding and ownership. These ongoing conversations also ensure that the draft plan for each fiscal year is familiar rather than a surprise.

The plan includes goals, strategies, and measures. There's a description of the special capital initiative and the infrastructure required to support a comprehensive fund development program. The plan also includes key resources for use in fund development.

WOMEN'S FUND OF RHODE ISLAND (www.wfri.org)   Rhode Island's Women's Fund began its fund development planning process with a board conversation. The Fund Development Committee facilitated the conversation, engaging board members in evaluation of previous activities and identifying new activities.

With board insights and ideas in hand, the Fund Development Committee drafted the plan. Then the Board reviewed and formally approved the plan. See Appendix 9-E on this book's website for the complete plan.

WOMEN'S FOUNDATION OF SOUTHERN ARIZONA (www.womengiving.org)   The Women's Foundation of Southern Arizona (WFSA) serves the unique needs of women and girls through grant making, enhancing philanthropy by and for women, and focusing community attention on the status of women and girls. Here, too, the fund development plan is a direct result of the organization's six-month strategic planning process.

A key element of the WFSA plan is the statement of assumptions. Located at the start of the plan, this section sets the context for the plan and clearly states what must happen for success. This plan also includes substantial financial data.

Look at the philanthropy and development portion of WFSA's vision in Appendix 6-K on this book's website. See the complete fund development plan, Appendix 9-G, posted on the book's website.

Your Fund Development Planning Process

It's up to you. Design a process that accomplishes the benefits listed earlier in this chapter. Your process must also produce a written plan. Use the previous chapters in this book as a resource. Keep in mind: In some way, your planning process and the resulting plan tackle the items in Appendix 9-A on this book's website, "Creating the Most Effective Fund Development Program for Your Organization."

Just like strategic planning, fund development planning is a back-and-forth process. Back and forth between staff and board. Back and forth between the fund development committee and the board of directors. Keep the following in mind as you execute the planning process for fund development:

- The fund development plan belongs to the organization. This is an organization-wide strategic plan and is adopted by the board.

   From this plan, staff develop operational plans for specific activities. These operational plans do not require the approval (or even the review) of the board. The operational plans belong to the development operation, and to specific fund development task forces that take on particular activities.
- Be very careful about drafting anything. Talk first. Engage people in conversation. Capture some of their perspective and concerns first.

   Only then do you draft elements of a very preliminary plan. Forget the theory of drafting for review. It doesn't build ownership or understanding. And you might step on some pretty big toes because you don't have the benefit of advance conversations.
- Creating the development plan actually happens throughout the 12 months of the fiscal year while you're implementing the current plan.

   A more intense effort—testing the proposed organization budget and actually drafting the plan—occurs three to four months before the start of the new fiscal year. The actual time frame depends on your organization's budgeting calendar.
- The plan is not written to meet a budget or to reach a goal. Instead, this is a process that tests the feasibility of a goal or budget and negotiates that goal or budget.

- Clearly distinguish between sources of charitable contributions and solicitation strategies.

    Sources include individuals, foundations, corporations, civic groups, faith groups, and government. Your organization's budget, monthly financial reports, and year-end audit should present charitable contributions by source.

    Solicitation strategies typically include personal face-to-face solicitation, direct mail (electronic and postal service), proposals (grant applications), telephone, and special events. Your fund development plan presents information both by source and by solicitation strategy.

Gathering the Right Information

Good planning starts with the right information. You remember that from Chapter 6, on strategic planning. You know that from your own experience.

So what's the right information? Things like: relationship-building and financial results from previous years; notes from your debriefing of previous strategies and activities; observations about what worked and what didn't and why; analysis of trends and implications; body of knowledge and best practices in the field; current research that offers more and new insights.

What else?

Maybe you did a self-audit about fund development. Maybe you have an independent audit of your development operation. Identify internal strengths and weaknesses. Pay attention to external opportunities and threats. Look at what's happening in your community.

Ask the strategic and cage-rattling questions. Talk and explore. Now focus a bit more. Consider, for example, these questions:

- What can you do immediately to enhance your fund development program?
- What must you do today that will improve your effectiveness and results tomorrow?
- What do you have to do today to prepare for the future?

Defining Criteria to Select Strategies and Activities

How do you pick which strategies and activities are most appropriate to your organization? Of course, you think about return on investment (ROI). But ROI often focuses on financial results only. That's bad.

You have to decide whether you have the capability (knowledge and skills) and capacity (resources—e.g., staff, database, etc.) to do the work. Avoid the all-too-common approach: Your boss or board just expects you to do it; so you try. That may not work so well. And, yes, it's the job of the fundraising leader to enable bosses and boards to understand all this.

I've been exploring a method to help organizations choose fundraising strategies and activities.

Step 1: Define the purpose of the strategy or activity: what it hopes to achieve. For example, the purpose of a fundraising event is to generate net profit; relationship building is a secondary purpose. The purpose of a cultivation gathering is relationship building; there's no expectation of gift giving.

Step 2: With a clear definition of purpose in hand, evaluate how well the proposed strategy or activity meets key criteria. Key criteria include things like cost, workload, and so forth. A rating scale (0 to 5, with 5 being high) can help. For example: cultivation gatherings do not net a profit and are rated 0 for raising money.

Review the criteria described below. Would you eliminate any? What additional criteria might you use? Even if you don't use this process and rating scale, you must establish criteria to evaluate which strategies and activities are most appropriate for your organization. See an example of this rating system and criteria in Appendix 9-F, the Steel Yard's fund development plan, posted on this book's website.

- *Mission alignment (e.g., demonstrating the organization's mission).*

  For example, a golf tournament doesn't relate to the Steel Yard's mission. But the Iron Pour certainly demonstrates the Yard's mission and raises money. This activity receives a 5 rating for mission alignment. (Visit www.thesteelyard.org to learn about the Iron Pour. This is an amazing event!)
- *Financial cost, both direct and indirect.*

  Overestimate expenses and underestimate income. That's what my managing director and finance committee at Trinity Rep taught me back when I was the chief development officer. This approach has never failed me. The Yard's Iron Pour received a rating of 3 in this criterion.
- *Projected net profit.*

  If the purpose of the activity is to raise money, then the rating better be close to 5. If the purpose is relationship building, then the rating can be low, even 0.
- *Relationship-building opportunity.*

  Ideally, pretty much everything done in fund development should nurture relationships. How do you intentionally design relationship building to happen at your programs and fundraising events? How do you engage your board members and staff in relationship building at fundraising events? What's your follow-up relationship-building plan after a fundraising event?

  Invent cultivation gatherings with the sole purpose of relationship building. For example, in its first few years, the Women's Fund of Rhode Island (WFRI) hosted a dozen cultivation gatherings, introducing some 300 people to the organization. A significant portion of these people—but not all—became donors. WFRI cultivating gatherings received a relationship-building rating of 5 and a projected net profit of 0.
- *Audience development and community outreach.*

  Ask yourself, how might our organization reach new audiences (e.g., the predisposed)? For the Steel Yard, the Iron Pour rates high in this criterion. So does the Yard's antique auto show.
- *Institutional capability/capacity.*

  Does your organization have the skills and resources to do this work?
- *Staff workload.*

  Is this the best appropriate use of the staff's time and skills?
- *Volunteer workload.*

  Are there enough volunteers to do help execute the activity? And will there be enough volunteers to do this again and again? Don't do something that is so onerous and time-consuming that no one wants to help do it again.

- *Risk analysis.*

    Identify every kind of risk. What can you afford or not afford? Remember the difference between a risk and a gamble, presented in Chapter 6 on strategic planning.

    How about the tornado during the three-day art festival I ran as the executive director of the Lansing, Michigan, arts council/art center? Not just rain, a tornado.

- *Opportunity cost.*

    For me, this is the really big criterion. What is your organization not doing because you're doing this activity? Picking this thing to do prevents you from doing something more important. And you know what usually seems to be the opportunity cost in organizations? Face-to-face personal solicitation and relationship building.

Imagine intentionally evaluating ideas based on these kinds of criteria. Imagine debriefing each strategy or activity. You identify how to improve the strategy to justify the return on investment. Then you decide whether to pursue the strategy for the next fiscal year.

You do this throughout the year. The accumulation of these decisions provides the general direction for fund development—and the written plan—in the subsequent fiscal year.

Establishing Goals and Strategies

First, remember the warning in Chapter 6, about strategic planning: Different people use different words. It doesn't matter if you use goals or directions. Or strategies or action steps. Or whatever. Just decide and then be consistent.

Another reminder, repeated over and over: Don't focus on money only. Other goals are equally important. In some cases, nonfinancial goals are more important. For example, if you're just starting a fund development program, process and infrastructure goals might be more important. If you're growing your fund development program, goals about capacity and capability might be more important.

The Steel Yard articulated the following three goals for its fund development plan:

1. Establish the necessary infrastructure to support an effective, comprehensive philanthropy and fund development program.
2. Operate as a donor-centered organization.
3. Develop a balanced mix of sources and solicitation strategies to support operations, special projects, and capital initiatives.

For each goal, the Yard outlined strategies, general time frames, and assignments of accountability. See Appendix 9-F, the complete plan posted on this book's website.

The Community Foundation for Greater New Haven (CFGNH) focuses on endowment building. The foundation's fund development plan defines six key results, not goals:

1. Top-quality customer service.
2. Top-quality development and stewardship operation.

3. Donor-centered relationships and communications.
4. Increased endowment for Greater New Haven.
5. Enhanced measures for service, engagement, stewardship, and giving.
6. More effective community nonprofits.

Each of the results includes a set of strategies and performance measures that demonstrate achievement of the particular result. CFGNH assigned a priority ranking and lead accountability to each strategy. In addition, the foundation projected allocation of staff time and additional administrative cost. See the foundation's strategy analysis grid in Appendix 9-D on this book's website.

The Women's Fund of Rhode Island organized its fund development plan into four areas of focus: Financial Investment, Community Growth, Branding, and Infrastructure. Each area of focus included strategies for the current fiscal year. The Women's Fund also proposed additional strategies for future years. See Appendix 9-E on this book's website.

Annualizing a Multiyear Strategic Fund Development Plan

Sound familiar? See Chapter 6, "The Second Relationship—With Your Community," which focuses on institutional strategic planning.

Obviously, your fund development program and process include many of the same strategies each year. In fact, you may not add any new strategies for several years. Your organization may focus on improving current strategies.

Every board member must take on a fund development activity. Put the members' names in the plan and together they can hold themselves accountable.

You may choose to create a multiyear strategic fund development plan with strategies extending over multiple years. You'll define measures that apply to multiple years. In this scenario, you annualize the plan.

Review the annualization process for the multiyear strategic plan in Chapter 6. Now think about these annual steps for your multiyear fund development plan:

- Based on the previous year's results (and the trends and implications over multiple years), define fiscal year benchmarks for the measures in your plan.
- Based on the previous year's performance and what you've learned, outline your time frames for your strategies and tactics.
- Based on performance by volunteers and your recruitment of new volunteers, figure who should do what—the assignment of accountability.

Measuring and Benchmarking for Fund Development

So much to measure, so little time. But for sure, don't measure money only. Please.

Measures describe what you want to evaluate. And evaluating results is more than money or retention rates or number of donors. Measuring results might include donor centrism, donor satisfaction, effectiveness of relationship building, and much more. Then you set benchmarks for a particular period. Benchmarks quantify and qualify your hoped-for results for the particular measures.

For example:

- The measure might be volunteer participation. The benchmark might be recruiting two new volunteers to participate in face-to-face personal solicitation.
- The measure might be newsletter effectiveness. The benchmark might be producing four issues with content, writing, and readability all adhering to the body of knowledge.
- The measure might be number of donors. The benchmarks might be increasing the number of donors by 10 percent and increasing retention rates to 75 percent.

You might set benchmarks compared to your own performance. You might also set benchmarks compared to standards in the sector or in your particular line of work.

What should you measure? Here are just a few ideas:

- Your organization's donor-centric quotient.
- Quality and effectiveness of your relationship-building program—from the donor's perspective, and based on your inputs into the process.
- Quality and effectiveness of your solicitation program—from the donor's perspective, and the results produced.
- Quality and effectiveness of your donor-centered communications—from content to writing to readability.
- Volunteer participation in relationship building and solicitation, including board members and others.
- Mix of sources of charitable contributions and solicitation strategies.
- Diversity of donors and volunteers.

And really, that's just the tip of the iceberg. Of course, you'll measure the money, too. Things like:

- Donor retention, acquisition, and attrition rates.
- Number of predisposed identified and then qualified as prospects.
- Number of qualified prospects who transition into donors.
- Number of first-time donors who give a second gift.
- Cumulative gifts given by a donor in a year.
- Lifetime value of donors.
- Diversity of donors.
- Gift ranges, gift sizes, and increases and decreases in gifts.
- Number of attendees and repeat attendees at cultivation and fundraising events.

And there's more to measure here, too.

Where do you get your ideas for measuring? Take a look at Exhibit 9.3, sample measures from the Steel Yard. Review the measures defined in the fund development plans posted on this book's website.

Exhibit 9.3   Sample Measures for the Steel Yard's Fund Development Plan

Goal 1: Establish the necessary infrastructure to support an effective, comprehensive philanthropy and fund development program.
   A few of the key measures for this goal:

- Staff, board, and other fundraising volunteers respect, accept, and use the most critical best practices in fund development.
- Participation rates of board members in pledging and pledge payment.
- Participation rates of board members and other volunteers in helping with fund development.
- Adoption of and adherence to key policies.
- Establishment of a formal Fund Development Committee.
- Breadth and depth of information in the Steel Yard database, with an emphasis on interests and disinterests, motivations and aspirations.
- Quality of reports to inform conversation and support strategic decision-making.

Need more ideas for useful and informative measures? Find out what others are doing:

- Talk with your professional colleagues. What do they measure and why? How do their measures add value to creating a quality donor-centered fund development program?
- Read the blogs and read the research.
- Read Chapter 24 in *Keep Your Donors: The Guide to Better Communications and Stronger Relationships*. You'll find lots of ideas for measuring relationship building—both from the donor perspective and from your perspective. Read Chapters 19 and 22 and 23 in *Keep Your Donors*. You'll learn about measuring your communications.
- Read Jim Greenfield's book *Fund-Raising Cost Effectiveness: A Self-Assessment Workbook*.
- See Sargeant, Shang, and Associates' book *Fundraising Principles and Practice*.
- Look at Mallabone and Balmer's *The Fundraising Audit Handbook*.

Honestly, it's not hard to identify things to measure—as long as you direct your attention beyond money. What's harder to do? Figuring out the process for measuring and then analyzing the trends and implications. What's still harder to do? Allocating the resources to do this critical work and engaging staff and board colleagues in strategic conversation. But this is important work. Do it. Demand that of yourself and your organization.

Here's another idea: project the likelihood of achieving your benchmarks. You could specify a percentage or use a numeric scale. For example:

- Measure: Board member participation in giving.
  Benchmark for this measure: 100 percent.
  Likelihood of achieving this benchmark: 100 percent. (And if the likelihood of achieving this benchmark isn't 100 percent, then remember enabling function #18: You need to enhance the attrition of some of your board members.)
- Measure: Donor retention rate.
  Benchmark for this measure: 75 percent, an increase of 10 percent from the previous year.
  Likelihood of achieving this benchmark: 50 percent (or 5 on a 10-point scale).

Interfacing Your Fund Development Plan with Your Budgeting Process

Here's the really big question: How does your organization set the charitable contributions goal for the fiscal year? Here's the really bad answer: The charitable contributions goal depends on how much money our organization needs to do our great work for the new fiscal year.

Why is that such a bad answer? Because many variables affect your ability to raise charitable gifts. And one of the least important variables—yes, least important—is how much money you want and need to do your work.

Why is "how much you want and need" so unimportant? Just because you want it doesn't mean you can get it. First, remember all those really bad choices that organizations make—and then reap what they sow? How does your organization compare to all those? Because how you compare to the really bad choices affects your ability to raise gifts.

Your fund development goal depends on internal and external variables. How much money you want and need is not the driving force.

There's more—what's happening in the outside world. Consider the effect of the external environment on your organization's ability to secure gifts. For example: the economy, societal trends, demographics, technology, government regulation and legislation, nonprofit/NGO sector credibility, and more.

Still there's more. Think about the factors within your organization (e.g., capacity and capability). For example: relevance of your mission and quality of your program; board recruitment and training; willingness of your board members to take on relationship-building and solicitation activities; your donor-centric quotient; staff capability (e.g., body of knowledge); organizational capacity (e.g., sufficient resources and the right resources); use of research in the field and within the organization; quality of your relationship-building program; number of predisposed and qualified prospects in the pipeline; effectiveness of your solicitation activities; and more.

Linking to Your Fiscal Year

Typically, your fund development plan coincides with your fiscal year and your budget. Organizations create an annual development plan or a multiyear plan. The best approach is to approve the fiscal year budget and the fund development plan at the same time. The fund development plan describes how your organization will secure the charitable contributions presented in the budget.

Staff and finance committee typically draft the budget. The charitable contributions portion of the budget usually reflects what the organization must raise in order to do what it wants to do. But rarely does the budgeting process test the likelihood of raising the money. Sure, the charitable contributions goal usually reflects actual results and trends from prior years. But often there's not sufficient examination of the many variables proposed at the start of this section.

Testing the Charitable Contributions Goal

Testing the charitable contributions goal means evaluating the organization's capacity and capability to raise money. Testing the charitable contributions goal means figuring out how much the organization is likely to be able to raise—and then comparing that to how much you actually want. And smart organizations adopt a budget based on what you can do, not what you want. Is your organization smart? Or not so smart? See the dismaying budgeting in Exhibit 9.4.

Exhibit 9.4   Dismaying Budgeting

Over and over I explain to clients how important it is to test the charitable contributions goal with a good fund development planning process. I remind them that adopting a budget without this testing process is risky.

Some organizations adopt a budget with how much they want and need. They disregard what good planning tells them. Here's what these organizations say:

- "Well, you know, we'll just work harder." Board members say that with a combined shrug and hands thrown in the air. But it doesn't work. The fund development plan already requires harder work, more time commitment, and tasks carried out by board members. The organization has to cut expenses in midyear. Or there's a deficit.
- "Maybe someone will die. Someone has for the past several years and we got a bequest." Yes, that's a direct quote. This organization (and others like it) wait for people to die. The bequest—hopefully unrestricted—compensates for bad budgeting and a faulty fund development plan that no one really intended to carry out. I don't know if someone died by year-end; I didn't bother to check.

(continued)

> *(Continued)*
>
> ■ "God will provide." Board and staff said that with solemn, pious faces. But I thought gods and goddesses helped those who helped themselves? What will your goddess think when she realizes that you planned poorly and expected her to take care of you? These organizations ran into trouble, too.

The testing process is the fund development planning process. The process covers 13 steps. The process:

1. Conducts a SWOT analysis for the organization and the fund development program, examining internal strengths and weaknesses and external opportunities and threats. Outlines ways to address the SWOT results and talks with the board about its willingness to address the results.

   This happens throughout the year. No need to wait until there's a draft budget.

2. Reviews the evaluation results of current-year fund development activities and examines the recommendations and decisions made. What did staff and board agree to do? Are these still likely and what is required to accomplish these?

   This happens throughout the year, too, at the conclusion of each activity. Then review again, as you begin to write the development plan for the new fiscal year or as you begin the annualization process.

3. Analyzes all donors (individually or by some form of segmentation into particular audiences) and determines the likely changes—for example, retention, gift increases or decreases and how they might happen, and attrition.

   This may happen throughout the year, but with greater focus near the end of the fiscal year, testing for the new year. Use this step to estimate potential income for the next fiscal year.

4. Evaluates the predisposed and qualified prospects to determine readiness for solicitation and potential new gifts for the new fiscal year and its plan.

   This may happen throughout the year, but with greater focus near the end of the fiscal year, anticipating the next year. Use this step to estimate potential income for the next fiscal year.

5. Figures out what has to be done to build relationships with diverse constituencies.

   This is an ongoing activity throughout the year. As the current year draws to a close, you project what to continue or discontinue, expand or add for the new fiscal year.

6. Explores new fund development activities and decides what resources are necessary to carry these out and what level of dollars might result.

   This is an ongoing activity throughout the year. As the current year draws to a close, you project what to continue or discontinue, expand or add for the new fiscal year.

7. Outlines the staff and volunteer resources necessary to enhance current-year activities and launch new activities.

   This is an ongoing activity throughout the year. As the current year draws to a close, you figure out if volunteers (including board members) will step up and perform. And if you don't have the staff and volunteers necessary, the organization does *not* increase its scope of work.

8. Estimates financial costs to do the work outlined.

    This is part of the budgeting process for the new fiscal year.

9. Synthesizes everything. Adds up the money, both income and expense. Adds up the human resources, volunteer and staff.

    Now you focus more intensely on the new fund development plan for the new fiscal year.

10. Compares the resulting likely money to be raised in charitable contributions to how much the organization wants and needs.

    This happens late in the current fiscal year, while developing the proposed budget for the new fiscal year. How do the two bottom lines compare—the money that can be raised and the money desired?

11. Shares findings from the planning process with the board and determines organization readiness to do what it takes.

    Look back at #7, for example.

12. Confirms or secures individual board member support to take on specific activities within the plan.

    A plan isn't a plan until people agree to take on the activities. Don't approve the plan—and the budget—without confirmation that specific board members and other volunteers will help carry out specific activities.

13. Recommends final budget figures for charitable contributions for the new year.

    Yes, it's the fund development planning process that recommends what the charitable contributions goal can be. Some organizations present a conservative income figure, with a more aggressive figure that is the hoped-for goal. The smart organization uses the conservative figure for actual budgeting.

USING A GIFT TABLE   Here's another strategy to help set your charitable contributions goal: Use a gift table. Fundraisers typically use gift tables for capital campaigns. Construction of a gift table depends on mathematical calculations gleaned from the analysis of hundreds and hundreds of capital campaigns conducted over decades and decades.

But gift tables are also useful for annual operating support. This approach can help your organization understand the context for raising contributions. The gift analysis can also help determine the likelihood of achievement.

First, construct a gift table representing your current donors. Pull these numbers from your current database for your current fiscal year. Put this together based on the cumulative gifts given by a donor during the fiscal year. Consider that total the donor's gift for the year. For example, Simone gave you four gifts of $25 each, which makes her a $100 donor.

How many donors do you have at what levels? There are no standard gift levels. Personalize the gift table to your gift levels (e.g., 100 gifts at $25; 57 gifts at $50; 32 gifts at $250, and so forth).

Analyze your gift table and the donors in it. Estimate how many donors might increase their gifts and to what level. Add it up. Examine the mathematical elements of the very traditional capital campaign gift table. For example:

- Fully 80 to 90 percent of the money comes from 10 to 20 percent of the donors.
- The top 10 gifts typically produce a minimum of 40 to 50 percent of the goal.

- About 35 to 45 percent of the goal comes from the next 100 gifts.
- An organization needs four times as many prospects as gifts needed because half of the prospects may give half of what they were asked for.
- The lead gift is typically 10 percent of the total goal.

Using this information, construct a traditional gift table to test how many contributions at which levels are necessary to raise your targeted goal. Now compare the two gift tables: the table with your current donors and contributions, and the version with traditional calculations. How close are these two tables? Next, identify donors and prospects for each gift level in the gift table you've constructed to make your goal. Fill in names for each gift level.

Identify where your current donors will fall within the gift table constructed to make your goal. Which of your donors are most likely to increase their gifts and to what level? Which of your donors might decrease their current gifts and to what level? Next, evaluate the likelihood that your qualified prospects are ready to be asked in the new fiscal year. Determine how much is appropriate to ask them to consider. Then evaluate again: What's the likelihood that the prospects will give what you ask for? If the likelihood isn't 75 percent or more, then don't count their gift at the requested amount; reduce the amount that might come in.

Here's that good old bottom line: If you cannot identify enough donors and prospects to fill out the gift table, how do you expect to raise the money? This is less hard to do—even becomes easier to do—the better you know your donors and prospective donors. And that, of course, is the purpose of relationship building, a key element of your fund development plan.

Summary

The fund development plan provides the framework for your development program. Develop a plan effectively and work that plan well. Then you'll see a difference in attitude, accountability, and productivity.

The process of creating the development plan is as important as the resulting plan. A good process produces ownership of the plan, assures shared accountability, and achieves your targeted results.

The challenge, of course, is the process itself. A good process depends on the four relationships described in this book. In particular, a good process requires highly effective enabling by the process manager, typically the development officer.

Your fundraising goal—the money goal—depends on the availability of donors and qualified prospects, and the capability and capacity of your organization to do the work.

Each of the prior chapters in this book contains ideas that are helpful to the development planning process. For example, see Chapter 8 for a review of values clarification, group process, conversation, and participatory decision-making. Take another look at managing change and leadership, Chapter 5.

See Chapter 6 for a detailed description of strategic planning. You can apply most—if not all—of this to your fund development planning. In Chapter 7, review the ways to engage constituents in the development process. Use some of these ideas for your planning. Finally, Chapter 8 describes your role as the principal enabler. The proverbial ball is in your court. Take it!

CHAPTER 10

Going Back to the Beginning
In Conclusion

The pressure to raise money is such that everyone seems content to overstep relationship bounds with the hope that the donor won't mind. . . . We see development as a chore rather than an exciting opportunity to grow a movement. . . .

We see donors as a means to achieving organizational goals, as opposed to a partner in organizational success. We're afraid donors are going to try to change us, and we don't think we can change, so we don't really want to hear their advice.

We don't think of their gifts as an action as valuable as our programmatic efforts. We think of their gifts as something that we earned because of our programmatic efforts, which means our donors shouldn't have a say in our programs.

—Brittany Janis, Cohort 19, Master of Arts Program in Philanthropy
and Development, Saint Mary's University of Minnesota

It was relationship building that really motivated my community members to reach out to one another. It was about the people as a whole, what we became when we joined together in a common cause. It was being the painters of the bigger picture and being painted into the bigger picture, thus creating a sense of belonging.

—Danielle Gines

Longing to belong. Isn't that part of human nature? Afraid of being forgotten. Isn't that part of being human, too?

Through relationships with others, we belong. Through commitment to community, we won't be forgotten.

No matter how difficult, millions of donors, volunteers, and staff around the world work together to build better communities. Together, people of every culture participate in philanthropy.

The philanthropic process brings people together in acts of giving. Participating in this experience enhances one's own life significantly. The act of giving is shared among the donor, the cause, and an organization that responds to both the cause and the donor.

Philanthropy's essential partner, fund development, is the means for nurturing relationships and securing contributions. But fund development depends on the entire organization for success. And, effective organizations—and their fund development programs—depend on four fundamental relationships:

1. The organization's internal relations—its values, culture, leadership, adaptive capacity, and so forth.
2. The organization's relationship with the community—its relevance to the community, articulated through strategic planning.
3. The organization's relationship with its constituents—in particular, its donor-centered behavior.
4. The organization's relationship with its volunteers—the ability to enable them to work well on behalf of the cause.

Each of these four relationships depends on the basic principle of marketing, which says: "It's not what you're selling that matters; it's what I'm buying that counts."

Even more simply put, this statement means that you must pay attention to your various constituencies, whether the "I" is a donor or volunteer, or the people working in your organization, or other organizations working in your community.

Make no mistake. The survival of your organization depends on developing these four relationships. Together, these relationships make a healthy organization. Together, these relationships can produce more philanthropic dollars.

The most successful organizations recognize that each relationship is a contributor to and a beneficiary of the other relationships. These organizations know that the four relationships interrelate into one interdependent system, each relationship adding value to the others.

The most competent professionals see the entire complex system. These professionals—including the fundraisers—are leaders, enablers, and managers. The most accomplished fundraisers are much more than master technicians. The best fundraisers are organizational development specialists, too. They understand, develop, and nurture the four relationships.

Do you want to raise more money? Does your organization want to thrive, not merely survive? Then make change. Don't get ready for it—do it!

Most organizations need to change in some way. Yours probably does, too. Most individuals can benefit from questioning, learning, and change. Get ready for your own personal change, too.

The reward is more than survival. With the four relationships in place, an organization can do everything better, including fund development. Without these relationships, nothing will be done well enough.

Why bother to do all this? Because the reward is an organization and constituents who react like the contestants in the Seattle stadium, watching the Special Olympics. Because the reward is organizational success, not just survival.

And the success of your organization matters only because of the difference to communities. Strong philanthropic organizations make a difference in their communities. That's what matters.

David Ben Gurion said, "In order to be a realist, you must believe in miracles." I do. Do you?

List of Appendices on the Companion Website

All appendices for *Strategic Fund Development* are posted on the book's companion website. Please visit www.wiley.com/go/strategic and enter password "strategic123" to download these materials.

Some of the documents are "read only." Other documents are available for you to access and modify for your own organization.

In some cases—as noted—you may find updated versions on my website at www.simonejoyaux.com. I regularly modify my materials and then post newer versions on my own website.

For more information, regularly visit www.simonejoyaux.com: Read my weekly blogs with professional tips, pet peeves, and personal rants. Check out the booklists and links. Visit my Free Download Library that includes materials on governance and other topics. Subscribe to my free e-newsletter (and visit the archive).

Chapter 1: Let's Start Here: An Important Introduction

Appendix 1-A: Basic Principles of Fund Development (Read only)
Appendix 1-B: Myth of More Visibility and "Greater Community Awareness" (Read only)
Appendix 1-C: The Donor-Centric Pledge (Read only)
Appendix 1-D: Nothing Can or Should Substitute for Philanthropy (Read only)
Appendix 1-E: Philanthropy's Moral Dilemma (Read only)

Chapter 2: Positioning Your Organization to Survive and Thrive: The Four Relationships That Are Critical to Effective and Productive Fund Development (and Healthy Organizations)

This chapter does not have any appendices or documents.

Chapter 3: The First Relationship—Within Your Organization: Creating the Infrastructure That Produces a Healthy Organization

Appendix 3-A: Questions for Building an Effective Board (Read only. Visit www.simonejoyaux.com for periodic updates to this document.)
Appendix 3-B: Tips for Consensus Decision-Making (Read only)

Chapter 4: The Fund Development Professional: Choosing Your Road—Organizational Development Specialist or Just Another Fundraising Technician

Appendix 4-A: Job Description for a Chief Development Officer (Available for you to access. Visit www.simonejoyaux.com for periodic updates to this document.)

Chapter 5: The Art of Leadership: A Critical Element of the First Relationship—Within Your Organization

This chapter does not have any appendices or documents.

Chapter 6: The Second Relationship—With Your Community: Ensuring Your Organization's Relevance through Strategic Planning

Appendix 6-A: Sample Governance Self- Assessment (Available for you to access. Visit www.simonejoyaux.com for periodic updates to this document.)

Appendix 6-B: Focus group and key informant questions for the Audubon Society of Rhode Island and the Steel Yard (Read only)

Appendix 6-C: Focus group and key informant questions for the Women's Foundation of Southern Arizona (Read only)

Appendix 6-D: Wethersfield (CT) Public Library Patron Survey (Read only)

Appendix 6-E: Member/Donor Survey for the Audubon Society of Rhode Island (Read only)

Appendix 6-F: Strategic planning kickoff agenda for the Steel Yard (Read only)

Appendix 6-G: Sample retreat formats (Read only)

Appendix 6-H: Strategic Planning Retreat agenda for the Steel Yard (Read only)

Appendix 6-I: Strategic Planning Retreat agenda for the United Way of Dutchess County (Read only)

Appendix 6-J: Sample tables of contents for information packets (Read only)

Appendix 6-K: Vision Statement of the Women's Foundation of Southern Arizona (Read only)

Appendix 6-L: Strategic Plan for the Audubon Society of Rhode Island (Read only)

Appendix 6-M: Strategic plan for the Steel Yard (Read only)

Appendix 6-N: Strategic plan for the United Way of Dutchess County (Read only)

Appendix 6-O: Strategic plan for the YMCA of Greater Providence (Read only)

Chapter 7: The Third Relationship—With Your Constituents: Nurturing Relationships to Build Loyalty

Appendix 7-A: Cultivation Ideas (Read only)

Chapter 8: The Fourth Relationship—With Your Volunteers: Enabling Them to Take Meaningful Action on Behalf of Your Organization

Appendix 8-A: Passionate Board Member Running Wild: A Real-Life Story with an Enabling Response (Read only)

Appendix 8-B: Assess Your Performance as an Enabler (Available for you to access)

Appendix 8-C: Questions of meaning about volunteerism (Read only. Visit www.simonejoyaux.com for periodic updates to this document.)

Chapter 9: Creating the Most Effective Fund Development Plan for Your Organization: A Plan That Produces Ownership and Results

Appendix 9-A: Creating the Most Effective Fund Development Program for Your Organization (Read only. Visit www.simonejoyaux.com for periodic updates to this document.)

Appendix 9-B: Job Description of the Fund Development Committee (Available for you to access. Visit www.simonejoyaux.com for periodic updates to this document.)

Appendix 9-C: Key Roles in Fund Development (Read only. Visit www.simone joyaux.com for periodic updates to this document.)

Appendix 9-D: Strategy analysis grid (with measures) for the Community Foundation for Greater New Haven (Read only)

Appendix 9-E: Fund development plan for the Women's Fund of Rhode Island (Read only)

Appendix 9-F: Fund development plan for the Steel Yard (Read only)

Appendix 9-G: Fund development plan for the Women's Foundation of Southern Arizona (Read only)

Notes

Chapter 1: Let's Start Here: An Important Introduction

1. Robert L. Payton, *Philanthropy: Voluntary Action for the Public Good* (New York: American Council on Education/Macmillan). For years, I've used the definition "philanthropy is voluntary action for the common good." I've attributed this to Bob Payton, based on my participation in the Executive Leadership Institute that he facilitated in February 1992, sponsored by AFP (then called NSFRE). And only now, while writing this third edition, did I notice that he actually says, "voluntary action for the public good." I wonder if, during the institute, Bob actually used the two phrases interchangeably? Or did I translate "public good" into "common good"? The concept of the commons does exist. And it does refer to community and public. Well, I just don't know. And no matter. I plan to continue using "voluntary action for the common good."

2. Robert H. Bremner, *American Philanthropy*, 2nd ed. (Chicago: University of Chicago Press), 3.

3. Chuck Collins and Pam Rogers with Joan P. Garner, *Robin Hood Was Right: A Guide to Giving Your Money for Social Change* (New York: W.W. Norton), 15.

4. Learn about social justice philanthropy, an essential element of philanthropy. Visit www.simonejoyaux.com for resources.

5. Collins and Rogers with Garner, *Robin Hood Was Right*, 15.

6. Henry A. Rosso and Associates, *Achieving Excellence in Fundraising*, edited by Eugene R. Tempel (San Francisco: Jossey-Bass, 2003), 3.

7. First published in 1996 as *The NSFRE Fund-Raising Dictionary* (editors Levy and Cherry), the dictionary is now online at www.afpnet.org. And speaking of AFP, visit the Resource Center, a valuable source of information and examples for your work.

8. Visit the Nonprofit Finance Fund at www.nff.org to learn more. Also read these articles: "Delivering on the Promise of Nonprofits," by Bradach, Tierney, and Stone, *Harvard Business Review* (December 2008); "Hidden in Plain Sight," by C. Miller, *Nonprofit Quarterly* (Spring 2003); and Miller's article "The Looking Glass World of Nonprofit Money," *Nonprofit Quarterly* (Spring 2005); and read "The Nonprofit Starvation Cycle," by Gregory and Howard, *Stanford Social Innovation Review* (Fall 2009).

9. Waldemar A. Nielsen, "The Third Sector: Keystone of a Caring Society," an Occasional Paper (Washington, DC: Independent Sector, 1990). Nielsen presented this paper at the 25th anniversary conference of the National Council on Philanthropy, Denver, Colorado, November 1979. At the time, he was Senior Fellow, Aspen Institute for Humanistic Studies.

10. Nielsen, "Third Sector," 1.

11. Ibid., 5.

12. Ibid., 8.

13. An epigram by Jean-Baptiste Alphonse Karr in the January 1849 issue of his journal *Les Guêpes* ("The Wasps").

14. Nielsen, "Third Sector," 4.

15. Read these great articles about the nonprofit sector and democracy, in the *Nonprofit Quarterly*: "Nonprofits Help Make Us Good Citizens," Arthur C. Brooks, Summer 2005; "Powerful Nonprofit Leadership: The D Factor," the editors, Spring 2008; "The Commons: Our Mission If We Choose to Accept It," Roger Lohmann, Summer 2003; "The Greatest Leadership Challenge: Renewing Our Belief in Democracy and Political Advocacy," Scott Harshbarger, Summer 2003; "Who's Promoting the *General* Welfare," Jeff Madrick, Summer 2003. Subscribe to the *Nonprofit Quarterly*. It's a great thinking magazine and regularly writes about social justice, democracy, and change (www.nonprofitquarterly.org). Read *Stanford Social Innovation Review*, too (www.ssireview.org).

16. Alexis de Tocqueville, *Democracy in America,* Chapter 11, "Political Associations in the United States," The Henry Reeve Text as revised by Francis Bowen and further corrected by Phillips Bradley (New York: Modern Library, 1945), 101.

17. Harvey C. Mansfield and Delba Winthrop, trans., ed., *Democracy in America* by Alexis de Tocqueville. Book II, Chapter 5 (Chicago: University of Chicago Press, 2000), 492.

18. Michael Edwards, *Small Change: Why Business Won't Save the World* (San Francisco: Berrett-Koehler, 2008, 2010). Edwards gives us some history and good explanations of key concepts. He dissects, questions, and compliments. He offers specific steps for reforming philanthropy and assuring social transformation. He makes us think—and that is good and necessary. Read this book. Read, too, Mal Warwick's letter to the editor commenting on Edwards's premise: "Power to the People!" *Stanford Social Innovation Review* 8, no. 3 (Summer 2010). In that same issue, read "The Mouths of Gift Horses: Nonprofits Should Court Contributions That Help Both Themselves and Society," by Henry E. Riggs.

19. Edwards, *Small Change*, 3.

20. Ibid., 2.

21. Ibid., 6.

22. Ibid., 8.

23. Ibid., 8.

24. Ibid., 24.

25. See the Donor-Centric Pledge in *Keep Your Donors* and at www.simonejoyaux.com. Click on Resources/Free Library/Fund Development/Relationship Building.

26. See the research of Dr. Antoine Bechara and Dr. Antonio Damasio, described in Tom Ahern's books on donor communications (www.aherncomm.com). Psychologist W. Gerrod Parrott identifies many more than seven emotions. See his full list in *Keep Your Donors: The Guide to Better Communications and Stronger Relationships*, where you can read all about emotions, why they matter, and how to use them appropriately and well.

27. Seth Godin, *Permission Marketing: Turning Strangers into Friends, and Friends into Customers* (New York: Simon & Schuster, 1999), 10.

28. See lots of details about identifying the predisposed, qualifying them as prospects, and nurturing the relationship in *Keep Your Donors*.

29. Visit CFRE International (www.cfre.org), the baseline certification for fundraisers worldwide. Click on the Test Content Outline, which describes the required knowledge for a fundraiser with five years of experience. See also *Fundraising Principles and Practice* by Sargeant, Shang, and Associates.

30. Read the *Donor Bill of Rights* and the *AFP Code of Ethical Principles and Standards of Professional Practice* at www.afpnet.org. Also visit www.simonejoyaux.com.

31. Visit www.cfre.org and learn about the baseline certification for fundraisers worldwide. Visit the Association for Healthcare Philanthropy (www.ahp.org) for the advanced credential of FAHP. Visit the Association of Fundraising Professionals (www.afpnet.org) to learn about the ACFRE, another advanced credential for fundraisers.

32. Authors William Landes Foster, Peter Kim, and Barbara Christiansen describe 10 funding models and encourage nonprofits to clearly identify and communicate their model.

33. I'm not referring to street fundraising. I use the term "personal face-to-face solicitation" according to the meaning in North America: Representatives of the organization (e.g., a staff and board member) meet personally with a qualified prospect, requesting a gift in a way that is personalized to the prospect. Remember the fundraising mantra: The right person(s) asking the right prospect for the right gift for the right project at the right time in the right way.

34. For more than 50 years, the Giving USA Foundation has researched giving. Its annual reports on U.S. philanthropy provide critical information for fundraisers and their organizations, policy makers and donors, and social observers (www.givingusa.org).

35. *Giving USA 2010* estimates a 3.2 percent decline in giving for the year 2009, not as dire as earlier recession years. For example, in 1974, giving fell by 5.5 percent, after inflation adjustment. Total estimated giving for 2009 was 2.1 percent of gross domestic product (GDP). The highest ever was 2.3 percent of GDP. One more point regarding the stickiness of philanthropy: *Giving USA*'s research finds that when compared to the Standard & Poor's 500 index, giving doesn't rise as quickly, nor does giving fall as steeply when the index declines. Visit www.givingusa.org. Every fundraiser should read this—and discuss the trends and implications with bosses and boards.

Chapter 2: Positioning Your Organization to Survive and Thrive: The Four Relationships That Are Critical to Effective and Productive Fund Development (and Healthy Organizations)

1. John W. Gardner, *Building Community* (Washington, DC: Independent Sector, 1991).
2. Ibid., 10.
3. Ibid., 9.
4. In response to the growth of the nonprofit/NGO sector, the UN developed recommendations for economic data gathering and reporting internationally. The UNSD enlisted the services of the Johns Hopkins Center for Civil Society Studies to produce a *Handbook on Non-Profit Institutions in the System of National Accounts*, issued in December 2003. In 2007, the Center for Civil Society Studies produced *Measuring Civil Society and Volunteering: Initial Findings from Implementation of the UN Handbook on Nonprofit Institutions.*
5. Social capital reminds me of "webs of connectedness," a phrase from Peter Senge, guru of learning organization theory. Read more about his theory in Chapter 3.
6. Robert D. Putnam, *Bowling Alone: The Collapse And Revival of American Community.* (New York: Simon & Schuster, 2000).
7. I used this specific example in my book *Keep Your Donors*, published in 2008. As of this moment, the global economic recession is over, although unemployment is still very high. General Motors is healthier. And yes, GM is apparently discontinuing its Hummer. But is that because GM wants to reduce the number of car models it produces—or is it because of peer pressure, social capital that demands cars with less environmental impact?

    Let me add this thought: Think about the implications of for-profit or nonprofit corporations in the building or destruction of social capital, and then the impact on civic capacity and civil society. I wonder if GM thought about that at all as it ran itself into the ground? How about your organization? As you think about going out of business—slowly or quickly—I imagine you think about the loss of services to clients and loss of jobs to employees. But do you think about the broader impact? On social capital in the community, on the community's civic capacity, and hence on civil society?
8. Putnam, *Bowling Alone,* 289.

9. In *Keep Your Donors*, I included the example: "Your donors assume you're using their gifts as directed." It's not included here because it seems our donors keep wondering how we're using their gifts. They're wondering how we're using their gifts because we are not clearly communicating how. So that makes me think that pretty soon, they'll move from wondering to being suspicious. And that's going to breach the social capital.

10. Alexis de Tocqueville, *Democracy in America,* Chapter 11, "Political Associations in the United States," The Henry Reeve Text as revised by Francis Bowen and further corrected by Phillips Bradley (New York: Modern Library, 1945), 404.

11. In an organizational setting, we call this ability "organizational capacity." There's an entire theory and approach called "capacity building" for the nonprofit/NGO sector. The intention of capacity building is to ensure that the organization has the capacity to achieve its mission. Unfortunately, the sector doesn't invest sufficient resources—both time and money—to build capacity. Instead, nonprofits allocate most resources specifically to mission, forgetting that without capacity, mission falters.

12. Ian I. Mitroff, Richard I. Mason, and Christine M. Pearson, *Framebreak: The Radical Redesign of American Business* (San Francisco: Jossey-Bass, 1994), 20.

13. Robert Coles, "Doing Well by Doing Good: Why We Volunteer," *Advancing Philanthropy* 2 (Spring 1994): 14–16.

Chapter 3: The First Relationship—Within Your Organization: Creating the Infrastructure That Produces a Healthy Organization

1. Daniel J. Boorstin (1914–2004) was a Pulitzer Prize-winning historian, prolific author, and university professor. He served as the Librarian of Congress from 1975 to 1987.

2. Mallabone and Balmer, *The Fundraising Audit Handook* (Toronto: Civil Sector Press, 2010). This handbook is useful. The audit tool includes eight modules critical to success:

    Module #1: Governance Environment
    Module #2: External Environment
    Module #3: Fundraising Track Record
    Module #4: Constituency Analysis
    Module #5: Program Maturity
    Module #6: Resource Availability
    Module #7: Fundraising Culture
    Module #8: The Donor Perspective

    Within each module, you'll find statements of best practices. Then you'll face the really big evaluation questions: Do we operate this way? Should we operate this way? You'll add up your responses and get your organization's score. You'll analyze the results and talk with your colleagues. Then ... you'll fix it. There's lots more to this handbook. Get your copy and try this assessment.

3. David S. Pottruck and Terry Pearce, *Clicks and Mortar: Passion Driven Growth in an Internet World* (San Francisco: Jossey-Bass, 2000), 26.

4. Ian Mitroff, Richard O. Mason, and Christine O. Pearson, *Framebreak: The Radical Redesign of American Business* (San Francisco: Jossey-Bass, 1994), 65.

5. Pottruck and Pearce, *Clicks and Mortar*, 245.

6. Posited by Kurt Lewin, American psychologist, 1896–1947.

7. See Shankar Vedantum's book *How Our Unconscious Minds Elect Presidents, Control Markets, Wage Wars, and Save Our Lives.* He describes overly cohesive, insular groups—for example, suicide bombers. It turns out that small, isolated groups can rewrite norms. Their intense loyalties, one to the other, trump the loyalties and norms of society.

8. Irving L. Janis, *Groupthink*, 2nd ed. (Boston: Houghton Mifflin, 1982), 9.

9. Frank E. Harrison, *The Managerial Decision-Making Process*, 3rd ed. (Boston: Houghton Mifflin, 1987), 271.

10. Jerry B. Harvey, "The Abilene Paradox: The Management of Agreement," *Organizational Dynamics* 3, Issue 1 (1974): 18, 63–80.

11. Ibid., 18.

12. Barbara H. Marion, "Decision-Making in Ethics," in *Ethics in Fund Development: Putting Values into Practice*, ed. Marianne Briscoe. *New Directions for Philanthropic Fund Development*, no. 6 (San Francisco: Jossey-Bass, 1994), 50–51.

13. Louis Edward Raths, *Values and Teaching* (Columbus, OH: Merrill, 1966).

14. James C. Collins and Jerry I. Porras, *Built to Last* (New York: HarperCollins, 1994).

15. Pottruck and Pearce, *Clicks and Mortar*, 222; February 1995 author interview with Larsen.

16. Marion, "Decision-Making in Ethics," 56.

17. Peter M. Senge, *The Fifth Discipline: The Art and Practice of the Learning Organization* (New York: Doubleday, 1990).

18. Peter M. Senge, Art Kleiner, Charlotte Roberts, Rick Ross, and Bryan Smith, *The Fifth Discipline Fieldbook: Strategies and Tools for Building a Learning Organization* (New York: Doubleday, 1994).

19. Cohort 20, Master's Program in Philanthropy and Development, Saint Mary's University of Minnesota.

20. Linda Ellinor and Glenna Gerard, *Dialogue: Rediscovering the Transforming Power of Conversation* (New York: John Wiley & Sons, 1998), 12.

21. Alan M. Webber, "Surviving in the New Economy," *Harvard Business Review* (September–October 1994), 7.

22. Juanita Brown and David Isaacs, "Conversation as a Core Business Process," *Systems Thinker* 7, no. 10 (December 1996–January 1997).

23. Senge, *Fifth Discipline*. The systems thinkers and learning organization theorists use Bohm's theory of dialogue. David Joseph Bohm (1917–1992) was an American-born British quantum physicist and philosopher. His work contributed to the fields of theoretical physics, philosophy, and neuropsychology.

24. Ellinor and Gerard, *Dialogue*, 21.

25. Ibid., 51.

26. Ibid., 52.

27. Sherrin Bennett and Juanita Brown, "Mindshift: Strategic Dialogue for Breakthrough Thinking," in *Learning Organizations, Developing Cultures for Tomorrow's Workplace*, ed. Sarita Chawla and J. Renesch (Portland, OR: Productivity Press, 1995), 173.

28. Brown and Isaacs, "Conversation as a Core Business Process," 4.

29. Ibid.

30. Peter F. Drucker with Jim Collins, Philip Kotler, James Kouzes, Judith Rodin, V. Kasturi Rangan, and Frances Hesselbein, *The Five Most Important Questions You Will Ever Ask About Your Organization*, Leader to Leader Institute (San Francisco: Jossey-Bass, 2008).

31. Pottruck and Pearce, *Clicks and Mortar*, 115.

32. Peter F. Drucker, *Managing the Non-Profit Organization: Principles and Practices* (New York: HarperCollins, 1990), 129.

33. Mary Parker Follett (1868–1933) was a pioneer in analyzing the human interaction of effective organizations.

34. Drucker, *Managing the Non-Profit Organization*.

35. William Bridges, *Managing Transitions: Making the Most of Change* (New York: Addison-Wesley, 1991), 4.

36. Carl Sussman, "Making Change: How to Build Adaptive Capacity," *Nonprofit Quarterly* (Winter 2003), www.nonprofitquarterly.org.

37. Ibid., 19.

38. Ibid., 21.

39. Think of this as "being crazy about asking questions." Embrace your own personal *folie du pourquoi* (asking why).

40. John P. Kotter and Leonard A. Schlesinger, "Choosing Strategies for Change," *Harvard Business Review* (March–April 1979), 107.

41. Jeanie Daniel Duck, "Managing Change: The Art of Balancing." *Harvard Business Review* (November–December 1993), 112.

42. Price Pritchett and Ron Pound, *High Velocity Culture Change: A Handbook for Managers* (Dallas, TX: Pritchett Publishing Company).

43. Robert H. Miles, "Accelerating Corporate Transformations (Don't Lose Your Nerve!): Six Mistakes That Can Derail Your Company's Attempts to Change," *Harvard Business Review* (January–February 2010), 70.

44. Ibid., 70.

45. Ibid., 71.

46. William Bridges and Susan Mitchell, "Leading Transition: A New Model for Change," *Leader to Leader*, no. 16 (Spring 2000): 31.

47. Eric Abrahamson, "Change without Pain," *Harvard Business Review* (July–August 2000).

48. Ibid., 76.

49. Cooperrider is a professor in the Department of Organizational Behavior, Weatherhead School of Management, Case Western Reserve University, Cleveland, Ohio.

50. David L. Cooperrider, *Appreciate Inquiry: A Constructive Approach to Organization Development* (Cleveland, OH: Department of Organizational Behavior, Weatherhead School of Management, Case Western Reserve University, 1993), 5.

51. Ibid., 4.

52. Ibid., 5.

53. Julia Kirby and Thomas A. Stewart, "The Institutional Yes: An Interview with Jeff Bezos," *Harvard Business Review* (October 2007), 81.

54. Ibid., 76.

55. Ibid., 76–77.

56. Ibid., 81.

57. Ibid., 82.

58. Pottruck and Pearce, *Clicks and Mortar*, 25.

59. Collins and Porras, *Built to Last*, 1.

60. Ibid., 202.

61. Saj-nicole A. Joni and Damon Beyer, "How to Pick a Good Fight," *Harvard Business Review* (December 2009), 50.

62. Ibid., 54.

63. Ibid., 52.

64. Denis E. Waitley is a motivational speaker and author of self-help books. Visit him at www.waitley.com.

65. At the time of his death in June 2010, Wooden was one of only three individuals to be enshrined in both categories, player and coach. Wooden developed his "pyramid of success" and wrote and lectured about this.

Chapter 4: The Fund Development Professional: Choosing Your Road—Organizational Development Specialist or Just Another Fundraising Technician

1. In *Keep Your Donors* (John Wiley & Sons, 2008), read Intermezzo #1 about the *folie du pourquoi* (asking why) and Chapter 2, "The Red Pants Factor: A Story about the Power of Questioning." Also see Chapter 3, which talks about organizational development specialists a bit.

2. Throughout this book, I use the terms fundraiser, development officer, and chief development officer. If your organization does not have a separate position responsible for the work, then your chief executive officer is responsible. For example, in small organizations, the chief executive (often called executive director) is the chief development officer, too.

3. Dr. Bryan is a retired human resources consultant from Rhode Island.

4. Yes, assertiveness can be risky. You may threaten your supervisor, your CEO, and others. Only you can decide how much risk to take. Only you can decide how to negotiate this. And you may have many different strategies and many different answers from moment to moment.

5. For more reading suggestions, check out my home page blogs and e-news at www.simonejoyaux.com.

6. I remind myself that the degree to which one is able and willing to take risks often depends on one's privilege. For example: If I have enough work as a consultant, I can risk disagreeing and arguing with a client—because if the client fires me, I'm okay. On the other hand, what kind of risk can the single father of six kids take? He may not be able to confront his employer about poor management. Or if you're a black lesbian, how risky is it for you to vigorously promote diversity and challenge homophobia and racism in your workplace?

7. For those of you who scoff at Wikipedia, I remind you, it's as good as an encyclopedia. We can verify the citations. We can be cautious. Yes, Wikipedia is still a good source.

8. Alan Bullock and Stephen Trombley, *The New Fontana Dictionary of Modern Thought* (London: HarperCollins Publishers, Ltd., 2000), 689, cited at Wikipedia.

9. Richard Barker, "No, Management Is *Not* a Profession," *Harvard Business Review* (July–August 2010), 52–60. Barker is a professor at the Judge Business School at England's Cambridge University. His article explains what makes a profession a profession, and why he doesn't consider management a profession. He does, however, believe in management and management education.

10. Barker, "No, Management Is *Not* a Profession," 56.

11. Ibid.

12. The CFRE certification program is accredited by the National Commission for Certifying Agencies, the accrediting arm of the Institute for Credentialing Excellence (ICE). ICE grants accreditation to a select group of organizations that demonstrate compliance with rigorous standards. This accreditation of the CFRE certification program assures the public—and fundraisers and their organizations—of the quality of the program. The accreditation acts as the seal of approval, confirming that the CFRE is a reliable tool for measuring that a fundraising professional has mastered the set of knowledge, skills, and abilities to be an effective fundraiser.

13. For more information, visit www.cfre.org. Also see the chapter entitled "International Perspectives on Fundraising" in the third edition of *Achieving Excellence in Fundraising*, released in December 2010 by Jossey-Bass. Sharilyn Hale, CFRE, describes the job analysis and certification process of CFRE International.

14. Sharilyn Hale, CFRE, "The Song of the River: A Study of Vocation in the Lives of Fundraisers" (MA dissertation, Saint Mary's University of Minnesota, 2004), 6. Sharilyn, a development officer from Toronto, was a member of Cohort 12 in the Master of Arts in Philanthropy and Development Program at Saint Mary's University of Minnesota (www.smumn.edu).

15. Ibid., 6.

16. Ibid., 11–12.

17. Ibid., 11–12.

18. Ibid., 79–80.

19. Martin E. P. Seligman is the Zellerbach Family Professor of Psychology at the University of Pennsylvania and an author of self-help books. His well-respected theory of "learned helplessness" describes the psychological condition when a human or animal acts helplessly in a bad situation—despite having the power to change the situation.

    Seligman writes about jobs, careers, and vocations in his book *Authentic Happiness: Using the New Positive Psychology to Realize Your Potential for Lasting Fulfillment* (New York: Free Press, 2002, 168): "Scholars distinguish three kinds of 'work orientation': a job, a career, and a calling. You do a *job* for the paycheck. ... You do not seek other rewards from it. ... A *career* entails a deeper personal investment in work. You mark your achievements through money, but also through advancement. ... A *calling* (or vocation) is a passionate commitment to work for its own sake. Individuals with a calling see their work as contributing to the greater good, to something larger than they are. ... The work is fulfilling in its own right, without regard for money or for advancement. ... But there has been an important discovery in this field: any job can become a calling, and any calling can become a job." (From the chapter entitled "In the Mansions of Life.")

Chapter 5: The Art of Leadership: A Critical Element of the First Relationship—Within Your Organization

1. Robert K. Greenleaf (1904–1990) founded the modern servant leadership movement. See his book, *Servant Leadership: A Journey into the Nature of Legitimate Power and Greatness* (New York: Paulist Press, 1991).
2. John W. Gardner, *On Leadership* (New York: Free Press/Macmillan, 1990), xi.
3. Peter Block, *Stewardship: Choosing Service over Self-Interest* (San Francisco: Berrett-Koehler, 1993).
4. Daniel H. Kim, "The Leader with the 'Beginner's' Mind," *Healthcare Forum Journal* (July–August 1993).
5. As I reflect on Kim's comment, I'm not so sure that leaders do or should learn faster than others. I think others in the organization might learn faster sometimes, and then lead the leader to learning. And I think leaders encourage this.
6. My colleague Wendy Zufelt-Baxter asks what is "truth" in a learning organization and with new-age leaders. "Is there just one truth?" questions Wendy. I think Kim means that leaders seek honesty. Leaders want and expect their colleagues to honestly and candidly share their insights, perspective, and questions. And, as Wendy implies, insights, perspective, and questions will differ. One person's truth may not be the same as another person's truth. But leaders want it all shared, honestly, with candor.
7. Refer to Chapter 3 for more about culture. Remember, culture refers to the beliefs, values, customs, traditions, norms—the way of life—of a group of people. A group's culture describes how its people see things, interact, behave, and make judgments about their world.
8. Dr. Prahalad, distinguished professor in the University of Michigan business school, died in April 2010, while I was writing this third edition. Dr. Prahalad coined the term *core competencies*. His most unconventional theory was "the fortune at the bottom of the pyramid." The *Washington Post* obituary notes that "his provocative books about business management and global marketing made him one of the world's most influential thinkers on corporate strategy."
9. Dee Hock, "The Art of Chaordic Leadership," *Leader to Leader* (Winter 2000), 25.
10. David S. Potruck and Terry Pearce, *Clicks and Mortar: Passion Driven Growth in an Internet World* (San Francisco: Jossey-Bass, 2000), 57.
11. Ibid., 62.
12. Hock, "Art of Chaordic Leadership," 25.

13. James C. Collins and Jerry I. Porras, *Built to Last* (New York: HarperCollins, 1994), 190.

14. McIntosh's writings are essential reading for anyone who claims to be a leader—and for any individual who wants to foster philanthropy, build community, and work for fairness and equity. Contact Peggy McIntosh and the National SEED Project at the Wellesley Centers for Women, Wellesley College, Wellesley, MA 02481 (mcintosh@wellesley.edu) for these articles: "White Privilege: Unpacking the Invisible Knapsack," "White Privilege: An Account to Spend," and "White People Facing Race: Uncovering the Myths That Keep Racism in Place."

15. One of my favorite stories is about the genie and picking the circumstances into which one is born. John Rawls developed the story to illustrate his theory of justice. Warren Buffett retold it. And I modified and retold the story in *Keep Your Donors*.

16. Yes, I'm privileged. Me, Simone Joyaux. I'm a white, heterosexual, well-educated, affluent woman. I win. Except for gender. Because it is a disadvantage to be a woman everywhere in the world.

17. Peggy McIntosh, "White Privilege: An Account to Spend."

18. Ibid.

19. I rant about this regularly in my "Personal Rants" blog on my home page at www.simonejoyaux.com. Look at the rant archives.

20. Peggy McIntosh, "White Privilege: An Account to Spend."

21. Ibid.

22. Saint Mary's University of Minnesota offers one of the oldest and best Master of Arts programs in Philanthropy and Development (www.smumn.edu).

23. Tracy Gary and Melissa Kohner, *Inspired Philanthropy: Creating a Giving Plan* (Berkeley, CA: Chardon Press, 1998), 2.

24. For more on this topic, read one of my favorite books: *Robin Hood Was Right: A Guide to Giving Your Money for Social Change*, by Chuck Collins and Pam Rogers, with Joan P. Garner. See also "Philanthropy's Moral Dilemma," Chapter 25 in *Keep Your Donors: The Guide to Better Communications and Stronger Relationships*, also posted on my home page at www.simonejoyaux.com.

25. Max DePree, *Leadership Is an Art* (New York: Dell Publishing, 1989).

26. Seth Godin, *Tribes: We Need You to Lead Us* (New York: Portfolio Hardcover, 2008), 138.

27. An American developmental psychologist, Gardner is the John H. and Elisabeth A. Hobbs Professor of Cognition and Education at Harvard Graduate School of Education, Harvard University.

28. Cited from Gardner's Frequently Asked Questions (FAQ) at www.howardgardner.com.

29. Ibid.

30. Muriel Barbery, *The Elegance of the Hedgehog*, trans. Alison Anderson (© Editions Gallimard, Paris, 2006; first publication 2008 by Europa Editions), 252.

31. Research of the late Dr. David McClelland, Harvard University psychologist, and Dr. Daniel Goleman, co-chairs of the Consortium for Research on Emotional Intelligence in Organizations, Rutgers University, described in "Leadership That Gets Results," *Harvard Business Review* (March–April 2000). For more information see also Goleman's book *Working with Emotional Intelligence* (New York: Bantam Books, 1998).

32. Daniel Goleman, "Leadership That Gets Results," *Harvard Business Review* (March–April 2000).

33. Ibid.

34. Ibid.

35. Daniel Goleman, *Social Intelligence: The New Science of Human Relationships* (New York: Bantam Books, 2006).

36. Ibid., 280.

37. Barbery, *Elegance of the Hedgehog*, 179.

38. Ibid., 277.

39. Jeffrey H. Dyer, Hal B. Gregersen, and Clayton M. Christensen, "The Innovator's DNA," *Harvard Business Review* (December 2009), 66.

40. Dyer, Gregersen, and Christensen, "Innovator's DNA."

41. Ibid., 63.

42. Ibid.

43. Ibid.

44. For more about questions and questioning, read: "Intermezzo #1—Why?" and Chapter 2, "The Red Pants Factor: A Story about the Power of Questioning", in *Keep Your Donors: The Guide to Better Communications and Stronger Relationships* (Ahern and Joyaux). Visit www.simonejoyaux.com and check out all the questions in the blogs, e-newsyletter, and in the Free Download Library.

45. Dyer, Gregersen, and Christensen, "Innovator's DNA," 64.

46. Seth Godin, "Fear of Bad Ideas," blog of December 21, 2009 (www.sethgodin.com).

47. Dyer, Gregersen, and Christensen, "Innovator's DNA," 63.

48. Ibid., 65.

49. Research from neurologist Kenneth Heilman, University of Florida, and author of *Creativity and the Brain* (2005), reported by Patricia Cohen in her May 8, 2010, *New York Times* article "Charting Creativity: Signposts of a Hazy Territory."

50. "Planning for the Sequel," *The Economist*'s "Schumpeter" column, June 19, 2010. In this issue, this business and management column talks about how Pixar's leaders support creativity. By the way, Joseph A. Schumpeter was an Austrian economist and political scientist (www.economist.com/blogs/schumpeter).

51. "Other communities" refers to regions and nations, faiths and generations, and so forth.

52. P. Christopher Earley and Elaine Mosakowski, "Cultural Intelligence," *Harvard Business Review* (October 2004), 140.

53. Ibid., 142.

54. Ibid.

55. For more about assumptions and mental models, see learning organization theory in Chapter 3. Read books and articles by Peter Senge and other learning organization theorists.

56. Dr. Richard Paul and Dr. Linda Elder, *The Miniature Guide to Critical Thinking, Fifth Edition: Concepts and Tools* (Dillon Beach, CA: Foundation for Critical Thinking Press, 2008), 41.

57. Ibid.

58. Ibid.

59. Robert Gunn, "Leading from Within: Strategies for and Reflections on Becoming a Leader of Leaders," *Perdido* (Winter 2000), 11. Reprinted from the September and October 1999 issues of *Strategic Finance*, Institute of Management Accountants (Montvale, NJ: 1999), 14.

60. Ibid., 17.

61. Dr. Paul C. Pribbenow, CFRE, is the president of Augsburg College in Minneapolis, Minnesota. He publishes a free e-news "Notes for the Reflective Practitioner," and is a well-respected speaker and author.

62. Pottruck and Pearce, *Clicks and Mortar*, 110.

63. Ibid., 112.

64. Ibid., 116.

65. Ibid., 115.

66. Noel M. Tichy is a leading authority on management and leadership development. Tichy is Professor of Management and Organizations at the University of Michigan's Ross School of Business.

67. Gary Kelsey is a consultant and the Program Director of the Master of Arts in Philanthropy and Development at Saint Mary's University of Minnesota.

68. Hock, "Art of Chaordic Leadership," 21.
69. Ibid.
70. Ibid.
71. Collins and Porras, *Built to Last*.
72. Hock, "Art of Chaordic Leadership," 21.
73. Ibid., 22.
74. Ibid., 23.
75. Jean Lipman-Blumen, "The Age of Connective Leadership," *Leader to Leader* (Summer 2000), 39.
76. Ibid., 40.
77. Ibid.
78. Ibid., 43.
79. Ibid.
80. Ibid., 44–45.
81. See descriptions and commentary on Wooden's pyramid of success on the Internet.

Chapter 6: The Second Relationship—With Your Community: Ensuring Your Organization's Relevance through Strategic Planning

1. Peter M. Senge, Art Kleiner, Charlotte Roberts, Rick Ross, and Bryan Smith, *The Fifth Discipline Fieldbook: Strategies and Tools for Building a Learning Organization* (New York: Doubleday, 1994), 302.
2. Beware of terminology. There are lots of words—goals, objectives, action steps, strategies, and so forth. Different people use these words differently. It doesn't much matter. Pick your words and clearly define them so everyone in your organization uses the same terminology and understands the agreed-upon meaning.
3. Senge et al., *Fifth Discipline Fieldbook*, 302.
4. Arie de Geus, speaker at Systems Thinking in Action Conference sponsored by Pegasus Communications, Boston, September 1995.
5. Peter F. Drucker, *Managing the Non-Profit Organization: Principles and Practices* (New York: HarperCollins, 1990), 120.
6. Philip J. Carroll, "Infrastructure for Organizational Transformation at Shell Oil," *Collective Intelligence* 1, no. 1, 1995.
7. Arie P. de Geus, "Planning as Learning," *Harvard Business Review* (March–April 1988), 71.
8. Ibid., 70.
9. See Seth's blog of May 24, 2010, "The Modern Business Plan," at www.sethgodin.com.
10. No matter the actual name of this group—board of directors, board of trustees, board of governors, whatever—this is your institution's legal corporate governing body. Of course it participates!
11. Call this person anything you want—his or her name works well! I'm using "planning process manager" to denote a particular function with skills and accountabilities. This is not an administrative function. This is a leadership function with requisite skills, expertise, and experience.
12. Henry Mintzberg, "The Rise and Fall of Strategic Planning," *Harvard Business Review* (January–February 1994).
13. Ibid., 113.
14. Ibid., 114.
15. Sometimes the planning process manager writes key informant and focus group questions, writes and tabulates surveys, and so forth. The planning process manager may outsource

some of this work, too. But the bottom line is the planning process manager ensures that this work gets done.

16. See the great book *The Trusted Advisor* by David H. Maister, Charles H. Green, and Robert M. Galford (New York: Touchstone, 2000).

17. Look back at Chapter 3, "The First Relationship—Within Your Organization," to distinguish between the various ways that individuals can have a voice.

18. Senge et al., *Fifth Discipline Fieldbook*, 299.

19. Some organizations invite their entire staff to participate in the decision-making retreat. Other organizations invite senior managers and, perhaps, additional representatives from each department. No matter which staff attend the retreat, all employees need to have a voice in the planning process by providing information and participating in conversations in various settings during the planning process.

20. Organizations sometimes confuse strengths and weaknesses, and opportunities and threats. Obviously, the economy can be an external opportunity or threat, depending. Another external opportunity or threat might be the political party in power. Other external factors include societal and technological trends. You cannot control these external factors but you must cope with them. Internal strengths and weaknesses might include things like the diversity of your staff and board, the size of your donor base, donor loyalty, or client satisfaction. Your organization can control all these items, even if you don't do so very well.

21. Step 7 requires the most time, often as much as three to six months or more, depending on the planning process. This step may also be the most expensive.

22. From www.entrepeneur.com.

23. For example, visit the Pew Research Center at www.pewresearch.org, a nonpartisan fact tank presenting information on issues, attitudes, and trends shaping the United States and the world. Visit the Indiana University Center on Philanthropy (www.philanthropy@iupui.edu) for research about giving and volunteering.

24. Deborah L. Duarte and Nancy Tennant Snyder, "Leadership in a Virtual World," *Leader to Leader* (Spring 2000), 43.

25. A little note about "competition": I don't support the concept in the nonprofit/NGO sector. First, if other organizations in your marketplace do the same work as you, why don't you partner? Why don't you merge? Service in the nonprofit/NGO sector is not about your organization and how it does things. The nonprofit/NGO sector is about community service and building community. What's best for the community should drive you—and your partnering. And yes, you should merge or get yourself acquired or go out of business if that's best for the community.

    Moreover, you are not competing for board members and donors and other volunteers. How many times do I have to yell out to the world: "People pay attention to what interests them. I have my interests and I have a whole lot of disinterests! I know where I want to give and volunteer—and it may not be with your organization or your cause. So you are not competing for my money or time." Actually, I think nonprofits use "competition" as an excuse for poor service, poor relationship building, and poor fund development. So please, stop talking about competition. Refocus your attention. Thank you.

26. For updates to this survey, visit Resources | Free Download Library at www.simone joyaux.com.

27. Peter M. Senge, *The Fifth Discipline: The Art and Practice of the Learning Organization* (New York: Doubleday, 1990), 128.

28. Senge et al., *Fifth Discipline Fieldbook*, Chapter 44.

29. Ikujiro Nonaka, "The Knowledge Creating Company," *Harvard Business Review* (November–December 1991), 104.

30. Karl-Henrik Robèrt, *The Natural Step: Simplicity without Reductionism* (Stockholm: Natural Step Environmental Institute, 1994).

31. Nonaka, "Knowledge Creating Company," 104.

32. Kenneth R. Andrews, *The Concept of Corporate Strategy* (Homewood, IL: Richard D. Irwin, 1971).

33. Peter F. Drucker, *Managing the Non-Profit Organization: Principles and Practices* (New York: HarperCollins, 1990), 46.

34. The board reviews and adopts the CEO's job description. See a copy of this important document posted at www.simonejoyaux.com. Click on Resources and visit the Free Download Library. There you'll also find a sample performance appraisal process for the CEO position.

35. Michael P. Mokwa, William M. Dawson, and E. Arthur Prieve, *Marketing the Arts* (Santa Barbara, CA: Praeger Publishers, 1980), 68–69.

36. www.sethgodin.com, July 16, 2010.

37. Campbell Robertson, "Efforts to Repel Oil Spill Are Described as Chaotic," *New York Times*, June 14, 2010.

38. Harry Dolan, *Bad Things Happen* (New York: Berkley Publishing Group, 2009), 84.

39. Daniel Silva, *The Rembrandt Affair* (New York: Putnam Adult, 2010).

40. Peter C. Goldmark Jr., "Toward a New Social Contract," 1991 Independent Sector Annual Meeting, Atlanta, Georgia. At the time, Goldmark was the President and CEO of the Rockefeller Foundation.

Chapter 7: The Third Relationship—With Your Constituents: Nurturing Relationships to Build Loyalty

1. G. T. (Buck) Smith developed this concept—first used in higher education—to measure the progress of major gift fundraising. Staff and volunteers execute a series of initiatives (called "moves") to build relationships with donors.

2. All the rage, seemingly everywhere—with software programs for support.

3. Carnegie, 1930s self-help guru, was an author and lecturer. He developed famous courses on self-improvement, salesmanship, public speaking, and interpersonal skills. His book *How to Win Friends and Influence People*, published in 1936, was a huge best seller and is still popular today.

4. Visit http://trustedadvisor.com.

5. Start with Adrian Sargeant's seminal research. My favorite is *Building Donor Loyalty: The Fundraiser's Guide to Increasing Lifetime Value*. Read more in *Fundraising Principles and Practice*. Follow the increasing amount of research about donors available through various sources. And for a specific example, see the donor/member survey of the Audubon Society of Rhode Island, posted on this book's website and printed in *Keep Your Donors*.

6. See Adrian Sargeant's research in *Building Donor Loyalty* and the data reported in *Fundraising Principles and Practice*, by Sargeant, Shang, and Associates.

7. See the Donor-Centric Pledge in *Keep Your Donors* and posted at www.simone joyaux.com.

8. www.marketingpower.com/AboutAMA/Pages/DefinitionofMarketing.aspx.

9. Ken Burnett, *Relationship Fundraising: A Donor-Based Approach to the Business of Raising Money* (London: White Lion Press, 1992), 48.

10. Read Ken's other books. Visit www.sofii.org, his Showcase of Fundraising Innovation and Inspiration.

11. Burnett, *Relationship Fundraising*, 48.

12. Peter F. Drucker, *Managing the Non-Profit Organization: Principles and Practices* (New York: HarperCollins, 1990), 84.

13. Don Tapscott, David Ticoll, and Alex Lowy, "Relationships Rule," *Business 2.0*, May 2000.

14. Lester Wunderman, *Being Direct: Making Advertising Pay* (New York: Random House, 1996), 279.

15. David S. Pottruck and Terry Pearce, *Clicks and Mortar: Passion Driven Growth in an Internet World* (San Francisco: Jossey-Bass, 2000), 224.

16. Ibid., 243.

17. Ibid., 247.

18. See *Keep Your Donors: The Guide to Better Communications and Stronger Relationships*. Visit www.neuroscience.org. Look at the research.

19. www.philosophersnotes.com.

20. Robert Bly, *The Copywriter's Handbook: A Step-by-Step Guide to Writing Copy That Sells* (New York: Henry Holt, 1995).

21. David R. Dunlop, "Special Concerns of Major Gift Fund-Raising," in *The Handbook of Institutional Advancement*, 2nd ed. (San Franciso: Jossey-Bass, 1986), 330.

22. Adrian Sargeant, Jen Shang, and Associates. *Fundraising Principles and Practice* (San Francisco: Jossey-Bass, 2010).

23. Seth Godin, *Tribes: We Need You to Lead Us* (New York: Portfolio Hardcover, 2008), 9.

24. Ibid., 125.

25. Ibid., 25.

26. Research by Elaine Chan and Jaideep Sengupta, Hong Kong University of Science and Technology. Reported in www.neurosciencemarketing.com, February 17, 2010.

27. That's the title of Jeff's August 12, 2010, blog. Jeff is passing on information from Brent Bouchez's "Engage:Boomers" media post blog of July 19, 2010, which reports on research from the Stanford Graduate School of Business.

28. See the final chapter in *Keep Your Donors*, "Philanthropy's Moral Dilemma," also posted at www.simonejoyaux.com.

29. See the work of Judith Nichols, PhD, CFRE. Judith is a researcher, author, and consultant specializing in the impact of changing demographics and psychographics on fundraising, marketing, and membership.

30. Jerry Weissman, *Presenting to Win* (Saddle River, NJ: FT Press, 2008).

31. Tom Ahern, ABC, Ahern Communications, Ink., www.aherncomm.com.

32. Bly, *Copywriter's Handbook*, 67.

33. Cialdini is the Regents' Professor Emeritus of Psychology and Marketing at Arizona State University. Visit him at www.influenceatwork.com. See, for example, *Influence: The Psychology of Persuasion* and *Yes! 50 Scientifically Proven Ways to Be Persuasive*.

34. See the September 30, 2009 article at www.sciencedaily.com.

35. "Emotional Ads Work Best," July 26, 2009, www.neurosciencemarketing.com, reporting on work from the UK-based Institute of Practitioners in Advertising and the book *Brand Immortality* by Pringle and Field.

36. Drake Bennett, "Easy = True: How 'Cognitive Fluency' Shapes What We Believe, How We Invest, and Who Will Become a Supermodel," *Boston Globe*, January 31, 2010 (www.boston.com).

37. Kurt Lewin was a German-American psychologist. He is considered one of the modern pioneers of social, organizational, and applied psychology.

38. Philip Kotler and Alan R. Andreason, *Strategic Marketing for Nonprofit Organizations*, 3rd ed. (Englewood Cliffs, NJ: Prentice-Hall, 1987), 69.

39. Roy H. Williams, *Secret Formulas of the Wizard of Ads* (Canada: Webcom Limited, 1999), 12.

40. R. Douglas Fields, "Of Two Minds: Listener Brain Patterns Mirror Those of the Speaker," *Scientific American*, cited by www.neurosciencemarketing,com, July 29, 2010.

41. David Ogilvy, *Ogilvy on Advertising* (New York: Random House, 1985), 7.

42. Richard A. Edwards, "Education: Our Legacy to the Profession," in *Fund Raising Management* (Garden City, NJ: Hope Communications, 1989), 85.

43. Dunlop, "Special Concerns of Major Gift Fund-Raising," 85.

44. According to Dunlop, as of 1986 each major gift staff person could manage approximately 70 to 80 prospects per year.

45. That's a question asked by Cohort 18, Master of Arts in Philanthropy and Development, Saint Mary's University of Minnesota. What's your answer? More importantly, how would your donors answer that question?

46. Learn about welcome packages at www.merkleinc.com. Also see description in *Keep Your Donors*.

47. Dunlop, "Special Concerns of Major Gift Fund-Raising."

48. Maggie Jackson, *Distracted: The Erosion of Attention and the Coming Dark Age* (Amherst, NY: Prometheus Books, 2008).

49. Theodore Zeldin, *Conversation: How Talk Can Change Our Lives* (Mahwah, NJ: Hidden-Spring, 2000). Zeldin is an English philosopher, sociologist, and historian. He is best known for his book *An Intimate History of Humanity* (1994), "which offered a unique and provocative perspective on human history by focusing on the evolution of feelings and personal relationships." (Cited from the book jacket of *Conversation*.)

50. Ibid., 3.

51. Ibid., 14.

52. Ibid.

53. Ibid., 12.

54. Ibid., 15.

55. It has been statistically proven that two individuals will be connected by no more than six different individuals. That means that in a nation of 300 million people, you can reach the President of the United States in only six calls. Yes, it's true.

56. *Strategic Fund Development: Building Profitable Relationships That Last* does not focus on asking. But lots of books and blogs and newsletters do. Here are a few of my favorites:

    Mal Warwick's books on direct-mail solicitation. Also see other books written by Mal.

    Laura Fredricks' books on asking: *The Ask* and *Developing Major Gifts*. Attend Laura's trainings, too (www.laura-fredricks.com).

    Brainchild of Andrea Kihlstedt and Brian Saber, the www.askingmatters.com website offers tips, videos, analysis of your asking style, and more.

    Kay Sprinkel Grace, *Beyond Fundraising: New Strategies for Nonprofit Innovation and Investment*. Attend Kay's trainings, too (www.kaygrace.org).

57. M. Anne Murphy, CFRE, and Deacon Larry A. Vaclavik, *The Dini Partners* (Houston, TX, 1996).

58. Seth Godin's blog on loyalty, September 9, 2010, at www.sethgodin.com.

Chapter 8: The Fourth Relationship—With Your Volunteers: Enabling Them to Take Meaningful Action on Behalf of Your Organization

1. Peter Block, *Stewardship: Choosing Service over Self-Interest* (San Francisco: Berrett-Koehler, 1993).

2. Joline Godfrey, *Our Wildest Dreams: Women Entrepreneurs Making Money, Having Fun, Doing Good* (New York: HarperCollins, 1992), 17.

3. Ibid., 18.

4. Ibid., 19.

5. Barry Bozeman and Mary K. Feeney, "Toward a Useful Theory of Mentoring: a Conceptual Analysis and Critique," *Administration & Society* 39, no. 6 (2007): 719–739.

6. Review Chapter 4 for details about organizational development specialists.

7. Max DePree, *Leadership Is an Art* (New York: Dell Publishing, 1989), 104.

8. Peter F. Drucker, *Managing the Non-Profit Organization* (New York: HarperCollins, 1990).

9. Block, *Stewardship.*

10. Regina Herzlinger, "Full Disclosure: A Strategy for Performance," in *Leader to Leader: Enduring Insights on Leadership from the Drucker Foundation's Award-Winning Journal*, Frances Hesselbein and Paul M. Cohen, eds. (New York: Peter F. Drucker Foundation for Nonprofit Management, 1999), 373.

11. Ibid., 376.

12. Debashis Chatterjee, *Leading Consciously: A Pilgrimage toward Self-Mastery* (Boston: Butterworth-Heinemann, 1998), 94.

13. Jay W. Lorsch, "Empowering the Board," *Harvard Business Review* (January–February 1995), 111.

14. Ian I. Mitroff, Richard O. Mason, and Christine M. Pearson, *Framebreak: The Radical Redesign of American Business* (San Francisco: Jossey-Bass, 1994), 44.

15. Martha Golensky, "The Board-Executive Relationship in Nonprofit Organizations: Partnership or Power Struggle," *Nonprofit Management and Leadership* 4, no. 2 (1993): 177–189.

16. Drucker, *Managing the Non-Profit Organization*, 126.

17. Robert Coles, "Doing Well by Doing Good: Why We Volunteer," *Advancing Philanthropy* 2 (1): 1994.

18. Charles Handy, "The New Language of Organizing and Its Implications for Leaders," Chapter 1 in *The Leader of the Future*, Frances Hesselbein, Marshall Goldsmith, and Richard Beckhard, eds., *Leader to Leader* (San Francisco: Jossey-Bass, 1996), 154. Handy, former professor at the London School of Economics, is an expert in organizational behavior and management.

19. Henry Rosso, *Achieving Excellence in Fundraising* (San Francisco: Jossey-Bass, 1991), 141.

20. John W. Gardner, *On Leadership* (New York: Free Press, 1990), 3.

21. Chapter 5—The Art of Leadership—talks about privilege. And, for further exploration of privilege and power in philanthropy, see the final chapter in *Keep Your Donors: The Guide to Better Communications and Stronger Relationships*, by Joyaux and Ahern. Also see "Philanthropy's Moral Dilemma," a monograph posted at www.simonejoyaux.com.

Chapter 9: Creating the Most Effective Fund Development Plan for Your Organization: A Plan That Produces Ownership and Results

1. What happens if your organization doesn't have a strategic plan? Hey, that's life. Use your fund development planning process to identify this lack. Use your fund development planning process to explain why a multiyear institutional strategic plan is important. Then include institutional strategic planning as a goal in your fund development plan. Use the power of fund development to fix organizational development issues in your institution.

2. Sheila Appel is Corporate Citizenship and Corporate Affairs Manager at IBM US. Sheila was a board member and then board chair of the United Way of Dutchess County when I consulted there.

3. Thanks to Daryl Eaton, Norfolk Land Trust, Norfolk, Connecticut, for the term *heartstorm*. Daryl remembers well what Tom Ahern and I taught at the workshop she attended: Emotions are the key decision-makers for us humans. So one day Daryl said, "We shouldn't

brainstorm; we should heartstorm." Daryl reminds us that everything is emotions. So it's our heart that does the storming.

4. See the Donor-Centric Pledge posted at www.simonejoyaux.com.

5. And if you've tried your best, over and over ... If you can honestly say that no matter what you do and how well you do it, they just won't play. Then maybe it's time to find another job.

6. *Keep Your Donors* devotes an entire chapter to measuring relationships and another chapter defines measures for newsletters.

Index